MATERIA~~LIZING DIFFERENCE~~

Consumer Culture, Politics, and Ethnicity among Romanian Roma

How do objects mediate human relationships? In what ways do they possess social and political agency? What role does material culture – prestige consumption, as well as commodity aesthetics, biographies, and ownership histories – play in the production of social and political identities, differences, and hierarchies? How do (informal) consumer subcultures of collectors organize and manage themselves? Drawing on theories from anthropology and sociology, specifically material culture, consumption, museum, ethnicity, and post-socialist studies, *Materializing Difference* addresses these questions via analysis of the practices and ideologies connected to Gabor Roma beakers and roofed tankards made of antique silver. The consumer subculture organized around these objects – defined as ethnicized and gendered prestige goods by the Gabor Roma living in Romania – is a contemporary, second-hand culture based on patina-oriented consumption.

Materializing Difference reveals the inner dynamics of the complex relationships and interactions between objects (silver beakers and roofed tankards) and subjects (Romanian Roma) and investigates how these relationships and interactions contribute to the construction, materialization, and reformulation of social, economic, and political identities, boundaries, and differences. It also discusses how, after 1989, the political transformation in Romania led to the emergence of a new, post-socialist consumer sensitivity among the Gabor Roma, and how this sensitivity reshaped the pre-regime-change patterns, meanings, and value preferences of prestige consumption.

(Anthropological Horizons)

PÉTER BERTA is an honorary research associate at the School of Slavonic and East European Studies at University College London, a visiting senior research associate at the Institute for Global Prosperity at University College London, and a senior researcher at the Institute of Ethnology at the Hungarian Academy of Sciences.

ANTHROPOLOGICAL HORIZONS

Editor: Michael Lambek, University of Toronto

This series, begun in 1991, focuses on theoretically informed ethnographic works addressing issues of mind and body, knowledge and power, equality and inequality, the individual and the collective. Interdisciplinary in its perspective, the series makes a unique contribution in several other academic disciplines: women's studies, history, philosophy, psychology, political science, and sociology.

For a list of the books published in this series see page 373.

Materializing Difference

Consumer Culture, Politics, and Ethnicity among Romanian Roma

PÉTER BERTA

With a foreword by FRED R. MYERS

UNIVERSITY OF TORONTO PRESS
Toronto   Buffalo   London

© University of Toronto Press 2019
Toronto Buffalo London
utorontopress.com
Printed in Canada

ISBN 978-1-4875-0057-3 (cloth)   ISBN 978-1-4875-2040-3 (paper)

∞ Printed on acid-free paper with vegetable-based inks.

(Anthropological Horizons)

Library and Archives Canada Cataloguing in Publication

Berta, Péter, 1972–, author
Materializing difference : consumer culture, politics, and ethnicity among
Romanian Roma / Péter Berta ; with a foreword by Fred R. Myers

(Anthropological horizons)
Includes bibliographical references and index.
ISBN 978-1-4875-0057-3 (cloth).   ISBN 978-1-4875-2040-3 (paper)

1. Romanies – Material culture. 2. Romanies – Social life and customs.
3. Romanies – Economic conditions. 4. Romanies – Ethnic identity.
5. Romanies – Politics and government. 6. Consumption (Economics) –
Romania. I. Title. II. Series: Anthropological horizons

DX115.B47 2019   305.891/497   C2018-906533-8

University of Toronto Press is pleased to acknowledge the financial support
for this book provided by the Hungarian Scientific Research Fund (PUB-K
114509) and the Research Centre for the Humanities of the Hungarian
Academy of Sciences.

University of Toronto Press acknowledges the financial assistance to its
publishing program of the Canada Council for the Arts and the Ontario Arts
Council, an agency of the Government of Ontario.

 Canada Council   Conseil des Arts
for the Arts   du Canada

 ONTARIO ARTS COUNCIL
CONSEIL DES ARTS DE L'ONTARIO
an Ontario government agency
un organisme du gouvernement de l'Ontario

Funded by the   Financé par le
Government   gouvernement
of Canada   du Canada | Canadä

 MIX
Paper from
responsible sources
FSC   FSC® C016245
www.fsc.org

For Marci and Dani

Contents

List of Illustrations   ix

Foreword by Fred R. Myers   xiii

Acknowledgments   xv

Introduction: Translocal Communities of Practice and Multi-Sited
    Ethnographies   3

Part One: Negotiating and Materializing Difference and Belonging

1   Symbolic Arenas and Trophies of the Politics of Difference   23
2   The Gabors' Prestige Economy: A Translocal, Ethnicized,
     Informal, and Gendered Consumer Subculture   53
3   From Antiques to Prestige Objects: De- and Recontextualizing
     Commodities from the European Antiques Market   82
4   Creating Symbolic and Material Patina   95
5   The Politics of Brokerage: Bazaar-Style Trade and Risk
     Management   118
6   Political Face-Work and Transcultural Bricolage/Hybridity:
     Prestige Objects in Political Discourse   150

Contents

Part Two: Contesting Consumer Subcultures: Interethnic Trade, Fake Authenticity, and Classification Struggles

7 Gabor Roma, Cărhar Roma, and the European Antiques Market: Contesting Consumer Subcultures 177
8 Interethnic Trade of Prestige Objects 208
9 Constructing, Commodifying, and Consuming Fake Authenticity 219
10 The Politics of Consumption: Classification Struggles, Moral Criticism, and Stereotyping 236

Part Three: Multi-Sited Commodity Ethnographies

11 Things-in-Motion: Methodological Fetishism, Multi-Sitedness, and the Biographical Method 261
12 Prestige Objects, Marriage Politics, and the Manipulation of Nominal Authenticity: The Biography of a Beaker, 2000–2007 266
13 Proprietary Contest, Business Ethics, and Conflict Management: The Biography of a Roofed Tankard, 1992–2012 281

Conclusion: The Post-Socialist Consumer Revolution and the Shifting Meanings of Prestige Goods 297

Notes 313

References 337

Index 359

Colour plates follow page 174

Illustrations

Map

0.1 Map of Romania   5

Tables

1.1   Some of the marriage payments paid between 2000
      and 2003   42
2.1   Movement of 10 Gabor Roma beakers between Transylvanian
      settlements and counties between the mid-twentieth century
      and 2012   58
2.2   Some of the prestige-object sales transactions carried out among
      the Gabor Roma between 1950 and 2011   64
2.3   A few silver beakers put up for auction on the Hungarian
      antiques market that could also be Gabor Roma prestige
      objects on the basis of their material properties   66
2.4   The most expensive Hungarian paintings sold at art auctions
      in Hungary (after 1990), and the most expensive silver beakers
      changing hands within the Gabor Roma ethnic population
      (after 1989)   71
10.1 Stereotypes of consumer patterns/value preferences and
      lifestyles in the discourses analysed   256

Colour Plates (following page 174)

1   Gabor Roma family members at a commemorative event (*pomana*) held six weeks after a funeral
2   Gabor Roma at the funeral of a prestige-object owner
3   Gabor Roma at a funeral waiting for the ceremony to begin
4   A Gabor Roma trader selling clothing items at a second-hand market in Mureş County
5   Political discourse among Gabor Roma at a funeral
6   Political discourse among Gabor Roma at a commemorative event held six weeks after a funeral
7   Political discourse between two influential Gabor Roma prestige-object owners at a funeral
8   Wedding of a young Gabor Roma couple in the home of the husband's family
9   An exceptionally valuable Gabor Roma footed beaker decorated with – among other things – "unexplainable animals"
10   A skillfully fire-gilt Gabor Roma footed beaker
11   A Gabor Roma footed beaker with a hunting scene below the girdle
12   A Gabor Roma *ščobo* beaker with two medallions and a finely elaborated surface pattern similar to snakeskin
13   A Gabor Roma *burikato* beaker decorated with a rearing horse and other animals
14   An exceptionally valuable, richly fire-gilt Gabor Roma roofed tankard decorated with vegetal motifs
15   An exceptionally valuable Gabor Roma roofed tankard decorated with biblical scenes
16   The Gabor Roma owner holding the footed beaker shown in photo 11
17   A richly fire-gilt Gabor Roma roofed tankard, held by the owner's son
18   The Gabor Roma owner and his grandson holding the roofed tankard shown in photo 14
19   A Gabor Roma footed beaker, held by the owner
20   A silver coin with a portrait of emperor Franz Joseph I, used to cover a repair at the lip of a Gabor Roma beaker
21   Decorations identified by the Gabor Roma as "unexplainable animals"

22 A Cărhar Roma prestige-object owner (possessing a valuable *ščobo* beaker)

23 A Cărhar Roma prestige-object owner (possessing five beakers)

24 Cărhar women and their children at a Cărhar Roma wedding in the Olt River area

25 A Cărhar Roma man with a copper kettle for distilling the local brandy

26 A Cărhar Roma family looking at photos of beakers and roofed tankards in the catalogue of an American art collector

27 An exceptionally valuable, richly fire-gilt Cărhar Roma footed beaker with numerous antique coins with portraits

28 A richly fire-gilt Cărhar Roma *ščobo* beaker with a finely elaborated surface pattern similar to snakeskin and a medallion bearing a Hungarian personal name and a date: 1683

29 A Cărhar Roma owner with his two large footed beakers purchased earlier from the Gabors

30 A Cărhar Roma owner with his footed beaker (richly decorated with vegetal motifs) purchased from the Gabors

31 A footed beaker (decorated with portraits of elderly, bearded men and vegetal motifs) bought earlier from the Gabors and now in Cărhar Roma possession

32 The Cărhar Roma owner of the beaker shown in photo 31 measures the height of his prestige object

33 Kuna with his beaker, and the Cărhar Roma broker mentioned in the case study in chapter 8

34 A Cărhar Roma wearing a necklace decorated with numerous *galbi*s with a portrait of Austrian emperor Franz Joseph I

Foreword

Some years ago, Daniel Miller made us pay attention to the way in which ordinary (or almost ordinary) commodities could take on transcendental value, overcoming a barrier that tended to exist between anthropological studies of material culture and other work on consumption. Péter Berta's *Materializing Difference* follows along this path. It is a detailed and determined account of the social life of antique silver objects among Romanian Roma. As part of the new generation of material culture scholars, Berta follows the pathways and significance of second-hand silver beakers and tankards as prestige objects that intersect the political rivalries, prestige, and personal relations of Gabor Roma. It is a fascinating story, where an ethnic population fashions its own prestige system out of materials that have considerably less value on the European antiques market, but imbue these materials with their own histories and significance in a system of partially restricted circulation. Annette Weiner would have loved to see the politics of inalienable possessions carried so directly into a class of objects that are undeniably made what they are by human activity.

Not only are differences among Gabor Roma such as prestige and standing constructed and represented through the process of collection, but what Berta describes as the patina-oriented consumer subculture organized around these silver objects constitutes a kind of "invisible ink" of ethnicity. At the same time, Berta refuses the potential exoticism of this structuring of difference. Instead, he places these processes and practices in a history of socialism and post-socialism, in which the value of ethnicized, small, portable, transferrable prestige objects changes and variegates in relation to the larger, encompassing political economy. It should be clear that this work interweaves a rich tapestry of topics pursued with care and thorough consideration. Berta eschews a simple big picture and attends to the complexity of the political lives and agency of prestige objects and their ownership histories.

Berta's knowledge of the diverging literatures of material culture and consumption studies combines with an extraordinary explication of Roma consumer taste and thinking about these objects, the collectors and markets through which they circulate, and the fluidity of these relationships. For those who want to see how to put theory to the test of research, Berta provides an exemplary case. Leaving no stone – or silver beaker or tankard – unturned, and no case with questions lagging, in this unique study Berta follows the objects, the contexts, and the information in which they are embedded with unflagging focus. It's as if the Gabor Roma make something out of nothing, make ethnicized value out of commodities of the European antiques market, as human beings make themselves through almost whatever comes to hand.

Fred R. Myers
Silver Professor of Anthropology
New York University

Acknowledgments

In the twenty years since the beginning of my research among Romanian Roma in April 1998, I have received invaluable professional, moral, and financial support from numerous individuals and institutions, enabling me to carry out the ethnographic research and write the chapters based on it.

My deepest gratitude goes to the Roma who have shared their everyday lives, time, and experience with me. Without their patience, trust, and generosity this monograph would never have been completed. I am enormously grateful to the members of my god-daughter's extended family for their continuous emotional support, encouragement, and intellectual guidance. Our deep friendship and hundreds of conversations contributed greatly to making me feel at home among the Roma.

Thanks are due to several institutions for providing ideal circumstances (a happy home) for writing the monograph:

Special mention must be made of the Institute for Ethnology of the Hungarian Academy of Sciences, where I have been a researcher since 1999. I am grateful to Attila Paládi-Kovács and Balázs Balogh, directors of the institute, for the generous assistance they provided in many ways throughout the research project on which this book is based.

During the past two decades, I was several times awarded an Eötvös Fellowship by the Hungarian State, and I spent many months on research and professional consultations in the Department of Anthropology at University College London. I wish to give special thanks to Michael Stewart for all the practical advice and unwavering professional support I received from him during the months in London.

Between 2015 and 2017, I spent two years on research as a Marie Curie Research Fellow (FP7-PEOPLE-2013-IEF; 628331) in the School of

Slavonic and East European Studies at University College London (UCL SSEES). I am especially grateful to Alena Ledeneva for her ceaseless efforts to smooth the path of my research project in countless ways: her insightful criticism, invaluable moral and practical support, optimism, and encouragement. I also benefited greatly from discussing some of the chapters with other colleagues working at UCL SSEES. In submitting my application for this fellowship funded by the European Commission, I received important professional help not only from Alena but also from the following colleagues, whom I would like to take this opportunity to express my gratitude: Nicholas Saunders, Christopher B. Steiner, and Nicholas Thomas.

Special thanks are owed to Henrietta L. Moore, director of the Institute for Global Prosperity at University College London, for providing a stimulating intellectual environment in the institute to further elaborate a research project focusing on the politics of arranged marriage among European Roma. This latter project is closely linked to my analysis of the practices that are the main focus of this monograph.

I am grateful to the colleagues who read all or portions of my manuscript (or one of the previously published articles a few chapters were based on) and shared their constructive criticism with me. I am particularly indebted to Éva Kovács and Andrea Szalai for their time, encouraging enthusiasm, and insightful comments. For their illuminating suggestions and questions, I am also thankful to Matti Bunzl, Chip Colwell, Tim Dant, Nicky Gregson, Jason Baird Jackson, Alena Ledeneva, Stephen E. Nash, Roberta Sassatelli, Alexander Smith, Michael Stewart, and Donald C. Wood.

I am especially indebted to Fred R. Myers for the foreword he has written to this book, and for his patience and support.

A special word of gratitude is owed to Andrea Szalai for the useful suggestions she shared with me during the transcription and interpretation of Romani conversations.

Financial assistance from many institutions at different times of the project enabled me to carry out the ethnographic research among Romanian Roma for this monograph. Special thanks must go to the Hungarian Scientific Research Fund; Balassi Institute; the Ministry of Hungarian Cultural Heritage; the Open Society Institute (Budapest); the Soros Foundation (Budapest); the Institute for Ethnology of the Hungarian Academy of Sciences; and UCL SSEES. Organizing and financing the first stage of the ethnographic research would not have been possible without the intellectual commitment of and support from Michael Stewart.

I received generous help for preparation of the manuscript from the Hungarian Scientific Research Fund (PUB-K 114509) and the Research Centre for the Humanities of the Hungarian Academy of Sciences, for which I am grateful. In connection with this latter support, I owe a debt of gratitude to Pál Fodor and Balázs Balogh.

Elayne Antalffy, Anna Babarczy, and Barbara Kamienski provided invaluable assistance in the translation of the monograph, and in streamlining its English. I am indebted to each of them for their infinite patience, inspiring commitment, and exceptional professional expertise. I wish to thank Ágnes-Éva Varga for her valuable help in the preparation of the photos for publication. I alone bear responsibility for any errors or shortcomings of this book.

I am also grateful to the team at the University of Toronto Press, especially my editors, Janice Evans, Douglas Hildebrand, and Jodi Lewchuk, who have been very helpful, flexible, and patient throughout the entire process of turning the manuscript into a book. I am truly thankful to Michael Lambek for his support in including this monograph in the Anthropological Horizons series, to the three anonymous reviewers, to the anonymous reader chosen by UTP's Manuscript Review Committee, as well as to the copy-editor of the manuscript, Jonathan Adjemian, for their insightful critical comments and advice. Portions of chapter 3 were previously published in 2009 as "Materialising Ethnicity: Commodity Fetishism and Symbolic Re-Creation of Objects among the Gabor Roma (Romania)," *Social Anthropology* 17(2): 184–97, and an earlier version of chapter 5 appeared in 2010 as "Shifting Transactional Identities: Bazaar-Style Trade and Risk Management in the Prestige Economy of the Gabor Roma (Romania)," in *Economic Action in Theory and Practice: Anthropological Investigations*, edited by Donald C. Wood (Bingley, United Kingdom: Emerald Publishing). Parts of chapter 9 appeared in 2011 as "Constructing, Commodifying, and Consuming Invented Ethnic Provenance among Romanian Roma," *Museum Anthropology* 34(2): 128–41, while an earlier version of chapter 10 was published in 2013 as "Classification Struggles, Moral Criticism and the Interethnic Trade of Prestige Goods between Two Romanian Roma Groups," *Journal of Consumer Culture* 13(3): 337–65. The first of the two extended case studies presented in part 3 appeared in 2015 as "Recreating and Materializing Social Differences through

Patina-Oriented Consumption: The Post-Socialist Ownership History of a Second-Hand, Luxury Commodity," *Museum Anthropology Review* 9(1–2): 1–33, and the second in 2014 as "Proprietary Contest, Business Ethics, and Conflict Management: A Multi-Sited Commodity Ethnography," in *Production, Consumption, Business and the Economy: Structural Ideals and Moral Realities*, edited by Donald C. Wood (Bingley, United Kingdom: Emerald Publishing).

Last but far from least, it is impossible to express the depth of my gratitude to my family members, who tirelessly supported me during the ethnographic research and the work of writing these chapters. Their understanding, patience, and love helped me through the moments when I doubted whether I would ever reach the end of this book.

MATERIALIZING DIFFERENCE

Consumer Culture, Politics, and Ethnicity
among Romanian Roma

Introduction
Translocal Communities of Practice and Multi-Sited Ethnographies

How do objects mediate human relationships? In what ways do they possess social and political agency? What role does material culture – prestige consumption, as well as commodity aesthetics, biographies, and ownership histories – play in the production and negotiation of social and political identities, differences, and hierarchies? How do translocal consumer subcultures of collectors – interpreted as communities of practice – organize and manage themselves?

Drawing on theories and case studies from anthropology and sociology – primarily material culture, consumption, museum, ethnicity, and (post-) socialist studies – this monograph addresses these questions via the analysis of the practices and ideologies connected to silver beakers and roofed tankards that are interpreted as ethnicized and gendered prestige objects[1] among the Gabor Roma[2] living in a multi-ethnic region of Romania (in Transylvania). The consumer subculture organized around these (ideally inalienable) silver pieces is among the contemporary second-hand cultures based on patina-oriented consumption. While the price of these beakers and roofed tankards on the European antiques market usually does not exceed US$11,000, they are traded among the Gabor Roma for several times as much; the price of the more valuable objects may reach, or occasionally even exceed, US$200,000 to US$400,000. (See colour plates: Photos 9–19.)

The theoretical approach used in this monograph builds largely on Appadurai's notion of methodological fetishism, the perspective of things-in-motion (the transnational or transcultural movement of things between various value regimes, for instance), and the biographical method. The chapters also rely heavily on recent theories developed in anthropology and sociology focusing on how symbolic conflicts between contesting consumer subcultures emerge and are managed; how the politics of ethnicized consumer taste and commodity aesthetics works; how values, meanings, and prices are constructed and contested on the globalized antiques market; and how an ownership history can possess a social and political agency of its own and become a scarce resource (that is, a sought-after symbolic pantheon, entry to which is greatly desired).

This book reveals the inner dynamics of the complex relationships and interactions between objects (silver beakers and roofed tankards) and subjects (Romanian Roma) and investigates how these relationships and interactions contribute to the construction, materialization, and reformulation of social, economic, and political identities, boundaries, and differences. It also discusses how, after 1989, the political transformation in Romania led to the emergence of a new, post-socialist consumer sensitivity among the Gabor Roma, and how this sensitivity reshaped the interpretations of an average standard of living and a good/normal/ideal life, as well as the pre-regime-change patterns, meanings, and value preferences of prestige consumption.

Setting the Context: The Romanian Gabor Roma

The Gabor Roma – also called simply "Gabors" – constitute one of the numerous Roma ethnic populations living in Romania. (See colour plates: Photos 1–8.) They are generally trilingual; while their mother tongue is a Vlach Romani variant, they additionally speak the regional Hungarian variant and learn Romanian as the official state language. The largest Gabor Roma local communities today are found in Mureş, Harghita, and Cluj Counties, while large numbers of Gabors also live in such Romanian cities as Oradea, Braşov, Arad, Satu Mare, and Timişoara (see Map 0.1). The great majority of the families I came to know were Seventh-Day Adventists, but a few families had joined the Pentecostals or the Jehovah's Witnesses, and others were Calvinists.

In interethnic encounters in Romania – that is, in the course of external self-identification – my interlocutors generally applied to themselves the ethnonyms *gábor cigányok/ţiganii gabori* (Gabor Gypsies/Roma), or *kalapos gáborok/gabori cu pălărie* (hat-wearing Gabors), and both Romanians and Hungarians used mainly those expressions when referring to them. However, in intraethnic discourses among themselves, the Gabors generally used another ethnonym: *amare feli r̓oma*, meaning "our kind of Roma/Roma like us" (see also Piasere 1985).[3]

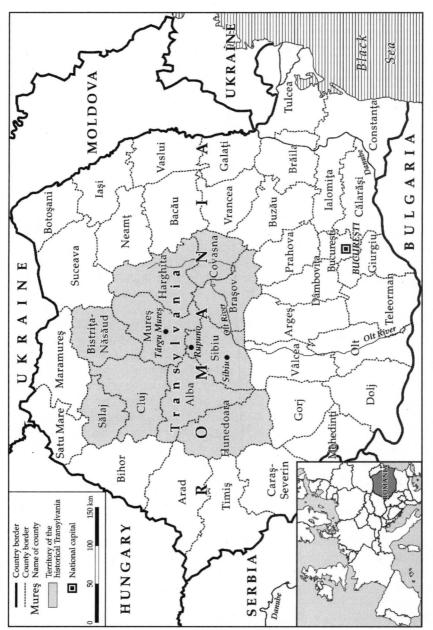

Map 0.1. Map of Romania

The dominant livelihood strategy among them today is intermediary trade (*bižnico*; see colour plates: Photo 4). Up until the political regime change in 1989, Gabor Roma entrepreneurs traded principally in Romania; after 1989, many of them began to extend their commercial activities to Hungary, while others regularly travelled to Turkey and imported various commodities, mainly carpets and curtains. Around the turn of the millennium, Gabor traders appeared in Croatia, Serbia, and Slovenia, and later in Slovakia and Austria. In the last few years, many of them have also tried their luck in other countries, including Greece, Macedonia, Albania, Bulgaria, Poland, Germany, Sweden, Italy, the Netherlands, Belgium, France, and the United Kingdom. Since 2010, Russia has also become a popular commercial destination for many merchants.

Among the various forms of intermediate trade practised within Romania, the Gabor Roma favour peddling, selling at second-hand markets, and selling goods imported in bulk to local retailers. What makes dealing with Gabor traders attractive is primarily their prices (which are usually lower than shop prices), the possibility of intense price bargaining, and, in the case of less mobile customers living in small settlements, the "home delivery" of commodities that are otherwise difficult to obtain.

In Romania – especially in regions where the supply of goods is weaker – the most extensively traded second-hand goods in markets are shoes, clothing (for instance, leather coats, jeans, jackets, shirts, and work clothing), and antiques (among other things, old clocks and watches, mortars and pestles, and inexpensive paintings). These traders also often stock new clothing articles (such as trousers, socks, and underwear), carpets, and curtains, as well as blankets, cookware sets, cutlery, mobile phones, and other commodities. The success of the Gabor Roma merchants can mainly be attributed to three factors: intense economic migration, rapid adaptation to changing market demands (the ability to flexibly change markets and the types of goods handled), and the effectiveness of the impression-management and trust-building strategies used in selling in markets and peddling.

The Gabor Roma making a living as tinsmiths mainly make eaves-troughs and downspouts for family homes, as well as for industrial facilities, churches, or schools; they roof buildings with tin sheets and produce customized hand-made roof ornaments, as well as buckets, watering cans, funnels, and other kitchen and garden implements. Some of them are craftsmen who make street garbage bins and also, with the help of Gabor Roma skilled in welding, large containers that can be lifted onto trucks for the transport of raw materials and rubbish. Others, with the help of subcontractors, undertake the restoration and construction of whole buildings (such as industrial facilities). Many Gabor entrepreneurs who make their livings as tinsmiths regularly participate in local and regional public procurement tenders.

The manufacture of various copper objects, once one of the major sources of income among the Gabors, gradually declined in the period before the political regime change in 1989 and has now almost completely lost its former economic significance. Nowadays only a few elderly persons still have coppersmithing skills and make – in their spare time – brandy stills, large pots for cooking and canning, and other copper objects intended as "curiosities" for market sale or as informal gifts for non-Roma in return for various favours (for instance, for help given in medical care or handling official affairs).

The above livelihood strategies make it possible for many Gabor Roma families to achieve a living standard similar to or higher than the average one of their non-Roma neighbours. It is largely due to the significant rise in the social and economic status of the Gabor Roma, beginning in the 1970s, that the previously typical non-Roma dominance in interethnic relations is now frequently reversed, at least in certain types of interactions. Some Gabor Roma families regularly employ non-Roma (or other, non-Gabor Roma) as drivers or as assistants in second-hand markets, or hire them to cater their social gatherings (for instance, weddings, betrothals, and funerals), clean their yards, or do other tasks around the family home. The fact that my Gabor interlocutors liked to refer to themselves as the "aristocracy of the Transylvanian Roma" and the frequent – often essentializing, idealizing, and exoticizing – reports in the Romanian and Hungarian media about their living conditions, religious orientation, and material culture can be primarily explained by this rise in their social and economic status.

Translocal Communities of Practice and Multi-Sited Ethnographies

In the course of my anthropological fieldwork among the Gabor Roma in Transylvania, it soon became clear to me that their prestige economy, organized around beakers and roofed tankards made of antique silver, was not a local or regional phenomenon; that is, it was not limited exclusively to a particular settlement or microregion but was an informal, ethnicized, and gendered practice that could be defined as translocal.

In other words, in many settlements and counties of Transylvania, there were Gabor Roma who participated actively in this economy in various roles, such as owner, broker, or creditor (see chapter 2).

It was because of this translocality that my fieldwork could not be limited to a single Gabor Roma local community or microregion of Transylvania. For my investigation, a detailed analysis of prestige consumption therefore required the use of the method of multi-sited ethnography (Myers 1991, 1998, 2002, 2004b, 2006b, 2006c, 2013; Nemeth 1991, 2002; Steiner 1994; Marcus 1995; Marcus & Myers 1995; Falzon 2009, 2015; Coleman & Hellermann 2011). This involved regular migration among Gabor Roma local communities as well as among contesting translocal consumer subcultures – that is, among the Gabor Roma and the Cărhar Roma[4] living in Romania, and several participants in the European antiques market – that were committed to collecting silver beakers and roofed tankards. George E. Marcus (1995, 106–8), one of the best-known theorists of this method, asserts that one technique of multi-sited ethnographic research is to "follow the thing" – that is, to trace the flow of things, such as gifts, money, or works of art, among different contexts. According to Marcus:

> The most explicit experimentation with multi-sited research using this technique seems to have emerged in studies of contemporary worlds of art and aesthetics … Notable examples include Myers's study of the circulation of Pintupi acrylic paintings in Western art worlds, Savigliano's study of Tango, Steiner's study of the transit of African curios into Western art markets, along with Taylor & Barbash's film based on Steiner's study, Silverman's study of taste in Reagan's America across three intensively explored sites, and Feld's mapping of "world music" and "world beat." (Marcus 1995, 106–7)

Multi-sited ethnographic research, just like the biographical method (see chapter 11), did not merely make it possible to map and investigate the movement of silver objects within and between social, cultural, and political contexts; it also required the documentation and analysis of changes in the material and symbolic properties associated with the travelling beakers and roofed tankards (such as meanings, values, and position in the ranking of available commodities), as well as a comparison of the various consumer subcultures and related value regimes affected by the migration of these silver objects.

Between 1998 and the completion of this book, I spent a total of over thirty-three months in Transylvania conducting multi-sited ethnographic research, mainly among Gabor Roma. In addition, when I was back home in Budapest, I often met Gabor families whose members were trading in Hungary; I joined them in mapping offers on the Budapest antiques market (looking for silver objects of the kind they found attractive), and in their intermediate trade.

Since an analysis of the motivations and consequences of the interethnic prestige-object trade between the Gabor Roma and the Cărhar Roma would have been unjustifiably one-sided had it been based exclusively on fieldwork carried out among the Gabors, I also built up long-term connections with Cărhar Roma families in numerous Romanian settlements. (It can be said of the Cărhars' prestige economy, too, that its active participants – such as owners, brokers, or creditors – live in many settlements scattered throughout Transylvania.) A significant part of my Cărhar interlocutors were persons who were themselves prestige-object owners and had participated as buyers, brokers, or creditors in one or more transactions organized between the Gabors and the Cărhars (e.g., in sales and purchases, or in credit deals that involved the pawning of silver beakers and roofed tankards).

Thanks to the frequent migration of silver objects between the European antiques market and Gabor Roma buyers, the antiques markets of Hungary and Romania also became a target of my ethnographic research. Over the past two decades, I closely followed the offers of the larger antique shops and auction houses in these countries that dealt in – among other things – silver beakers and roofed tankards. I was also in regular contact with some antiques dealers working in Hungary and Romania who are marginal participants in the Gabors' prestige economy, primarily as occasional sellers. Furthermore, I made significant efforts to compare assessments made by museums and participants in the antiques market in Hungary and Romania of objects that had the material properties popular among the Gabor Roma with the evaluations of Western European and overseas art collectors, antiques dealers, and auction houses. To this end, I regularly followed auctions in major transnational auction houses, such as Sotheby's and Christie's, where silver pieces were put up for sale, and met a number of antiques dealers in Western European cities such as London or Paris trading in, among other things, silver beakers and roofed tankards made by European silversmiths.

In concurrence with contemporary, constructivist critiques of (ethnic) "groupism" and the traditional concept of community, (a) I do not regard the Gabor Roma as an externally rigidly bounded, internally socially undifferentiated, fixed, and unquestionably given social formation; and (b) in this book I primarily examine practices, ideologies, and strategies, the analysis of which can contribute to a deeper understanding of the inner dynamics, and processual and relational nature, of the *groupness* or *communityness* characteristic of the Gabors. In other words, I focus on practices, ideologies, and strategies frequently applied by the Gabor Roma in order to conceptualize, experience, and perform their own ethnic identity and belonging. This perspective draws primarily on the following two trends of critical reinterpretation of analytical categories:

(1) One is the critique of groupism elaborated by Rogers Brubaker (1998, 2002, 2004, 2009; see also Billig 2002; McLaughlin 2007; Osei-Kofi 2012; Rhodes 2012; Ang 2014). Brubaker argues that groupism is an attitude, widespread in both public and scholarly discourses, that takes "discrete, sharply differentiated, internally homogenous and externally bounded groups as basic constituents of social life, chief protagonists of ethnicity, nationalism and race" (Brubaker 2002, 164) and "fundamental units of social analysis" (Brubaker 2009, 28).

Brubaker's writings throw light on the fact that the level of existing as a group – that is, the intensity of groupness – is a changing and context-sensitive quality. Consequently, social scientists need to make a more self-reflexive critical analysis of the concept of "group," which has often been used in a simplifying, essentializing, and overgeneralizing way. In the absence of such a shift in perspective, investigations can continue to overemphasize the significance of social groups and unwittingly obscure the inner dynamics, diversity, and ephemeral character of groupness. Brubaker stresses the need for social scientists to elaborate "ways of analyzing ethnicity without invoking bounded groups" in place of "analytical 'groupism'" (Brubaker 2004, 3). One way of doing this is to focus the analytical gaze not on "groups" but rather on "groupness," "as a contextually fluctuating conceptual variable" (Brubaker 2004, 11):

Shifting attention from groups to groupness, and treating groupness as variable and contingent rather than fixed and given, allows us to take account of – and, potentially, to account for – phases of extraordinary cohesion and moments of intensely felt collective solidarity, without implicitly treating high levels of groupness as constant, enduring, or definitionally present. (Brubaker 2004, 12)

This approach primarily takes groupness "as an *event*, as something that 'happens'" (Brubaker 2004, 12), and argues that it is more expedient to think of "ethnicity, race, and nation not in terms of substantial groups or entities but in terms of practical categories, situated actions, cultural idioms, cognitive schemas, discursive frames, organizational routines, institutional forms, political projects, and contingent events" (Brubaker 2004, 11).

(2) The analytical perspective of the book also owes much to social scientists who have elaborated the theory of *communities of practice* and have been strongly critical of the concept of community interpreted as an unchanging, *per definitionem* existing social unit (see, among others, Lave & Wenger 1991; Eckert & McConnell-Ginet 1992a, 1992b; Wenger 1998; Holmes & Meyerhoff 1999; Bucholtz 1999; Eckert & Wenger 2005; O'Sullivan 2009; Maida & Beck 2018).[5] The theory of communities of practice has had a significant career in the social sciences, partly because it has drawn attention to the context-dependency and variability of communityness, and partly because – as Bucholtz (1999, 210) has also pointed out – a community of practice "may be constituted around any social or linguistic practice." This theory became particularly popular in the theory of learning, in linguistics (e.g., in anthropological linguistics and in sociolinguistics), and in sociology. Eckert and McConnell-Ginet (1992b, 96) argue that the community of practice "is an aggregate of people who come together around mutual engagement in some common endeavor. Ways of doing things, ways of talking, beliefs, values, power relations – in short, practices – emerge in the course of their joint activity around that endeavor." The authors go on to point out that the novelty of this theory lies above all in the fact that the community of practice

is different from the traditional community, primarily because it is defined simultaneously by its membership and by the practice in which that membership engages … A community of practice might be people working together in a factory, regulars in a bar, a neighborhood play group, a nuclear family, police partners and their ethnographer, the Supreme Court. Communities of practice may be large or small, intensive or diffuse; they are born and they die, they may persist through many changes of membership, and they may be closely articulated with other communities. Individuals participate in multiple communities of practice, and individual identity is based in the multiplicity of this participation. Rather than seeing the individual as some disconnected entity floating around in social space, or as a location in a network, or as a member of a particular group or set of groups ... we need to focus on communities of practice. (Eckert & McConnell-Ginet 1992b, 96)

Elsewhere Eckert (2009, 109) states that "the value of the notion *communities of practice* ... lies in the fact that it identifies a social grouping not in virtue of shared abstract characteristics (e.g. class, gender) or simple co-presence (e.g. neighborhood, workplace), but in virtue of shared practice."

Recognizing the explanatory power and intellectual significance of the above critiques of analytical groupism and the traditional concept of community, (a) the practices that are the focus of this monograph – the prestige economy developed around silver objects and Roma politics as the wider framework for that economy – are interpreted as important means and contexts of the experience of being Gabor Roma (i.e., of *Gaborness*) as an "event"; and (b) the individuals involved in these practices are regarded as persons constituting translocal, ethnicized communities of practice. The members of these communities of practice are bound together by shared interest and shared (passive or active) participation, by a consensus on the meanings, patterns, and value preferences associated with the latter, and by the intense flow of information – regardless of where they may be in Europe at any particular time.

What Does This Book Offer?

Why is it worth writing and reading a monograph on prestige consumption among the Gabors and the related Roma politics?

Anthropological and sociological research focusing on the Roma has devoted very little attention to studying the ideologies and practices through which social, economic, and political inequalities and hierarchies are organized within individual Roma ethnic populations or communities, and what Roma interpretations are associated with them. When examining social relations and interactions among Roma, the majority of analyses have focused mainly on the ideologies of equality-centrism, describing in detail its manifestations, causes, and consequences (see, for instance, Stewart 1994, 1997, 1998; Kertész Wilkinson

1997; Blasco 1999; Engebrigtsen 2007; Ries 2007). This asymmetry in research highlights the need for a more detailed, processual, relational, dynamic, and context-sensitive understanding of how the politics of difference works among Roma people.

In harmony with that need, this monograph primarily examines the role played by the politics of difference – in particular practices such as prestige consumption and marriage politics – in the construction and representation among the Gabor Roma of social and political identities, values, hierarchies, and boundaries, and their continuous negotiation. The chapters devote special attention to how these Roma create, strategically use, and shape certain categories and mechanisms of categorization related to social, economic, and political differences.

This monograph starts from the theoretical viewpoint that for a deeper and more balanced understanding of the social relations and interactions among Roma it is necessary to simultaneously investigate the ethics of sociability[6] and the politics of difference, and the ways in which they impact each other. It argues that observance of the ethics of sociability and adherence to Roma politics are practices, the simultaneous presence of which is not qualified by the Gabor Roma as risky, inappropriate, or undesirable – they do not necessarily exclude or extinguish each other. On the contrary, among the Gabors both the ethics of sociability and Roma politics are considered to be morally approved phenomena that in numerous contexts mutually interpret, explain, reinforce, and shape each other. In other words, the Gabor Roma discourse of the ethics of intraethnic similarity does not regard political differences as either morally stigmatized social constructions or dangerous anomalies to be eliminated; achievements in the symbolic arenas of Roma politics are important and highly valued elements in the Roma concept of success. It was precisely for this reason that my Gabor Roma hosts considered not egalitarianism but the creation and maintenance of harmony and balance between the ethics of sociability and the politics of difference as the ideal model of intraethnic social and economic relations.

These chapters offer the reader a picture of Roma families that in many respects show successful social and economic integration, typically have balanced relationships with the majority society, in many cases have accumulated significant economic capital, and have a standard of living comparable to or higher than that of non-Roma living in their vicinity. This monograph could therefore serve as an alternative to the dominant analytical perspective that tends to associate Roma

communities mainly with stereotypes of social marginalization, poverty, deprivation, defencelessness, interethnic conflict, and subordina-
tion, and to characterize social relations within these communities as
only slightly differentiated (see, for example, Stewart 1997, 1998; Barany
2001; Scheffel 2005). Several of the symbolic arenas of Roma politics
among the Gabors – for example, their prestige economy, marriage
politics, or the hierarchies of patrilines – are unequivocal proof that the
Roma do not necessarily construct and represent their identities *against*
the negatively defined majority society (with the intention of differenti-
ating themselves from that society and creating social distance); rather,
they can also be characterized by highly valued intraethnic identity
practices that are inseparable from the Roma interpretations of social
success and respectability and in which non-Roma either play no part
or are participants of only marginal significance. Through the analysis of the intraethnic politics of difference practised among the Gabors,
these chapters can also contribute to deconstructing and reconceptualizing the dominant negative image of Roma in Romanian and Western
European media reports and public discourses – an image that is usually disquietingly fragmentary, essentializing, and homogenizing.

The Gabor Roma are an excellent example of how, when a minority
in many respects integrates into the majority society, certain ethnicized
practices of this minority may at the same time operate independently
and successfully. In the case of the Gabors, Roma politics (as a whole)
and certain of its symbolic arenas, such as prestige consumption focused
on silver objects or marriage politics based on endogamous, arranged
marriages, can be included among these practices. This monograph
also demonstrates that these practices have multiple, context-sensitive
usability and significance in identity management. On the one hand,
my Gabor Roma interlocutors frequently defined them as important
means of creating intraethnic differences. On the other hand, in the contexts of comparison between themselves and the non-Roma or other,
non-Gabor Roma, they tended to identify these practices – because of
their ethnicized character – as symbolic resources that to a considerable
degree contribute to the conceptualization, experience, and representation of their own shared Roma ethnic identity and belonging.

The Structure of the Book

This introduction, "Translocal Communities of Practice and Multi-Sited
Ethnographies," began with some key questions and other elements of

the analytical approach taken in the monograph, then briefly outlined the ethnographic context of the research. It went on to highlight the analytical significance and explanatory power of the method of multi-sited ethnography, which proved indispensable and illuminating in the course of this project, and to discuss what the problem sensitivity of this book's chapters owes to the growing critique of groupism, associated particularly with the name of Rogers Brubaker, and to the theory of communities of practice.

The first part of the monograph, "Negotiating and Materializing Difference and Belonging," which deals with intraethnic aspects of prestige consumption, begins with the chapter "Symbolic Arenas and Trophies of the Politics of Difference," which analyses the values around which, as well as the ideologies and practices by which Roma politics characteristic of the Gabors is organized. The chapter investigates in detail the symbolic arenas of Roma politics – mainly the achievements in these arenas that are taken into account when the Gabors negotiate and define prestige relations between individuals, families, local communities, and patrilines. It also examines the symbolic trophies – certain honorific titles – that are the principal goal of Roma politics. Finally, the chapter draws attention to the dynamic character and complexity of the relationship between the politics of intraethnic difference and the ethics of sociability, and the intensity and significance of their interactions and interdependence.

The second chapter, "The Gabors' Prestige Economy: A Translocal, Ethnicized, Informal, and Gendered Consumer Subculture," discusses the interpretation of authenticity constructed by the Gabor Roma and associated by them with their beakers and roofed tankards[7] made of antique silver, which they regard as prestige objects. It then provides many examples to show how the prestige economy that has arisen around these pieces can be interpreted as a translocal, ethnicized, informal, and gendered consumer subculture. The chapter explores why the Gabors define these beakers and tankards as luxury goods, why they regard inalienability as their ideal state, and what main functions – such as political trophies and multiple identity symbols – are associated with them. Finally, it compares the most important features of patina-based prestige objects (beakers and roofed tankards) with those of novelty-oriented prestige goods (such as Western cars or new family houses).

The third chapter, "From Antiques to Prestige Objects: De- and Recontextualizing Commodities from the European Antiques Market," follows the ways in which the Gabors – as new owners – "erase" most of the meanings and values previously associated with these ethnic-border-crossing beakers and tankards by non-Roma – that is, by the value regimes of the antiques market and art history (decontextualization through deaestheticization and dehistoricization); it also outlines the processes through which the Gabor Roma endow these objects with new, usually ethnicized meanings and values (recontextualization through reaestheticization and rehistoricization).

The fourth chapter, "Creating Symbolic and Material Patina," argues that when assessing the value and price of a beaker or tankard changing hands among them, the Gabors attribute special significance to two factors: the political renown accumulated by the previous Gabor Roma owners of the piece (symbolic patina)[8] and the set of material properties (material patina). The chapter highlights how the ownership histories of sought-after silver objects become interpreted as ethnicized symbolic pantheons and acquire their own political agency; the Gabor Roma regard entry into these pantheons as a means of representing economic power and resources and shaping social and political differences and identities. At the same time, remarkable changes that occur in the social and economic situation of the current owner can also have an impact on the significance and value associated with the ownership history of the piece in his possession and on certain processes relating to that object (e.g., the intensity of proprietary contests focusing on it). In addition to the dynamics, agency, and politics of ownership histories, the chapter also discusses in detail the ethno-aesthetics on the basis of which the Gabor Roma determine the values and meanings of the material properties of their prestige objects.

The fifth chapter, "The Politics of Brokerage: Bazaar-Style Trade and Risk Management," deals with the activity and importance of the brokers often employed in prestige-object transactions – sales and purchases, certain credit deals – among the Gabors. It explores in detail the factors justifying the employment of intermediaries, especially the sources of uncertainty that accompany these transactions (for instance, the relative lack of standardization of material properties or the politics of [in]visibility connected with prestige objects), and analyses the strategies most frequently used by brokers as risk managers.

The sixth chapter, "Political Face-Work and Transcultural Bricolage/Hybridity: Prestige Objects in Political Discourse," focuses on strategies and techniques used by the Gabors to "frame" (i.e., to mitigate the consequences of) the public mention of beakers and tankards in political discourse (including songs with political content). These strategies and techniques are inseparable from Gabor Roma interpretations of social person, success, and respectability, and from the need for a continuous search for balance between the ethics of sociability and the politics of difference. First, the chapter investigates how the ethics of public face-work shape discourses on intraethnic political achievements and differences at various social gatherings. Through the analysis of several short examples, a song excerpt, and a whole song, the second part of the chapter concerns face-saving strategies and techniques used in discursive political self-representation that concentrates on prestige objects – with a special focus on linguistic indirectness.

The second part of the monograph, "Contesting Consumer Subcultures: Interethnic Trade, Fake Authenticity, and Classification Struggles," deals with interethnic aspects. It begins with the seventh chapter, "Gabor Roma, Cărhar Roma, and the European Antiques Market: Contesting Consumer Subcultures," which describes two consumer subcultures that also show an intense interest in the silver beakers and roofed tankards sought after among the Gabor Roma, and make considerable sacrifices in order to collect and possess them. Following some paragraphs on the European antiques market, the chapter discusses in detail the main features of the prestige economy that has developed around these types of silver objects among the Romanian Cărhar Roma, and compares the Gabor Roma and Cărhar Roma interpretations of the symbolic and material properties of beakers and tankards. In summing up the differences between the two Roma prestige economies and value regimes, it devotes special attention to the question of inheritance and to the role that prestige objects play in marriage politics among the Cărhars.

The eighth chapter, "Interethnic Trade of Prestige Objects," outlines the main causes for and characteristics of the prestige-object trade between the Gabor Roma and the Cărhar Roma, while the ninth chapter, "Constructing, Commodifying, and Consuming Fake Authenticity," deals with a practice – money-oriented fraud – that owes its existence in part to that interethnic trade. The aim of the latter chapter is to explore in detail the strategies and practices (such as the manipulation of material patina, ownership history, and the context of the transaction) used by some Gabor individuals in attempts to acquire substantial profit by misleading Cărhar Roma buyers and creditors – trying to sell to or pawn with the latter silver pieces of modest value, only recently purchased from the antiques market but disguised as highly valued prestige objects with long and attractive Gabor Roma ownership histories. The chapter also investigates the sporadic cases where non-Roma entrepreneurs living in their vicinity or the anthropologist doing research among them were the targets of money-oriented fraud initiated by Gabor Roma.

The tenth chapter, "The Politics of Consumption: Classification Struggles, Moral Criticism, and Stereotyping," examines how the Gabor Roma and the Cărhar Roma, when explaining their consumer choices with regard to beakers and roofed tankards, attach partially different interpretations to the concept of a good/normal/ideal life and to such dichotomies as an average standard of living versus luxury, morally approved versus morally stigmatized patterns of consumption, and consumer modernism versus conservatism. The chapter also highlights how these two Roma ethnic populations construct their rival interpretations of consumer moral superiority, primarily through practices such as classification struggle, stereotyping, and moral criticism focusing on consumption.

The third part of the monograph, "Multi-Sited Commodity Ethnographies," opens with the eleventh chapter, "Things-in-Motion: Methodological Fetishism, Multi-Sitedness, and the Biographical Method," which sums up a few of the main methodological and theoretical features and novelties of the anthropology of things-in-motion. It also proposes that analyses based on multi-sited research that concentrate on tracking commodities-in-motion and on their – often transnational or transcultural – social lives, should be defined as multi-sited commodity ethnographies. The chapter argues that examining the biographies and agency attributed to things-in-motion is crucial to a deeper understanding of the political, social, and cultural contexts, processes, and relations surrounding them, as well as of the interdependence and complex network of interactions between things and subjects.

The twelfth and thirteenth chapters are based on case studies; drawing on the methods and problem sensitivity of the anthropology of things-in-motion, they trace and analyse the post-socialist Gabor Roma social career of a silver beaker and a roofed tankard respectively.

Finally, the conclusion, "The Post-Socialist Consumer Revolution and the Shifting Meanings of Prestige Goods," seeks an answer to the question of how patterns, practices, and value preferences related to prestige consumption among the Gabor Roma have changed as a consequence of the post-socialist transformation – especially the post-socialist consumer revolution. It summarizes the reasons for the political, social, and economic popularity of silver beakers and roofed tankards before 1989, investigates which of these changed and in what way after the regime change, and then explores the influence these changes had on the Gabors' prestige economy. The chapter devotes special attention to the growing symbolic conflict between traditional, patina-based prestige objects (the silver beakers and tankards) and post-socialist, novelty-oriented prestige goods (such as Western cars and new family houses), and the deepening division in Gabor Roma opinions with regard to the social value and significance of beakers and tankards that has arisen since 1989, in part along generational lines.

PART ONE

Negotiating and Materializing Difference and Belonging

1

Symbolic Arenas and Trophies of the Politics of Difference

Roma Politics (*Romani Politika*)[1]

Roma politics characteristic of the Gabors is a "tournament of value" (Appadurai 1986, 21) composed of a series of – mainly ethnicized – symbolic arenas, practices, and ideologies used to create, perform, and redefine social and economic differences. To quote one of my acquaintances, Roma politics is "a contest … The Gabors are deeply absorbed in politics." My interlocutors relied primarily on the successes achieved in the symbolic arenas of Roma politics to conceptualize prestige relations between individuals, families, local communities, and patrilines.

Roma politics is not part of national party politics in Romania; it is not affiliated with any political organizations and is independent of the activities of both county-level and settlement-level local governments, as well as central government institutions and the various offices in their employment. Nor does it have ties with the various forms of ethnic self-organization or pressure groups; it is separate from the activities of civic organizations concerned with the enforcement of Roma rights and interests in Romania, from Roma nation-building efforts, and from the issue of the representation of ethnic minorities in parliament. In other words, Roma politics is an ethnicized, relatively closed and informal subsystem of the politics of difference, largely invisible and unknown to the majority society. The link between party politics in Romania and Roma politics consists of a few Gabor men joining one of the Romanian parties, and a lot of people regularly following political news in the Romanian media. Most of my interlocutors who are members of a party were not motivated to join because of the prospect of a political career among the non-Roma. Rather, they saw this step as a way of augmenting their local or regional non-Roma relational capital – adding mayors or headmasters, for instance, to their networks of Roma acquaintances who may contribute (as customers or brokers) to the growth of their business activities in commerce or the construction industry.

Roma politics is therefore not a "smaller version" of national party politics in Romania, and not even one of its subsystems; they exist in parallel, independently of each other. While there are no major obstacles to Gabor men participating in national or regional party politics, and nobody sees anything objectionable about it in their own Roma ethnic population, the active participation of non-Roma in Roma politics is essentially unimaginable. The main reason for this is that the symbolic arenas of Roma politics are organized primarily around ethnicized goods and ideologies of value; that is, most of them are closely tied to Gabor Roma ethnic identity and history. For this reason – with the exception of a few anthropologists and antiques dealers – only the Gabors are interested in these arenas and the successes achieved here (such as purchases of prestige objects or marital alliances established with influential Gabor families), and the reputational profit accompanying them cannot be converted into social respectability or prestige in the non-Roma world (e.g., in Romanian party politics). The only exceptions are some of the principles of the ethics of sociability (such as expectations of sharing and solidarity) and the accumulation of cash and assets (such as new family homes and expensive cars), the value of which is calculated in the same way by both the Gabors and the non-Roma.

When conceptualizing, and from time to time redefining, prestige relations between individuals, families, local communities, and patrilines, my Gabor Roma acquaintances took into account the following symbolic arenas:

(1) *The accumulation of economic capital*: with special emphasis on successes achieved in the prestige economy.

(2) *The politics of kinship, 1*: the prestige hierarchies of Gabor Roma patrilines at local, regional, and ethnic population levels. The position occupied in them derives from the political fame inherited from patrilineal forebears.

(3) *The politics of kinship, 2*: the accumulation of relational capital among Gabor Roma. In their case, the sources of relational capital with special significance are marital alliances (*xanamikimo*) established with influential Gabor families through arranged marriages (often of children), and a social network consisting principally of consanguineous

male relatives (brothers, sons, and grandsons), co-fathers-in-law, and brothers-in-law who can be mobilized in case of need.

(4) *The Gabor Roma ethics of sociability*: behaviour (*phirajimo*) and honour, respectability, and social appreciation (*patjiv*). In this fourth symbolic arena, individuals, families, and patrilines compete with each other for the construction, preservation, and enhancement of their own positive public images. The social evaluation of this image depends first and foremost on "behaviour" – that is, the extent to which the given individual, family, or patriline respects the Gabor Roma ethics of managing social relations and interactions.[2]

Let me quote just three comments revealing the conditions that must be met for someone to be successful in Roma politics.

[According to one of my middle-aged Roma interlocutors, "there must be several records in the file"[3] of people who would like to be successful in politics. These "records" that the Gabor Roma "score" or "weigh" (evaluate) are the following:] One – the rank, the birth [patrilineal prestige]; two – he must have a good beaker [or a roofed tankard]; three – he must have a good wife [one coming from an influential family]; four – he must have wealth [cash] beyond his beaker [or roofed tankard]; five – he must have a good son; and six – he must have good behaviour [he must respect the Gabor Roma ethics of sociability]. (25 July 2003)[4]

If you want to be a widely honoured, esteemed person in the meetings[5] and want everyone to give you your right [show respect towards you], you must have a rank [high patrilineal prestige; be from a politically successful patriline]; you must be rich, not only with a *taxtaj* [silver beaker; you must also have substantial cash reserves]; you must be strong, you must have a few backs behind your back; you must have good co-fathers-in-law so people can't get up your nose [have a social network supporting you in conflict situations]. (1 August 2003)

We fight [compete] to buy a good beaker. We fight for the good Roma [marital alliances with influential families]. We fight for the wealth [silver prestige objects and cash accumulation]. We fight for the honour [*patjiv*] ... We fight for the big houses ... That is Roma politics. (1 August 2003)

The major past and present events and achievements associated with the political arenas – for instance, memorable marital alliances, prestige-object transactions, or local and regional prestige hierarchies of patrilines – are common and often dominant topics of conversation at social gatherings (organized for weddings, betrothals, wakes, funerals, and memorial rituals) and in spontaneous discourse among Gabor Roma.[6] This is only one side of the coin, however. Political discourse is also a constitutive means as well as a context of Roma politics; it not only represents the successes and failures achieved in the prestige economy or in marriage politics, among other arenas, but it also gives an opportunity to shape, redefine, and negotiate current prestige relations. That is, a substantial number of the strategies and techniques used in political discourse – for instance, bringing up topics that threaten the positive public image of rival individuals (mentioning and exaggerating their political failures, and so on), or symbolically devaluing their successes – themselves function as means aiming at modifying prestige relations.

Within the Gabor Roma ethnic population, it is not the typical non-Roma forums of political (self-)representation – such as national or regional newspapers, the various television channels, or political party events – that provide the most significant contexts of political publicity but rather the types of social gatherings mentioned in the previous paragraph, and the male discourses that take place at those gatherings. The gatherings considered to be the most important, the ones that mobilize the largest crowds and receive the most intense attention, are wakes and funerals,[7] which are open to everyone to attend (in contrast to weddings and betrothals, for instance, where participation is by invitation only). (See colour plates: Photos 1–3, 5–7.)

The dialect of the Gabors uses synonyms for the concept of political discourse, such as "talking politics" (*politikazin*); "counting each other" (*djinenpe jăkhavrăh*) – that is, the participants evaluating and comparing each other's political achievements; "weighing each other up" (*merlegezin jăkhavrăh*); "rating each other" (*pontozin jăkhavrăh*; in the words of one of my Roma interlocutors, "with smiley faces and sad faces like in a school"); and "counting people's strengths and weaknesses [political successes and failures]" (*djinen le manušengo djengo ponture, the vi lengo zurale ponture*). The tropes and paraphrases that my Roma acquaintances often used for wakes give an idea of the special social and political significance attached to such gatherings: a "Roma parliament," or a "Roma lyceum or grammar school," where people "learn more than in ten years anywhere else. You see everyone's behaviour, how they behave, how they speak, how they think. [At a wake everybody] makes his/her own school report."

What do men talk about when they talk politics at a wake? The content of the answers given below – only a few of many – is in line with my experiences during participant observation. Several of these comments focus on only one or a few arenas of Roma politics. An outstandingly high proportion of answers associate politics primarily with genealogical memory and discourse: with the recalling of political successes of fathers, grandfathers, and other patrilineal forebears, and negotiations about past and current prestige relations among patrilines or families belonging to the same patriline. This practice is called *nemzetezinpe* ("talking nations," that is, talking about Gabor Roma nations [patrilines]) by my Gabor interlocutors. In their Romani dialect, the term "nation" (*nemzeto*) is used as a synonym of patriline, while the noun "rank" (*rango*) refers to the prestige of an individual's patriline or, in other words, the position of that patriline in the local, regional, or ethnic population-level prestige hierarchies of Gabor patrilines.

When we talk, we start with the families: what nation [patriline] your grandfather is from, what nation [patriline] your father is from, where I am from, where did I receive my wife from, where did I bring my daughter-in-law from, what marital alliances I've formed. How I fitted my family well [whether I managed to establish marital alliances with influential families], like my father did with his children, or I couldn't … They weigh [compare and evaluate] each other up. (2 August 2003)

[They talk about] ranks [patrilineal prestige], origin [descent, the patrilines], the beakers, wealth, behaviour. (20 September 2000)

There are a lot of things in politics … Politics comes up when the Roma gather together at a wake or funeral to talk about each other: "One is richer, the other is poorer!" … They continue their nations [they talk about their patrilineal past] because they know where you are from, where I am from … That you are from a poor rank [a patriline with modest prestige] or from a great nation [an influential and respectable patriline]. They talk nations. (5 August 2003)

They mention how their grandfather's grandfather lived because they go that far, they go back to their fifth grandfather [the grandfather of their grandfather]. How it was, how he left his sons [what material and symbolic inheritance he left to his sons], and how the other man left his sons … what beakers they had, how they behaved [to what extent they abided by the ethics of sociability] ... They bring out [bring up] the grandfather of their grandfather and other important things: wealth, behaviour. (31 July 2003)

Politics is not the only significant and prevalent topic of male conversations taking place at wakes, funerals, memorial rituals, weddings, betrothals, and other social events. The discussion and interpretation of the principles of the Gabor Roma ethics of sociability and religious – in our case mostly Adventist – lifestyle strategies, and the citing and debating of passages from the Bible are similarly common phenomena. In addition, frequent elements of the wakes are the mainly Romani or Hungarian-language "wake songs" (*žalniko djili*, literally, "slow songs"), that often themselves have political content, as well as "holy songs" (*sento djili*) from the Adventist hymnal. A natural feature of conversations at social gatherings is that the central discourse of the event – followed by the majority of those attending, but participated in mainly by elder men and led by one or more of them – occasionally stops for a while. When this happens, the participants organize themselves into smaller groups and converse quietly within their groups until one of them raises his voice again and captures the attention of the others, putting an end to the parallel conversations.

Roma politics, as a topic and discursive practice, is not only a typical element of male discourses arising at the social gatherings mentioned earlier but also an important and often even dominant part of informal conversations that take place within the family or with the participation of a few non-kin individuals who come together in a public space. That is, political discourse is also a frequent element of everyday meeting situations such as a visit to relatives, joint intermediary trade, recesses in Adventist worship services, or visits to second-hand markets, coffee shops, pastry shops, or shopping centres, where the Gabors are likely to run into two or three acquaintances at any time.

In the Gabor Roma local communities I got to know, the ideology of hierarchy played a crucial role not only in the evaluation and comparison of achievements in the arenas of Roma politics but also in the conceptualization of relations between genders and generations. Opinions regarding these achievements and relations are usually conceptualized in the form of prestige hierarchies (see, for example, the discussion of the concept of "rank" later in this chapter). Since Roma politics permeates several spheres of social and economic life and is an important source of their inner dynamics, the vast majority of my Gabor hosts were characterized by intense hierarchy awareness and status sensitivity. Also, they regarded the skillful use of morally approved techniques of creating and shaping social and economic differences as an esteemed competence. At this point, it is worth separating the concepts of "hard" and "soft" hierarchy, which are distinguished by their differing relations to personal autonomy. While "hard" hierarchies often openly question, threaten, and constrain personal autonomy, "soft" hierarchies regard respect for personal freedom of decision and autonomy as an important value. In the case of the latter, individuals prefer to use indirect techniques of exerting coercion (e.g., persuasion) in their effort to influence personal choices. The prestige hierarchies resting on the political performance of Gabor Roma individuals, families, and patrilines belong to the category of "soft" hierarchies.

Roma politics is an intensely gendered practice: it is primarily dominated – controlled and directed – by men. To give only a few examples: in determining the prestige associated with the descent of children, the prestige of the father's patriline is regarded as dominant (the political performance of the mother's patriline is often also taken into account); beakers and tankards are owned exclusively by men; and decisions regarding marriages and marital alliances are made principally in line with the political plans and interests of the fathers and paternal grandfathers. Women are also frequently active participants in politics, especially in political decision-making within their own nuclear families and in maintaining a positive public image of their families. However, the political agency of women is generally manifested indirectly (e.g., through informal influence on the husband's public stand), and is more limited in scope – for the most part to matters related to the selection of the children's marriage partners and the formation of marital alliances, and the accumulation of *patjiv*. In the case of women, the degree of individual political agency depends to a significant extent on how successful the husband and his father and patriline are in politics, how harmonious the connection between husband and wife is, and how familiar the wife is with the discursive and other techniques and strategies of Roma politics.

The Symbolic Trophies of Roma Politics

The participants in Roma politics do not compete for political offices and positions invested with formal power but rather for the accumulation of renown, social esteem, and prestige in their own Roma ethnic population, and for the acquisition of honorific titles – interpreted as symbolic trophies – reserved for those most successful in politics.

It is common practice that the politically most successful brother is given honorific titles such as "family leader" (*čaladvezetăvo*), the brother who "leads/heads/raises the family" (*vezetil/inkărăl opră o čalado*), who "goes at the front of the family" (*źal maj anglal dendo čalado*). The verb "lead" is also frequently used to describe dominance relations within a patriline – for example, the man/family who "leads the *vica*[8] [patriline]."

In a patriline that is markedly successful in Roma politics, there may be more than one person with the honorific title of "big Gabor Roma man" (*baro řom*; henceforth "big man"), which generally becomes widely used only after the death of the person meriting the title.[9] Big men are individuals from high-prestige patrilines who owned one or more valuable prestige objects; formed several marital alliances with influential Gabor families when marrying off their children and grandchildren; were able to rely on their extensive social network of male relatives for support in conflict situations; and were exemplary in respecting the ethics of sociability.

Finally, a widely respected, outstandingly influential individual whose name is associated with the most important political successes in his own local community is often referred to as "village leader" (*faluvezetăvo* or *bulibaš*).[10] The social significance of these individuals is highlighted by expressions such as "he is the Gabor man who leads the village" (*o řom kon vezetil o gav*) or "he is the foot [foundation] of the village" (*vov-i e talpa le gavehko*). Just as in the case of *čaladvezetăvo* and *baro řom*, an intense contest may develop among potential candidates and their supporters for the honorific title of village leader. The latter title is given in only some Gabor communities; it is rare for it to be used, for example, in settlements with only a few Gabor families who belong to the same patriline.

Before the change of political regime in Romania in 1989, in many Gabor Roma local communities the person who was chosen informally by the local authorities to manage communication between the majority society and the Roma was also called village leader. These cultural, social, and economic brokers participated with more or less success in the implementation of central and local government decisions, the coordination of information flow across ethnic boundaries, and the distribution of various allowances (social benefits and the like) allocated to the Roma. In some settlements, the broker chosen by the non-Roma local government was in fact the Gabor individual most successful in local Roma politics, while in other settlements the two roles were held by two different people.

In line with the requirement of respecting individual autonomy, none of the titles of family leader, village leader, or big man invests its bearer with formal power or entitles him "to give orders in other people's courtyard" or make decisions about other people's property. To quote one of my interlocutors: "A stranger has no right [to order others around] because everyone orders his/her own self around. You see? All it is, is that the man who has a title [who is respected as a village leader or big man] is talked about by every Gabor Roma." The bearers of these honorific titles, therefore, have powers limited to their own households just like those of every other Gabor individual. As one comment about the possibilities and limits of a village leader explains, "He doesn't have any [any direct power]. All it is, is that he's got a bigger *patjiv*, he's respected more, he's listened to more, he's invited to every meeting [wedding, christening, and so on], people want to be *xanamika* [co-father-in-law] with him [they want to form marital alliances with him], they want to be *tjirve* [fellow-godparents] with him, they want to sit at the same table with him." The village leaders and big men are, therefore, often asked to participate as social, economic, and political brokers in the management of various disputes, such as divorces that turn into conflicts or disagreements over economic transactions.

The holders of these honorific titles, like the rest of the Gabor Roma, can count primarily on their social capital – the renown and prestige arising from their successes in Roma politics – if they wish to represent their interests effectively. That is – assuming they insist on employing morally approved strategies – they can invoke only indirect techniques of coercion such as persuasion to influence social and economic relations and processes. It would be misleading, however, to pass over the fact that even village leaders and big men may occasionally resort to morally ambivalent techniques of political manoeuvering. It happens, for instance, that the village leader may threaten an individual intent on rejecting his advice with sanctions such as public shaming – through the symbolic devaluation of the person's political achievements, for example – at the next social gathering (a wake or wedding), dissolving their previously established marital alliance, or preventing a marital alliance the person in question is planning with someone else. Since my interlocutors were aware of the political significance of these threats, requests by the most influential men tended to meet with positive responses without their having to mention any possible sanctions.

No one among the Gabor men would define himself as the ruler of his own Roma ethnic population or of all the Roma in Romania or

Transylvania, or perhaps as the "International King of Gypsies" or the "Emperor of Gypsies" (see Fosztó 2007). In accordance with this, every single one of my Gabor acquaintances agreed that none of the self-declared Roma leaders associating the titles listed in the previous sentence with their own persons had the power to limit other people's personal autonomy (ordering them to do something, for example), and the mention of their names or media coverage of them was usually accompanied by reactions such as laughter and mockery.

The fact that the individuals who are really successful in Roma politics constitute a small elite can be attributed to the uneven distribution of resources or, in a few exceptional cases, the absence of individual political ambitions. In symbolic arenas such as the prestige economy or the competition for the most influential co-fathers-in-law, most Gabor men participate as merely marginal actors or passive onlookers.

The Symbolic Arenas of Roma Politics

The Accumulation of Economic Capital

An important factor in determining prestige relations between individuals, families, and patrilines is the size of their economic capital. Besides large marriage payments[11] and accumulation of cash, the Gabors regard consumer goods and services such as quality Western cars and minivans, big new houses equipped with costly and fashionable household appliances, the latest models of consumer electronics (colour televisions, mobile phones, and the like), and frequent visits to fast-food restaurants and shopping centres as the most important socially approved and respectable forms of wealth representation. The elite sphere of consumer goods, however, encompasses not the commodities and services mentioned above but silver prestige objects. (See colour plates: Photos 9–19.) As will be explored in more depth in the chapters that follow, the Gabors pay the highest purchase prices for the latter pieces, and their purchase gives them the promise of the highest level of social appreciation, renown, and prestige.

The Politics of Kinship, 1: Position in the Prestige Hierarchies of Gabor Patrilines[12]

Anthropological analyses focusing on Roma often argue that the past and the question of descent do not play a central role in shaping their social relations and identities; they are at best marginal factors, and these relations and identities are mostly constructed in the context of interactions taking place in the present. The identity projects characteristic of the Roma – at least according to this professional stereotype – concentrate dominantly on the present, while their ethnic and genealogical memory is short-term and of marginal significance. Stewart, for instance, concludes from his experiences with a Masari Roma community in Hungary that, for the Roma, the past is "truly another country" (Stewart 1997, 60); therefore, "essential aspects of one's identity did not derive from the past but were learned for oneself in conjunction with one's contemporaries" (Stewart 1997, 58; see also Stewart 2004). According to Stewart's interpretation, the Roma he stayed among did not attribute any special significance to past prestige relations between descent groups, just as they did not consider the generational differences between men to be socially marked (Stewart 1994, 120). Another passage from the same author expresses this with much more general wording:

> There are no formalized kin groups among the Vlach Rom, nor is an ideology of shared descent important in conceiving social relations. Rather, shared identity is talked of primarily in terms of shared activity at the present time. If one lives like a Rom, sharing one's life with other Rom, one is a Rom. In line with this ideology of identity through shared activity, Gypsies think of themselves as a "brotherhood" open to anyone who fully participates in the communal rituals. (Stewart 1996, n.p.)

Blasco reaches a similar conclusion with regard to the Gitanos in Madrid. She argues that the Gitanos' social memory is "rudimentary" (Blasco 1999, 15), the past has no significance for them (50–1), and they do not show any interest in it (143). Their genealogical memory is "extremely shallow, going back no more than three or at most four generations. People know that they are related, but often not the exact nature of the kinship tie that links them" (52; see also 142). Blasco also claims that the Gitanos "focus on the present rather than on the past as source of shared identity" (15; see also 14, 53, 175); that is, their model of identity "denies that a shared memory may play a role in the constitution of Gypsyness" (39; see also Blasco 2001). This explains why the Gitanos define social memory as a characteristic feature of the non-Roma and argue that it does not contribute to their existence as Gitanos.

Stewart's and Blasco's interpretations of the identity-forming capacity of descent and ethnic past deviate from my field experiences to a considerable extent. Besides the fact that we studied different Roma ethnic populations in different regions and at different times, there are two further interrelated explanations for this divergence of opinions. First, both Stewart (1997, 28) and Blasco, while recognizing the significance of personal memories and remembrance, focused on the notion of common origin. Second, both authors primarily looked at how the past and, within that, the notion of common origin contributed to the being of their hosts as Roma – that is, to the processes of constructing ethnic identity, boundaries, and differences. That is to say, both Stewart and Blasco approached the question of descent and ethnic past mainly from the perspective of interethnic relations.

When it comes to the question of the origin of the Gabor Roma ethnic population as an "imagined community" (Anderson 1991, 5–7), my experiences were similar to those of Stewart and Blasco: it interested only a fraction of my Gabor Roma interlocutors, and the theories of Indian, Egyptian, or other origins that often appear in contemporary professional and lay discourses played no role at all in their identity projects – they did not serve, for example, as ideological pillars of their ethnic identity and belonging (their *Gaborness*). In the Gabors' case, however, personal memories – in connection, for example, with deceased relatives – also played a key role in conceptualizing their relation to the past.

What is the most striking difference between the interpretations of the past in the communities studied by Stewart and Blasco and those of the Gabor Roma known to me? The latter attribute special social significance to a dimension of the past that lies between the notion of common origin ("Where do we Gabor Roma come from?") and personal memories/remembrance, while neither the members of the Masari Roma community discussed by Stewart nor the Gitanos in Madrid studied by Blasco showed special interest in that dimension. This intermediate dimension of the past is the (recent) history of the Gabor patrilines, which focuses primarily on the political differences and prestige relations between the various patrilines. In other words, the vast majority of my interlocutors showed an intense interest not only in the decades covered by personal memory but also in the major changes of political relations among the Gabor patrilines over the past hundred or hundred and twenty years, as well as in the more important political events of that period.[13] As mentioned, evoking and interpreting these political events – such as memorable prestige-object transactions, marital alliances, and the conflicts and rivalry associated with them – is a practice that often dominates formal and informal male conversations.

Accordingly, during conversations focusing on the ethnic past, genealogical discourse tends to play an outstandingly important role. It primarily involves "counting" (*djinen*) fathers, grandfathers, and other patrilineal forebears – that is, evoking, comparing, and discussing their political achievements and significance; in short, the already mentioned practice of "talking nations." The political importance of patrilineal forebears and identity and of genealogical memory is aptly illustrated by the previously cited commentaries about the content of political discourses at wakes. My Gabor acquaintances thus regarded their own ethnic history, and especially the past of their patrilines, not as a "foreign country" (Stewart 1997, 60) but rather as one of the inescapable and often strategically useful sources, or "raw material," for their identity projects in the present.[14]

The relationship between the political achievements and social prestige of descendants and those of their patrilineal forebears is characterized by intense interaction and interdependence. The position a patriline has held in the local or regional prestige hierarchy of patrilines in the past usually has a considerable impact on the political ambitions, plans, and possibilities of its descendants. A high patrilineal prestige going back a long time is a political heritage/resource/capital that can be converted into renown and money in several contexts. If, in contrast, a patriline has persistently remained at the bottom of the local or regional prestige hierarchy of patrilines, this fact will probably become a social stigma impeding the achievement of political successes for upward-aspiring descendants. To be a member of a patriline that was of low prestige until the recent past can bring about a series of face-threatening insults and limit political self-representation (participation in genealogical discourses at social gatherings, etc.); it has a negative effect on the social evaluation of certain political successes (buying prestige objects, for instance) and on their hoped-for reputational profit. In short, it can be an impediment to fulfilling political ambitions and to upward social mobility. Patrilineal prestige acquires considerable significance, among other things, when the value of a prestige object's symbolic patina is estimated (in the course of the deal, the buyer also pays for the reputation of the previous Gabor owners of the piece), and it is also often of importance when a choice has to be made between potential co-fathers-in-law and when the sum of a marriage payment is determined. According to the interpretation of my Gabor hosts, patrilineal identity is, therefore, one of the identities imbued with outstanding social and political significance.

Most of my interlocutors in their forties could "count back" (*djinen palpale*) five to seven generations in their patrilines. Their genealogical memory – understandably – became more detailed and differentiated as they moved closer to the present, while their information about the first forebear(s) in their memory was limited to a few personal details and memorable political events. My acquaintances knew most about the past of their own patrilines and had a slightly less detailed knowledge of patrilines with which their patrilineal forebears maintained long-term, harmonious cooperation (usually manifested in marital alliances). Their genealogical knowledge also proved to be fairly detailed and differentiated for patrilines that were considered dominant in their own local communities and were consequently often discussed during political discourses at local social gatherings.

The use of the term "rank" by my Gabor interlocutors when comparing the political successes of patrilines is a clear indication of the political significance of patrilineal past and prestige. "Rank" is a category associated with the concept of patriline in their political discourse – that is, it "goes for the nation [refers to/depends on the patriline]" (*nemzetre megyen*). The comparative "ranks" of two patrilines ("low[er]-ranking" versus "high[er]-ranking"; "having a rank" versus "not having a rank") are determined on the basis of the political achievements of their past and present members. In the case of larger Gabor Roma communities where members of several patrilines live together, prestige relations are often expressed by organizing the "ranks" assigned to the individual patrilines into a hierarchical system. My hosts often talked of patrilines of "first" (*dintuno*), "second" (*dujto*), "third" (*trito*), etc. "rank," or "high rank" (*baro rango*), "middle rank" (*kăzepeša*), and "poor/low rank" (*čoŕŕo/cino rango*); or, less frequently, of "first-order/first-class," "second-order/second-class," and "third-order/third-class" patrilines.[15] The Romani term "coat of arms" (*cimero*) is occasionally used as a synonym of "rank": someone may, for instance, come from a "great coat of arms" or a "poor/small coat of arms."

The "rank" of an individual refers to the degree of prestige or renown achieved by his/her own patrilineal forebears in Roma politics. A man who has proved to be similarly successful in politics as his father, grandfather, and so on – that is, who is capable of reproducing his heritage of patrilineal prestige or renown – is often referred to as a person who "carries on the rank of his father" (*lengă dadehko rango folytatin*), "sits on his father's wagon" (*pe lengă dadehkă vurdon bešen*), or "carries on his father's, grandfather's [carries on the prestige earned by his father, grandfather]." Descriptions such as "having a rank" versus "not having a rank" and "high rank" versus "poor/low rank" may apply not only to individuals and patrilines but are occasionally also used to express political differences between Gabor Roma local communities.[16]

Let me quote just one excerpt from an interview that shows the political significance of patrilineal prestige differences. The commentary below, made by a middle-aged man from a patriline considered to be dominant ("first rank," *dintuno rango*) in a Gabor Roma community in Transylvania, describes how members of the local upward-aspiring patriline (referred to as of "second rank," *dujto rango*) attempted to reduce the social distance between the two patrilines with the help of two strategies: the purchase of valuable prestige objects and marrying into the families of "first rank." However, my interlocutor maintains that not even the success of these strategies can eliminate – at most they can partly counterbalance – the negative political heritage of the living members of the upward-aspiring local patriline: their forebears[17] were "poor Roma" who often had to endure privations, did not possess prestige objects, and had at most a marginal role in local politics. For this reason, my host argued, the members of this upward-aspiring patriline have to prove their respectability much more frequently and more convincingly (through political successes) to compensate for the low patrilineal prestige stemming from the marginalized social and economic position of their forebears:

> *Bară ŕomehko śavo*: this Romani expression could be translated as "there is a big ["first rank," politically outstandingly successful] man's son" ... Then there are these second-rank Roma as well. Péter, you know, our Lord raised them up so that they became a bit better off and they don't consider themselves to be at the level where their forebears had been [they believe they merit a higher social status than their forebears]. Because, Péter, just watch, if my father lists for you ten *bară ŕomen* [big men]. And if you go and see the sons of those Roma, you're sure to see that they are *bară ŕomengă śave* [the sons of big men]. From their character. Even if they are dressed in used clothes, you can see that they have nobility of character. You go and see a rich second-rank Roma. He's rich. Everything's new and shiny in his house. But you can see that he's not the same descent as the first-rank Roma. There's a difference ... The way these second-rank Roma are, if they don't do either a *xanamikimo, dintuno, ke le bară ŕomengă śave* [if one of them doesn't establish a first-class marital alliance with a big man's son] or if they don't buy a beaker every second or third year, the rust will eat

their signet [the renown accompanying their previous political successes will decline] and it will be destroyed. Theirs [the prestige objects and patrilineal forebears of "second-rank" men] are not talked about [during political discourses at wakes, etc.], and they [their prestige objects and the members of their patriline] sleep. That's how, you understand? ... And they fight to always buy the first beaker [the most valuable beakers], they give out *mita* [cash gifts][18] so they can marry into the great ["first rank"] families; otherwise they'll be left behind because their forebears were poor Roma. (28 August 2004)

Men who were born to a patriline considered to be of "first rank" and who have also achieved significant individual successes in the arenas of Roma politics are often described by the phrase "He's good [is doing well] both in rank and in situation" (*Meg-i vi rangilag, vi helyzetileg*). That is, while the Gabors consider the political performance of all members of a patriline when defining patrilineal prestige (the "rank"), they focus only on the present and the political achievements of a given individual when characterizing his "situational" position. Since patrilineal segments, families, and individuals belonging to the same patriline are not equally successful in politics, they can have very different "situational" positions.

The Gabor Roma interpret individual successes achieved in the present in the accumulation of economic capital, in marriage politics, and in the competition for *patjiv*, argues Szalai (2010, 25), as "important factors influencing but not eliminating rank-differences" in the short term. That is, the local or regional prestige hierarchies of patrilines are dynamic social constructions that can change in the long term – for instance, as a result of the mass impoverishment and decline in the size of families belonging to the dominant patriline, in time a patriline once regarded as "second rank" can move into a dominant position (becoming "first rank"). The dynamics of Roma politics is, in part, ensured on the one hand by the possibility (in the long term) of upward social mobility within the prestige hierarchies of patrilines and on the other by the fear of losing the position currently occupied in those hierarchies.

Unlike the Roma communities studied by Stewart and Blasco, for the Gabors, their joint activities in the present – the prestige economy, marriage politics, and so on; that is, their simultaneous participation in communities of practice – and their patrilineal history both possess a significant identity-forming capacity.

The Politics of Kinship, 2: Marriage, Marital Alliance (Xanamikimo), *and the Social Network of Male Kin*

The Gabor Roma are characterized by arranged marriages (often of children), patrilocality, and ethnic endogamy (choosing spouses from their own Roma ethnic population). First marriage generally takes place between the ages of thirteen and fourteen for girls and between fourteen and sixteen for boys, with only the young couple, their closest relatives, and a few invited Gabor Roma guests present – and with the complete exclusion of the churches and the registry office. (See colour plates: Photo 8.) Girls who reach eighteen or nineteen years of age without being married off by their parents, usually because of a health problem of some kind, are regarded as spinsters, and as the years pass fewer and fewer fathers of sons show any interest in them.

The spouse is chosen and the betrothal (*tomnjală*) and the wedding (*bijav*) are arranged and performed under the direction and supervision of the fathers and paternal grandfathers. According to the most common Roma ideology, this division of labour between generations is justified, because young people have only superficial knowledge of the social and economic situation of the families of potential husbands or wives and cannot decide on their own "who will be a good, the right, spouse for them." Although there are parents who ask for and, to some extent, take into consideration their children's opinion on which potential spouse to choose, generally little social significance is attributed to the personal preferences or desires of the future wives and husbands; as a result, young people are not often able to influence events.

Parents and grandparents do not usually wait until their children/ grandchildren reach the age considered to be ideal for marriage to look for a suitable co-father-in-law. Future co-fathers-in-law frequently come to an agreement on the marriage of their children years before the wedding, and in some cases even a betrothal ceremony takes place. The purpose of the latter is to reinforce and demonstrate the future co-fathers-in-law's solidarity and commitment to each other, and to symbolically monopolize the chosen individual/family. Part of the function of a betrothal, therefore, is to reduce the possibility of somebody subsequently thwarting the marriage plans; that is, someone might persuade the chosen co-father-in-law – through cash gifts given in secret or other means – to establish a marital alliance with him instead.

As a general rule, spousal considerations do not focus on the personal characteristics of potential husbands and wives, but on the possible marital alliances between Gabor Roma families and patrilines, and the political, economic, and other advantages expected from these alliances.[19] When choosing a co-father-in-law from among potential candidates,[20] fathers and paternal grandfathers with significant political ambitions mainly aim to establish a marital alliance with someone who has gained significant renown in Roma politics, and may thus contribute to the realization of their own political and status plans. Arranging a marriage therefore means that, just as the children to be married are given a spouse, the fathers and grandfathers choose a partner (co-father-in-law, *xanamik*)[21] for themselves.

In an ideal case, *xanamikimo* is a relationship resting upon greater-than-average political, social, and economic cooperation, and a moral obligation of mutual help; that is, it creates the possibility to build, represent, and reproduce social closeness. The most common forms of cooperation are assistance in economic transactions (such as giving a loan, acting as a guarantor, or undertaking joint commercial activities), regular visits and intense exchange of information, help with the management of conflicts affecting the other party, and participation in temporary political alliances that support the status plans of the co-father-in-law. Although balanced reciprocity is the ideal model for a relationship between co-fathers-in-law, it is not realized in all cases. The nature of the relationship between them – the existence or lack of reciprocity or symmetry, for instance – is subject to constant negotiations. It is also highly status-sensitive; that is, it is dependent to a considerable extent on how successful the two co-fathers-in-law are in politics compared to each other.

For a marital alliance to become permanent, the wedding must be held and the young wife must move in with the young husband's parents, but these are not sufficient conditions in themselves. A further condition is that the young couple soon have a son, who will ensure the continuity of the husband's patriline. According to comments made by my interlocutors, the arrival of a son is the event that gives meaning to the existence of the young couple as an independent family and stabilizes both the marriage and the *xanamikimo*, which are merely temporary social formations up to that point. (Not only the absence of a son but several other factors may also be the cause of the dissolution of a marriage.)[22] The special social significance attributed to the arrival of a son is clearly expressed by my hosts who spoke of daughters-in-law who had given birth to one or more sons as having thereby become "stabilized" members of their husbands' families.

If the young couple does not have either a son or a daughter within the period considered to be ideal – namely, the first few years of marriage – the marriage and the marital alliance are usually dissolved. Except for a few exceptional cases, marriages in which only daughters are born meet the same end. How long the husband's family is prepared to wait for the arrival of the first child depends on a number of factors, the most important of which is the extent to which the husband's family has an interest in maintaining the *xanamikimo* (in order to pursue its political ambitions, for instance). In asymmetrical marital alliances, where the co-father-in-law providing the wife is of significantly higher prestige, it can happen that the husband's father waits for as long as six to eight years before breaking up the *xanamikimo* and the marriage.

In contrast with the vast majority of Roma ethnic populations,[23] the practice of paying a bride price is not followed among the Gabors. In their case, when a marriage is arranged the husband's family neither makes a payment in cash nor counterbalances in some other way the costs, emotional work, and so on involved in bringing up the wife.

According to the Gabor Roma ideology, the dowry (*zestre*) given with the wife primarily serves to compensate for the status difference between genders – that is, the higher prestige associated with masculinity. In the words of one of my Gabor interlocutors, "We buy the boys, pay for them." The dowry comprises three types of gifts that flow from the parents of the wife to those of the husband.

The most important element of the dowry is the marriage payment (*juššo*; see Table 1.1). This sum may vary on a large scale, and in the determination of the actual amount the parties take into account several factors, particularly successes in Roma politics, often through a lengthy process of negotiation. The marriage payments that I observed between 1998 and 2014 – between well-to-do families – were generally in the range of US$10,000 to US$30,000, and the highest was €100,000.

The second type of gift given with daughters on their marriage is clothing intended for the wife's personal use, generally calculated in sets (*rîndo*) or full sets (*setto*). A set of clothing consists of a skirt and an apron, while a full set additionally contains a headscarf, a blouse, a pair of stockings, a pair of shoes, an underskirt, and a piece of underwear. The skirts and aprons in the style, colours, and patterns characteristic of Gabor women are an indispensable part of their everyday wear that cannot be bought in any clothing shop. There are only two ways of procuring them: purchasing the necessary materials and having a local tailor sew them, or buying used or new skirts and aprons from the Gabor

Table 1.1. Some of the marriage payments paid between 2000 and 2003

	Year of Marriage and the Handover of Marriage Payment	Amount of the Marriage Payment	Number of Times the Marriage Payment Exceeded the Gross Average Monthly Salary in Romania for the Year of the Marriage
1.	2000	DM15,000	54.63
2.	2000	DM20,000	72.84
3.	2000	DM20,000	72.84
4.	2000	DM20,000	72.84
5.	2001	DM20,000	62.76
6.	2001	DM30,000	94.15
7.	2001	DM20,000	62.76
8.	2001	DM100,000	313.83
9.	2001	DM20,000	62.76
10.	2001	DM10,000	31.38
11.	2002	US$10,000	62.12
12.	2002	US$30,000	186.38
13.	2002	US$10,000	62.12
14.	2002	US$15,000	93.19
15.	2002	US$5,000	31.06
16.	2002	US$10,000	62.12
17.	2002	US$5,000	31.06
18.	2003	US$100,000	500.16
19.	2003	US$10,000	50.01
20.	2003	US$20,000	100.03
21.	2003	US$60,000	300.09
22.	2003	US$10,000	50.01

Note: "DM" = German mark.

Roma women who sell such pieces from door to door or in Transylvanian second-hand markets. (The average cost of having a set of clothing made was around 570 to 830 new Romanian lei[24] – US$170 to US$247 – in December 2011.) At the weddings I observed, the wives generally received ten sets of clothing from their parents. It is worth taking into consideration that the clothes given to the future wife to take with her usually also include several other items (sweaters, jackets, and the like) and auxiliary pieces (towels, blankets, and so on).

Finally, the third type of gift is something related to the house or the separate part of the house that the young couple will use as their personal space, the purchase or building of which is the responsibility of the husband's parents. The parents of the daughter-in-law are expected to furnish one or two rooms of this house or part thereof and – if they can afford it – to equip it with various extras.

The political dimension of *xanamikimo* is rooted not only in the economic significance of the money changing hands before and during the wedding – the marriage payment and the cash gifts often given in secret to encourage the marriage and marital alliance – but also in the fact that the process of choosing a co-father-in-law and negotiating the marriage payment provides an opportunity to represent, reproduce, and shape the social relations between individuals, families, and patrilines. Choosing a co-father-in-law from among potential candidates may be an important means, for instance, of representing social closeness and reinforcing solidarity, furthering upward social mobility and increasing renown, reproducing or enhancing status distance, finding a political supporter, and managing conflicts. It may even on occasion be used as a livelihood strategy.

Due to limitations of space, I shall discuss only four of the more important motivations that my interlocutors defined as political and that often play a decisive role in the choice of a co-father-in-law.[25]

(1) *Marital alliance as a means of representing social closeness and reinforcing solidarity.* The establishment of many *xanamikimo*s can be explained by the fact that both of the parties involved seek an opportunity to institutionalize or reinforce the mutual regard that has arisen between them or to reproduce their already existing social ties. Wedding the children of parents belonging to the same patriline or patrilineal segment is a frequent strategy, for instance, when one of the major objectives of the future co-fathers-in-law is to represent their solidarity and social closeness within their descent group.[26] It is also quite common for a family to pick an individual from a different patriline as co-father-in-law because the families are of similar social status and their forebears have previously made one or more *xanamikimo* that proved beneficial to both parties.

(2) *Marital alliance as a means of upward social mobility and accumulation of renown.* When looking for a co-father-in-law, many of my

acquaintances thought the most important goal was to form a *xanami-kimo* with someone more successful in Roma politics than they were, and thus have their renown enhanced and their social status raised to a certain degree. Upward-aspiring families with plenty of wealth but low patrilineal prestige attempt to marry into politically more success-ful families mostly by offering higher-than-usual marriage payments – that is, outbidding their rival co-father-in-law candidates. Since a *xanamikimo* allows the parties to appear regularly in each other's com-pany, and its Roma definition includes an expectation of solidarity and mutual assistance, a co-father-in-law marrying upward has every rea-son to hope for a decline in the frequency of public insults addressed to him – referring, for example, to the marginal social status or poverty of his forebears. Once a marital alliance has been formed, open expression of such insults would threaten the face of the new co-father-in-law – a person of higher prestige – and his family much more seriously, and would be seen as significantly more shameful, since the two families are now also bound together morally by the *xanamikimo*.

The few parents who break up the recent marriage of their children and the *xanamikimo* accompanying it because they have in the meantime been given an opportunity to establish another marital alliance with much more political significance and profit (promising greater renown, for instance) are also motivated by political ambitions and the chance to enhance their reputation. This strategy is usually limited to the first few years of marriage, since once the young couple have already "sta-bilized" – that is, they have one or more sons – and "they are a good match" – that is, they have a harmonious relationship – breaking up the marriage unilaterally often brings lengthy conflicts with it and is considered to be morally questionable (mostly because of uncertainties relating to the fate of the separated couple's children). For these rea-sons, this happens extremely rarely.

(3) *Marital alliance as a means of finding political supporters.* For affluent but "soft" (*kovlo*) men – that is, individuals who have little power to enforce their political interests and thus prefer to avoid conflicts – the dominant motivation for their choice of co-father-in-law may well be to find an influential and widely respected supporter in the person of a co-father-in-law "who many people listen to" and who can hopefully provide effective support in economic or social conflicts or in bargain-ing situations.

(4) *Marital alliance as an occasional livelihood strategy.* Due to tem-porary financial difficulties, influential men belonging to patrilines

of high prestige are occasionally forced to find a co-father-in-law among ambitious and affluent members of families with more modest patrilineal prestige, hoping that the large marriage payment they receive for their son and the cash gifts often given to ensure that the marriage comes about will help them recover from their economic crisis situation. If there is a substantial social distance between the co-fathers-in-law and the party with the lower prestige is prepared to make significant sacrifices to maintain the *xanamikimo* (because of the reputational profit he hopes to gain from it), it can occasionally happen that even after the marriage the latter will need to ensure that his more prestigious co-father-in-law continues to have an interest in maintaining the marital alliance – for instance, by doing him little favours or giving him cash gifts disguised as loans or supplements to the marriage payment. It also happens on occasion that the party having higher prestige but struggling with financial difficulties defines these hoped-for cash gifts not as loans or supplements to the marriage payment but as "shame payments." That is, he argues that the daughter-in-law moving in with his family has brought shame to his house (for instance, by raising suspicions of unfaithfulness), and he will allow the *xanamikimo* and the marriage to continue on condition that his co-father-in-law "compensate" him – that is, transfer a certain amount of money to compensate for the public loss of face caused by his daughter. For his part, the father of the wedded young man may also attempt to force a cash gift out of his less influential co-father-in-law by temporarily "throwing back" his daughter-in-law – that is, sending her back to her parents and thus putting pressure on his co-father-in-law by threatening to dissolve the *xanamikimo*, which would cause a loss of renown for the latter.[27]

A *xanamikimo* can also occasionally be used as a livelihood strategy by a politically successful man struggling to cope with financial difficulties if he wants to marry off his daughter. In this situation, it is not unusual for him to pay only a nominal marriage payment and to receive in secret cash gifts of substantial value in return for accepting the marriage proposal of the lower-prestige, aspiring, and wealthy father of a boy. (In some cases the father of the wife gives back some of the cash gift received from his co-father-in-law just before the wedding ceremony as the marriage payment.) That is, the politically more successful party comes into some money by partially or fully saving his marriage payment and by receiving cash gifts from the parents of the future husband for the *xanamikimo*.

As also shown by some of the above strategies used in choosing a co-father-in-law, a position of dominance in the local or regional prestige hierarchies of patrilines is a political resource or capital and a goal at the same time. In several cases, the successful members of a patriline considered to be "first rank" in a given settlement or region can demand and receive marriage payments of higher-than-usual value (as well as cash gifts of persuasion), based on the position of dominance of their patriline, in return for their agreeing to establish a *xanamikimo*, or they may persuade the father of the boy – the future co-father-in-law – to be content with a strikingly modest marriage payment.

The above cases aptly illustrate why and how the choice of a co-father-in-law and negotiations concerning the amount of marriage payment can acquire a political meaning and significance among the Gabors, and why many co-fathers-in-law cannot take it for granted that their marital alliance will in fact be harmonious or balanced.

The Ethics of Sociability: Behaviour (Phirajimo) and Honour, Respectability, and Social Appreciation (Patjiv)

The Gabor Roma ethics of managing social relations and interactions encompass several socially approved preferences. These include, for example, expectations of solidarity, sharing, helping behaviour, and similarity; the requirement of respecting individual autonomy and business ethics;[28] a set of moral expectations concerning age and gender roles; and the group of principles coordinating participation in the symbolic arenas of politics. Although political successes enjoy social appreciation in the same way as adherence to the ethics of sociability, participation in politics is only an optional practice, and declining to be involved is not accompanied by major negative symbolic consequences. Respecting the ethics of sociability, in contrast, is expected from every individual, and failure to comply results in moral disapproval.

According to my interlocutors, it is mainly on the basis of the individual's *phirajimo* (behaviour) in social interactions that Roma society regards him or her as having more or less *patjiv* – that is, as being honest, respectable, and deserving of social appreciation.[29] The evaluation of *phirajimo* mostly depends on the extent to which the individual respects the Gabor Roma ethics of managing social relations and interactions. Adherence to these ethics is called *lašo phirajimo* (proper – that is, morally approved, supported – behaviour). Persons who can hope for only modest social appreciation and honour because they frequently fail to respect the ethics of sociability are often characterized by phrases such as "He/she consumed [lost] his/her own *patjiv*" (*Tele xalah lehki patjiv*).

The Gabor Roma interpretation of *patjiv* and the set of efforts to create, save, and enhance it is best captured by the theory of face-work developed by Goffman (1967) during his analysis of interpersonal interactions. I argue that *patjiv* is a crucial – but far from the only – component of the Gabor Roma concept of individual face. Efforts made to construct and maintain this face are practices belonging to the category of face-work, and Goffman's "line" (Goffman 1967, 5) corresponds to the ethics of managing social relations and interactions in the case of *patjiv*. *Patjiv* is specifically interactive; it is a quality created, reproduced, and shaped in the context of interpersonal interactions, and its existence is unimaginable without the active participation of other Gabor Roma as co-authors. *Patjiv*, like face, is therefore a symbolic property "on loan ... from society" (Goffman 1967, 10).

Let me discuss just a few principles that are significant elements of the Gabor Roma ethics of managing social relations and interactions.

(1) *The expectation of solidarity, sharing, and helping behaviour* involves practices such as:

- Providing help (in the form of, for instance, granting interest-free or low-interest loans, acting as a guarantor, participating in the organization of mortuary rituals, or mobilizing non-Roma relational capital) in economic or other crisis situations; help of this type is expected mainly from consanguineous and affinal male relatives.
- Regular cooperation among the households of brothers, usually involving goods of small value: exchange of labour services (personal transport, for instance), tools and materials of tinsmithing, kitchen equipment and ingredients, small loans, and so on.
- Sharing of some economic resources with the favourite brother, brother-in-law, or co-father-in-law: these resources may include, among other things, information on current market conditions (such as the whereabouts of wholesalers, repositories, potential landlords, and promising buyers) and the availability of regular clients (e.g., school headmasters or mayors) for men working as building contractors.
- Participation in temporary factions in Roma politics: giving support to brothers and co-fathers-in-law in contests for the purchase of prestige objects and the establishment of marital

alliances, in managing social and economic conflicts (related to loan transactions, repayment of marriage payments, purchase of lots and houses, and the like), and in public face-work aiming at the preservation of a positive public image in political discourses at social gatherings such as wakes, weddings, and so on.

- Receiving close relatives and acquaintances who visit as guests (offering food and drinks), and giving them accommodation and transport if needed.
- Distributing cash gifts interpreted as "representations of joy" (*mita*) that accompany individual successes such as the purchase of prestige objects, the establishment of marital alliances, or the receipt of substantial lottery winnings.

(2) *The ethics of similarity* exert a considerable influence on the construction of social (among others, ethnic, gender, and patrilineal) identities and belongings, and on choosing morally supported ways of performing these identities and belongings. The practices preferred by the ethics of similarity include, for instance, men sporting moustaches and broad-brimmed hats and married women wearing ankle-length skirts and headscarves, choosing a spouse from their own Roma ethnic population, rewarding the accumulation of ethnicized goods such as silver prestige objects and marital alliances with influential Gabor families with social esteem, and using their own Romani dialect almost exclusively in communication among themselves. The ethics of similarity, however, can be followed only within obvious limits; they do not apply to practicing politics, for instance, and in accordance with this, the discourse of the ethics of similarity does not regard political differences either as morally stigmatized or as dangerous anomalies to be eliminated. In addition, my Gabor Roma interlocutors did not link the similarity expected and supported in certain contexts with the concept of egalitarianism.

(3) *Individual autonomy: the expectation of respecting the individual's freedom of action and decision.* The ethics of sociability usually hold the restriction of an individual's autonomy by another person to be morally unacceptable, but in some situations – in the case of certain kinship relations characterized by age differences, for instance – they define it as self-explanatory. An excellent example is the relationship between father and son. Let me support this statement with reference to the process of arranging a marriage and the practice of income distribution within the family.

As mentioned before, the responsibility for finding a spouse and negotiating the amount of the marriage payment falls not on the young people getting married but on the fathers and paternal grandfathers who acquire a political ally – a co-father-in-law – through the marriage. However, they do not participate equally in organizing the events; the exploratory conversations to try to discover the intentions of potential co-fathers-in-law, the choice of the most promising co-father-in-law, and the bargaining over the marriage payment are mainly under the control and supervision of the paternal grandfathers. Another example for the restriction of individual freedom of action and decision is the dominant logic of income distribution. When father and son share their trade business or work in the same family-based construction business, the sons usually yield their incomes to their fathers for a long time, sometimes until they are in the mid-thirties – that is, they "work for the same pocket." In this case, it is mostly the father who decides what share of their income will be spent on household bills, saved towards marriage payments, or spent on buying new work tools. In both of the above cases, the primary and often overtly declared ideological basis of socially approved restriction of personal autonomy is the age (generational) difference.

However, the requirement of respecting individual autonomy – see also the section on the ethics of similarity – does not mean that my Gabor interlocutors considered egalitarianism to be the ideal and dominant organizing principle of social and economic relations. For them, individual autonomy is a flexible and context-sensitive social construction, the applicability of which is constrained by several morally approved and normalized gender-, age-, and generation-based hierarchical relations. (See, for instance, the previous discussion of the relationship between father and son.)

(4) *The Gabor Roma definition of business ethics* regards the public formation and maintenance of business respectability and trustworthiness (*patjiv le lovengi*) as important values that can be achieved, provided, for example, that an individual:

- meets his/her obligations created by agreements in connection with economic transactions;
- does not resort to the tools of misleading or intimidation based on physical superiority in order to procure some asset for less than its market value, thus wronging the seller; that is, he/she avoids trying to make dishonest profit;

- as a creditor, refrains from charging socially stigmatized interest rates – that is, rates too high to be morally acceptable; and
- shows no undue partiality when taking a stand in estimating the value of assets (such as silver beakers and roofed tankards) or managing economic conflicts (for instance, in connection with a divorce).

People with considerable *patjiv* are welcome guests in most households and their company is sought at public social gatherings; they are trusted in business transactions and have less difficulty taking a loan; and people are more ready to establish a marital alliance with them or to ask for their advice in the management of economic and social conflicts. "When someone has *patjiv*, people lend him money, they respect him, too. They say, 'Yes! This is a man!'"

According to the ideology of the ethics of sociability, the social significance of *patjiv* cannot be surpassed by that of any prestige object or any marital alliance with even the most influential Gabor families.[30] The importance of *patjiv* and the related public face-work is accurately illustrated by the following phrases that are often heard in discourses – at wakes, for example – thematizing the ranking of social values: "Your greatness [your political achievements] may be princely but you also have to have good/fine behaviour"; "Wealth is a good thing, but if there is no honour with it then wealth is worth nothing"; "Neither the beaker nor the money is worth as much as *patjiv*"; "If your behaviour is not right, you may have two beakers, but they are not worth five cents"; and "No money could buy *patjiv*."

Frequently disregarding the ethics of sociability – that is, the relative absence of *patjiv* – is, of course, not enough in itself to nullify an individual's achievements in marriage politics or the prestige economy, but it undoubtedly is a factor affecting their social evaluation. Let us remember that Roma politics involves symbolic arenas that are ethnically closed, and performances achieved in them are only very rarely – for example, in the case of wealth measured in money – seen by non-Roma as results worthy of esteem or respect. That is, an individual buying a valuable beaker or forming a marital alliance with an influential Gabor family can hope to be rewarded with a positive social response exclusively by the members of his own Roma ethnic population, several of whom are his competitors in politics and may view his achievements with ambivalent feelings.

Because of this ethnicized character of Roma politics, the Gabors can count only on each other's support, approval, and ratification in their attempts to transform their political achievements into socially authenticated successes, differences, and fame. In other words, this transformation cannot take place without the supportive cooperation – co-authorship – of many other Gabor Roma.

One of the most efficient means of mobilizing the above-mentioned support, approval, and ratification is engaging in conduct that earns social respectability (that is, *patjiv*). Having significant *patjiv* makes it substantially easier – and not having it considerably harder – to gain the goodwill and sympathy of influential Gabor Roma. Therefore, *patjiv* may significantly contribute to an individual's political achievements being rewarded with appreciation and honour by other Roma, and in this way, it assists and catalyses the transformation of these achievements into successes, differences, and renown authenticated by social consensus.[31]

It is thanks first and foremost to this catalytic capacity that *lašo phirajimo* and *patjiv* or social respectability are imbued with political significance, and that individuals and families having political ambitions compete with each other to accumulate them. I myself – in harmony with the interpretation of my Roma hosts – consider this competition to be one of the symbolic arenas of Roma politics.

The degree of *patjiv* associated with an individual and the degree of *patjiv* associated with his/her patrilineal forebears are not independent of each other. If the *phirajimo* of the forebears left much to be desired, this could turn into a face-threatening symbolic "inheritance" for their politically ambitious descendants; it gives an opportunity for their rivals to, for instance, insult and shame them at public social gatherings. At the same time, substantial *patjiv* "inherited" from patrilineal forebears and reproduced by descendants can be used as a symbolic resource or capital in the same way as high patrilineal prestige. *Patjiv* is therefore another good example that shows the degree and significance of the political interdependence and interaction between the individual and his/her patrilineal forebears among the Gabors.

This chapter has argued that adherence to the ethics of sociability and participating in Roma politics are practices the simultaneous presence of which is not qualified as risky, inappropriate, or undesirable (at least not when they are applied in socially approved ways) – they do not necessarily exclude or extinguish each other. On the contrary, both the ethics of sociability and Roma politics are considered to be morally approved phenomena that in numerous contexts mutually explain, reinforce, and shape each other. For individuals competing to accumulate social appreciation, honour, and fame, one of the most important challenges is to balance the relation between these two phenomena, so that when personal decisions must be made they do not come into conflict with each other more than absolutely necessary. Unlike, for example, the Masari Roma community in Hungary studied by Stewart (1998, 28, 34, 39), the Gabor Roma do not define the politics of difference as a dangerous anomaly best eliminated; for them, the results achieved in politics are important and highly esteemed components of the concept of success.

The ethics of sociability and Roma politics are not of equal importance, however; when their simultaneous presence leads to a conflict of values and interests – that is, when they give contradictory guidance in a situation that requires a decision – preferring the ethics of sociability is regarded as the morally approved choice. Since it happens that an individual, swayed by political ambition, nevertheless gives preference to his/her own political interests, it is not infrequent at the level of individual decision-making that Roma politics and the ethics of sociability come into conflict with each other.

My Gabor interlocutors regarded not egalitarianism but the creation and maintenance of harmony and balance between the ethics of sociability and the politics of difference as the ideal model of social and economic relations. During my fieldwork, as mentioned, I did not meet a single Roma person who equated observance of the ethics of similarity or the respect of individual autonomy with the concept of egalitarianism. (As was noted by several of my hosts, it does not follow purely from the principle that everybody "gives orders only in his/her own courtyard" that all Roma are equal or that all Roma should be equal.) When I asked whether the expectation of similarity or the requirement of respecting individual autonomy could perhaps be interwoven with the notion of equality, Rupi, a man in his twenties, was nonplussed and answered with a laugh, "You think we [the Gabor Roma] live in the Garden of Eden?!?"

2

The Gabors' Prestige Economy: A Translocal, Ethnicized, Informal, and Gendered Consumer Subculture

Inventing Authenticity

My Gabor Roma interlocutors distinguished two classes of silver pieces defined as prestige objects: beakers (*taxtaj*, pl. *taxta*)[1] and roofed tankards (*kana*, pl. *kăni*). These items are highly singularized; each beaker and tankard has its own Gabor Roma proper name and cultural biography (ownership history, for instance) and a unique composition of material properties.

What qualities are included in the Gabor Roma concept of an "authentic prestige object"? There can be no interpretation of authenticity without a definition of its criteria and markers. The criteria are conditions that must invariably be satisfied for an object to be labelled as a piece belonging to the category of, say, "authentic African art" or "authentic Gabor Roma prestige objects." The markers are clues confirming that the piece meets the criteria of authenticity; that is, they serve to verify authenticity.[2]

The Criteria of Authenticity

For a beaker or roofed tankard purchased from a non-Roma owner[3] – from the European antiques market, for instance – to eventually become an authentic Gabor Roma prestige object, it must meet four conditions: (a) The piece must be made of silver. (b) As my acquaintances explained, an item produced in the recent past, which is "not old" (*na-j phurano*), that is, not made of antique silver, cannot become a prestige object. Recently produced pieces are labelled "new beakers/tankards" (*njevo taxtaj/njevi kana*) in prestige-object discourse, where the adjective "new" refers to the age of the piece in question. (c) It must have the right shape. The Gabors do not consider every item that fulfils the above two conditions to be a potential prestige object; this label is only used for beakers of certain kinds of shape and roofed tankards. (Among these types of beaker shape, trumpet-shaped footed beakers are considered to be the most valuable.) I will henceforth refer to the above three criteria with the term "material patina." (d) The fourth – symbolic – criterion for an item coming from the non-Roma to be qualified as an authentic Gabor Roma prestige object is that it must have acquired an ethnicized ownership history by "passing through the hands" of at least two or three Gabor Roma owners. I shall use the term "symbolic patina" for this Gabor Roma history of ownership, and refer to the pieces satisfying all four criteria as Gabor Roma prestige objects of complete value.

When a beaker or tankard fulfils all material criteria, it is described by adjectives such as "proper" (*bevalovo*), "valid" (*valabilo*), "genuine" (*valodivo*), and "original" (*eredetivo, oridžinalo*). These words are often heard when, for instance, the Gabors browse auction catalogues or museum or art history books – which is by no means a rare occurrence – containing photographs of objects that have the material properties they are looking for. If a beaker or tankard fails to meet one or more of the material criteria, terms such as "foolish" ("foolish beaker/tankard"; *dilo taxtaj/dili kana*) or "untruthful" ("untruthful beaker/tankard"; *xoxamno taxtaj/xoxamni kana*) are used to describe it. The expression "foolish beaker or tankard" as a carrier of irony also frequently refers to objects that satisfy all criteria of prestige objecthood but represent an unquestionably modest value.

The Markers of Authenticity

What are the clues indicating that a beaker or a tankard is a "proper" piece? While it is simple enough to identify the shape and material through a short examination,[4] my interlocutors used several markers to assess the age of objects. These are discussed below.

When mapping the choices offered by the European antiques market, the Gabors take a conspicuously and homogenously bright surface to be a clue that the object is newly made, and prefer pieces with a surface that is darker in tone and appears almost black in depressions. The only parts of the item exempt from this requirement are the handle of a roofed tankard and the place on a beaker's body where it is most often touched.

Another group of indexical representations of embeddedness in history are minor damages visible on the body of beakers or tankards: scratches, dents, thinning of the silver (in the case of footed beakers, such thinning tends to happen just above the ring articulating the object's cylindrical body), a tear at the lip, or partial detachment of the base. When faced with a completely undamaged surface – just as when the silver was mirror bright and light in tone – my interlocutors concluded that the item must have been made recently and was therefore not suited to become a Gabor Roma prestige object.

Since fire-gilding was gradually displaced by electro-gilding in the middle of the nineteenth century, the technology of gilding is also an important marker of age. The only gold-decorated objects the Gabors look for and consider "proper" are those that were made using fire-gilding technology. They regard the bright and shiny, homogenous, and mostly undamaged gilding achieved by galvanizing to mean that the item is not old enough, in contrast to the unevenly distributed, deep gold tone of fire-gilding, faded in places, that they take to be an obvious sign of embeddedness in history.

Age is also considered to be shown by various decorations. These include, for example, antique coins with portraits, biblical scenes, "indecipherable inscriptions" engraved on the mantle of the beaker or tankard (which my Gabor interlocutors often interpreted to be in "Hebrew," "Latin," or "Greek") or "unexplainable [meaning unknown] animals." The latter tend to be mythological creatures that are typically defined as members of "long extinct" species. A frequently used value-increasing strategy is that the owner dates the supposed time of manufacture of his object to match the historical period associated with some of the decorations, and thus describes his beaker or tankard as a piece "from biblical times or the time of Christ" or made in "Greek" or "Roman" antiquity.

Finally, various dates inscribed on the objects are also interpreted as age markers.

The Gabors' Prestige Economy as a Translocal, Ethnicized, Informal, and Gendered Consumer Subculture

The analysis of the practices and ideologies of prestige or luxury consumption, as well as of its causes and effects, is a prominent area of research on contemporary consumer society and culture. Several studies are concerned, for instance, with the complex relationship between prestige or luxury consumption on the one hand and status representation and mobility on the other (Yoon & Seok 1996; Han, Nunes, & Drèze 2010; Nelissen & Meijers 2011; Wang & Griskevicius 2014), with the changing patterns and regional or national characteristics of prestige or luxury consumption (Wong & Ahuvia 1998; Frijters & Leigh 2008; Gupta 2009; Yeoman 2011; Fuh 2012; Zhan & He 2012; Zhang & Kim 2013), and with the reception, impact, and reinterpretation of Veblen's classic theory (Campbell 1995; Bagwell & Bernheim 1996; Trigg 2001). Some studies argue that consumer subcultures specializing in art works, vinyl records, vintage cars, and so on (Mandel 2009); the world of universities and scientific academies (Blackmore & Kandiko 2011); and the Olympic movement should also be regarded as prestige economies.[5]

Any type of activity can be discussed in the conceptual framework of the prestige economy that the members of a community of practice regard as a symbolic arena serving to construct, represent, legitimize, and (re)negotiate social, cultural, political, or economic differences in socially agreed-upon ways. The following features are common in all prestige economies: (a) The primary form – or at least one of the dominant forms – of profit drawn from success in them is prestige itself. (Prestige can of course be converted into further forms of profit: money or relational capital, for instance.) (b) A further shared feature of such economies is their competitive nature, which partly derives from the fact that the prestige goods at the centre of these economies constitute a scarce resource. (c) Finally, we must not forget that prestige can be created, maintained, and shaped only in the context of interpersonal interactions and that the existence of prestige is inconceivable without the active participation of others as co-authors. That is, prestige is a quality "on loan ... from society" (Goffman 1967, 10), and therefore prestige economies cannot exist without some degree and form of publicity.[6]

For most prestige economies, the following components can be distinguished: the prestige goods; the participant framework (the active participants competing in the symbolic arena as well as the audience); the resources; the transformations; and the definition of morally approved versus disapproved strategies available to the participants – that is, the rule book of participation.

In the case of the Gabor Roma, the term "prestige economy" is a comprehensive label for the passion of collecting beakers and roofed tankards (*prestige goods*) and proprietary contests for them, and various other practices and ideologies connected with these objects. As mentioned in the introduction, this economy is not limited to a single local community or microregion but constitutes a translocal community of practice involving Gabor Roma inhabitants of several counties and settlements in Romania as owners, brokers, creditors, and so on. All my Gabor acquaintances followed the major events of this economy and took them into account as an important factor in calculating the prestige relations between individuals, families, and patrilines (*active participants, audience*). Silver beakers and tankards, however, can only be found in families where there is both political ambition and the economic resources needed to buy, possess, and accumulate them (*transformations*). The two most important types of resource are economic capital, manifested primarily in money, and the possibility of inheriting a prestige object (*resources*). The relatively small number of prestige objects and the scarcity of resources explain why only a small group of Gabor individuals participate in this economy as owners and why the spatial distribution of beakers and tankards is far from even: in some Gabor Roma communities in Transylvania numerous silver objects can be found, while in other local communities there are none at all.

What evidence is there to support the claim that this prestige economy is not merely a local practice or one limited to a small region but one in which Gabor Roma inhabitants of several Transylvanian settlements participate in various roles?

An apt illustration of the prestige economy's translocal character is the participant structure – and, within that, the places of residence of the people involved – of a prestige-object transaction that took place in 2006 (discussed in more detail in chapter 12). The owner who was planning to sell his beaker was living in a small town in Cluj County, but he had pawned his beaker with a Gabor Roma lender living at a distance of 190 kilometers in a city near the border between Romania and Hungary. One of the potential buyers was a resident of Târgu Mureş, and his number-one supporter (broker), whom he invited to participate in the bargaining process, lived in a neighbouring village. The other potential buyer – the future owner of the beaker – had been living in the county seat of Cluj County for years, and the broker he commissioned lived in a settlement in the vicinity of Târgu Mureş. The six participants, therefore, were residents of six different settlements, located in three different Romanian counties: three in Mureş, two in Cluj, and one in Bihor.

The translocal character of this economy is also shown by the data in Table 2.1. The table displays the place and county of residence of the Transylvanian Gabor owners of ten beakers during the period between

Table 2.1. Movement of 10 Gabor Roma beakers between Transylvanian settlements and counties between the mid-twentieth century and 2012

Beaker	Movement
1st beaker	Vălureni (*Mureş County*) → Târgu Mureş (*Mureş C.*) → X (*Mureş C.*)
2nd beaker	Cluj Napoca (*Cluj C.*) → Hărţău (*Mureş C.*) → Cluj Napoca (*Cluj C.*) → Turda (*Cluj C.*) → X (*Cluj C.*)
3rd beaker	Atid (*Harghita C.*) → Şiclod (*Harghita C.*) → Hodoşa (*Mureş C.*) → X (*Mureş C.*)
4th beaker	Hărţău (*Mureş C.*) → Vălureni (*Mureş C.*) → Cluj Napoca (*Cluj C.*) → X (*Mureş C.*)
5th beaker	Maia (*Mureş C.*) → Crăciuneşti (*Mureş C.*) → Vălureni (*Mureş C.*) → Timişoara (*Timiş C.*) → Crăciuneşti (*Mureş C.*) → X (*Cluj C.*)
6th beaker	Atid (*Harghita C.*) → Vălureni (*Mureş C.*) → Crăciuneşti (*Mureş C.*) → Oradea (*Bihor C.*) → X (*Mureş C.*)
7th beaker	Murgeşti (*Mureş C.*) → Vălureni (*Mureş C.*) → Crăciuneşti (*Mureş C.*) → Budiu Mic (*Mureş C.*) → X (*Mureş C.*)
8th beaker	Crăciuneşti (*Mureş C.*) → Măgherani (*Mureş C.*) → Budiu Mic (*Mureş C.*) → Vălureni (*Mureş C.*) → Timişoara (*Timiş C.*) → Vălureni (*Mureş C.*) → X (*Mureş C.*)
9th beaker	Cluj Napoca (*Cluj C.*) → Hodoşa (*Mureş C.*) → X (*Mureş C.*)
10th beaker	Măgherani (*Mureş C.*) → Praid (*Harghita C.*) → Târgu Mureş (*Mureş C.*) → X (*Mureş C.*)

Note: The settlement names are not pseudonyms and refer to the places of residence of the previous owners; X = the place of residence of the current owner.

the middle of the twentieth century and 2012. The data provide clear evidence for the translocal flow that characterizes several prestige objects and thus for the statement that the economy in question is not restricted to a single settlement or microregion in Romania. (Many beakers and tankards are passed down or sold to people who have had the same place of abode for a long time.)

How long have the Gabors owned beakers and tankards? This is not easy to ascertain. One obstacle we have to overcome when attempting to map the distant past of their prestige economy is that although the cultural biographies (ownership histories, etc.) of the more valuable objects often come up in conversations at various social gatherings such as wakes and weddings or family events, written documents (sales contracts, for instance) are available only from the recent past. The oldest sales contract I have seen regarded a transaction between two Gabor Roma men on 8 November 1943. The gilded beaker for sale, which is currently owned by the son of the buyer at the time, was sold for 5,000 pengos,[7] which corresponds to 383.4 days' wages for a tailor in Budapest that year.

Our knowledge of the distant past of the prestige economy must therefore rely primarily on oral history. Within this source, the most detailed and reliable data come from the cultural biographies of silver objects (primarily ownership histories and ownership disputes). During my fieldwork, I paid special attention to documenting in detail the biographies of the more valuable pieces, checking my information against the memories of several of my interlocutors and then comparing it with the data I obtained from the mapping of family trees. The results of this process clearly indicate that the predecessors of today's Gabor Roma owned beakers and tankards as far back as the middle of the nineteenth century. Unquestionable evidence is provided by the pieces that my hosts unanimously agree were passed down in the same family through five or six generations.[8]

What we have seen about the spatial distribution of prestige objects gives rise to the question of how many beakers and tankards may currently be in Gabor Roma ownership. Due to the translocal nature of this economy, it is impossible to give a precise answer to this question. In a Mureş County village (Bigvillage),[9] home to one of the most populous Gabor Roma communities, for example, the local Roma owned thirty-eight silver objects – of which thirty-five were beakers and three tankards – in 2012. This figure includes not only the prestige objects located in Bigvillage at the time but also items that were owned by local Roma but recently pawned in another settlement. It excludes, however, pieces pawned with a Roma creditor in Bigvillage but owned by a nonlocal Roma possessor. If we add this figure (thirty-eight) to the number of objects that had at some point been owned in this settlement but passed into the ownership of Roma living elsewhere before 2012, we get a surprising result. The number of silver objects that are known to me to have ever belonged to a possessor in Bigvillage exceeds seventy. The number of pieces to have ever actually belonged to an owner in this settlement is, however, presumably even larger, since I could learn only of items that were still part of local memory and that, in addition, happened to be mentioned during the discourses in which I participated.

The great majority of prestige objects currently in Gabor Roma ownership are beakers. During my fieldwork, I documented the biographies of around a dozen tankards and well over a hundred beakers that are presently in the Gabors' possession. According to the interpretation of my hosts, if only the shape is considered, the object class of beakers is more important than the group of roofed tankards. Most of them knew of no more than a few – at the most three –tankards whose value and attractiveness were equal to those of sought-after and precious beakers. Let me quote just one commentary in this context: "The roofed tankard is less [valuable], it doesn't have that name [the fame of beakers]" (*E kana maj cini-j, na-j la kodo anav*). The difference in value between the two classes of prestige objects is also aptly reflected in their differing social popularity and the different intensity of proprietary contests for their possession.

The prestige economy in question is a translocal, ethnicized, informal, and gendered segment of the Romanian economy – it is a consumer subculture that can be interpreted as a community of practice similar to groups of competing collectors specializing in other types of antiques or various artworks. In contrast with those communities of collectors, however, typical forms and arenas of public representation such as exhibitions (musealization), auctions, and their related publications (such as catalogues) are not at all characteristic of the Gabor Roma.

The Gabors' prestige-object market is characterized by a lack of institutionalization, and it cannot be linked to one or more regularly visited physical locations, as in the case of Moroccan bazaars, auction houses, or shopping centres. This is an invisible market or, in other words, a market without a marketplace. My interlocutors acquired their knowledge about the current supply-and-demand conditions as well as the material properties and cultural biographies of prestige objects from their conversations with each other and through viewings of these pieces.

While the feature of translocality needs no further explanation, those of ethnicization, informality, and genderedness undoubtedly do.

(1) *Ethnicization.* The fact that these beakers and tankards are intensely ethnicized – that is, they are important means of, among other things, conceptualizing, performing, and materializing Gabor Roma ethnic past and identity – can be traced back primarily to the circumstance that many characteristics of the prestige economy organized around these objects can be regarded as ethnic-population-specific features.

- In transactions taking place within their own Roma ethnic population, what the Gabor buyers primarily pay for (besides the pieces' material properties) is the political renown of the previous Gabor owners – that is, for a type of symbolic goods inseparable from their own ethnic belonging, history, and identity. The embeddedness of these beakers and tankards in Gabor Roma ethnic history is a symbolic property regarded exclusively by the Gabors themselves as valuable and worthy of esteem.

- The practice of basing the estimation of value attributed to the material properties of beakers and tankards exclusively on an ethno-aesthetics constructed by the Gabors is characteristic only of the Gabor Roma ethnic population (see chapter 4).
- Another reason why these objects have become markers of ethnic identity is that the exceptional social and economic significance attached to them is also an ethnic-population-specific feature; neither the European antiques market nor the members of the Romanian majority society in general attach the same significance to beakers and tankards as the Gabor Roma do.[10]
- Finally, because of the three factors mentioned above, the participation structure of the prestige economy in question – the ideal sellers, buyers, and audience – and the prestige and fame deriving from the successes achieved in it must also be regarded as ethnicized.[11]

In short, only the Gabor Roma define the political renown of the previous Gabor possessors of a prestige object as a distinguished source of value and are prepared to pay for it. They are also the only ones willing to pay a substantial sum for those material properties that are regarded as precious and sought after on the basis of the preferences of their prestige-object aesthetics. It follows that only the Gabors reward with social appreciation, honour, and renown the purchase and possession of the beakers and tankards that are in great demand among them and regarded as highly esteemed.

(2) *Informality.* Despite the fact that the existence of prestige objects occasionally became known to certain Romanian anthropologists, journalists, or other non-Roma individuals participating in the handling of some ownership disputes and sales transactions (solicitors, police, and judges, for example), the Gabors' prestige economy did not become an economic segment supervised or regularly monitored by state authorities either during the period of socialism or since. As will be discussed in detail in the conclusion, the informal character of this economy – that is, the fact that the transactions taking place in it were mostly "invisible" to the members of the majority society and the Romanian state – was

one of the major factors that accounted for its social popularity among the Gabor Roma before the change of political regime in 1989. (On the economic and social significance of informal practices in other socialist and post-socialist contexts, see Ledeneva 1998, 2006; Morris 2012, 2016; Morris & Polese 2013, 2015.)

(3) *Genderedness.* In addition, the prestige economy is a gendered phenomenon: it represents and reproduces at multiple levels the Gabor Roma ideology of prestige difference between genders (where higher prestige is associated with masculinity). Let me discuss briefly here just three examples in support of this claim.

The gendered character is aptly illustrated by the social distribution of ownership rights related to prestige objects and by one of the organizing principles coordinating their inheritance. The beakers and tankards, which are often symbols of patrilineal identity, may be possessed by men only and are passed down from father to son. The prestige object of a deceased husband cannot be inherited by his widow; she has it only for safekeeping (*garal*) until her son comes of age and becomes able to care for himself and for his paternal inheritance. In a few – exceptional – cases, a father used one of his less valuable prestige objects in lieu of marriage payment; that is, he handed it over to the family of his daughter's future husband at the time of the wedding. This could happen if the father had more prestige objects than he had sons and, because of temporary financial difficulties, could not pay the marriage payment for his daughter's marriage in cash. The silver object changing hands in such a case would become the property not of the newlywed daughter but of the husband, and would be inherited by a son born from the marriage of the young couple (I learnt of three such cases altogether).

Participation in prestige-object-related activities such as value estimations, the organization and implementation of various transactions (e.g., sale, inheritance, or pawning), the prestige-object discourses emerging at public social gatherings, and the management of conflicts of ownership rights were defined by my Roma acquaintances, both men and women, as primarily masculine practices – that is, activities associated with men.

Finally, a further example of genderedness is the practice of anthropomorphizing the difference in value between the object classes of beakers and tankards, which may be interpreted as an indirect reproduction of the prestige difference between genders. My interlocutors often referred metaphorically to the beakers as men and the tankards as women. The personification and genderization of silver objects in these commentaries is the result of an interconnection between two social practices of making distinctions: the value consensus that beakers are more valuable than tankards is expressed through the ideology of the prestige difference between men and women; that is, the latter ideology illustrates and explains the former one. To quote just one interview:

> He [a Gabor Roma man] had so much money that he surpassed all the Roma in the matter of money. Understand? There wasn't a single Roma, a single family that would have been richer than him. He bought this beaker, he also had a ... tankard. You know, tankards are not as precious with us as beakers because the tankard means the woman and the beaker means the man. (23 February 2001)

Beakers and Tankards as Luxury or Prestige Goods

Nothing illustrates the special social and economic significance of beakers and tankards among the Gabors better than the conspicuous difference between the price range associated with them on the antiques market and the prices paid for them among the Gabor Roma. While on the antiques market the price of these pieces currently rarely exceeds US$9,000 to US$11,000, within the Gabor Roma ethnic population prestige objects of complete value usually change hands for many times that sum. The price of the more valuable pieces may reach, or occasionally even exceed, US$200,000 to US$400,000 (see Table 2.2). Of the prestige-object sales transactions I analysed, the highest purchase price was handed over in 2009: one of the most influential and wealthy Gabor men paid US$1,200,000[12] for a beaker that had been in pawn for a long time and was considered to be exceptionally valuable (this case is described in more detail below).

The considerable difference between the prices of "proper" beakers paid within the Gabor Roma ethnic population and the prices on the antiques market can be clearly seen if we compare the figures in Tables 2.2 and 2.3, especially those showing the magnitude of the prices in relation to the gross average monthly salary for the year of the transaction in Romania and in Hungary. The most expensive of the "proper" beakers the sale of which I followed in the various auction houses in Budapest changed hands for 1,700,000 Hungarian forints (US$8,692).

Table 2.2. Some of the prestige-object sales transactions carried out among the Gabor Roma between 1950 and 2011

	Year of Transaction	Purchase Price Excluding Subsidiary Costs (cash gifts, the broker's success fee, etc.)	Number of Times the Purchase Price Exceeded the Gross Average Monthly Salary in Romania for the Year of the Transaction
1.	1950	oRON115,000	314.2
2.	1952	oRON10,000 +2 exchange beakers	24.8 (excluding the value of the exchange beakers)
3.	1961	oRON105,000	116.9
4.	1964	oRON240,000	229.4
5.	1964	oRON50,000	47.8
6.	1968	oRON130,000	104.1
7.	1968	oRON160,000	128.2
8.	1970	oRON300,000	209.2
9.	1972	oRON600,000 +2 exchange beakers	400.5 (excluding the value of the exchange beakers)
10.	1972	oRON450,000	300.4
11.	1973	oRON800,000 +1 exchange beaker	511.8 (excluding the value of the exchange beaker)
12.	1975	oRON200,000	110.3
13.	1980	oRON500,000	192.1
14.	1980	oRON1,000,000	384.3
15.	1982	oRON1,700,000	579
16.	1984	oRON2,000,000	620
17.	1984	oRON1,400,000	434.2
18.	1985	oRON600,000	182.6
19.	1985	oRON700,000	213.2
20.	1986	oRON1,200,000	361.7
21.	1988	oRON250,000	73
22.	1989	oRON3,500,000 +1 exchange beaker	989 (excluding the value of the exchange beaker)
23.	1990	oRON5,000,000	1,246.8
24.	1990	oRON3,000,000	748.1

	Year of Transaction	Purchase Price Excluding Subsidiary Costs (cash gifts, the broker's success fee, etc.)	Number of Times the Purchase Price Exceeded the Gross Average Monthly Salary in Romania for the Year of the Transaction
25.	1994	DM100,000 (US$62,631)	559.1
26.	1995	DM75,000 (US$54,158)	399.9
27.	1996	DM300,000 (US$197,014)	1,368.1
28.	1996	DM30,000 (US$19,701)	142.4
29.	1997	DM100,000 (US$57,485)	486.7
30.	1999	DM75,000 (US$39,596)	328.6
31.	2000	DM300,000 (US$135,954)	1,215
32.	2004	US$87,000	264.5
33.	2005	US$10,000	30.8
34.	2006	US$400,000	961
35.	2008	US$300,000	392.9
36.	2009	US$600,000	785.8
37.	2009	US$250,000	393
38.	2009	US$1,200,000	1,886.7
39.	2010	US$1,000,000	1,876.8
40.	2011	US$220,000	316.9

Notes: (1) All objects changing hands are beakers. (2) "oRON" = old Romanian leu. (3) "DM" = German mark.

The most spectacular example of the considerable difference between the value regime of the antiques market and that of the Gabor Roma is provided by the comparison of a court-ordered auction in Mureş County in 2006 and a sales transaction among the Gabors in 2009. Both events involved the previously mentioned exceptionally valuable beaker, which changed hands for the highest purchase price in the history of the Gabors' prestige economy.

The previous owner left this beaker as a security with a Gabor Roma creditor at Christmas time in 2002, when he borrowed US$121,000 from him for a year. Although another year was later added to the loan period, the financial situation of the debtor had not improved at all, and

Table 2.3. A few silver beakers put up for auction on the Hungarian antiques market that could also be Gabor Roma prestige objects on the basis of their material properties

Type of Object (date of production in brackets)	Date of Auction	Starting Price in Hungarian Forints (HUF)	Hammer Price in Hungarian Forints (HUF)	Number of Times the Hammer Price Exceeded the Gross Average Monthly Salary in Hungary for the Year of the Transaction
Footed beaker (17th century)	4 Dec. 2003	HUF750,000 (US$3,355)	HUF800,000 (US$3,579)	5.6
Footed beaker (17th century)	12 Dec. 2004	HUF1,100,000 (US$5,828)	HUF1,100,000 (US$5,828)	7.1
Sčobo beaker (1670–94)	3–5 May 2005	HUF600,000 (US$3,068)	HUF1,700,000 (US$8,692)	10.2
Footed beaker (around 1640)	17 May 2005	HUF650,000 (US$3,254)	HUF750,000 (US$3,755)	4.5
Footed beaker (around 1650)	17 May 2005	HUF480,000 (US$2,403)	HUF650,000 (US$3,254)	3.9
Sčobo beaker (17th century)	17 May 2005	HUF650,000 (US$3,254)	HUF650,000 (US$3,254)	3.9
Footed beaker (end of 16th century)	9 Nov. 2006	HUF1,200,000 (US$5,875)	HUF1,500,000 (US$7,344)	8.3
Footed beaker (17th century)	8 Dec. 2007	HUF280,000 (US$1,633)	HUF750,000 (US$4,373)	3.8
Footed beaker (around 1650)	21 May 2009	HUF250,000 (US$1,239)	HUF1,000,000 (US$4,956)	5
Footed beaker (end of 17th century)	10 Dec. 2011	HUF420,000 (US$1,825)	HUF800,000 (US$3,477)	3.7

he could still not repay the loan. To delay putting his pawned beaker on the market, the debtor sued the creditor in 2005, arguing that they had originally agreed on a five-year loan period; however, because he wanted to buy the pawned object himself, the creditor now claimed that it was a one-year period. The court decision made in the winter of 2005–6 was in favour of the creditor, and the debtor was told to pay his debts back in full without delay. Since he was unable to do so, the court ordered the auction of the beaker left as a security for the loan.

The bailiff entrusted by the court with the auction was, however, faced with the almost impossible task of determining the starting price, taking into account both the Gabor Roma and the antiques market interpretations of the value and significance of the beaker. That is, while being bound by legal regulations, the court bailiff had to manage and supervise the sale of the beaker as not only an economic but also a cultural broker. On top of all that, he had to fulfil this double-broker function with virtually no previous knowledge of the Gabors' prestige economy.

The court bailiff therefore asked for official value estimates from two non-Roma antiques experts, one Hungarian and one Romanian, in order to be able to determine the starting price. My Gabor Roma acquaintances were deeply shaken and outraged when they heard that one expert estimated the beaker's current antiques-market value at €8,000 and the other at €3,650. Both estimates were based exclusively on properties regarded as sources of value by the participants in the antiques market, with no mention at all of those aspects of value – such as the renown of the previous Gabor Roma owners or the preferences of the Gabors' prestige-object aesthetics – on the basis of which the Gabor Roma determine the current value and social significance of beakers.

The auction took place on 17 July 2006 at the gallery of the Mureş County Artists' Association in Târgu Mureş. The court bailiff and his wife arrived a few minutes before twelve in a vehicle escorted by two police cars with blaring sirens. Since no one had any idea of how many people would turn up for the auction and who they would be, the gallery was surrounded by police, who had arrived at the scene before the bailiff in two minivans. Once the creditor's solicitor had also arrived, the creditor, his sons, and I took our seats in the gallery, where the authorities were filming the auctioning. Besides the people already mentioned, the event was attended by two other Gabor Roma men (both supporters of the creditor), two employees of the gallery, and three non-Roma onlookers. In other words, there were many more policemen and other official persons at the auction than there were Gabor Roma people. (The explanation given by my Roma interlocutors was that most of the Gabors found the declared starting price to be extremely low and therefore did not consider the auction to be "valid" or "serious.")

The beaker was displayed on the desk in front of the court bailiff throughout the procedure; everyone could see it, but no one could touch it. When the bailiff had informed the audience of the legal process leading to the auction and of the rules of the auction, the bidding started. The only person to make a bid was the creditor, who bought the debtor's beaker for the starting price of €8,000. (When preparing for the auction, when no one yet knew if he would have a serious rival in the bidding, the creditor argued that he would be prepared to offer between US$200,000 and US$250,000 so that he could become the legal owner of the beaker according to Romanian law.) My acquaintances explained the absence of the debtor, saying that no one would lend him enough money to outbid the creditor at the auction because he had "eaten his *patjiv*" (lost his business credibility among the Gabor Roma); he had therefore decided to stay away to demonstrate that he did not consider himself bound by the result of the auction. When the purchase price had been paid, the events were recorded in the proceedings and the document was signed by the creditor and two other Roma men as witnesses. The creditor then slipped the beaker into the inside pocket of his jacket and, evading the curious journalists waiting outside the gallery, took it back with his sons to its hiding place: a safe at the police station of a settlement in Mureş County.

Although according to the laws of the Romanian state the beaker was now the inalienable property of the creditor, he knew that for the members of his own Roma ethnic population to recognize him as the new rightful owner, he would also have to buy it in the manner and at a price customary among the Gabors. This was because, as most of my Roma hosts agreed, the ownership situation had not in effect been altered by the court-ordered auction. They supported this conclusion by three arguments.

In their view, the starting price was ridiculously low, compared to the prices the more valuable beakers and tankards changed hands for among the Gabor Roma. They interpreted the striking difference between the price range of the Gabors' prestige economy and the price range of the antiques market as an encouragement for them to completely ignore the result of the auction.

The rejection of the new ownership situation was also justified by the unusual participant framework of the change of owner, namely that this process had taken place under court order and supervision and in the absence of the debtor, which is completely contrary to Gabor Roma business ethics. It is worth noting that the Gabors emphatically prefer a social or economic conflict to be managed and resolved *within* their own Roma ethnic population as far as possible. This is especially true for the prestige economy, a highly ethnicized symbolic arena of Roma politics regarding which the non-Roma are thought to be ignorant and incompetent. More precisely, my acquaintances are convinced that the non-Roma are familiar only with the antiques-market logic of value estimation/attribution, which is entirely uninteresting for the Gabor Roma. The participation in this case of non-Roma authorities and experts therefore called forth moral stigmatization, suspicion, and rejection.

The final factor that led to the outcome of the auction being questioned was that the creditor was known among the Gabors as a "soft" person, who avoided conflict when possible and had limited power to enforce his political interests. It therefore seemed evident to most of my interlocutors that if he wanted to be recognized by the Gabor Roma as the new owner of the beaker, he could not be satisfied solely with the official document, issued by the authorities, that validated his ownership rights. He must also buy the beaker "the Gabor Roma way" – that is, in conformity with the requirements of Gabor Roma business ethics, and for a price corresponding to its Gabor Roma market value. If he failed to do so, most of the Gabors would not acknowledge him as the rightful new owner; he would be faced with a series of conflicts between himself on the one hand and the debtor and his supporters on the other; and, moreover, he would lose a significant part of the symbolic profit (growth of fame, for instance) that he had accumulated through his previous commitment to business ethics and that he had hoped to augment by buying the prestige object in question.

For this reason, in the years following the auction, the creditor made a number of attempts to buy the beaker "the Gabor Roma way," while it continued to be under his supervision, but all without success. The debtor finally sold the beaker to another affluent Gabor man for US$1,200,000 in 2009, and the creditor was given US$350,000 as capital and interest. Thus, the loan transaction was closed – after almost seven years.

To put the economic significance of this record purchase price in perspective, let us compare the Gabors' prestige economy to another translocal consumer subculture: art collectors specializing in the works of Hungarian painters. The latter community of practice is itself a contemporary prestige economy, where the highest purchase price in the history of Hungarian auctions since the change of political regime in Hungary in 1990 – 240 million Hungarian forints (about US$1,062,370) – was paid for Tivadar Csontváry Kosztka's painting *Landscape in Trau at Sunset* (1899) at an auction in Budapest in 2012. The data in Table 2.4 clearly show that some of the highest purchase prices paid in the Gabors' prestige economy since the change of political regime in Romania approach (or even exceed) the highest sums paid for Hungarian paintings at auctions in Hungary after 1990.

During the period of my fieldwork, the lowest purchase price among the Gabors – US$10,000 – was paid for a four-decilitre footed beaker that had only recently come into the possession of a Gabor Roma man from an antiques dealer in Budapest (which explains why it had an unusually low price). This piece was sold by its first Gabor Roma owner to the elder son of one of his brothers in January 2005, because of financial difficulties he was experiencing while waiting for a kidney transplant. The only reason why Bango (the seller's brother) agreed to the transaction – which he monitored and controlled – was that brothers are morally expected to show solidarity and mutual support for each other; that is, his primary aim was to alleviate his brother's financial worries. The latter would have had great difficulty selling his beaker outside his own family, since it did not yet have an extensive Gabor Roma ownership history and, besides, it did not have particularly notable material properties. Bango was well aware of this: that is why he instructed his elder son to buy the object, as he – thanks to his young age – did not need to feel ashamed of this transaction. Bango himself, however, was not prepared to buy this beaker of strikingly modest value, since that act may well have exposed him to scorn and ridicule ("Is this measly beaker all he managed to acquire?"), even though everybody knew that the sole purpose of the transaction was to provide help. That was because he already owned an exceptionally valuable beaker and substantial cash reserves sufficient to buy any of the more precious prestige objects. The purchase of this piece of modest value would have therefore been irreconcilable with his own political achievements, interests, and ambitions.

Among all the goods – silver objects, houses, or automobiles, for instance – that change hands from time to time among the Gabors, it is

Table 2.4. The most expensive Hungarian paintings sold at art auctions in Hungary (after 1990), and the most expensive silver beakers changing hands within the Gabor Roma ethnic population (after 1989)[13]

The Most Expensive Hungarian Paintings Sold at Art Auctions in Hungary (after 1990)			The Most Expensive Silver Beakers Changing Hands within the Gabor Roma Ethnic Population (after 1989)			
Year of Auction	Hammer Price of the Painting in Hungarian Forints (HUF)	Number of Times the Hammer Price Exceeded the Gross Average Monthly Salary in Hungary for the Year of the Transaction		Year of Transaction	Purchase Price of the Beaker	Number of Times the Purchase Price Exceeded the Gross Average Monthly Salary in Romania for the Year of the Transaction
1. 2012	HUF240 million (US$1,047,440)	1,076	1.	2009	US$1,200,000	1,887
2. 2003	HUF220 million (US$944,287)	1,540	2.	2010	US$1,000,000	1,877
3. 2006	HUF180 million (US$811,615)	998	3.	2008	US$600,000	786
4. 2007	HUF180 million (US$985,329)	922	4.	2006	US$400,000	961
5. 2008	HUF170 million (US$1,135,149)	807	5.	2009	US$250,000	393
6. 2003	HUF160 million (US$686,754)	1,120	6.	2008	US$300,000	393
7. 2007	HUF120 million (US$656,886)	614	7.	2000	DM300,000 (US$135,954)	1,215
8. 2008	HUF120 million (US$801,282)	569	8.	2011	US$220,000	317
9. 2008	HUF110 million (US$734,509)	522	9.	1996	DM300,000 (US$197,014)	1,368

Note: "DM" = German mark.

the more valuable beakers and tankards for which the highest purchase prices have been paid. For individuals with significant political ambitions who wish to gain the renown that accompanies successes in the prestige economy, these objects represent the elite sphere of goods: they are regarded as the most valuable and most sought-after commodities. In other words, these individuals are prepared to make the greatest financial sacrifices and take the greatest risks to be able to buy and possess an important beaker or tankard, while having to sell one of these pieces involves the most serious loss of prestige or face for them.

My Gabor hosts were obviously well aware of the fact that there is a conspicuous difference between their own value regime and that of the antiques market concerning the silver objects in question. This is clearly illustrated by a commentary made by an influential Gabor trader, who owned five prestige objects at the time of writing. The sentences quoted here were said as my host was carefully unwrapping the beaker he had recently bought – this was the piece with the most modest value in his collection of five beakers – removing the towels protecting it so that I could have a look.

> Look here, Péter, what wealth means to us! A Hungarian man wouldn't give 100 [US] dollars for it! ... Our Lord knows! There are people, like you are now, who know [the Gabor] Roma history, stay with us and have heard [a lot of things], they'd say, "I'll buy it because it's valuable. I'll give you something for it." But not as much as it's worth!! You'd never give that much! But there are other [non-Roma] people, who say, "What shall I do with it? I wouldn't even put it in my display cabinet. I'd throw it away." They certainly wouldn't give money for it! It won't be bought by a Hungarian man or a Romanian man or a German man. It is only ... there are these [individuals] ... who are knowledgeable about antiques, who collect them, you know? ... And if one of these antiques collectors saw it, he'd say "I'll give you 5,000 [US] dollars for it" ... But our Lord knows that it's not worth more than a glass of water to a Hungarian man. And with us [in the Gabor Roma ethnic population], 65,000 or 70,000 [US] dollars ... Here, with us, if I say in the night, "I'll sell it," there'll be ten buyers for it, Gabor Roma. They wouldn't give [US] 5,000 dollars for it, they'd never even mention sums like that, because we wouldn't even bargain with such a person. I'd say, "[I'm asking] 150,000 [US] dollars." [One of the people showing an interest replies,] "I'll give you 60,000 or 70,000 [US dollars]." I'd easily get that price, I'd get it in half an hour, they'd pay and that's that. I'd get that 65,000 or 70,000 [US] dollars [among the Gabor Roma] as easily as I'd get 100 [US] dollars from a Hungarian man. (15 December 2004)

Inalienability as the Ideal State

The owners never put their prestige objects up for sale merely because they think they can sell them for more than they paid to acquire them. That is, they do not purchase these pieces to resell them as soon as possible at the highest possible profit. The idea of selling does not even occur to anyone when his financial circumstances are in order or show only a temporary declining trend. Possessors only part with the more valuable beakers and tankards if their financial situation is beyond hope – because of debts or for other reasons – and no other solution is available to them. Even in a situation like that, it is still common practice to employ various strategies to delay the sale of the prestige object as long as possible. The most common of these strategies is to take a loan by pawning the beaker or tankard.

While the high purchase price paid for one of the more precious pieces increases the buyer's prestige and renown in itself, and he – together with relatives and acquaintances loyal to him – is eager to bring up this purchase price in conversations at social gatherings, the seller and his supporters have a fundamentally different attitude towards the same price. Public mention of the purchase price (at wakes or weddings, for instance) together with the seller's name is in most cases interpreted as a political insult addressed to the seller, as the loss of face and prestige accompanying a sale is intensified by attention being publicly drawn to the fact that he had to part with his prestige object. Two groups of cases, however, often constitute an exception to this: transactions in which the purchase price is extraordinarily high in comparison to prices usually paid for valuable beakers and tankards, and those in which the purchase price paid by the buyer is unreasonably high in comparison to the market value most Gabor Roma attach to the piece in question.

The significant difference in social evaluation between the sum spent on and the sum received for prestige objects is also reflected in Romani terminology. The purchase price paid for a more precious piece is often referred to as "famous money" (*vesteko love*), that is, expenditure that has its own fame and will bring renown for the new owner as well.[14] The income acquired through the sale of a beaker or tankard was, however, never qualified by similar positive terms in the commentaries of my interlocutors. The ambivalent social evaluation of incomes earned through the sale of prestige objects is clearly indicated by the frequent use of the phrase "silent money" (*muto love*) to refer to the amount received for a beaker or tankard. It was regarded as an income inseparable from the shame associated with the sale, something best not talked about publicly.

The money received for these pieces is, therefore, not a marker of economic success and prosperity; it is neither defined as respectable income nor referred to as profit deserving the envy of others. None of my acquaintances talked about selling their prestige objects as a trans-action that proved to be profitable for him or contributed to his reputation as a successful businessman. They did not see the sale this way, even if the purchase price was substantially higher than the price they had paid to acquire the object in the past, or if they had not had to pay a single penny to become a prestige-object owner because the piece they had sold had been inherited from their fathers. The only situation in which the money received for a beaker or tankard does not have negative connotations is where the owner makes the decision to sell his prestige object because he is planning to buy another, more valuable beaker or tankard and needs the proceeds from the sale of the former to raise funds for the purchase of the latter.

The income from the sale of a piece might have exceeded its previous purchase price; what is more, the sale might have given rise to a signifi-cant margin that could constitute a respectable sum if it was looked at from the perspective of the "restricted definition of economic interest" (Bourdieu 1977, 177). Even so, the purchase prices received from the sale of prestige objects were still usually shrouded in silence among my Gabor interlocutors, and they scrupulously avoided linking them in any way to the concepts of increase in renown or social appreciation. As Bourdieu recommends, in order to understand such phenomena we need to take into account all possible types of profits (economic capital, reputational profit, and so forth).

Since by purchasing a valuable prestige object the buyer publicly dis-plays the economic surplus he has accumulated, his person tends to be associated with positive concepts such as economic prosperity, afflu-ence, and the prospect of rising social status (the buyer "may acquire a great name/fame" [baro anav] for himself). The sale of a prestige object, in contrast, is plain-to-see proof of serious financial difficulties – scar-city of resources and savings – and is accompanied by a greater or lesser loss of prestige for the seller ("the [seller's] name/fame falls" [tele perel lehko anav]). Generally, the higher the value of the piece offered for sale or the stronger the political ambition of the seller to be successful in the prestige economy, the greater the symbolic loss. The parties in a pres-tige-object sale are therefore not participants in an exchange where the buyer and the seller benefit equally – that is, where they have the same degree and type of profit. My interlocutors did not see the two parties as equal beneficiaries, even when they considered that the buyer paid a fair price – that is, when he offered a sum matching the estimated Gabor Roma market value of the object. Its estimated market value might be the same as the purchase price paid for the piece, but the reputational consequences for the buyer and the seller are never regarded as equal.

The differing social evaluation of the sum invested in and the sum withdrawn from the prestige economy and the fact that these objects are put up for sale only in the event of an economic crisis clearly show that, for the Gabors, the ideal mode of being for these pieces has nothing to do with commodity status based on the concept of alienability. On the contrary: their objective is to keep the more valuable beakers and tankards out of the circulation of commodities for as long as possible. This explains why they do not define prestige-object sales as successful deals – that is, an ideal way of maximizing monetary profit – and why the social evaluation of the sum received for a beaker or tankard is ambivalent. The individuals who decide to participate actively in the prestige economy see the social esteem and prestige (the "great name/fame" mentioned above) – rather than the margin they acquire if the object is sold for more than its previous purchase price – as the ideal form of profit they hope to gain from buying and possessing these ethnicized pieces. (This does not mean, however, that an owner who is forced to sell will not do everything to negotiate the highest possible purchase price.)

The Gabor Roma definition of the ideal mode of being for a prestige object is akin to Annette Weiner's interpretation of inalienable goods (1985, 1992, 1994; see also Weiss 1997; Miller 2001; Myers 2001, 2004b; Curasi, Price, & Arnould 2004; Mills 2004; Colwell 2014). According to Weiner, certain things, like Maori woven cloaks or Kula shells,

> are perceived to belong in an inherent way to their original owners. Inalienable possessions are imbued with affective qualities that are expressions of the value an object has when it is kept by its owners and inherited within the same family or descent group. Age adds value, as does the ability to keep the object against all the exigencies that might force a person or a group to release it to others. (Weiner 1985, 210)

Inalienable possessions deserve special attention due to the role they play in the construction, reproduction, and authentication of social identities and hierarchies. As Weiner (1985, 210) notes, "The primary value of inalienability … is expressed through the power these objects have to define who one is in an historical sense." Weiner examines these goods mostly in social contexts where the legitimation of the elite is based on events or differences rooted in the past (myths, for instance), and thus where members of the elite must continuously demonstrate their close relationship to this past to reproduce social distance and hierarchies in the present. Weiner (1985, 210) argues that inherited, inalienable possessions are interpreted as the materialization and evidence of this relationship – of the interplay and interdependence of the past and present – and as such they acquire political significance. "The object acts as a vehicle for bringing past time into the present, so that the histories of ancestors, titles, or mythological events become an intimate part of a person's present identity" (Weiner 1985, 210).

For the Gabors, the embeddedness in ethnic and family history of their silver prestige objects is also an important identity-shaping factor. These pieces play a significant role in the conceptualization and materialization of ethnic and patrilineal identity, history, and belonging, and also have considerable influence on the (continuous re-)evaluation of prestige relations in the present. When buying or inheriting valuable beakers or tankards, the owners regard it as their aim to make these objects inalienable – that is, to keep them in their possession for as long as possible and bequeath them to their sons.[15] This practice is also indicated by the phrase "traditional [hereditary] asset" (*hadjomanjošo vadjono*) used as a synonym for the term "prestige object," which refers to the generally held opinion that, ideally, the fate of the more valuable pieces is inheritance from fathers to sons; that is, for as long as possible they "should not leave the family." The most well-to-do and ambitious men strive to bequeath a silver object to each of their sons.

The act of passing a beaker or tankard down from generation to generation within a family creates a symbolic link between its owners, which gives rise to a new meaning associated with that object: it becomes a patrilineal identity symbol, an indexical representation or objectification of family history (see Miller 1987; Myers 2001; Tilley 2006). This new meaning tightens the relationship between the object and its owner, increases the object's emotional and identity value in the eyes of the owner, and prompts him to make greater economic and other sacrifices if he has to struggle to keep the piece in his possession.

There are at least two significant differences between Weiner's examples and the Gabors' prestige economy. (a) The Gabor beakers and tankards do not "belong in an inherent way to their original owners." That is, the relationship between a silver object and its previous Roma owners is limited to the incorporation of these possessors into the Gabor Roma cultural biography of the piece. (b) The beakers and tankards are not connected with any concept of sacredness or "cosmological authentication" (Weiner 1992, 4); the social agency attributed to them is of a different nature. The inheritance of a precious piece within a family influences the power or prestige relations between families exclusively in that the Gabor Roma usually consider the process of inheritance to be a symbol of the *permanence* of economic stability and affluence associated with the family in question. That is, the inheritance of a sought-after silver object does not automatically reproduce the Roma political position of the heir's predecessors, nor does it grant the heir power over others.[16] As a result, significant emotional value is attached to the fact of inheritance from father to son solely by the members of the heir's family, who consider the inherited piece a symbol of their family and patrilineal identity, history, and belonging.

Since there is no way of predicting the future economic situation of owners, and because intense proprietary contests often arise for the acquisition of attractive pieces, my interlocutors were well aware that there was only a small chance of being able to maintain the inalienability of sought-after objects in the long term (for four or five generations). This knowledge explains why even short-term possession of the valuable beakers and tankards that frequently end up as the targets of political manoeuvres that aim to force their sale is spoken of as an achievement worthy of respect, and generates considerable social prestige and appreciation. The possession of the most important pieces often "becomes part of [ethnic] history [that is, it qualifies as a memorable political event]" (*istorije aśel*) among the Gabors, even if it only lasts for a decade or two. This is exactly what is suggested by the commentary below concerning the Gabor Roma biography of one of the most valuable beakers:

> The Hungarians either make an ultramodern home or buy the latest car model. We too have houses and cars, but the beakers are our wealth. Understand? For us, the beakers. If you have a good [valuable] beaker, you'll talk differently … even in a hundred years' time or two hundred years' time [your descendants will talk differently] if you ever owned that beaker! Take for example the beaker from X [X = the name of the settlement where a former owner of the piece in question lived and from which the

Gabors created its unique proper name], this world-class beaker. That village [X] is such a hopeless village that you can't drive in there by car. You need to have a carriage and two good horses and then you can go in, that kind of end-of-the-world village ... And that beaker raised the fame of that village so that when people talk about it as "the beaker from X," it gives the village wings! You understand? The Roma who lived there, God doesn't like it and neither do people if we look down on each other but the Roma who lived there are third-class, not even second-class [they are of low patrilineal prestige]. And the beaker raised one of them [the person who possessed it for a while then sold it in 1952] so much that they still say, his grandchildren still say [proudly talk about it] that "That beaker belonged to my grandfather!" (23 February 2001)

Lasting inalienability as the ideal mode of being is not the same as passivity or inactivity, however. It is certainly not the same for the more precious pieces that manage to stay in the centre of social interest and that more than one potential buyer would be pleased to buy at a moment's notice.[17] As Weiner (1992) has noted in her discussion of the key element of her critique of exchange theory, the strategy of "keeping-while-giving," inalienability should not be thought of as a static property; researchers should instead direct their attention towards the dynamics of the processes that are embedded in the contexts surrounding seemingly immobile objects. That is, the essence of the inalienability of Gabor prestige objects is best captured through – among other things – the strategies and practices aimed at acquiring them (forcing their sale, for example) or keeping them in one's possession (see also Myers 2001, 9). Such a perspective allows us to recognize that in the case of the more valuable pieces, the maintenance of inalienability is an activity requiring continuous political and economic exertion – constant vigilance against the challenges posed by potential buyers and efforts to maintain the stability of the owner's economic situation, for instance – and a degree of risk-taking.

Aspects of the Significance Attached to Beakers and Tankards

(1) *Political trophy.* Beakers and tankards play a crucial role in the construction, representation, and reconceptualization of prestige relations between individuals, families and patrilines – that is, in Roma politics. The more valuable objects are sought-after political trophies: they are pieces invested with political meaning and significance, the

materializations of social and economic success. This is clearly indicated by comments in which these pieces are referred to using the metaphor of a "cheek." To quote just one of these: "Many Roma keep [in their possession] them [the beakers and tankards] as a cheek. Because that is their cheek and that is their glory, the beaker." The noun "cheek" is a metaphorical term for public social image (or face, in the sense of Goffman 1967, 5) and is synonymous with *patjiv* and fame. When my interlocutors argued that they buy and possess prestige objects to use them as "cheek," they were really saying that these pieces and transactions are an important means of achieving and increasing the respectability, social appreciation, and prestige that can be earned among the Gabors.

(2) *Materialization of ethnic identity.* Corroborating the discussion earlier in this chapter about the ethnicized character of beakers and tankards, many of my acquaintances defined their prestige economy as an ethnic-population-specific social, economic, and political practice: a marker of their own Roma ethnic identity and belonging, or in other words, a materialization or proof of the authenticity of their *Gaborness*. This is well demonstrated by the fact that they often characterized themselves as "beaker Roma" (*taxtajale Řoma*), referring to their passion for collecting silver prestige objects as a feature that distinguished them from most of the Transylvanian Roma ethnic populations. (My hosts usually used the same phrase to describe the Cărhar Roma as well.)

(3) *Materialization of patrilineal identity.* As mentioned in the section on inalienability, the prestige objects passed down from father to son contribute significantly to the creation and experience of patrilineal identity, belonging, and history.

(4) *Economic asset: reserve* (tartalîko, rezerva). The purchase and long-term possession of precious pieces in high demand are interpreted as a manifest symbol of economic prosperity and affluence. Although the ideal mode of being of beakers and tankards is inalienability, their owners do not forget that they change hands for substantial purchase prices within their own Roma ethnic population. That is, these pieces are potential commodities and – apart from their political and other functions – are also useful as assets or reserves that can be easily converted into cash in the event of an economic crisis. This economic reserve function is also an important factor when an object of great value is inherited, since the heir becomes the owner not only of a piece invested with political significance and emotional and identity value but also of an easily marketable asset.

Patina-Oriented versus Novelty-Oriented Prestige Goods

The Gabors, however, spend only part of their disposable surplus on silver beakers and tankards. Since the beginning of the post-socialist consumer revolution, following the change of political regime (see also Ngai 2003), many costly commodities and services that were previously unavailable or in very short supply in Romania have become increasingly popular among the Gabor Roma, especially within the generations socialized after 1989. Many of these expensive goods – in much the same way as silver beakers and tankards – are ideally suited for representing wealth through conspicuous consumption and possession; my interlocutors therefore considered them to be prestige goods as well. These include, for instance, new and fashionable – mostly Volkswagen, Mercedes, and Opel – automobiles and minivans, new family homes with several rooms and expensive domestic appliances demonstrating affluence, costly home entertainment products (such as colour televisions) and mobile phones, and regular visits to popular restaurants (McDonald's, for instance) and shopping centres. I refer to these expensive commodities and consumer practices as post-socialist prestige goods since their newly acquired popularity and their mass consumption are inseparable from the process of post-socialist economic and social transformation (for more on this, see the conclusion).

These two types of prestige goods differ from each other in several respects: in their identity value (e.g., ethnicization), embeddedness in history, (in)alienability, visual accessibility, singularization, and market availability. While the consumption of post-socialist prestige goods is generally characterized by novelty-oriented value attribution, the dominant factor of the purchase and collection of silver beakers and tankards is patina-centred value attribution (see also chapter 4).

Post-socialist prestige goods can be characterized by the following properties:

(1) They are not endowed with an identity value by the Gabor Roma; that is, they do not play a part in their ethnic, patrilineal, or other (social) identity projects.
(2) Embeddedness in history – ownership history, second-handedness – is not a source of value, but rather a factor that decreases their value and the degree of social reputation and esteem that can be expected from their ownership. (Who could hope to achieve renown by driving a second-hand, battered car?)
(3) In their case, temporary possession – "to be alienated"-ness – is the commodities' ideal mode of being. In other words, they are

an efficient way of representing economic capital only until a
new model of the given type of product appears on the market,
at which point the owners make significant efforts to replace the
model in their possession with the latest one.

(4) They can be viewed frequently and by many people.

(5) They are not or are only slightly singularized mass products, usually without a proper name, unique material properties, or a well-
known cultural biography.

(6) They are not a scarce resource: they can usually be purchased at
any time and in an unlimited quantity, their purchase generally
limited only by the buying power of the prospective owner.

The beakers and tankards of the Gabors are, in contrast, patina-based
prestige goods that can be characterized by the following attributes:

(1) They are endowed with multiple identity values: they are an
important means of constructing, representing, and materializing ethnic and patrilineal identity, past, and belonging (they are,
among other things, ethnicized), etc.

(2) Their Gabor Roma ownership history – embeddedness in ethnic history, interpreted as symbolic patina – is one of their most
important sources of value.

(3) The ideal mode of being of the more sought-after pieces is inalienability. In other words, owners make every effort to maintain possession of these objects as long as possible.

(4) Although the beakers and tankards are common and popular conversational topics among Gabor individuals, their owners rarely
make them accessible – viewable and touchable – to others. The
social life of these silver items stored in hidden places is therefore
mainly limited to discourse: the dominant way the beakers and
tankards are used among the Gabor Roma is not the sight of these
pieces but talk about them.

(5) They are intensely singularized: each object has its own proper
name and cultural biography, and a unique composition of material properties.

(6) Finally, they constitute a scarce resource: the more valuable pieces
are put up for sale only rarely and at unpredictable times. This
partially explains why the news of an impending sale often trig-
gers an intense proprietary contest among potential buyers in the
Gabor Roma ethnic population.

3

From Antiques to Prestige Objects: De- and Recontextualizing Commodities from the European Antiques Market

Objects Moving between Value Regimes

The Gabor Roma do not make silver objects, nor do they have them made by silversmiths living in their vicinity. All of the beakers and tankards they possess were originally made some time ago by non-Roma – mostly Transylvanian Saxon and Hungarian – silversmiths, and at the very beginning of their transnational social career, before reaching the Gabors, they were the property of non-Roma aristocrats, burghers, guilds, congregations of the Reformed Church, and so on. In other words, all of them have reached the Gabor Roma from beyond the boundaries of their own Roma ethnic population.

On its way from one value regime to another – that is, during the process of turning from an antiques-market commodity[1] into a Gabor Roma prestige object of complete value – each silver item goes through a major symbolic transformation affecting its meaning and value. I call this process the "symbolic alchemy" (Bourdieu 1998, 99–102) of recreating meaning and value. This process does not involve any sort of modification of the material properties of the pieces; that is, their first Gabor owners do not change material features in order to suit the value preferences of their prestige-object aesthetics. They do not, for instance, have their especially desirable decorations engraved into them or replace fire-gilding that has faded over time. (The only modification they may occasionally make is repairing or hiding smaller cracks by tinning or some other procedure.)

At the beginning of their identification with them, when they take them into their possession, the Gabors symbolically empty these beakers and tankards; that is, they remove most of the meanings and value associations linking these pieces to the earlier, non-Roma period of their transnational biography (when their characteristics were interpreted on the basis of the value regimes of the antiques market and art history), decontextualizing them through practices such as deaestheticization and dehistoricization. As a result the objects become partially deethnicized and desingularized.

The Gabors then recreate these beakers and tankards, assigning to them new meanings and value preferences; that is, they recontextualize them. This process includes two practices. One is reaestheticization – that is, the substitution, based on a prestige-object aesthetics constructed by and characteristic exclusively of the Gabor Roma, of many of the antiques-market meanings and value preferences previously associated with the material properties of the silver object bought from non-Roma. The other practice – rehistoricization – involves the integration of the piece into the ethnic history of the Gabors; that is, the construction of its Gabor Roma social career or biography. This is realized through such processes as creating a Gabor Roma ownership history, giving the piece a Romani proper name, and defining its biographical character. While all prestige objects have a Gabor ownership history and a Romani proper name, only certain beakers and tankards have permanent attributes representing biographical characters. Through reaestheticization and rehistoricization these beakers and tankards become partially reethnicized and resingularized.[2]

For an item coming from the non-Roma, the acquisition of a Gabor Roma social career is a lengthy process. There is, therefore, a liminal phase between the time of purchase from the European antiques market or other source and the state of becoming a Gabor Roma prestige object of complete value – a transitional period of the object's change of identity, characterized by gradual increase in its value. During this period, the social and cultural identities associated with the beaker or tankard are still ambivalent; the piece no longer belongs wholly to the value regime of the antiques market, nor is it yet a Gabor Roma prestige object of complete value. No matter how attractive the material properties of a beaker or tankard, the significance attributed to it by the Gabors during this transitional period remains very modest compared to the social and economic importance associated with most prestige objects of complete value. (At the beginning of this period, the value attributed to a piece coming from the non-Roma is barely more than its current antiques-market value.) The same applies to the prestige associated with the act of acquiring an item from the antiques market; such a transaction is not accompanied by significant social appreciation or reputational profit among the Gabors. On the contrary, it may be associated with a sense of shame, since the fact that the buyer did not attempt to purchase one of the much more expensive prestige objects – well-known and much desired among the Gabors and with a long Gabor Roma ownership history – suggests that his financial means are limited. Fearing insults related to his financial situation, the first Roma owner of a beaker or tankard coming from the antiques market therefore usually does his best to avoid the fact of the purchase becoming a topic of conversation at public social gatherings.

In the Romani dialect of the Gabors, the terms "new beaker/new tankard" (*njevo taxtaj/njevi kana*) refer to silver objects in the transitional period. In this case, the adjective "new" denotes not the time when the object was made but the fact that the piece is at the very beginning of its Gabor Roma social career. To refer to the development of an object's embeddedness in ethnic history and to the accompanying increase in value, my interlocutors often used phrases such as saying that over time the piece "grows old" in the possession of its successive Gabor owners. Another synonym of integration into ethnic history is the phrase "native beaker," whereby the term "native" refers to the circumstance that the object in question has been changing hands among the Gabor Roma for a long time.

Although the beakers and tankards bought on the European antiques market are *completed* objects with respect to their material properties, the Gabors regard them as merely raw material for their identity projects, *half-finished* goods in need of significant symbolic elaboration. The process of symbolic recreation occurs not only in the case of pieces bought from non-Roma but also with items purchased from other, non-Gabor Roma. The Gabors do not regard an object biography constructed by another, non-Gabor Roma ethnic population as a source of value, just as they do not see an antiques-market pedigree as such a source;[3] that is, in their eyes beakers and tankards of either origin are "without a past worthy of preservation or mention."

External Sources for the Acquisition of Silver Objects

Despite the large number of silver pieces in the possession of members of their own Roma ethnic population, it still happens from time to time that Gabor individuals buy "new" beakers or tankards made of antique silver but with no previous Gabor Roma ownership history. There are three reasons why they may decide to purchase "new" objects.

One reason is that there are substantial differences between the purchase prices of "proper" silver pieces put up for sale on the European antiques market and those of the objects of complete value that have been changing hands among the Gabors for a long time. Gabor buyers motivated by this consideration choose the antiques market because they want to join the prestige economy but do not have sufficient cash reserves to buy one of the beakers or tankards with a "great name" that are sold among the Gabors for many times the antiques-market price. These buyers of pieces with no more than an antiques-market pedigree hope that once the objects have "been through the hands" of two or three owners belonging to their own family – ideally the buyer, his son, and grandson – they will become sought-after prestige objects of complete value; that is, their social significance and value will increase. This is a cost-efficient but more time-consuming and – from the point of view of future reputational profit – risky strategy for becoming a prestige-object owner.

Some Gabor Roma purchase "proper" silver pieces on the antiques market because they want to sell them on within a short time to other Gabor men who regard them as future prestige objects. In such cases, the buyers are intermediary traders who become only temporary owners of the beakers or tankards from the antiques market. This activity is best defined as an occasional livelihood strategy.

Finally, some Gabor individuals attempt to sell "proper" pieces bought from non-Roma sellers in another Transylvanian Roma ethnic population – the Cărhar Roma (see chapter 7) – pretending that these pieces are highly valued and much-desired Gabor Roma prestige objects of complete value.

It was principally due to a substantial change in the economic and social importance of silver objects in the eyes of the non-Roma majority society in the nineteenth century that large numbers of beakers and tankards were able to pass into the possession of Transylvanian Roma. The increasingly widespread use of cash and banking services gradually took over the place of the "family silver," and as a consequence silver pieces that for centuries had been a preferred way of storing surplus wealth in part lost their earlier social popularity and economic significance, and a great many were sold by their non-Roma owners. Many of these pieces made available for sale in the nineteenth century were purchased by Transylvanian Roma families.

It is worth distinguishing six main external – that is, non-Roma or other, non-Gabor Roma – sources of object acquisition. I found no examples for the use of the first four following the 1989 collapse of socialism in Romania, and the sixth source of pieces became accessible to my hosts mostly after the political regime change. The fifth source, the possibility of buying silver objects from antiques dealers and collectors, was frequently used by my interlocutors both before and after 1989.

(1) According to recollections of the decades before the Second World War, *banks and pawn shops* in the Transylvanian regions inhabited or regularly visited by Gabor Roma were frequently used sources of such objects. The silver pieces deposited there and never redeemed were acquired either secretly through informal channels, or at public auctions organized to sell them.

(2) According to stories of prestige-object acquisitions during the socialist era, *public museums* with beakers and tankards in their collections were another important source. Since the items on display were the inalienable property of the socialist Romanian state, they could pass into the possession of Gabor Roma buyers only via informal paths.

(3) The *congregations of the Reformed Church* in Transylvania were a further source of silver objects; besides other types of "proper" beakers, beakers in the shape valued highest according to Gabor Roma prestige-object aesthetics – trumpet-shaped footed beakers – could often be found among the Communion vessels. The Gabors made regular and sometimes successful attempts to buy one or more "proper" pieces that had the material properties they found attractive. As the transnational biographies of the prestige objects with ecclesiastic origin reveal, opportunities to buy them often arose when congregations wished to remedy their financial difficulties by selling some of their valuables, publically or informally.

(4) In very rare cases, silver pieces were purchased by the Gabors from *members of another Transylvanian Roma ethnic population*: the previously mentioned Cărhar Roma.

(5) The Gabors also bought, and still buy, "proper" silver objects from *antiques dealers and collectors* in Romania and elsewhere.

(6) Finally, it occasionally happens that Gabor individuals acquire – in person or with the help of a broker – pieces with material properties they find valuable at *antiques auctions* in Hungary.

Noting my interest in prestige objects, many of my Gabor acquaintances asked me to find places – museums, antique shops, or auction

houses – in Hungary with beakers and tankards for sale. (They sometimes made quick sketches to illustrate the kinds of material properties they were looking for.) Others charged me with finding museum
or auction house catalogues and art history publications containing –
among other things – photographs of "proper" pieces.

Decontextualizing Objects Coming from Non-Roma:
Commodity Fetishism or Strategic Amnesia

The beakers and tankards coming to the Gabors are objects that already
have a social career; they are imbued with a series of values and meanings (ownership history, for instance) constructed by non-Roma, of
which my Roma acquaintances have some degree of knowledge. To
become representations of ethnic and patrilineal identity and history
among the Gabors, the pieces must be symbolically emptied; that is,
most of the meanings and value associations linking them to their former, non-Roma contexts of use must be removed (see also chapter 4).

How does decontextualization – the process of symbolic emptying or
divestment – happen? What happens with the earlier, non-Roma period
of the object's transcultural biography, after it comes from the European
antiques market into the possession of its first Gabor Roma owner?

The dominant attitudes among my interlocutors regarding the non-
Roma past of these pieces are best characterized by concepts such as
lack of interest, indifference, and conscious forgetting. As has been
mentioned, the Gabors do not consider an object's non-Roma or other,
non-Gabor Roma social career (its ownership history, for instance) as a
source of value or a factor worth remembering or talking about when
they compare the values and determine the purchase prices of prestige objects changing hands within their own Roma ethnic population.
They also ignore most of the value preferences of the antiques market or art history concerning material properties. These preferences are
replaced by meanings and value associations belonging to the Gabors'
own prestige-object aesthetics.

The two value regimes and communities of practice identify with
two different phases of the transnational biographies of these pieces;
for the participants in the antiques market, the only source of value is
the period during which the object's owners were not Roma, while for
the Gabors, the only source of value is the phase of the piece's biography that is linked with the Gabor Roma ethnic population. The non-
Roma silversmiths and former owners are outside the Gabors' social

world and memory, and neither knowledge nor a detailed record of them have any attraction or benefit for these Roma.

As a consequence, it does not occur to the Gabors to take their beakers or tankards to nearby gallery owners, silversmiths, antiques collectors, or museum experts, for example to get some help with deciphering the makers' marks found on them in order to shed some light on who made them or on other elements of the pieces' non-Roma social life. They do not spend long hours in the library or archives poring over old pattern books or the literature on the history of silversmithing, researching the non-Roma past and art-historical significance of their prestige objects. Even though it would pose no difficulties for many owners to hire a non-Roma expert to conduct the research for a fee, none of them allocate any money for this purpose.[4]

It is worth noting that in communications with members of the majority society, the non-Roma origin of prestige objects is occasionally mentioned. In these situations the Gabors like to emphasize to their Hungarian or Romanian interlocutors that several of their beakers and tankards were previously owned by "barons and counts" – that is, members of the Transylvanian aristocracy – thus attempting to temporarily establish a continuity between the phases of the transcultural object biographies linked to different ethnic populations.[5] (The quest for continuity is restricted to similar topics and to interethnic communications.) Let me mention just one example:

> In the old days counts, barons, kings … [owned beakers and tankards]. Have you seen in the museum how they drink from the beakers? From the *taxtajs*! … They drank wine from the top and turned the beakers round and [filled] the bottom with brandy. They drank from that. You understand? The one with the better beaker, with the finer figures [richer decoration] took it out [and said], "Do you have one like this?" They boasted of it, it was their pride. (28 February 2004)

Mentioning during interethnic encounters that these objects were once non-Roma status symbols is clearly a more effective way of representing the current social significance of the beakers and tankards among the Gabors than citing the names of influential Gabor Roma owners whom the vast majority of Transylvanian Hungarians or Romanians have never heard of.

Indifference towards the non-Roma social career of prestige objects is, however, not the same as unconscious forgetting; that is, it is not simply a case of new meanings and values necessarily and imperceptibly displacing old ones. In our case, forgetting is a conscious and self-reflective practice, a type of strategic amnesia, that acquires a constitutive power through its effect of erasing or removing meanings. In other words, intentional forgetting based on ethnicity – symbolic emptying or divestment – accelerates the marginalization and disappearance of the antiques-market and art-historical meanings and value associations that could otherwise unsettle the identification of the Gabor owners with objects from the antiques market. It thus allows new meanings and values – those characteristic of the Gabor Roma – to be associated with the pieces travelling between value regimes.[6] As was noted by Weiss (1997, 164), forgetting is often not "merely an ineffective attempt to retain information, or an unintended consequence of the production of new forms of knowledge. Rather, forgetting can in some instances be seen as an intentional and purposive attempt to create absences that can be crucial to the reconstruction and revaluation of social meanings and relations." This is exactly the case with the Gabor Roma attitude towards the previous social career of beakers and tankards purchased from non-Roma.

When the Gabors choose and buy on the antiques market objects with the material properties they find desirable, they employ a strategy that can be interpreted as a peculiar form of "commodity fetishism." This concept was elaborated by Marx (1909) as a criticism aimed at the political economists of his age who – in his view, incorrectly – attributed too much importance to exchange value; that is, they derived the value of commodities primarily from their relation to each other rather than from the amount of labour needed for their production, or from the human relations connected with the process of production (Lury 1996, 40–2; Slater 1997a, 111–12; Dant 1999, 45). Commodity fetishism is, in Marx's view, a misleading and deceptive form of value representation (Slater 1997a, 114).

The essence of the strategic "commodity fetishism" characteristic of the Gabors is that, in the course of acquiring a beaker or tankard from the European antiques market, its non-Roma social career is held to be unimportant and is therefore "erased," while all attention is focused on the object's material properties. Just as the political economists criticized by Marx trace the value of commodities back primarily to the commodities themselves and to the relation of the commodities to each other, the Gabor Roma likewise focus on nothing but "commodity form" (Dant 1999, 45) – that is, material properties – when selecting from the pieces available on the antiques market those that fulfil the criteria of their own prestige-object definition. And just as the political economists mentioned disregard the process of production (the person producing the commodity, the amount of labour invested, and so on), the Gabors similarly show no interest in identifying either the masters who made the silver objects or the previous non-Roma owners, thus marginalizing and erasing most of the meanings and values that once linked the acquired pieces with the non-Roma majority society.

Recontextualizing Objects Coming from Non-Roma

(1) *Reaestheticization.* As mentioned, the Gabors do not alter the material attributes of objects coming from non-Roma but transform most of the antiques-market and art-historical meanings and values associated with these attributes according to the preferences of the prestige-object aesthetics they have developed themselves (see chapter 4).

(2) *Rehistoricization: constructing a Gabor Roma social career or biography for the piece.* This part of the process of recontextualization is the integration of a beaker or tankard into ethnic history. The practices described below focus primarily on the Gabor social careers of objects and are employed in different ways or not at all by participants in the antiques market in the case of "proper" silver pieces. Their common feature is that they are more time-consuming than the process of checking material properties, which is a matter of just a few minutes.

(2.1) *Ethnicized ownership history: the Gabor Roma possessors.* As previously discussed, a piece cannot become a Gabor prestige object of complete value immediately after its purchase on the antiques market, since it has had only non-Roma owners. To be of complete value, the item must have been changing hands within the Gabor Roma ethnic population for a while: it must "pass through the hands" of at least two or three owners; that is, the vacant – or more precisely, intentionally emptied – places of the former non-Roma possessors must be occupied by Gabor Roma owners. The latter will form the ethnicized, unique ownership history of the prestige object, the symbolic patina that the Gabors consider one of the most important factors when assessing the value and bargaining over the prices of these pieces.

(2.2) *Giving a Romani proper name.* Beakers and tankards are objects having Romani proper names (*Řomano anav*).[7] Many of the techniques of giving a piece a proper name described below are akin to the process of naming Kula objects (Weiner 1983, 1992, 1994; Munn 1986, 105–9; Damon 2002) and to giving titles to works of art.

For many pieces, naming is based on some element of their Gabor Roma social careers. Many of these objects bear the name of one of their previous Gabor owners ("Doja's Beaker," *le Dojahko taxtaj*), but it is also a common practice to create the proper name from the name of a settlement. In the latter case, the chosen settlement is one where a former Gabor Roma owner of the beaker or tankard was living. Such names tend to take the form of a possessive adjective construction such as "the Beaker from Găieşti" (*le Găčehko taxtaj*) – that is, the beaker once owned by a Gabor Roma resident of Găieşti.[8]

For many of the prestige objects, naming is based not on their Gabor social careers but on a conspicuous material property. The pieces may be named after the decorations on their surface: figural representations, plant motifs, inscriptions, coins, and so on. Some examples are "the Monkey Beaker [the beaker with engravings depicting monkeys]" (*o taxtaj le Majmonenca*); "the Thaler Beaker [the beaker with thalers]" (*o taxtaj le Tellerenca*); "the Mountains Beaker [the beaker with decorations identified as mountains]" (*o taxtaj le Plajinahko*); "the Leafy Beaker [the beaker with leaf motifs]" (*o taxtaj le Patrengo*); or the object called "the Forest" (*o Văš*), which has a motif of long leafy tendrils identified as "groups of trees" on its side. On this last beaker, besides the three "groups of trees" – reminiscent of sheaves of reeds – there are three flower motifs on the mantle with an oval representing a pistil in the centre of each. My acquaintances, however, did not interpret these decorations on the basis of pattern books used by silversmiths of the period or of descriptions found in the catalogues of auction houses or in art historical publications – that is, according to the value regimes of the antiques market and art history. The current owner of the object from Mureş County argued that the tendril-like leaf motifs were "clusters of trees" symbolizing the "jungle," and he defined the pistils in the flower motifs as "shaven human heads, the heads of savages living in the jungle. Look! These are the savages, the savages who live in the forests. Ancient people!" The fact that this piece was given the proper name "the Forest" and that its decorations were explained by the above historicizing interpretation (highlighting its age) are excellent examples of the way in which the Gabors remove and alienate these objects from their former contexts of use and interpretation (the non-Roma ethnic populations, and the antiques market and art history) and the meanings associated with them in those contexts. This case also aptly demonstrates that the partial reconceptualization of the meanings and values attached to an object's material properties can contribute to its symbolic recreation in the same way as, for example, the formation of a Roma ownership history can.

Some of the objects are named after the damages or alterations on their bodies. One example is "the Nicked Beaker" (*o Stîrbo taxtaj*), which has a nicked lip.

Rich gilding may also become a characteristic that gives a piece its name, as was the case with the beaker called "the Yellow" (*o Galbeno*), the gilding of which is in such a good state that, according to one of my hosts, "It shines like a light bulb in the dark" (*Phabol sar o villanjo ando tunjariko*). My acquaintances used the proper name "the Yellow" for more than one beaker, due to their excellent fire-gilding, and distinguished these objects from each other by adding the name of a well-known former Gabor owner: "Bango's Yellow" (*o Galbeno le Bangohko*).

The individuals from whom the beakers and tankards got their proper names are therefore integral parts of their Gabor Roma social careers; these objects are never named after ethnic others (Hungarians, Romanians, or the like). In my experience, there was only one exception and, after a brief investigation, even that soon turned out to be merely apparent. One of the large-capacity beakers bought by a Cărhar individual from Sibiu County from its last Gabor owner in the mid-1980s bears the Romani proper name "*Tornai Borbála – Alacsony István* [two sets of Hungarian first and surnames]." The Gabors, however, did not use the names of these two Hungarian aristocrats to create a proper name for the beaker because they attributed special significance to its non-Roma social career and wanted the proper name to be a memorial to these two people. The sole reason for the choice of name was that they regarded the two proper names engraved in the beaker's mantle as singularizing decorations – just like many figural representations or plant motifs decorating other prestige objects. (This is clearly shown by the fact that many of my acquaintances referred to this piece using variations on its name, suggesting that they were not aware that they were dealing with first names and surnames of people.) The former non-Roma owners' names thus became the raw material for creating a Romani proper name without this constantly reminding the Gabors of the non-Roma phase of the object's biography and delaying or interfering with the symbolic process of removal of its antiques-market meanings and value associations.

For some of the pieces, the naming focuses on the transnational or transcultural character of their biographies. One example is the item called "the Beaker from Pest" (*o Pešticko taxtaj*) which got its name because its first Gabor owner bought it in the late 1960s in Budapest, and another is "the Beaker from the Olt River area" (*o Volticko taxtaj*), which came from the Transylvanian Cărhar Roma in the mid-twentieth century. (The latter proper name can be traced back to the fact that the Cărhar Roma seller lived in one of the Cărhar local communities in the Olt River area.) The objects recently bought by the Gabors from non-Roma individuals or from other, non-Gabor Roma also belong in this category; until they acquire their own, permanent, name, they are temporarily called "the New Beaker/Tankard" (*o Njevo taxtaj/e Njevi kana*). In this case, the adjective "new" expresses not the age of the item but its lack of embeddedness in Gabor Roma ethnic history.

The cases of Romani naming linked to a piece's Gabor social career aptly demonstrate that the naming itself significantly contributes to the recontextualization of objects coming from the European antiques market and to their becoming efficient means of constructing and representing Gabor Roma ethnic identity and history.

(2.3) *The dominant feature of the object biography.* In addition to the proper name and the ownership history consisting of Gabor possessors, some beakers and tankards are also assigned a permanent attribute that represents a dominant feature of their Gabor Roma social careers.

One of these attributes – "fighter" (*harcošo*) – is associated with an object if it is considered to be especially valuable and sought after, and intense proprietary contests have often arisen among potential buyers for its acquisition.

Other pieces are qualified in prestige-object discourse by attributes such as "unlucky" (*bibaxtalo*) or "cursed" (*armandino*). A piece is labelled "unlucky" if "it left in its wake [that is, it 'caused']" one or more misfortunes during its Gabor Roma social life – at least according to the Gabors' interpretation. These may include the death or sudden impoverishment of one or more former owners during the time the object was in their possession. In the case of some of the pieces regarded as *bibaxtalo*, my interlocutors attributed the misfortunes to the owners being overly attached to their silver objects – that is, to the possessors stubbornly refusing to sell them in time in spite of the accumulation of family conflicts and increasingly hopeless debts.

A beaker or tankard is labelled "cursed" if it has been cursed by one or more of its former owners or their close relatives. The spoken curses are usually addressed to the new owner, mainly in cases where he came into possession of the object using strategies contrary to Gabor Roma business ethics: in a dishonest manner (e.g., by deception) or by threatening to make use of superior physical force. (To cite only one of the frequently used curses: "May this beaker never bring good fortune to X [that is, to the new owner], and may it be inherited by the dogs [that is, may the new owner's son die before he could inherit the object concerned]!") The curse is therefore a verbal sanction initiated by the seller who has suffered damages or his immediate relatives and, according to the Roma ideology of cursing, is fulfilled by God – but only if its target is in fact guilty of seriously violating the business ethics of prestige-object transactions.[9]

Since the attributes "unlucky" and "cursed" – in contrast to "fighter" – do not enhance the renown and value of the beakers or tankards (on the contrary, they call them into question or diminish them), their owners would never dream of associating them with their own prestige objects, and should another person attempt to do so (either at a public social gathering or during an informal conversation) it would very probably be interpreted as a face-threatening political insult.

4

Creating Symbolic and Material Patina

When assessing the value and price of a beaker or tankard changing hands among them, my Gabor interlocutors attributed special significance to two aspects. One of these was the political renown that the former Gabor Roma owners of the silver object had accumulated (symbolic patina), while the other was the set of material properties of the piece (material patina), the value of which was estimated in accordance with the prestige-object aesthetics the Gabors had constructed. In what follows, I will take a closer look at these two dominant sources of value.

Symbolic Patina

Consumer Interpretations of the Ownership History of Second-Hand Goods

Although the symbolic boundary separating second-hand commodities from new may vary according to the social context and – as noted by Setiffi (2011, 12) – is often left subjective and vague, there is at least one criterion of second-handedness commonly adopted in both professional and everyday discourses: the piece acquired by someone has already been owned by at least one possessor. (Let us set aside the consideration of producers or retailers of goods being regarded as owners.) In what follows, I combine Kopytoff's (1986) concept of object biography and McCracken's (1986) definition of patina,[1] and regard the ownership history of commodities – the identity and memory of previous owners – as a marker or manifestation of second-handedness.

In order to understand the significance of ownership history as a symbolic property affecting consumption, let us consider the concept of "extended self," which was introduced by Belk (1988, 2013, 2014a, 2014b; Ladik, Carrillat, & Tadajewski 2015) in connection with the analysis of interactions between consumer goods and identities. From the point of view of understanding the effects of commodities on the lives of their owners (i.e., the agency of commodities), Belk (1988, 139) considers it crucial to recognize that

> knowingly or unknowingly, intentionally or unintentionally, we regard our possessions as parts of ourselves. As Tuan argues, "Our fragile sense of self needs support, and this we get by having and possessing things because, to a large degree, we are what we have and possess." That we are what we have ... is perhaps the most basic and powerful fact of consumer behavior ... [P]ossessions are an important component of sense of self.

The objects we possess, Belk continues, can literally extend the limits of our self and agency (see also Gell 1998). This is what happens, for instance, when "a tool or weapon allows us to do things of which we would otherwise be incapable" (Belk 1988, 145). At the same time, in many cases, we define our possessions – such as various collections, pets, or family heirlooms – as an extension of our own selves in a metaphorical sense; that is to say, we regard them as a representation or materialization of our personality, the loss of which would be a very sensitive issue and a source of great pain. There is no reason to doubt the accuracy of Belk's argument that "the functions that possessions play in the extended self involve the creation, enhancement, and preservation of a sense of identity. Possessions help us at all ages to know who we are" (Belk 1988, 150).

I argue that not only a rare and in-demand object itself but also the place occupied by its possessor in the ownership history of the given object can be seen as a dimension of the owner's "extended self." Ownership histories are often regarded as symbolic pantheons – halls of fame – providing an opportunity for consumers to construct, reconceptualize, and represent their identities. They can also serve as a means and context of the politics of difference. Integration into the ownership history of a sought-after, expensive piece not only allows the new owner to conspicuously advertise the economic and other resources he/she has accumulated but also provides an opportunity for invidious comparison between him/her and (a) the previous possessors – who had no choice but to sell the object – as well as (b) the rivals over whom he/she triumphed in the contest for the piece.

In recent decades, the focus of consumption studies has partially shifted to counterbalance the dominance of analyses dealing with the acquisition of new commodities and the related social impacts. As a result of this process, an increasing number of researchers have raised the question of what happens to goods after the owners decide they no longer wish to use them (Lastovicka & Fernandez 2005, 813; Parsons & Maclaran 2009, 301). Focusing on this question, many studies have devoted special attention to the various ways (gifting, selling, and so on) and contexts (flea markets, garage sales, charity shops, auctions, and the like; see Herrmann 1997, 2004; Gregson & Crewe 2003; Cheetham 2009; Denegri-Knott & Molesworth 2009) of disposing of used commodities, the related rituals and their impacts on consumer identities (McCracken 1986; Belk 1988, 1995; Strahilevitz & Loewenstein 1998; Gregson & Crewe 2003; Lastovicka & Fernandez 2005; Gregson, Metcalfe, & Crewe 2007), and the ways in which the symbolic properties (meanings, functions, and values) associated with used goods are transformed in the process of recycling (Korom 1996; Gregson, Crang, Ahamed, Akter, & Ferdous 2010; Newman, Diesendruck, & Bloom 2011; Alexander & Reno 2012) or permanent withdrawal from use (Miller & Parrott 2009; Gregson 2011).

As noted by several researchers, potential buyers may display a variety of attitudes towards the ownership history of second-hand goods. Two of these are discussed below.

(1) *The ownership history of second-hand commodities as a pollution to be removed.* For many consumers, the purchase of second-hand goods carries negative associations: low purchasing power; the forced substitution of used for new goods; and the potential risks, such as physical and symbolic pollution, that may derive from previous use. They therefore regard these goods as commodities that have suffered significant devaluation and arouse aversion (see also Argo, Dahl, & Morales 2006). Such negative associations mean that when second-hand goods are put up for sale, it is not uncommon for their biographies to be manipulated and, as far as possible, traces of their previous use concealed. Let us call this view of the value and meanings of goods – which interprets previous ownership as a negatively defined symbolic property, one that leads to loss of value and should thus be hidden – *novelty-seeking consumption*; it prefers the purchase of new commodities that follow the current fashion, and regards this choice as a socially respectable and esteemed consumer decision.

Arguments to explain the decrease in value and negative meanings associated with second-hand goods often emphasize changes in material properties, such as wear and tear, scratches, or stains. In other cases, they focus on negative associations attached to previous owners, known or unknown. These may include, among others, risks that derive from earlier physical contact between the commodity and its prior possessors – for instance, the possibility of physical or symbolic pollution, disease, or misfortune arising from resale due to the death of the previous owner.

Thus, those purchasing second-hand commodities often employ meaning-eliminating and depersonalizing practices (or divestment rituals) which "rely on the consumer's historical and geographical imagination, about who has owned, used and worn the commodity before, when, where and under which conditions" (Gregson & Crewe 2003, 144). They do this in the hope of removing the material or symbolic traces of previous use, including physical pollution and ill fortune as well as the memory of the former owner; the purchased object, be it a piece of clothing or a house, thus ceases to be a part of the previous possessor's "extended self." The symbolic emptying – the partial or complete erasure of the meanings and values associated with the piece – enables the new owners to substitute their own preferred meanings and values for the previous ones. Thanks to this process – and to the often-applied modification of material properties by such means, for example, as mending faults and decorating surfaces – the second-hand object can be repersonalized and will become part of the new owner's "extended self." In the words of Gregson and Crewe (2003, 144), frequently the "problem is ... that there is too much trace of previous ownership, traces that need to be expunged, removed."

One of the earliest analyses focusing on the significance of symbolic divestment practices related to second-hand goods is McCracken's (1986) work, which argues that consumers resort to using these practices in two cases. First, new possessors of second-hand commodities make an attempt in this way to "erase meanings associated with the previous owner. The cleaning and redecorating of a newly purchased home, for instance, may be seen as an effort to remove the meanings created by the previous owner" (McCracken 1986, 80). Second, consumers often use depersonalizing practices to remove meanings and emotional value before putting up for sale or withdrawing from use their own precious commodities regarded as a part of their "extended self." "In moments of candor, individuals suggest that they feel 'a little strange about someone else wearing my old coat'" (McCracken 1986, 80). These practices, McCracken argues, "suggest a concern that the meaning of goods can be transferred, obscured, confused, or even lost when goods change hands. Therefore, goods must be emptied of meaning before being passed along and cleared of meaning when taken on" (1986, 80).

Gregson and Crewe (2003; see also Lastovicka & Fernandez 2005) also devote considerable attention to consumer rituals – employed primarily in the case of second-hand goods purchased at charity shops – that are aimed at removing meanings and emotional value from commodities. The most common of these rituals are careful washing and dry cleaning. They argue that cleansing rituals or practices are tools "by which the bodily presence of the unknown previous owner/s is erased; the means through which the taboos of wearing other people's clothes are countered; and … a means of personalizing … The rituals of cleansing purchases, then, are practices of erasure and reincorporation" (Gregson & Crewe 2003, 163).

(2) *The ownership history of second-hand commodities as a source of value.* In the case of many second-hand commodities, however, ownership history – that is, the fact that someone has possessed them before – does not lead to any decrease in value. On the contrary, it is the primary basis of the economic value associated with these goods, and of the social interest in and market demand for them. These commodities are regarded as attractive principally because of their biography and, within that, their ownership history or, more precisely, because "they retain a part of the extended self of valued others" (Belk 1988, 149).

This is exactly the case with family heirlooms, or various objects previously owned by celebrities – film stars or musicians, for instance – or other famous people, such as monarchs, politicians, scientists, and so on (O'Guinn 1991; Giloi 2011; Newman et al. 2011; Dawdy 2016), and identity symbols acquired from a rival political group (Harrison 1995, 1999). These goods owe their specific emotional and economic value primarily to their ownership history and the symbolic interactions that may take place between the new owner and the former possessors.

Citing Belk's line of reasoning, when we find second-hand pieces attractive because of their previous owners, in reality we are trying to identify with those owners; a frequent aim of "owning artifacts that once belonged to famous historical figures" is "to share in the glory of a superstar" (Belk 1988, 149). Newman, Diesendruck, and Bloom (2011, 216) note that the ownership-history-oriented consumption of second-hand goods may be inspired by two further motivations. The first of these has to do with the ever-growing and increasingly globalized market of the personal belongings of celebrities and other famous people;

many believe that purchasing these objects is a profitable investment, since after a period of time they can be sold at a higher price. The other motivation is rooted in the possibility of indirect physical contact with the previous celebrity possessor, namely, the assumption that "a person's immaterial qualities or 'essence' can be transferred to an object through physical contact" (Newman et al. 2011, 216). Newman, Diesendruck, and Bloom argue that it is often difficult to determine the order of importance of these three motivations, and note that in some cases there may even be considerable market demand for second-hand goods owned by celebrities with a negative social evaluation (criminals, for instance).

The situation is similar when it comes to the possession of family heirlooms or memorabilia; their emotional and identity value for the current owner derives primarily from the possibility of symbolic contact and identification with his or her own forebears. Objects passed down from generation to generation, together with their ownership histories, hence play a constitutive role in the conceptualization, representation, and materialization of descent and family past and history (see also Myers 2002, 2004a).

Second-hand commodities acquired through ownership-history-oriented consumption are therefore desirable and attractive primarily due to their biographical value (Hoskins 1998, 2006), which derives from the fame and prestige of the previous owners or shared descent-group membership. Thus, in the case of many commodities, ownership history is a positive property – in fact, it is often one of the most important sources of value – and therefore an intense proprietary contest frequently arises among potential buyers to acquire these goods and become integrated into their ownership histories.[2] I use the term "patina-oriented" or "patina-seeking" consumption for the type of consumption where ownership history – regarded as a highly estimated symbolic patina – significantly increases the value and desirability of a commodity and is the primary reason why the current market price of the piece exceeds its original purchase price.

The social, economic, or emotional significance of ownership history can be clearly seen in the fact that many patina-seeking consumers make a considerable effort to carefully reconstruct, display, and advertise the biography of the second-hand goods they have acquired. Gregson and Crewe (2003, 144) use the term "recovery rituals" to refer to the group of practices by which "the former meanings and traces of ownership are retrieved, recaptured and reimagined" by the present owners.

To sum up, previous possession and the resulting ownership history may constitute a value-decreasing factor for many second-hand goods, motivating sellers to hide their former social career from buyers (*novelty-oriented consumption*). Often, however – as in the case of the personal belongings of celebrities or precious Gabor Roma beakers and tankards – ownership history is an important value-, desire-, and price-increasing property that sellers and owners strive to highlight and emphasize (*patina-oriented consumption*). While the market price of second-hand goods whose value is determined by a novelty-oriented consumer attitude tends to be lower than their original purchase price, in patina-seeking consumption second-hand commodities often change hands for several times their original purchase price because of the biographical value deriving from their ownership history, and the possibility of a symbolic contact and interaction between the new owner and the previous possessors.[3]

The Political Renown of Previous Gabor Roma Owners as Symbolic Patina

As previously mentioned, because it has so far been in the possession of only non-Roma owners, a beaker or tankard bought from the European antiques market will not become a prestige object of complete value immediately after the partial reconceptualization of the meanings and value associations linked with its material properties. To be of complete value, a piece must have changed hands within the Gabor Roma ethnic population for a considerable while; it must "accumulate" at least two or three Gabor owners. The political renown of the latter constitutes the symbolic patina of a beaker or tankard, which my Gabor hosts considered – together with material patina – to be the most important factor in value estimates and price negotiations. In other words, in sales transactions among the Gabors, what the buyers primarily pay for is in part the Gabor Roma ownership histories of prestige objects – that is, "who [in their Roma ethnic population] had owned" (*kahkă sah*) the piece being offered for sale, and what political performance and prestige they had. The comment below clearly confirms the truth of these claims:

A *njevo taxtaj* [a "new beaker" = a beaker with no Gabor Roma ownership history] is worthless ... The value of the beaker is rooted in who left it as his legacy [among the Gabors]. Whose beaker it was! There must be at least two or three generations [two or three Gabor Roma owners]. Who

owned it before. Who, and what kind of Gabor Roma were they! Because
a beaker has to have its nobility [fame] deriving from who it belonged to!
It's not that bit of silver that carries the beakers [makes them valuable]
or that little bit of gilding on them. It's that *veste* [the renown due to
their Gabor Roma ownership history]! Who it belonged to! They are not
valuable because they have a lot of gold on them. [But because of] who it
belonged to! (19 March 2005)

The importance of the Gabor Roma ownership history in estimating
an object's value and price is clearly shown by the conspicuous difference in social and economic significance between "proper" beakers
and tankards recently purchased from the antiques market (i.e., those
still in their transitional period) on the one hand and prestige objects
of complete value on the other. Since the pieces recently acquired from
the antiques market do not yet have a Gabor Roma pedigree, they are
regularly referred to as "orphan beaker/tankard" (*arvona taxtaj/kana*)
or "fatherless and motherless [beaker/tankard]" (*na-j le či dad, či dej*),
phrases which are interpreted pejoratively as synonymous with having little value. A woman compared the beakers and tankards recently
purchased from the antiques market to children adopted from an
orphanage:

It has no owner. [That is, the object only recently bought on the antiques
market has no Gabor Roma owners.] You know what it's like? Like when
children are put in an orphanage. A lady may put them in, too, because
she can't support them or for some other reason. So, if you take them out
[of the orphanage], their rank's fallen a little because people say they are
from an orphanage. You understand? So the material properties of the
new beaker [one with no Gabor Roma pedigree] are good, everything
is good about it; its shape is good, its workmanship is good, the only
problem with it is that people say, "It hasn't been inherited [or changed
hands through sale transactions] among the Gabor Roma." (28 February
2004)

The metaphors of "having no parents" or "being an orphan" express
the view that such pieces are at the very beginning of the process of
being integrated into the Gabor Roma ethnic history. In the words of
middle-aged Bandi from Mureş County:

A beaker with neither father nor mother [without a Gabor Roma
ownership history] is worthless. If ... we don't know whose it was [among

the Gabors] and where it came from and what sort of beaker it is, it's seen as just a new beaker that has no value at all. (19 March 2005)

Rupi, a man in his twenties, made a similar comment in connection with an object that had been recently acquired by the Gabors from the Hungarian antiques market and was still in its transitional period:

> It's a good beaker [in terms of its material properties]. But the thing is that it never had our moustache on it. You understand? [We can't say] "It came from X [it was bought from this or that Gabor Roma owner]." It has neither father nor mother, that is, we can't say that it is a native [piece], we can't say that it was in the possession of X or Y [of anybody among the Gabors] … But the beaker from Z [village Z] does! There we know that it was bought from this or that Gabor Roma. (27 August 2004)

The moustache is one of the most important symbols of masculinity and ethnic identity among the Gabor men. In expressions such as "Our moustache wasn't on it [the beaker or tankard in question]," "It doesn't have a moustache," or "It's a beaker with a moustache," often heard in prestige-object discourse, the word "moustache" is used as a synonym of Gabor Roma ethnic identity or, in a narrower sense, stands for the piece's embeddedness in the Gabor Roma ethnic history.

The quotations below not only support the previous statements about the central role of Gabor ownership history in determining an object's market value, desirability, and price but also indicate that my interlocutors knew exactly that the value regimes of the antiques market and art history define the value and significance of beakers and tankards quite differently from the way they do.

> [The Gabor Roma] do not pay for the material of the beaker, that it contains this much gold or that much silver! But [what they pay for is] the renown! Whose it was! "It was this Gabor man's or that Gabor man's." The renown! The great name [fame]! … The [Gabor Roma] history. Because it's said, "This beaker was big X's, big Y's or big Z's." It has a name [fame] because that beaker changed hands among the [Gabor] Roma. (19 March 2005)

> If it was already known among the Gabor Roma that it was a new beaker [one that had only recently been purchased from the antiques market], nobody bought it. Because it was worthless. Because even if somebody bought it, the others said [to him], "What have you bought? A new beaker? What good is that for? It's good for nothing!" No, nobody bought

it. [They bought] only native beakers. The beakers that the [Gabor Roma] forefathers left behind as their legacy. Those ones were bought! The ones about which they said, "These beakers have a father and a mother, these beakers have a moustache!" Those were the valuable beakers and if somebody bought one of those, that had value and fame, it was said, "That Gabor man bought a [precious] beaker, he's a big man!" Not all beakers are the same, either. (19 March 2005)

Expressions such as "orphan beaker," "an object with neither father nor mother," "a piece with no moustache," or "an object with no owner," used to describe beakers and tankards recently purchased from the European antiques market, also indicate that the Gabors do not consider previous non-Roma (or other, non-Gabor Roma) possessors and their renown to be a source of value, nor do they regard these people to be "fathers and mothers"; these ethnicized roles can be fulfilled only by Gabor Roma.

The biographies of the more important prestige objects, especially their ownership histories and any associated memorable events (such as rivalry and conflicts between potential buyers or exceptionally high purchase prices), were followed and discussed over and over again by my hosts at various social gatherings with the same intense interest and passion that they showed towards past prestige relations among the Gabor Roma patrilines. The relationship of individuals with their ethnic, and often local and patrilineal, past is partially constructed, experienced, and performed through the prestige-object biographies themselves. The following comments made by Rupi, who owns several prestige objects, give a clear illustration of the above:

A gaźo [a non-Roma individual] doesn't know anything about them [Gabor prestige objects]. A gaźo doesn't know anything about our Gabor Roma history. I'm telling you the truth, he doesn't know what it is. We know where it [a beaker or tankard] comes from and for how many years it's been with the Gabors. It's not just what we see [it's not only the material properties of a beaker or tankard that make it valuable] but also the history, that it's been with the Gabor Roma for so many years. The Gabor Roma history makes it so precious and expensive! ... If you, say, bought one [a beaker] from one of us. Another [Gabor man] comes and says, "Show me the beaker you've bought!" You show it to him. And that Roma man may not know [which is why he asks you], "So where is this beaker from?" "It was Z's and Z bought it from this man and this man bought it from that man. Five or six hands back!" ... These [the prestige objects] have a history like that, the same as if it was written down. You know? On paper. That's why they're so expensive ... These [that is, the ownership histories] are counted back in detail [memorized carefully by the Gabors]: who owned it [the given prestige object] in the past and where it came from. (5 September 2004)

What has been noted about the modest significance of pieces recently acquired from non-Roma (or other, non-Gabor Roma) sellers is aptly illustrated by the remarkable difference observed between the antiques-market prices of "proper" beakers bought recently by some Gabor Roma and the purchase prices of the sought-after, important beakers of complete value within their own Roma ethnic population. While the latter may sell for US$200,000 to US$400,000 or occasionally even more (see chapter 2), "proper" beakers were purchased on the antiques market by my hosts during my fieldwork for the following prices: (a) €10,000 (place of purchase: an antique shop in Western Europe; time of purchase: 2003); (b) €20,000 (an antique shop in Budapest; 2004); (c) US$8,300 (an antique shop in Western Europe; 2004); (d) HUF900,000 ([US$4,311]; an antique shop in Budapest; 2004). The figure in (b) only appears to contradict the previous statement that the antiques-market price of the silver beakers wanted by the Gabors generally does not exceed US$9,000 to US$11,000. If an antiques dealer had precise knowledge of the Gabors' prestige economy and its typical price range, he/she would probably attempt to sell his/her objects for a higher price than is usual on the antiques market to any Gabor Roma showing an interest; this is exactly what happened in transaction (b) above.

As the above quotations strikingly illustrate (see also chapter 2), the Gabors' beakers and tankards are patina-based prestige goods, and the consumer subculture organized around them is one of the contemporary second-hand cultures based on patina-oriented consumption.

Ownership History as a Symbolic Pantheon and Other Motivations for Purchasing

Potential buyers (as previously discussed) often regard the most important component of object biography – ownership history – as a scarce resource, a sought-after symbolic pantheon, entry to which is fiercely contested. In many cases, to become an inalienable part of the ownership history of a precious commodity is one of the primary goals of the competing potential buyers, such as collectors or museums. This aspiration is driven by the agency of ownership history, which can be traced back primarily to the fact that integration into it is often interpreted as a means of representing economic and other resources and shaping social and political differences and identities. In other words, major changes in ownership history, for example, may influence some of the relations between subjects and certain processes, such as the intensity of proprietary contests, organized around the given commodity.

This is exactly the case for subcultural economies based on patina-seeking consumption, such as the Gabor Roma prestige economy. The *reputational profit* that a purchaser hopes to gain by buying a valuable beaker or tankard derives – at least in part – from the prestige of the object's previous Gabor owners or, more precisely, from the fact that the buyer himself can become an inalienable part of an ownership history that comprises highly esteemed former possessors and is regarded as an ethnicized symbolic pantheon or hall of fame.[4] Taking possession of an important prestige object allows the buyer to indulge in *self-glorification*, presenting himself as someone on a par with the former influential and successful owners of the piece and attempting to identify with them symbolically.

As mentioned before, integration into the ownership history of a valuable beaker or tankard also provides its new Gabor possessor with an opportunity for *invidious comparison* between himself and those who failed in their attempt to buy the object in question on the one hand, and between himself and the individual who was forced to sell the piece on the other.

The purchase/sale of a precious item *may trigger a significant shift in various dimensions of political relations*. It may affect, for example, the comparative evaluation of the political achievements of brothers competing for the role of family leader or of individuals attempting to win the honorific title of village leader, just as it may influence the dominant interpretation of social differences between families and patrilines.

A potential buyer's political ambitions, his willingness to take risks, and the renown he hopes to gain from the transaction may be increased by an opportunity to purchase a highly esteemed beaker or tankard from *one of his most important political rivals*. The reputational profit expected from the transaction may further be enhanced if the object for sale is considered to be *the rival seller's patrilineal identity symbol* – that is, if it has been passed down from father to son in his family for a long time and therefore has substantial emotional and identity value for the seller. Since both types of transactions are accompanied by an extra loss of face for the seller, he will very likely tend to agree to a considerable price cut during negotiations just to find an unrelated buyer who is not one of his political rivals, or to make sure that the object passes to one of his own close relatives – his brother or son-in-law, for instance – and thus "remains in his family." The goal of both strategies is to diminish the intensity of the shame and loss of prestige as well as of the political insults, directed at the seller, that will inevitably accompany the transaction.

The prospect of integration into the ownership history of a valuable piece may also intensify an individual's propensity to buy, and he is promised extra fame if he can come into possession of a sought-after object that *was once owned by members of his own patriline* (i.e., was once regarded by his forefathers as a family heirloom and patrilineal identity symbol) but then passed into the ownership of others. Many of my Gabor interlocutors interpreted the transactions in this category as acts of repurchasing – of familial or patrilineal repatriation – emphasizing that the purchase gave the buyer an opportunity to restore the status of the object as a patrilineal identity symbol and to counterbalance, at least partially, the loss of face caused by the sale of the piece by one of his forebears.

Beyond the possible effects that integration into ownership history may have on the prestige of the new owner and the evaluation of his political performance, the new possessor's social and economic position and any subsequent major shifts in it may also influence the value and significance of the ownership history of the object he has just bought.

The acquisition of a valuable beaker or tankard by an individual with only modest success in politics and a social status substantially lower than that of most of its previous owners will have a negative effect on the value of the ownership history and the renown of the piece. This is not only because the new possessor will have less opportunity to bring up ("to pluck," *megpenget*) the object in conversations at social gatherings but also because others will speak about it less often – which, according to my Roma acquaintances, will lead to some degree of loss of value ("the value of the piece will fall"). The loss of value attributed to the low social prestige of the new owner was often expressed by pejorative phrases such as "sleeping beaker" or "the beaker is asleep and so is its owner" (*sovel vi o taxtaj, vi lehko gazda*). The words "sleep" and "asleep" are synonymous here with a partial exclusion of the object in question from Gabor Roma social publicity. When, however, a beaker or tankard with excellent material properties is acquired by a new owner whose political achievements surpass by far those of the previous possessors, the social significance and desirability associated with the ownership history of the piece changing hands increase, and the object – in the words of my Roma hosts – "ranks up" (becomes of "higher rank," more valuable).

There is, therefore, a dynamic relationship between the ownership history of a prestige object and the current social and economic position of its owner; a complex interaction and interdependence can be observed in terms of value and renown.

Material Patina: Prestige-Object Aesthetics

Gabor Roma prestige-object aesthetics comprises a series of value preferences with respect to the social and economic significance of various material features: which material properties should be taken into special consideration when estimating a piece's value and price, how those properties relate to each other, which of the different variations of a given material property are more valuable, and which are less valuable.

Value-Increasing Material Properties

(1) *The shape of the object.* As previously mentioned, the word *kana* denotes only tankards (see colour plates: Photos 14–15, 17–18), while *taxtaj* refers to beakers of a few particular shapes. The value preferences with regard to the various object shapes available on the European antiques market are themselves part of the prestige-object aesthetics that allows the Gabors to symbolically remove these pieces from the value regimes of the antiques market and art history by reaestheticizing them, endowing many of their material properties with new meanings and values.

The shapes of beakers regarded as "proper" by my interlocutors were the following. One of these is the footed beaker with a girdle articulating its cylindrical body (*taxtaj kuštikasa*).[5] (See colour plates: Photos 9–11, 16, 19.) Another type of shape is the *ščobo* beaker (*ščobo taxtaj*), which is shaped like a flowerpot and has a hollow foot a few millimetres in height. (See colour plates: Photo 12.) The third type, similar in shape to the *ščobo* beaker, is the *burikato* beaker (*burikato taxtaj; burik* means "navel" in Romani), which is also a flowerpot-shaped object but does not have a hollow foot. (See colour plates: Photo 13.) The *burikato* beaker got its name from the depression in the centre of the bottom, which my acquaintances described as a "bellybutton." *Burikato* pieces originally had a solid silver stem, which was removed, together with the foot, by the Roma when put in use; only the upper, flowerpot-shaped vessel was kept as a prestige object. (The navel-like depression in these beakers has the function of hiding the traces of the soldering that joins the solid stem to the bottom of the vessel.) Another type of "proper" beaker shape is the octagonal beaker (*njolcsegîvo taxtaj*), named after its octagonal form. (Very rarely, pieces of modest value that did not belong to any of the above shape types were also mentioned in recollections.)[6]

The great majority of prestige objects currently in the possession of the Gabor Roma are beakers. The most popular and valued type is the footed beaker, followed by *ščobo* objects, of which there are substantially fewer; and – as far as I know – the *burikato* and octagonal beakers, deemed the least important and attractive, now number fewer than fifteen each.

(2) *The material: the age and quality of the silver.* As mentioned in chapter 2, according to my interlocutors, one of the indispensable material conditions for a beaker or tankard to become a prestige object of complete value is that the piece should be made of antique silver and no other materials. The purity of the silver is also an important aspect of value. The higher its silver content – that is, the lower its copper content – the more valuable the silver is considered to be.

(3) *Minor damages.* My hosts attributed a partially different meaning and significance to minor damages on the objects than do experts of the value regimes of the antiques market and art history. These damages include, for example, silver erosion, cracks, dents, and minor changes in the colour of the silver (signs of wear where the piece is most likely to be held, a darkening or "blackening" of grooves in the object's body, and so on). While these damages are regarded as factors that decrease the value of a piece when it is estimated on the antiques market, my Gabor acquaintances saw them as evident proofs of their age and therefore value-increasing factors. This practice has its roots on the one hand in the past-oriented character of the Gabors' prestige-object definition and on the other in their fear of forgery. They feel confident that pieces with clearly unblemished and injury-free surfaces are of recent manufacture; that is, they are not of antique silver, and thus they cannot become prestige objects of complete value in the near future. Such beakers and tankards available on the antiques market are therefore avoided by the Gabors.

(4) *Decorations*. The most sought-after decorations include whole-figure representations or portraits of old, bearded men, and such men wearing crowns or laurel wreaths (my acquaintances liked to define the latter persons as "kings," "emperors," or "princes"); decorations depicting soldiers or armed animals; aristocratic coats of arms; figures of wild animals (e.g., lions, bears, wolves) and horses; and biblical or hunting scenes. (See colour plates: Photos 9–21.) Since the valuable objects are considered to be political trophies and symbols of economic prosperity, my interlocutors gave preference to decorations that they associated with the concepts of aristocracy, social elitism, and respectability. Due to the associations attached to them, several of the above-mentioned decorations are well suited to represent excellence, power, prestige, and dominance.

The popularity of portraits of "monarchs" as decorations is also indicated by another practice: the method frequently used in repairing an injured lip. If a beaker's lip is cracked or nicked in a few places, the damages are often hidden by attaching a silver coin – depicting Austrian emperor Franz Joseph I – to the outside of the lip, slightly thinning the edge of the coin so that it almost blends into the body of the beaker. (See colour plates: Photo 20.)

Another group of decorations are sought after among the Gabors because – according to their interpretation – they are proof of the age of the object. As mentioned, old age – the quality of being antique – is a major source of value for both beakers and tankards. Since these objects are held to be the indexical representations of a distant past, decorations whose ages are difficult or outright impossible to determine with any accuracy are in great demand. These include, among other motifs, legendary creatures such as the unicorn, the griffin, and the dragon. My hosts did not define these decorations as unicorns, griffins, and so on but used the collective label of "unexplainable animals" when referring to them. (They also often included in this category animals – for example, greyhounds – that were not entirely unknown to them but whose breed they were uncertain about, or animals that were represented on the mantle of objects in unusual ways, for instance, "armed" and "dressed in military uniform.") The cause of their being "unexplainable" was often seen in their "extinction a long time ago," as a result of which "there were no written records on the basis of which their identity could be precisely determined." (See colour plates: Photos 9, 21.) In the words of middle-aged Kalo from Mureş County, "The really good beakers are the ones with animals on them that we can't explain … The valuable ones are the ones that have these fanciful [mysterious] animals on them, so you can't tell what they are." Zoltan, who is a prestige-object owner himself, argued that "there are unexplainable animals ... on the beakers sometimes ... My brother's got one, a beaker, there are these animals on it that we can't recognize what animals they are ... Those objects are valuable ... These are not recent beakers, you know ... these beakers were made before the time of Lord Jesus."

A similar historicizing practice of my acquaintances was the frequent identification of portraits on the antique coins or other parts of the objects as the images of ancient "Roman or Greek aristocrats."

Antique coins built into or fixed on the beaker mantle or attached to the bottom of the foot are similarly important value-enhancing decorative features. In prestige-object discourse they are called "silver coins" (*rupune love*) or "thalers" (*talleri*). For instance, a precious beaker currently located in Cluj County, which was exchanged by one of its previous owners for two smaller footed beakers and a modest sum of cash in 1952, was described by one of my interlocutors as follows:

> This beaker belonged to the prophets, before Christ. And there are twelve coins on it, on that beaker ... And one of the twelve, the bigger one, is so [valuable] that a museum expert in Bucharest said, "Give me that beaker! I'll remove that coin and give the rest back. I'll give you as much [money for it] as you want, in US$ or German marks!" But the Roma man [the owner of the piece] didn't sell it, and he won't sell it. That's how [valuable] this beaker is. (16 June 2000)

Further value-increasing properties are medallions (*pažga*) inscribed with initials, dates, proper names, a coat of arms, or some kind of portrait, or especially rich, well-preserved fire-gilding. When they could not decipher the meaning of inscriptions on medallions or beneath the lip, my Gabor interlocutors liked to identify them as being written in "Latin," "Hebrew," or "Greek." The aim of this technique of historicization is also to demonstrate the prestige objects' age and embeddedness in history. The languages mentioned above were often interpreted as icons of past ages (such as "biblical times") and my acquaintances frequently argued that the object with an "indecipherable inscription" was made in the historical period associated with that inscription.

The prestige-object aesthetics in question also defines the wealth of vegetal decorative motifs – stylized leaves, tendrils, flowers, and so on – as a value-increasing factor, primarily because it is held to be an

evidence of craftsmanship and meticulous care. The presence of numerous non-figural and non-vegetal decorations also enhances the value
of an object (at least when compared to the entirely or almost entirely
undecorated surface). Decorations in this category include, for example, surface patterns of different shapes described in prestige-object
discourse as snakeskin (*sapani morči*, a beaker body with a surface pattern similar to snakeskin), fish scale (*maśani morči*, an object decorated
with a fish-scale-like pattern), and bean (*babošo*, a piece decorated with
a small bean-shaped pattern). The value-enhancing richness of these
decorations was frequently characterized by my hosts in such terms as
"There's nowhere to put a hair [on the beaker's body]" or "You have
nowhere to put a needle, it's [the surface of the object] so detailed."
Almost or completely undecorated pieces are often called "white beakers" (*parno taxtaj*). The attribute "white" conveys the mirror-like,
homogenous appearance of the object's decoration-free surface.

(5) *The size expressed in capacity.* The issue of size expressed in capacity
is also a major component of the Gabors' prestige-object aesthetics. At
the time of my fieldwork, a capacity of one litre (*ekh kofako*) was considered to be the ideal and most sought-after beaker size. Of the prestige
objects I documented, the smallest had a capacity of three and a half
decilitres while the largest had a capacity of more than three litres.[7]

Value-Decreasing Material Properties

The ethno-aesthetics in question also specifies a set of material properties that have a negative effect on the value of a piece. These properties include decorations associated with morally stigmatized evil spells
(*čoxajimo*), such as snakes (*sap*) or frogs (*źamba*), as well as suspiciously
flawless and new-looking gilding (which has a different shade from fire-
gilding), and conspicuously damage-free and bright silver. The owner
of an item that has either of the latter two properties must anticipate that
his political rivals will spread rumours about his prestige object being
not actually a "proper" piece but a "new beaker" – that is, one recently
produced in a silversmith's workshop and therefore decidedly less
valuable than its owner claims it is. My hosts showed a similar attitude
towards decorations that they themselves identified as depicting livestock typical of a village environment (horses are the only exception).
Their prestige-object aesthetics also frowns upon the appearance on an
object of exclusively feminine decorations (female figures or portraits,
for example) since this property is at odds with the gendered character

of their prestige economy – that is, the close connection between prestige objects and masculinity. For beakers, a lip with a markedly outward curving shape is also a disadvantage; many of my interlocutors associated this with female pudenda, considered by the Gabors' ideology of the body to be impure. Finally, especially small or unusually large sizes are further unfavourable features of a beaker or tankard. My acquaintances often referred ironically to very small beakers using the metaphorical label *tripidjili* (a small punch used by tinsmiths).

The material properties listed in the previous paragraph are regarded as disadvantageous because they carry negative associations – evil spells, immorality, "new beaker," feminine dominance, impurity – that provide an obvious opportunity for the possessor's political rivals to symbolically devalue his object. That is, they offer an opportunity for informal rumours or the expression of open insults, which may result in a partial loss of face for the owner.

The Scope of Validity of Value Conventions

The value conventions of the prestige-object aesthetics constitute an ethnicized, translocal type of cultural capital that is widespread among the Gabor Roma. In my experience, individual value preferences are rare and are generally related to the type or numerousness of decorations – for some of my interlocutors, "unexplainable animals" were the most valuable decorations, while others attached the greatest value to antique coins with portraits of "monarchs" on them, and so on.

When mapping how aesthetic preferences shape the significance of a piece, it is worth taking into account that the influence of the value associations attached to individual material properties on the value of an object as a whole may be highly varied and context-dependent. To take just one example, two of the three Gabor footed beakers currently considered to be the most valuable have a completely undecorated (reeded) girdle, while the third piece has a wriggle-work girdle. According to the value convention regarding the types of girdles, the reeded girdles are less prized. In the cases of the two beakers with reeded girdles mentioned above, however, this disadvantage is completely marginalized by a large number of sought-after and highly esteemed material properties held to be much more important than the shape of the girdle (ideal beaker size and shape, "unexplainable animals" as decorations, antique coins with portraits of "monarchs," and rich fire-gilding in good condition).

As to the question of whether symbolic or material patina is more important, no single answer is valid for all objects. All my acquaintances attributed a high degree of significance to Gabor Roma ownership history *and* material properties evaluated on the basis of their prestige-object aesthetics; that is, in general, the relationship between these two sources of value was considered to be balanced. It goes without saying, however, that during our conversations the owners of pieces with a social career of modest renown but highly esteemed material properties liked to argue in favour of the dominance of material patina as a primary source of value, while the possessors of objects with an excellent pedigree but average material properties did the same in the opposite direction, arguing for the priority of ownership history. Both practices had the objective of "retouching" the performance of the owner in the prestige economy by highlighting his object's more valuable properties and downplaying or under-representing the significance of its less valuable ones. Whether the symbolic or the material patina has primacy in a transaction must be decided by the participants on a case-by-case basis.

The dynamics of the value associated with an object's symbolic patina differ to a considerable extent from that attached to material patina. While it may happen that a piece with sought-after material properties "acquires" influential Gabor owners in the short run – thus increasing the value associated with its ownership history – the material properties of the same object remain unaltered throughout its social career and their value is unlikely to change to a significant degree (see also the next section).

This difference is one of the major motivations behind a large share of purchases from non-Roma; many influential Gabor buyers hope that their "new beakers" (objects bought recently from the antiques market) with several attractive material properties will "age" with time in the possession of their family members (sons, grandsons, and so on); that is, "time will give them a name [renown]" and these pieces may become sought-after prestige objects thanks to the gradual growth of their Gabor Roma ownership histories.

Fashion and Prestige-Object Aesthetics

The fact that the group of aesthetic value conventions can be regarded as a dynamic social construction is due not only to the marginal presence of individual preferences. In recent decades there have also been a few changes in value preferences concerning certain material properties that have affected the whole of the Gabor Roma ethnic population as an aesthetic community of practice. Let me discuss three of these changes.

(1) *Size.* An analysis of recollections and the object biographies known to me indicates that up to the 1950s the Gabors were keen to buy and collect pieces with large capacities of well over one litre – one-and-half-, two-, or three-litre beakers – and held these to be more valuable than the richly decorated one-litre beakers that are much more popular today. In the words of one of my middle-aged hosts, "The Gabor Roma used to prefer the big *parno taxta* [the large "white beakers" – that is, pieces with few or no decorations], with no work on them." Another of my acquaintances – in somewhat exaggerated terms – claimed that "the old people [who lived in the mid-twentieth century] … say, there was a six- or seven-deciliter beaker, it wasn't worth anything to them. Only the two-liter ones or the one-and-a-half-liter ones! And nowadays those [the latter beakers] are not worth a quid of tobacco." The smaller – about one-litre – beakers started to become more valuable and sought after from the end of the 1950s, and this process reached its peak around the time of the change of political regime in 1989; by that time, there was little social interest in or demand for large-capacity prestige objects. The few large beakers – with a capacity of two to three litres – still in Gabor Roma ownership after 1989 are practically unsellable among the Gabors but fairly popular in several Cărhar Roma communities (particularly those in the Olt River area in Sibiu and Brașov Counties).

(2) *The value attributed to the decorations.* In parallel with the process mentioned above, another shift in preferences occurred during the decades preceding the change of political regime. For the interpretation of this shift we should remember that the beakers with decidedly large capacities tended to have little or no decoration at all, in contrast with most of the one-litre or smaller beakers, which were more or less richly decorated. The gradual devaluation of large capacity over the second half of the twentieth century, together with the increase in the popularity of and demand for the more richly decorated pieces with a capacity of about one litre, led to an important shift in the evaluation of the significance of decorations; much greater emphasis than before came to be placed on rich decoration as an important source of value when determining an object's price and value.

(3) *Preferences regarding the shape of a beaker and the number of prestige objects.* Recollections unquestionably indicate that in the mid-twentieth

century, unlike today, there was no substantial difference between footed and *ščobo* beakers in terms of either their social significance or their numbers. During the years of socialism, the Gabors had many more *ščobo* beakers in their possession than they do now, and there was a much more intense demand for them than around 1989 and thereafter. These pieces are typically decorated considerably more modestly than are footed beakers, and a substantial proportion of the large prestige objects had a *ščobo* shape.[8] As a consequence of the shifts in value preferences regarding ideal size and quantity of decorations discussed above, the *ščobo* shape has undergone a gradual devaluation, and many of these beakers were sold by the Gabors to the Transylvanian Cărhar Roma in the decades preceding the political regime change. None of the prestige-object sales transactions among the Gabors documented by me since 1989 involved *ščobo* beakers.

The shifts in preferences mentioned in this section, along with the intense Cărhar Roma interest in buying large *ščobo* objects, explain why footed beakers have become dominant in the Gabor Roma ethnic population not only in terms of the value associated with their shape but also numerically.

Prestige-Object Aesthetics as an "Invisible Ink" of Ethnic Identity

Many of the preferences of the Gabors' prestige-object aesthetics mentioned above provide excellent examples of how, by modifying many of the meanings and values attached by the non-Roma to their material properties, the Gabors distance these beakers and tankards from the antiques market and art history and how they recreate (reethnicize, and so on) them on an aesthetic level.

The politics of aesthetics/aestheticization is a widespread practice, the significance of which has been repeatedly noted in sociological and anthropological literature. The relevant studies can be divided into at least two groups on the basis of their problem sensitivity. Some of them focus on the role played in identity politics by consumer taste as a cultural competence monopolized by a given community, asking first of all how community-specific tastes are used strategically in the processes of authentication, representation, and reproduction of social and cultural identities, differences, and boundaries (see, for example, Bourdieu 1984; McCracken 1988). Other investigations deal with the increasing aestheticization of everyday life in the context of (post)modernity – that is, the causes and consequences of the pervasive presence of "signs and images" – examining such phenomena as the blurring of the boundary between high art and mass culture or the influence of the media, advertising, and fashion industry on consumer sensitivity and preferences (Featherstone 1991, 65–82; Scott & Urry 1994, 54; Lury 1996). My interpretation shows similarities with the former of these research perspectives.

Knowledge of the Gabors' prestige-object aesthetics constitutes an ethnicized type of cultural capital accessible primarily in discourse, the acquisition of which is a time-consuming process (it requires, among other things, a detailed analysis of the associated terminology and value preferences). With the exception of a few non-Roma anthropologists and antiques dealers and a number of Cărhar Roma individuals, it is a competence possessed by only the Gabor Roma. This is why many of my hosts interpreted familiarity with their prestige-object aesthetics – like the passion for collecting beakers and tankards – as a marker of their own Roma ethnic identity and one of the attributes that can be deployed as an "invisible ink" of ethnic identity in managing social relations, interactions, and boundaries. I have borrowed this term from McCracken (1988, 34), who argues that certain communities use their own aesthetic tastes or sensitivities[9] as an "invisible ink" – that is, as a means of supervising community membership. With the help of a community-specific taste, in conversations about its value preferences, individuals attempting to represent themselves as members of a community to which they do not belong can be exposed without their being aware of it. The Gabors' prestige-object aesthetics fulfils a similar function, although in their case there are no ethnic others who would be willing to create the impression that they are Gabor Roma themselves. In terms of ethnic identity politics, the significance of familiarity with their prestige-object aesthetics comes from the fact that this knowledge marks and links the members of the Gabor Roma ethnic population like an "invisible ink." This ethnicized aesthetic competence pertains to the repertoire of ideologies and practices aimed at creating a sense and experience of ethnic belonging (that is, of *Gaborness*) – it enabled my interlocutors to conceptualize, represent, and reproduce themselves as a special type of community of practice: a translocal taste community or aesthetic community.[10]

5

The Politics of Brokerage: Bazaar-Style Trade and Risk Management

Who Are the *Cenzar*s?

The Gabors make use of brokers often and in a variety of situations, such as house purchases or the forming of marital alliances. The term *cenzar*[1] in their Romani dialect primarily refers to individuals acting as intermediaries in prestige-object transactions. The *cenzar* is an entrepreneur engaged in occasional income-generating activity, participating in the flow of beakers and tankards without becoming an owner himself.

Gabor *cenzar*s coordinate either transactions in which only Gabor Roma individuals participate or interethnic deals, which in the great majority of cases take place between Gabor Roma and Cărhar Roma. Sometimes a Gabor broker helps to pawn a Gabor prestige object with a Transylvanian Roma – neither Gabor nor Cărhar – creditor whose Roma ethnic population neither collects silver beakers or tankards nor defines them as prestige goods but nevertheless accepts them as securities because its members are aware of the fact that both the Gabors and the Cărhars greatly value these objects.[2]

It is often not a simple task for a seller or buyer to decide whether or not to employ a *cenzar*. The atmosphere of uncertainty that accompanies prestige-object transactions usually prompts participants to make use of the services of intermediaries, since they can thereby diminish the risk of doing "a crazy sale [making a bad deal]." The participation of a *cenzar*, however, involves considerable expenditure that the client would much rather avoid. The decision to engage one, therefore, is preceded by careful deliberation, with special regard to the balance between the expected return and the costs of his employment.

When do the Gabors use the services of a broker in connection with beakers and tankards? First, during prestige-object sales transactions, and second, when an owner in an economic crisis situation takes a substantial loan from a creditor and pawns his beaker or tankard with him as a security. In a loan transaction, a broker may be needed in the planning of loan arrangements, in which case he is expected to find the most suitable creditor for the owner – that is, a person who possesses the hoped-for sum, is likely to respect all conditions of the loan agreement, and considers the prestige object offered as a security to be a valuable piece. Another situation concerning loan transactions that frequently results in a *cenzar* being engaged is one in which the indebted owner's pawned beaker or tankard has already "sunk in the debt" – that is, the combined sum of the capital and interest has reached 80 per cent of the estimated value of the security – and there is intense demand for it; that is, several individuals would be keen to purchase it. In this case, the broker's job is to find the potential buyer who offers the highest purchase price and to represent the debtor's interests during the price bargaining, or to find at least one person among those interested in the pawned object who considers it more valuable than does the current creditor and who is prepared to buy the debt. In the eyes of this new creditor, the piece has not yet entirely "sunk in the debt"; that is, the debtor can expect to gain some more time before his whole debt has to be repaid.[3]

An agreement between a *cenzar* and his employer is made according to one of two scripts. (a) Contact is often initiated by the person forced to sell or pawn his beaker or tankard or by the individual planning to buy a prestige object; he visits one of the men known to be successful brokers and entrusts him with the task. (b) In other cases, the potential broker visits the would-be seller or buyer and – in the hope of the substantial profit he expects to make from the deal about to be clinched – offers his services. The commission usually comes about when the sentence "Stand by me [that is, in the planned deal]!" or "Will you stand by me?" is uttered and the request is accepted; this is always supplemented by an agreement on the fee to be paid to the *cenzar*. An employer may engage more than one *cenzar* in a transaction, entrusting them with either the management of the deal or some subtask, such as mapping supply-and-demand conditions or pushing prices up. This is especially true in sales of the more valuable pieces. Since many people see their participation in such an event as a one-off source of substantial income, several individuals with varying degrees of brokering experience visit the would-be seller or buyer when news of the planned transaction reaches them and offer their expertise and support.

Not only cash-oriented brokers may contribute to the organization of the deal. Prestige-object transactions are accompanied by a mobilization of the social network supporting the interests of the buyer or seller, especially the group of brothers and co-fathers-in-law who maintain a harmonious relationship with him.[4] Some of the latter, in accordance with the moral expectation of mutual support, may volunteer to give their assistance without being asked and do not (or at least not openly) ask for financial compensation. The helpers in this category who undertake some of the brokering tasks may do so either with or without the seller or buyer's prior consent; they may participate in the search for the most suitable buyer or seller or "raise" the value of the object offered for sale by praising its symbolic and material properties in male conversations.

In some of the cases, the job of brokering is therefore undertaken not by a single person but by a small group of individuals, including both cash-oriented brokers and supporters who interpret their participation primarily as a moral obligation. It can also happen that the *cenzar* himself engages a few helpers and carries out his tasks with the help of, for example, his sons or brothers.

Being a *cenzar* – at least in the case of the more valuable objects – is inseparable from the concept of competition. The *cenzar* may be affected by the following contexts of potential rivalry: (a) *Cenzar* candidates compete with each other to be chosen for the task. (b) The *cenzar* makes every effort to gain the upper hand over the broker(s) engaged not by his employer but by other stakeholders. (The seller's broker competes with the buyer's broker; often, when the object for sale is popular and much sought after, the various *cenzars* engaged by potential buyers become each other's competitors, and so on.) (c) It can happen that competition develops between the brokers employed by the same party in the transaction with respect to which one of them will be the first to arrange the deal the employer wishes.

While only Gabor Roma brokers participate in the organization of a transaction between a Gabor seller and a Gabor buyer, interethnic transactions show a much more varied picture. When a Gabor seller decides to sell his beaker or tankard among the Cărhars, he may directly visit a Cărhar man he regards as a potential buyer or turn to one of the Cărhar *cenzars* known to him. If he does not know who to turn to in the Cărhar Roma ethnic population, he will probably entrust the task to a Gabor broker who has already had some contact with the Cărhars – someone who has either lived for some time in one of the settlements also inhabited by Cărhar Roma or has participated in the organization of interethnic deals before. If this Gabor *cenzar* knows a Cărhar person who could be a potential buyer, he may get in touch directly with that individual, or, as is often the case, he may first turn for advice to a Cărhar man who himself sometimes acts as a *cenzar* in his own Roma ethnic population; together, the two of them would then try to find the most suitable buyer. From the point of view of the Gabors, the Cărhar *cenzar*s are the gatekeepers of their own prestige-object market, who – in return for a fee – assist orientation in another translocal, informal, and ethnicized segment of the Romanian economy, the current supply-and-demand conditions of which are only superficially known even to most Gabor brokers. The engagement of Hungarian or Romanian intermediaries in transactions among the Gabors or between the Gabors and the Cărhars is not an option, since they lack most of the competencies needed to be a *cenzar* (see later in this chapter). (Gabor brokers are never entrusted with the coordination of transactions taking place between a Cărhar seller and a Cărhar buyer.)

The participation of a broker is, however, not an indispensable element of prestige-object transactions.

Deals not involving a *cenzar* may take place between close relatives – between brothers or between a nephew and his paternal uncle, for instance. Since in such a case the object changing hands "remains in the family," the factors that influence the price bargaining tend to be more predictable, since the parties involved have a higher-than-average trust in each other and are quite familiar with the piece in question. In other words, the mediation of a broker is made partially redundant by the social closeness and solidarity between the relatives.

In other cases, the parties manage without a *cenzar* because the creditor holding the debtor's beaker or tankard – which has already "sunk in the debt" – as a guarantee makes the best offer for the purchase of the pawned object. The creditor and the debtor have already estimated the value of the piece at least twice: first when it was pawned (i.e., when the capital was determined) and then at the time when both parties acknowledged that the object had "sunk in the debt." The price bargaining seems to be more predictable in such cases because of the advanced state of the value assessment process.

A further type of transaction in which a broker is often dispensed with is one in which the owner forced to sell or pawn his beaker or tankard is an influential Gabor individual with considerable experience in acting as a *cenzar*. In this type of case, the seller himself represents his own business interests.[5]

Sources of Uncertainty in Prestige-Object Transactions

Why is a broker employed in a substantial share of transactions? The primary reason is the high degree of uncertainty that characterizes the seller or buyer (or both). This attitude may stem from the following:

(1) Difficulties in quantifying the monetary value of the object;
(2) Difficulties in verifying its nominal authenticity;
(3) A scarcity of reliable information on the current supply-and-demand conditions of the Gabor (or Cărhar Roma) prestige-object market; and
(4) A relative lack of persuasive ability.

It is primarily due to the uncertainty surrounding prestige-object deals that the significance of price bargaining and the scope for action, as well as the economic importance of brokers coordinating it, are remarkably large. The support of an experienced broker can secure a savings or additional profit amounting to as much as tens of thousands of US dollars for his client, and it is often thanks to the activities of the broker that a buyer or seller chooses precisely his client to do business with. While the latter two of the causes of uncertainty mentioned above do not need further explanation, the first two most certainly do.

Why Is It Hard to Express an Object's Value in Money?

The quantification of the object's value is an indispensable part of each and every change of ownership (with the exception of inheritance), but it is seldom free of difficulty. Certain characteristics of the value discourse around prestige objects, and the singularity of the pieces, make predicting the final purchase price – and estimating a reasonable price – problematic.

Dominance of the Discourse of Qualitative Value

The Gabor participants in the conversations I observed, whether these took place in closed groups – among family members, for instance – or at public social gatherings, often brought up the subject of prestige objects. Among other things, they discussed the comparative importance of two or more pieces, describing in detail their value-increasing properties or their shortcomings; ranked the beakers and tankards in the various families, Transylvanian settlements, or regions; and talked about the more important value conventions of their prestige-object aesthetics, or which of the former Gabor owners had made the greatest contribution to the increased renown or value of a particular item. An important thematic unit of their prestige-object discourse concerned the interpretation of current sales and pawn transactions, and the discussion of memorable past business deals (often even from decades earlier), with special reference to the impact of these transactions and deals on the prestige of the buyers or sellers, the evaluation of the purchase prices, and the participating parties' attitudes towards business ethics.

The Gabors' prestige-object discourse is characterized by a dominance of qualitative rather than quantitative expressions of value. When my interlocutors spoke about the properties of a specific beaker or tankard, they did not apply any common unit of measurement that could make the qualitative value of one property precisely comparable with that of another; that is, they did not express the value relations among the individual properties of a piece in quantitative terms, such as money. It is thus effectively impossible to decide what proportion of the value or purchase price of an object is due to any given feature (unlike in discussions about, for example, automobiles, the parts of which are themselves products with prices attached to them). In discourses dealing with prestige-object properties, there is no way of expressing part–whole relations in quantitative terms.

In the following I shall mention only three types of the value relations associated with certain attributes of a given piece that are left unquantified by the Roma.

(1) *The value conventions of the prestige-object aesthetics*. The Gabors do not quantify the qualitative value differences between material properties, for instance. Thus they express in quantitative terms neither how much more valuable monarchs' portraits are than tendril and leaf decorations, nor how the significance associated with the shape of a beaker or the quality of silver relates to the value attributed to gilding or capacity.

(2) *The relationship between symbolic and material patina.* They do not use the language of numbers to express the relative proportions of the

groups of material properties versus the symbolic ones, such as ownership history, within the value of any given object.

(3) *The group of former owners.* Finally, they do not quantify the extent
to which former Gabor owners contributed individually to the renown
and social significance of a given piece.

The situation is similar when attempts are made to compare the values of two or more objects. When establishing the ranking of beakers
and tankards in terms of their economic and social significance, my
hosts tended to use qualitative terms such as that one is "more valuable," "worth more," or "more famous," or value metaphors such as
"the father of beakers" (a positive value metaphor) or "a tin can" (a
negative value metaphor).

The relative lack of quantitative terms is also characteristic of the sales
transactions and price bargaining. When the value of an object offered
for sale is quantified, those present bargain over a single (end) sum: the
purchase price encompassing the totality of the value components. This
sum is not divided into parts either during the price bargaining or in
later discussions evaluating the transaction or the reasonability of the
purchase price.

The dominance of qualitative expressions of value is closely connected to the social definition of these objects. As previously discussed,
they are primarily defined not as commodities but as symbols with
multiple meanings, the ideal state of being of which – at least in the case
of the more valuable ones – is long-term inalienability. The ideal type
of profit hoped to be gained through the possession of an important
beaker or tankard is therefore not the cash profit margin that could be
acquired if the piece were to be sold for more than its earlier purchase
price, but rather the renown and respectability that derive from maintaining the object's inalienability and from the social significance attributed to the piece. Therefore, these objects are not sold unless the owner
finds himself in an economic crisis situation; that is, the decision to put
a piece up for sale is not determined by, for instance, current favourable trends in the prestige-object market. In keeping with this, the value
associated with a beaker or tankard is generally quantified only when it
is already obviously very close to being pawned or sold.

This does not mean, however, that the owner of a valuable object is
not proud of having paid a large sum for it or that he does not occasionally attempt to demonstrate his economic power by stating in the
presence of others that, if he were forced to sell his beaker or tankard,
he would be paid an outstandingly large sum of money for it. Although

statements of this sort may include quantitative expressions of value, these tend to be unrealistically high figures rather than the results of careful value estimates based on current market conditions.

The Relative Lack of the Standardization of Material Properties

As mentioned before, only three material conditions must be met for a silver piece coming from the European antiques market to become, over time, a Gabor Roma prestige object of complete value. These are related to material, age, and form. Beakers and tankards, however, are hand-made items also possessing numerous other material properties that considerably affect their value. These may be differentiated along the dimensions of quality, quantity, or shape, among others. Some objects are only sparsely decorated, while others exhibit a whole series of highly esteemed decorative elements; some beakers have a capacity that is regarded as the ideal size (one litre), while the capacity of others may be as little as five or six decilitres or as much as two litres. The singularity of beakers and tankards is further increased by the random occurrence of certain properties (including fire-gilding, for instance), while other attributes (such as capacity) are common to all objects. Many decorations – such as inscriptions, portraits, animal representations, or ancient coins – can be found only on a single piece and are therefore considered to be unique distinguishing features. My interlocutors often also interpreted the various damages, or the repairs thereof, as singularizing attributes. The above phenomena explain why every single prestige object has a unique set of material properties; that is – as my acquaintances unanimously agreed – no two pieces found in their Roma ethnic population have identical material features.

Singularity is also characteristic of the Gabor ownership histories associated with the beakers and tankards. Since – as far as I know – no two pieces exist that were acquired by the same first Gabor owner from the non-Roma (or other, non-Gabor Roma) and subsequently always sold to or inherited by the same person and at the same time, the ownership histories of prestige objects differ from each other to varying degrees.

The beakers and tankards are therefore highly singularized; each piece can be characterized by a unique composition of material properties and an individual series of Gabor Roma owners.[6] Their singularity prevents the substitution of one object for another and makes it more difficult to compare two or more pieces or the values attributed to them. The beakers and tankards are therefore clearly distinct from commodities – household appliances and the like – the properties of which are generally standardized, making the various models of any given product marketed by different manufacturers relatively easily interchangeable and allowing them to function, at least partially, as reliable reference points for each other in value and price comparisons. The low level of standardization of properties is one of the reasons why the values and purchase prices of prestige objects vary so widely.

Singularity is, however, a characteristic feature of not only the Gabor ownership histories and the set of material properties of the individual items but also individual sales transactions; each transaction is a unique "microcosm" characterized by a continuously changing combination of circumstances.

It is worth making a brief digression at this point on the question of the role of the purchase price in the construction of the value associated with an object (see also chapter 2). My Gabor acquaintances did not typically use purchase prices previously paid for a beaker or tankard to express or calculate its current market value (objects recently sold for outstandingly large sums are exceptions to this). Accordingly, when bargaining over the current purchase price of a piece, they rarely attribute much significance to either the purchase prices paid for beakers and tankards in other people's possession or the previous purchase prices of the piece about to change hands. This latter statement also applies even to the great majority of cases where the given object has recently changed hands a few times and estimating the purchasing power of the prices it has sold for causes no difficulty. If we also consider what has already been said about the dominance of qualitative expressions of value, it becomes obvious that purchase prices are not the primary social representations of value in the case of these objects.

In addition to singularization, other circumstances may also make it difficult to use previous purchase prices as reliable reference points in quantifying an object's current value. Some of the pieces had last changed owners for money in the 1950s or 1960s, when the Gabors had considerably more modest living standards than they do today. According to the recollections of my interlocutors, many of them lived in tiny adobe huts, the members of older generations usually wore traditional moccasins, and prestige objects sometimes changed hands not for money but for assets, such as pigs. The substantial rise in the standard of living and economic status of many Gabor Roma since the 1970s has also contributed to the fact that the purchase prices paid around the middle of the twentieth century have by now completely lost their ability to function as a benchmark in quantifying the present value of a beaker or tankard. For other prestige objects, no relatively recent purchase prices are available at all because they have been passed down in the same family for some time, and in this type of change of ownership, as previously mentioned, there is no need to quantify the piece's value.

Another frequent obstacle to taking previous purchase prices into consideration is the problem of converting currencies. Until the mid-1990s, the purchase prices of beakers and tankards – like the sums of marriage payments given with daughters – were primarily determined in old Romanian leu; these prices and marriage payments were usually given and paid in German marks from the mid-1990s until 2002, when the mark was replaced by the euro; since then, either euros or US dollars have been used for these purposes. (On the politics of currencies in socialist and post-socialist contexts, see, for example, Lemon 1998; Pine 2002; Rogers 2005.) The most important source of uncertainty with regard to currency conversion is the fact that during the decades of socialism, ordinary citizens had no access to the exchange rates set by the National Bank of Romania. For this reason, I encountered many cases during my fieldwork – not only related to prestige objects – where my interlocutors were hard-pressed to determine what the sums paid in old Romanian leu, for example, in the 1960s or 1970s would be worth today in US dollars or euros.

Another factor contributing to the prevalence of uncertainty is that the Romanian leu was not always a stable currency in terms of purchasing power. The problem of estimating the current value of purchase prices given in old Romanian leu during the first few decades of socialism is exacerbated, for instance, by the hyperinflation that followed the change of political regime in Romania: 170.2 per cent in 1991, 210.4 per cent in 1992, 256.1 per cent in 1993, and 136.7 per cent in 1994. The spectacular decline in the value of the Romanian leu following the regime change and the ensuing loss of trust are the primary explanations for why the Gabors preferred to use the German mark in their more important economic transactions from the mid-1990s.

Among the sales transactions that came to my knowledge, there was only one in which the participants attributed great significance to a purchase price previously paid for an object when determining its current purchase price. The deal, a clear example of the difficulty of estimating the current value of an old purchase price, was reached between two brothers. In 1984, the younger brother (Zoltan) bought a beaker from his older brother (Pista) for 1,400,000 old Romanian lei. In that year, this purchase price was equivalent to 434 times the gross average monthly salary in Romania. Around the turn of the millennium, Zoltan got into debt, and in 2004, desperately needing cash, he convinced his brother to buy the beaker back from him. Referring to the moral expectation that close kin should help each other, Zoltan argued that he had bought the object from his brother in 1984 primarily to support the latter's political ambitions, so that Pista would have enough cash to buy a more valuable beaker. (Zoltan had not inherited a prestige object and had not previously bought one. Since the piece he had bought from Pista in 1984 was considered to be one of middling value among the Gabors, the one-time deal had been far from a purely selfless act of helping; it also served to raise Zoltan's social status.) Zoltan, then, specified that Pista was to buy the beaker from him for the same price that he had sold it to him in 1984. After a lengthy discussion, to ensure that his political rivals would not be able to accuse him of causing his brother financial damage, Pista finally accepted this condition. However, the brothers, who because of their close kinship did not use the services of a *cenzar*, faced an extraordinary challenge: How could the current value of the old purchase price be determined?

The uncertainty was mostly due to the lack of reliable procedures and reference points: the value of the purchase price paid in 1984 could not be defined automatically in euros or US dollars – that is, in the currencies that were generally used in 2004 to calculate the prices of prestige objects. The uncertainty regarding the establishment of value equality left a great deal of room for rivalry and manoeuvring. The problem immediately triggered a wave of speculation with respect to possible techniques of conversion and to the question of what could be considered a fair or reasonable price in the current case; for weeks these questions were among the leading topics of conversation among my Gabor Roma acquaintances. Zoltan's supporters – his affinal relatives and friends – wanted the 2004 purchase price to be as high as possible, while those loyal to Pista invariably calculated much lower sums as the ideal purchase price.

The problem of conversion between the different currencies – the pre-regime-change Romanian leu and the euro or US dollar – was finally resolved with the help of an impromptu unit of measurement (Dacia automobiles), which was present at the time of the use of each of these currencies. The Gabor Roma often use this method – "This house was worth this or that number of Dacias at the time" – when they wish to represent the one-time economic significance of certain commodities or of sums of money paid during the decades of socialism. The brothers, however, had different interests. For Zoltan, the most advantageous calculation of the current value of the 1984 purchase price would have been made with reference to new, standard-model Dacias without extras, which in 1984 cost 65,000 to 70,000 old Romanian lei. In contrast, Pista strove to achieve the highest possible unit price. Since he was the buyer and the older and more influential of the brothers, he agreed to continue the price bargaining on the condition that more expensive Dacia models, those that had been the most popular among the Gabors in the 1980s, be taken as a reference point in calculating the worth of the old purchase price. After these automobiles rolled off the conveyor belt, their first owners typically equipped them with accessories to enhance their comfort and aesthetic pleasure and then sold them on the used car market. In the mid-1980s, these upgraded Dacias had cost about 100,000 to 110,000 old Romanian lei.

The brothers finally came to an agreement: they determined the 1984 purchase price of a Dacia to be 100,000 old Romanian lei, which allowed them to calculate that exactly fourteen automobiles could have been bought with the 1,400,000 old Romanian lei paid for the beaker at the time. Zoltan could therefore expect a sum from Pista that would allow the purchase of at least that many Dacias when the deal was concluded in 2004.

At this point, however, another disagreement arose between the two brothers, this time with respect to which of the Dacia models available around 2004 should be regarded as their point of reference when calculating the purchase price. Understandably, Zoltan voted for the latest and therefore more expensive model – the Dacia Solenza – while Pista's choice fell on the cheaper Dacia Supernova manufactured between 2000 and 2003. Pista's choice was accepted in the end and, taking current automobile market prices into consideration, the price of an automobile was taken to be US$6,000. The outcome of the several-weeks-long negotiations aimed at establishing value equality was a total purchase price of US$87,000[7] for the beaker, US$84,000 of which was paid by Pista in cash in December 2004. This purchase price was made up of the price of fourteen Dacias and a sum of US$3,000 that Zoltan had borrowed from Pista years before but had not yet repaid, and that Pista now cancelled by adding this sum to the price of the fourteen Dacias.

The Embeddedness of Value Creation and
Price Setting in the Social Context

Difficulties with the quantification of value are, however, not in themselves enough to justify the employment of a broker. This is because
the problem of singularity and the dominance of the qualitative expressions of value in discourse are challenges in the face of which brokers
are almost as helpless as their employers. Why, then, is it worth the
principal's while to engage one?

It is worth the effort because while the uncertainty leaves plenty of
room for bargaining, the participants are not equally well equipped to
represent their political and economic interests; some are a great deal
more effective in impression management and persuasion than others.
The source of efficacy may be the individual's experience and widely
recognized expertise in the prestige economy on the one hand, and his
social prestige on the other. Let me clarify the relationship between
prestige and bargaining power through a brief discussion of the cultural logic of value creation and price setting, and of the way in which
this logic is embedded in the system of social differences.

When estimating and quantifying the value of their prestige objects,
the Gabors rely on advice only from individuals belonging to their own
Roma ethnic population, deliberately and consistently ignoring the
opinions of the non-Roma (or other, non-Gabor Roma). When making
deals among themselves, they never even consider seeking professional
advice from non-Roma art historians or antiques dealers, since they are
well aware that these experts define the meanings and significance of
these objects on the basis of a value regime different from their own.
Therefore, the only people who may have a say of any consequence in
determining the value and purchase price in a transaction among the
Gabors are members of their own Roma ethnic population.

For the Gabor Roma, value estimation and price bargaining are processes characterized by negotiation (often lengthy and accompanied by
heated debate), the constraint of reaching social consensus, a high level
of subjectivity, and intense political rivalry. The central arena of value
creation and estimation is the discourse organized among influential
Gabor men, while the basis of the relatively permanent social existence
of value is a fairly broad social consensus with regard to individual
prestige objects. That is, an indispensable component of value creation
is ratification by others; it is no use for the owner alone to declare that
his beaker or tankard is a sought-after piece or to designate its position

in the local or regional ranking of prestige objects. For his opinion to become a more or less permanent social fact, it must be confirmed and approved by numerous respectable Gabor men. The value of a beaker or tankard is, therefore, not a static property but rather a variable and often contested quality in need of continuous maintenance.

The ratifying power indispensable for creating and "stabilizing" value is, however, far from evenly distributed in society; it is closely related to current political and prestige relations. In public conversations about the significance and ranking of beakers and tankards, the individuals with the greatest power to influence public opinion are the very same ones to whom people turn for support or advice during marital conflicts or financial disagreements – that is, respectable, influential, and wealthy family heads generally in their early fifties or older. Since "it's their words that the most people listen to," it is essential for owners to procure the support of as many of these individuals as they can in their efforts to reach a social consensus about the value of their own prestige objects.

The considerable effect that influential voices in prestige-object discourses can have on the process of value estimation is aptly illustrated by the statements below, some of which are slight exaggerations. In the words of one of my interlocutors, these individuals "can wash away [take away the value of] or raise a beaker with a single word, they can turn an empty can into gold." Describing the power of a successful Gabor broker, a middle-aged man said, "If he puts his seal on [if he claims] that it's a good beaker, it could be an empty can [even if it was worthless], it would still become good [valuable]." Turning to the broker in question, the speaker continued, "An empty can turns into gold in your hands, because of your seal!" The word "seal" is used here as a synonym for the broker's expertise and outstanding social prestige. Another expression often used by my acquaintances is "Their words [the words of respectable individuals having substantial ratifying power] stick" (*lipilpe lengi vorba*), that is, their opinion "leaves its mark on the beaker or tankard," and few people are prepared to question it (at least in public).

Successful brokers tend to come from among these influential and prestigious men. A seller, if he is regarded as "a weak or soft owner" – that is, if he "cannot determine the price" (cannot offer persuasive arguments for the significance and value of his beaker or tankard) – can benefit greatly from employing a broker who is not simply an expert on prestige objects but also a respectable and much-honoured individual.

As a number of transactions have shown, a buyer who is more successful in politics may succeed in convincing a seller who is less skilled at
representing his own interests that the piece offered for sale is worth
much less than the seller's asking price; the buyer can thus acquire the
object at a lower price than current market conditions would justify.
A less influential seller, therefore, often chooses to employ a broker in
order to avoid the vulnerability arising from such an asymmetrical status relation and, thus, to improve his bargaining position. He hopes
that the respectable broker will be able to exalt the precious properties
of his beaker or tankard more convincingly than he himself could and
that the broker's expert opinion will have a greater effect on quantifying its value. This would make it easier to convince the buyer to make
a substantial financial sacrifice. Conversely, if the significant status
asymmetry between the bargaining parties favours the seller, it is in the
interests of the buyer to use the support of a broker, since this can help
reduce the chance of paying an unjustifiably high purchase price for the
desired object.

In prestige-object pawn transactions, the social reputation of a broker may also be of use in other ways. Creditors and borrowers often
lack trust in the business honesty of their partners and worry about the
other party failing to fulfil some of the agreed-upon obligations. An
influential broker can provide at least some protection against possible
immoral economic manoeuvres or tricks, since one of his moral responsibilities is to confirm the details of the agreement in the event of future
conflicts and, if necessary, put pressure on his employer's business
partner to abandon any attempts to breach the agreement. We must
not underestimate the economic significance of a broker's support. At
times of conflict among themselves, financial or otherwise, the Gabors
turn to the Romanian authorities only as a last resort. They first attempt
to find a resolution within their own Roma ethnic population, in which
endeavour they can primarily count on the intervention and assistance
of influential Gabor individuals.

The above description is reminiscent of Stewart's (1997, 176) argument that in economic transactions among themselves, the members of
the Roma community he studied in Hungary employed intermediaries
"similar to the *cincars* in Roma-peasant transactions" because the parties did not want to bargain directly with each other and wanted to
avoid the impression that one dominated the other. The Gabors also
often use the services of a broker because his presence makes communication between the parties indirect; however, the benefit hoped to be

gained from indirectness is not the same in the two cases. It is not in order to maintain an impression of equality or to avoid appearing subordinate to the other party that a Gabor seller or buyer with a modest ability to represent his own economic interests employs a broker when he enters into a bargaining situation with a more influential individual; he employs a broker because he is aware that the existing status asymmetry is unfavourable to him and he wants to counterbalance it in order to further his own business interests to the greatest possible extent.

The Politics of (In)Visibility: The Partial Dematerialization of Objects

A potential buyer often employs a broker because he is not confident that during the pre-purchase viewing he can identify beyond all doubt the nominal authenticity of the prestige object he wishes to buy. He is worried that the seller may attempt to sell him a piece similar to the one he is hoping to acquire but that has been recently bought on the antiques market or is a copy that has been secretly made to appear aged. Individuals undertaking the purchase of a beaker or tankard therefore place great emphasis on verifying nominal authenticity. When choosing a broker, one common consideration is whether he has previously seen the desired object and will be able to identify it.

What may make it difficult for a potential buyer to verify a piece's nominal authenticity? The primary source of uncertainty is the special way in which prestige objects are used for conspicuous consumption or possession.

As has been shown by Veblen, in his classic work (1899), and other authors, the message conveyed through conspicuous consumption or possession reaches the addressees primarily via the visual channel. The most efficient method of representing purchasing power and related community membership is undoubtedly the display of consumption to the broadest possible public – that is, showing one's positional or status goods in person or with the help of the media to the widest possible audience.[8] While the beakers and tankards are common and popular topics of male conversation, their owners only rarely make them accessible for viewing or touching by other Gabor Roma. The Gabors, unlike the vast majority of non-Roma antiques collectors, do not organize public exhibitions for their beakers and tankards, nor do they publish catalogues with photographs of these pieces. If an owner keeps his prestige object in his home, he stores it in a secret place – a hidden corner of the apartment, for instance – where visitors will not see it, not even by chance. Another frequent strategy is to secretly entrust the piece to a non-Roma neighbour or some other acquaintance on whose loyalty and discretion the possessor can count. The non-Roma keepers usually receive small amounts of money and other gifts in return.

It is not unusual for a possessor not to show his prestige objects to anyone, apart from the members of his immediate family, for years. This relative invisibility may apply not only to the less valuable pieces that attract little social interest, and that the owner's acquaintances and friends rarely express a wish to view, but can also be observed in the case of sought-after and highly esteemed objects. For many owners of these latter pieces, keeping them provisionally invisible is a strategic decision made with the aim of manipulating their renown; they want to maintain and increase the interest and curiosity shown by others regarding their beakers and tankards.

Any given prestige object is rarely shown to the same Gabor individual more than once within a short period of time; many of my interlocutors who had been given the chance to inspect a certain beaker or tankard had been able to do so only once, unless the item belonged to someone in their immediate family. A person who asks a host to show him his prestige object every month or every year is an unknown phenomenon. The restrictions on viewing are naturally relaxed when a piece is offered for sale and potential buyers and brokers visit the owner to have a look at it. This is also the case when an object has just changed hands and several relatives, acquaintances, and friends visit the new owner to congratulate him on the transaction and have a glimpse of the new acquisition. Respectable and influential men who are frequently asked to participate in prestige-object transactions as brokers or witnesses are given more opportunities than anyone else to see various beakers and tankards.

An object's relative invisibility may be temporarily suspended for reasons other than its sale or pawning. Before a large share of the Gabors joined the Seventh-Day Adventist Church in the late 1990s, the ceremony of blessing Paschal food, held at Easter in the Orthodox and Greek Catholic Churches, had been an opportunity to view prestige objects, when many Gabor families used their own beakers or tankards to bring the Paschal food home from the church (*sacral use*). In his own home, an owner may occasionally fetch his prestige object and show it for a few minutes to his guest to demonstrate his respect and esteem for him (*honorific use*), to underscore the social closeness between them (*networking use*), or to enhance his own renown (*conspicuous use*).[9]

The main red-letter days (Christmas, Easter) and social events such as weddings also offer an opportunity to view these pieces. The host may bring out his prestige object and show it to his guests, who will then respond to this gesture by praising the piece and expressing various good wishes. The host may further demonstrate his esteem for those present through a practice that has now become exceedingly rare: pouring some wine or other alcoholic beverage into the silver object and offering it to the guests.

A situation in which the host fetches and displays his beaker or tankard at the explicit request of his guest is referred to as a "request to view" (*előkérés*). This may happen not only during gatherings on certain red-letter days or at some social events, but also when a guest visits the home of a prestige-object owner alone or as a member of a small group.

A "request to view" is a socially marked event of just a few minutes' duration, and initiating it calls for great circumspection on the part of the guest. The most important reason for caution is that the making of a "request to view" and the compliance with or refusal of such a request are – according to my interlocutors – an indirect means of representing and negotiating prestige relations between individuals, families, and patrilines. The motivation for a "request to view" is usually curiosity about the material properties of a prestige object, mainly aroused precisely by its relative invisibility. For most of my acquaintances, it was primarily these events that offered opportunities to increase their knowledge of the material features of beakers and tankards and to accumulate some practical experience with the various procedures aimed at verifying the authenticity of material patina (the age of the object, for instance).

A "request to view" is met with the least resistance when it comes from individuals in a close relationship of trust with the owner – brothers, co-fathers-in-law, or neighbours – or from respectable and influential men; that is, when it is made by current or potential future members of the social network supporting the owner and his family. Political rivals, in contrast, never ask to view each other's prestige objects, because they can be quite certain of a refusal. Compliance with a "request to view" is also unlikely if the social distance between the owner and the individual making the request is significant and to the advantage of the former. I have not heard of a single case of a "request to view" being made by a woman visiting the host alone and not closely related to him.

In most cases, a refusal sends the political message that the owner does not regard the guest as someone who could have a significant influence on the value and fame of his prestige object or on his own renown and relational capital. Since it might damage their positive public image, possessors rarely express this message openly, preferring instead to use various indirect strategies of refusal. Here is just one example: the host announces that he would be pleased to show his beaker or tankard to his guest and then, citing a momentarily insurmountable – and often fictitious – obstacle, finally refuses the "request to view." Countless excuses can be made in such a situation: the non-Roma acquaintance who is looking after the object is not at home, the owner's son who could fetch the piece from its hiding place cannot be reached at the moment, and so on. Anxiety about the loss of face a refusal would result in can be so intense that men who consider themselves too young or of significantly lower social prestige than the owner often prefer not to make a "request to view" at all.

As mentioned in chapter 2, the most important marker of the value and social significance of a beaker or tankard is not how many people have already viewed it but rather how many influential Gabor men speak in praise about it among themselves, and how often they do so. The social life of prestige objects is primarily tied to words; the dominant medium or context of publicity used by the Gabors is not visibility but discourse. This practice can be defined as *discursive conspicuous possession*.[10]

These pieces are hidden from the outside world – that is, are partially dematerialized by being made invisible – and often become subjects of strategic (political and economic) secrecy, which in itself contributes greatly to the reproduction of social interest shown in them. Relative dematerialization – that is, limited visual access – is the primary reason for the existence of the politics of (in)visibility concerning beakers and tankards, and also why a potential buyer will often entrust a broker with verifying the nominal authenticity of an object offered for sale.[11]

Purchasing as a Bazaar-Style Transaction: *Cenzars* as Risk Managers

The Gabors' knowledge of the quantified value and nominal authenticity of beakers and tankards and of current supply-and-demand conditions on the prestige-object market shows a great deal of similarity with the kind of knowledge possessed by the bazaar customers studied by Geertz. He argues that information about commodities in a bazaar

> is poor, scarce, maldistributed, inefficiently communicated, and intensely valued ... The level of ignorance about everything from product quality and going prices to market possibilities and production costs is very high, and much of the way in which the bazaar functions can be interpreted as an attempt to reduce such ignorance for someone, increase it for someone, or defend someone against it. (Geertz 1978, 29; see also Geertz 1963, 1979)

It is often very difficult for buyers to know whether or not they can acquire something for a moderate (or for a reasonable) price. Because of this, the

> search for information – laborious, uncertain, complex, and irregular – is the central experience of life in the bazaar ... The main energies of the bazaari are directed toward combing the bazaar for usable signs, clues as to how particular matters at the immediate moment specifically stand ... the most persistent concerns are with price and quality of goods. (Geertz 1978, 30)

According to Appadurai (1986), scarcity of information about the quality and value of commodities as well as the considerable effort made for its collection characterize not only buyers in the Moroccan bazaar but also some segments of modern industrial societies. Appadurai (1986, 43) therefore argues for the necessity of a more general application of the bazaar as an analytical category: "Bazaar-style information searches are likely to characterize any exchange setting where the quality and the appropriate valuation of goods are not standardized, though the reasons for the lack of standardization, for the volatility of prices, and for the unreliable quality of specific things of a certain type may vary enormously." The "complex and culturally organized information mazes" and the "bazaar-style information search" (Appadurai 1986, 43) that helps a buyer to find his or her way in these mazes also characterize, among others, the market of Oriental carpets and that of used cars in industrial societies (Rees 1971, 109–18; Geertz 1978, 31; Fanselow 1990; Alexander 1992, 84–5; see also Ichinosawa 2007).

In Fanselow's (1990, 251) interpretation, the uncertainty afflicting buyers in a bazaar is primarily due to the "information asymmetry" between them and sellers. According to him, in the bazaar money has a special status as the most standardized and therefore most reliable commodity. It is the value of money that is the most predictable, in contrast to all other commodities that "are unstandardized and therefore unpredictable and unreliable," and whose "inspection is difficult, time-consuming and therefore costly" (Fanselow 1990, 251). The seller, who receives money, has more reliable knowledge about its value and quality than does the buyer about the goods of dubious origin he or she has bought. Bazaar studies reveal that customers use two methods in their attempt to reduce uncertainty – that is, as risk management. One of these is the strategy of "intensive information search" (Fanselow 1990, 255), and the other is clientelization – that is, an effort to build a long-term business relationship of mutual trust with certain vendors.

I argue that prestige-object deals taking place among the Gabors are in several respects – such as the high degree of uncertainty, the absence of fixed prices, and the great significance of price bargaining – similar to bazaar-style transactions. Potential sources of uncertainty in our case include the difficulty of quantifying qualitative value and verifying nominal authenticity, the scarcity of information on current supply-and-demand conditions, and the relative lack of persuasive ability. The information asymmetry between the buyer and the seller applies only to the question of nominal authenticity[12] in prestige-object transactions but not to the problem of uncertainty regarding the quantification of value ("What does the concept of fair or reasonable price mean?"), because the latter is a problem for both the buyer and the seller.

Gabor Roma sellers and buyers attempt risk management primarily through the strategy of employing brokers who are experts in intensive information searches and who also provide a number of other services in the course of the transactions to support their clients (or, more precisely, to act in their place). Since prestige-object transactions are infrequent and irregular, there is a relatively meagre chance of a regular business relationship developing between the seller or buyer and any of the brokers. Therefore, for the most part, the Gabors cannot rely on the advantages of clientelization.

Sources of Mistrust in a *Cenzar* and Methods of Ensuring His Loyalty

The attitudes of principals towards their intermediaries may often be ambivalent. Although they use their services in an effort to reduce uncertainty accompanying the transaction, they often see the brokers themselves as a source of potential uncertainty. This attitude is related to the problem of loyalty and can be traced back to two causes.

First, the main motivation for the broker is the success fee. His employer can never be quite sure that the potential business partners contacted by the broker will not surreptitiously attempt to persuade the broker to change sides by offering him substantial sums of money for his support. As already mentioned, in the hope of increased profits, the intermediary may make a secret deal with some of the people – other than his employer – whom he contacts. It is essential for the broker to keep quiet about his hopes of a success fee from someone other than his employer, since this is the only way to keep the latter's trust and maintain the impression that he is continuing to represent the employer's interests to the best of his knowledge. The fact that the figure of an intermediary is often associated with stereotypes of moral untrustworthiness and corruptibility can be partially explained by the risk of informally offering a success fee and the constraints of the related economic secrecy.

There is a further source of uncertainty, however: in addition to participating in Roma politics as an intermediary, the broker may have various other political roles. He may be the owner of one or more prestige objects himself, in which case the impending deal may have a negative effect on the social evaluation of his own achievements in the prestige economy. He may be (and often is) a member of political interest groups that could be affected by the upcoming transaction, in which case loyalty and interest tie him not only to his employer but also to other Gabor individuals (his co-fathers-in-law or brothers, for instance) and social units. The mistrust often felt by principals is partially the result of these parallel – and often conflict-ridden – political loyalties or, more precisely, of the fact that the broker must (re)rank his loyalties from time to time. One dilemma I frequently observed during my fieldwork was this: who should the broker, having studied the market conditions, name as the ideal buyer – his own co-father-in-law, whose solidarity lies with him but who possesses modest purchasing power, or the wealthiest of the potential buyers, who makes the highest offer but has long been one of the broker's political rivals? Principals often maintain that there is a disturbingly short distance between a broker's parallel political roles, and the potential conflict of interest may result in the broker ultimately not giving priority to his employer's interests in his management of the transaction.

In their efforts to persuade the broker to do his very best to answer the questions they are most concerned with – "Who would be the ideal buyer or seller?" and "What does the concept of a fair or reasonable price mean in the given situation?" – principals may use the following strategies:

(1) The most important means of ensuring a valid value estimate and loyalty is the attraction of a high success fee.

(2) To avoid being given a misleading expert evaluation, the principal may call upon the broker to "go on faith" (to swear) – that is, to demonstrate by uttering conditional self-curses threatening himself and members of his family with death and other misfortunes[13] that his expert opinion regarding market conditions, the value of the available prestige objects, and so on reflects the best of his knowledge. According to the Gabor Roma ideology of swearing, if the broker attempts to mislead his employer, the conditional self-curses in the oath will very likely be fulfilled.

(3) Finally, the principal often tries to ensure the validity of the expert opinion by selecting a broker from among his close kin, whose solidarity lies with him. In this case, the principal tries to turn the parallel existence of loyalties to his advantage; in addition to the attraction of the promised success fee, the broker's commitment is also boosted by the moral expectation of solidarity between close relatives.

Practising Brokerage

(1) *The broker as a tout.* The potential buyer or seller often has only limited knowledge of current supply-and-demand conditions in the prestige-object market and would either not be able to find his ideal business partner alone or be able to do so only with great difficulty. Such individuals often engage a broker to act as a tout and find the ideal buyer or seller for them. Such potential buyers are not sufficiently well or reliably informed about where, at that precise moment, there are prestige objects for sale in their own Roma ethnic population and how valuable the available pieces are; as potential sellers, they are not adequately informed about who has the necessary political ambitions and sufficient money to buy their beakers or tankards.

When searching for potential buyers, the broker usually gives priority to certain groups. One of these is made up of well-to-do individuals whose parents or grandparents once owned and highly esteemed the object currently for sale but were forced to part with it at some point. The well-to-do descendants of former owners are an obvious target for the broker, since they usually attribute special emotional and biographical value to the object and are willing to make a higher-than-usual economic sacrifice to acquire it. Buying back a piece is a symbolic act of remedy aimed at counteracting – at least in part – the loss of face suffered by the descendants' families. Another group at the top of the imagined list of potential buyers is wealthy men whose predecessors had in the past made an attempt to acquire the object now offered for sale but who ultimately lost out in the competition among buyer candidates.

In their search for potential buyers, brokers are also keen to contact individuals who are known to "have a burning desire for a good beaker" – that is, who are ready to jump at the opportunity to purchase a valuable object because they have been trying to join the prestige economy or to improve their position in the ranking of owners for quite some time. Since prestige-object sales transactions are relatively rare among the Gabors and years may pass without any of the valuable beakers or tankards changing hands, affluent individuals wishing to acquire one of the most important objects may have to wait for decades before a piece they consider ideal for themselves is offered for sale.

In some cases, the intermediary's choice of potential buyer or seller is limited, because his employer specifies a set of individuals with whom he does not want to do business under any circumstances. When the transaction is a sale, the principal's most important political rivals tend to belong to this group, since – giving rein to their political ambitions – they usually consider it an important mission to shame the seller and his family from time to time at public social gatherings following the transaction. They may, for example, make various face-threatening comments such as "Your father's fur coat [that is, prestige object] is now in my possession!" Principals also try to avoid potential buyers or sellers about whose business honesty they have their doubts and who they fear would not respect the agreement.

Some sellers decide to sell their beakers or tankards to nobody but the Cărhar Roma – either because they see this as a way of making sure the pieces do not end up in the hands of any of their Gabor Roma rivals or because they are convinced that due to certain material properties (such as large capacity), the objects up for sale will be more appreciated by the Cărhars than by the members of their own Roma ethnic population. In this situation, the broker must assess the market conditions among the Cărhars. He also must do this if, although the Gabor owner does not have a problem in principle with choosing a buyer from his own Roma ethnic population, the intermediary cannot find anyone there who the owner would willingly bargain with.

Finding the ideal buyer or seller may take no more than a few telephone calls – that is, a few minutes or hours. In other cases, however, the broker has no choice but to go and visit potential business partners living in various regions of Romania and to either covertly gauge their interest or openly ask them whether they would be willing to participate in the imminent transaction. If the intermediary meets with a series of rejections or if a business partner with whom he has already made some progress unexpectedly decides to withdraw from the purchase or sale, market research may go on for weeks (or longer).

(2) *The broker as an estimator.* After having mapped supply-and-demand conditions in the prestige-object market, a broker will inform his employer about the persons who should be contacted for bargaining. If the employer is a potential buyer, the broker needs to explain the quality and estimated value of the pieces up for sale and to give guidance on which ones are worthiest of consideration. If the principal wants to sell an object, the broker has to give an estimation of the piece's value and information on any offers he has received that should be considered. Whether the broker is working on behalf of a buyer or seller, the key questions are the same: "What is a reasonable price, and what is an advantageous deal at the given moment?" and "Which concessions are worth making during price bargaining?" As I have already noted, an employer often commissions a broker partly because of uncertainty surrounding quantifying qualitative value and a lack of clarity regarding the relationship between quantified value and purchase price, in the hope that in this way he can avoid making an unfavourable deal.

(3) *The broker as an agent of persuasion.* As I have already indicated, prestige-object sales transactions are usually inseparable from the concept of competition. One reason for this is that an imbalance in the relationship between supply and demand sides is a relatively common phenomenon; it often happens, for instance, that several influential individuals compete for the acquisition of a highly regarded piece offered for sale. The broker in this case must persuade the chosen potential seller or buyer to ignore the offers from others and instead do business with his employer.

An intermediary may need to bring persuasion skills to bear not only in this situation but also when assessing market opportunities. If, for instance, there are no beakers or tankards for sale on the prestige-object market or none of the pieces for sale is valuable enough for the broker's employer to buy, the broker must contact individuals who own the kind of objects his employer desires and who are very likely to have to sell those pieces (because of their debts, for instance) in the near future. The broker's aim is to convince one of the latter possessors that by postponing the sale he is harming his own bargaining position – in other words, that it would be to his advantage to complete the deal now. When an intermediary's task is to contact hesitant potential buyers, he is expected to mobilize or increase their political ambitions and willingness to buy. His primary strategy is detailing the significance of the reputational profit of purchasing a prestige object; he may note, for instance, that the target person has almost everything needed to be numbered among influential and respectable individuals and "lacks only one thing: a valuable beaker." The job of the broker may, therefore, include having to persuade a potential seller to part with his prestige object as soon as possible or convince a potential buyer to go ahead with the purchase.

(4) *The broker as an expert on nominal authenticity.* As mentioned before, the visual accessibility of beakers and tankards is a scarce resource among the Gabors; that is, an object offered for sale may have been seen in the previous years or decades by only a small number of people other than the owner and his close relatives. Unless he is one of the few, the individual planning to buy needs a broker who has had at least one opportunity to examine the piece for sale and is in a position to establish with confidence whether the beaker or tankard shown to him as part of the bargaining process is indeed the same object that his employer wishes to acquire. Anyone who has held several prestige objects in his hands is at an advantage when competing to be engaged as broker, since he has greater-than-usual experience in comparing the material properties of the various pieces and is better equipped to identify fakes.

(5) *The broker as a price bargaining manager.* After identifying potential business partners, the principal embarks on the bargaining process with the individual who has given the best offer. At this stage of the transaction, the activities of the intermediary representing the seller are primarily focused on persuading the prospective buyer to pay a sum surpassing or equal to the minimum purchase price set by his employer. If the broker is employed by one of the potential buyers, his main goal is to reduce the asking price and present his employer's offer as the perfect sum.

Once the broker has also asked his employer's prospective transaction partner what his final price is, he meets the two of them separately and attempts to reduce the difference between the two sums to a minimum.[14] When the two offers have moved much closer to each other, the broker arranges a meeting at which both parties are present. Here he emphasizes the benefits of the imminent transaction and the negligibility of the remaining difference between the final prices, and tries to persuade the parties to halve – or share in some other way – this difference and agree on a purchase price. Whether agreement is reached after a lengthy process of negotiation or at the very first meeting depends on the circumstances of the transaction, as does the question of whether the buyer and seller try to assert their interests through direct participation in the bargaining process or through intermediaries.

What arguments can a broker use to persuade the seller to reduce the minimum purchase price he initially set and the buyer to be prepared to make a greater financial sacrifice than he originally meant to?

The most efficient way of raising a buyer's willingness to make sacrifices is listing and extolling the valuable properties of the beaker or tankard. The intermediary may detail at great length the political significance of former owners, the renown that the object has therefore acquired, and the piece's rare and highly esteemed material properties. Other elements of the object's social career may also increase its desirability and value. One such element, for instance, might be the association of the attribute "fighter" with a beaker or tankard for the possession of which there has recently been intense competition among a number of influential individuals. Another convincing argument emphasizes the prestige to be gained by the purchase – that is, the fact that the buyer is about to acquire a piece that will be the envy of many of his political rivals and could be a significant source of reputational profit.[15] The broker may also cite current market conditions, arguing that there is no other, more valuable beaker or tankard presently on the market, and if the potential buyer delays the transaction for too long, other people may well set their heart on the object. As well, some urgent cost may come up and part of the money put aside to buy a prestige object may need to be used to pay for it. That is, if he refuses to modify his final price, he may well have to forgo the present opportunity to buy.

Reducing the minimum price set by the seller tends to meet with less reluctance. Let us remember that the Gabors will part with their more valuable beakers and tankards only if they are facing serious financial difficulties, which, by the time an object is put up for sale, limit the seller's room for manoeuvring during the price bargaining. In contrast with potential buyers, who may decide to withdraw and postpone buying at any time, the seller usually must find a buyer for his piece within the foreseeable future.

(6) *The broker as an eyewitness and a manager of publicity and renown.* When the purchase price is handed over, those present include not only the parties to the agreement but also a group of witnesses consisting of the broker(s) and other individuals – mostly consanguineous or affinal relatives of the buyer and the seller (usually brothers, sons, and co-fathers-in-law). The witnesses first of all verify that the buyer hands over the total sum contained in the agreement and receives the prestige object he has chosen to buy. They have an equally crucial role in the event of possible future conflicts between the parties – that is, if one of the parties later accuses the other of a breach of contract. Their presence is needed at the handover in part because their personal memory of the event is used as "documentation" of the details of the agreement, which are not always recorded in writing.

The witnesses have the further role of disseminating the news; they are the managers of publicity – indispensable for prestige economies – who describe the details of the agreement between the parties and the circumstances of the transaction to all those who could not be present at the event. Because, of all the witnesses, the broker has the most detailed information on the deal and what led up to it, he is regarded as the most important witness, to be called upon first in case of need.

Since his employer pays him a substantial sum as a success fee, Gabor Roma business ethics place the broker under a moral obligation to enhance the renown of the buyer and the prestige object that has changed hands at various social gatherings. Positive publicity also benefits the broker, since the transaction is another convincing piece of evidence for his expertise. The successful deals associated with his name function as symbolic trophies and constitute an efficient means of building trust; they help him to enhance his reputation as a broker and to gain further employment.

The intermediary of the buyer and that of the seller do not, however, have the same possibilities and constraints regarding public talk about the transaction. As was discussed before, the social evaluations of buying versus selling a prestige object are fundamentally different; while the former is accompanied by an increase in renown, the latter is a face-threatening (shameful) process, which the seller would much rather keep a secret. For this reason, the seller's broker cannot publicize the deal without causing symbolic harm to his earlier employer and drawing attention to the loss of prestige he has suffered. While the intermediary engaged by the buyer is free to boast of the transaction and his own role in it essentially without any constraint, the discursive possibilities of the broker assisting the seller are far more limited.

Shifting Transactional Identities

What are the characteristics of a successful intermediary? Or, in other words, what factors do principals consider when choosing a broker for a transaction?

(1) *Business trustworthiness, experience, and reputation.* The popularity of an intermediary increases with potential employers' confidence that he will respect any agreement between them and with the number of successfully concluded prestige-object transactions in which he has participated and which have attracted substantial publicity among the Gabors. Since business trustworthiness, expertise, and reputation based primarily on these two factors are important considerations when choosing a broker, intermediaries place a great deal of emphasis on building up and preserving these qualities.

(2) *Types of ethnicized knowledge.* The responsibilities of an intermediary would be impossible to fulfil without certain types of ethnicized knowledge. For the successful completion of a transaction, the broker must possess:

(a) Thorough knowledge of Gabor prestige-object aesthetics and the various value preferences that form part of it. Without such knowledge, the broker would be unable to estimate or compare the values of beakers and tankards. Detailed knowledge of this aesthetics is far from being evenly distributed in the Gabor Roma ethnic population; even many ambitious individuals planning to purchase prestige objects possess only a portion of that knowledge.

(b) Familiarity with the ethnic history of the Gabors. This is indispensable for value estimation and for success in persuading a potential buyer. The broker must possess thorough knowledge of the previous Gabor owners of the piece for sale and must be familiar with their political achievements, which might "raise" the attractiveness of the object in question and serve as an effective argument to increase a potential buyer's willingness to buy and to mobilize his political ambitions. Since, through the transaction, the buyer pays in part for the renown of previous possessors, the broker can credibly present to the potential buyer the value of the piece for sale and successfully represent his employer's interests only if he is familiar with the Gabor Roma ethnic past and the object's ownership history.

(c) Knowledge of major events and trends in the Gabors' prestige-object market and economy. The intermediary must possess up-to-date knowledge, for instance, of supply-and-demand conditions (who has sufficient cash and political ambitions to make the purchase, and who is likely to have to sell his beaker or tankard in the near future) and of major conflicts emerging in the wake of prestige-object deals.

All of the above types of knowledge are ethnicized; with the exception of a few anthropologists, Cărhar Roma individuals, and non-Roma antiques dealers who have been in contact with the Gabors for quite some time, only the Gabor Roma have access to them.

(3) *Intraethnic and interethnic relational capital.* The accumulation of intraethnic and interethnic relational capital – that is, what Boissevain (1974, 147) calls "strategic relationships" – is indispensable for a broker and can benefit him in two ways. First, if he is a welcome guest at the tables of many Gabor families, he is unlikely to have any difficulty rapidly and reliably mapping supply-and-demand conditions. The more families he can contact without any restrictions, the easier it will be for him to find the right business partner for his employer. Second, an intermediary who numbers several Cărhar men and brokers among his acquaintances and whose name is associated with successful interethnic transactions is a more attractive choice for owners who specifically wish to sell their prestige objects among the Cărhars. Relational capital is one of the symbolic goods that can make a broker sought after and increase his chances of being chosen to manage the next transaction.

(4) *Rhetorical skills and experience.* Finally, an intermediary must possess the rhetorical skills and experience needed to first gauge potential buyers or sellers' intentions and persuade them, and then to manage the price bargaining.

The above list of competences clearly explains why – unlike in the horse sales investigated by Stewart (1997) – we never see non-Roma (such as Hungarian or Romanian) brokers involved in transactions within the Gabor Roma ethnic population or between the Cărhars and the Gabors: the intensely ethnicized character of the prestige economy precludes their involvement.

The anthropological and sociological literature mostly classifies brokers according to the identities associated with the goods mediated by them and the nature of the symbolic and non-symbolic borders crossed by the migrating goods. The best-studied intermediaries are undoubtedly economic brokers. Political brokers coordinate the management of political conflicts and the interpersonal or intergroup flow of political goods (votes or party donations, for instance), while cultural brokers do the same with cultural conflicts and goods (for example, with types of culture-specific knowledge interpreted as identity symbols; see Steiner 1994; Myers 2002).

It would be a mistake, however, to conclude from the above classification that a certain type of goods behaves the same way in all transactions – that is, to assume that political commodities always remain exclusively political and cultural commodities remain cultural. The Gabors' prestige objects are a good case in point. They demonstrate that, since the goods changing hands are frequently characterized by transactional identities appearing in context-sensitive combinations, the identity of the brokers mediating their flow should also often be interpreted as a multiple, context-sensitive quality. Let us have a closer look at this claim.

(1) *Brokering symbols of economic prosperity.* Whether they change hands among the Gabors or through interethnic trade between the Gabor Roma and the Cărhar Roma, beakers and tankards are luxury goods for which customers often pay as much as hundreds of thousands of US dollars. Intermediaries are therefore economic actors, and the objects' identity as assets can be regarded as the permanent transactional identity of migrating beakers and tankards.

These pieces, however, not only possess economic significance but also play an important role in certain identity projects. As a result, further identities are associated with them. To understand this proposition, let us distinguish two types of transactions. One is the group of intraethnic transactions that take place within the Gabor Roma ethnic population, where these objects – while retaining their identity as assets – also acquire political meaning and significance. The second type are interethnic transactions that occur between the Gabors and the Cărhars, where in addition to the economic significance associated with the beakers and tankards, the knowledge and management of ethnic and cultural differences also play a decisive role.

(2) *Brokering symbols endowed with political identity value (intraethnic trade).* For the Gabors, as discussed before, prestige objects are symbols imbued with political meanings and importance and constitute a scarce resource – they are political trophies, and intense competition often arises among potential buyers for their possession. The intermediaries

themselves are influential agents of Roma politics, since their activities have a substantial impact on the flow and social distribution of prestige objects (at the same time that a broker helps one person to buy a valuable piece, he is preventing others from purchasing it). They are occasional entrepreneurs who broker, among rival individuals and social units, goods interpreted (among other things) as representations of political success, catalysts of obtaining certain honorifics (family leader, *baro rom*, village leader) and raw materials suitable for materializing patrilineal identity. Brokers are therefore managers of political identity projects and, to a certain extent, are also sources of the dynamics of these projects, since several of the prestige-object transactions would probably never come about without them.

(3) *Brokers as managers of cultural otherness (interethnic trade)*. The Gabors, however, do not always sell their beakers and tankards among themselves; they often sell them to the Cărhars. In this context, the objects continue to be assets above all; but another of their potential identities, as symbols of cultural identity, also comes to the fore.

For a Gabor Roma intermediary to be able to present a Gabor beaker or tankard for sale among the Cărhars in accordance with their value preferences and thus obtain the highest purchase price possible, he must also possess sufficient cultural background knowledge of the workings of the Cărhar Roma prestige economy and consumer culture. A thorough knowledge of the similarities and differences between the Gabor and the Cărhar prestige economies (e.g., between the two prestige-object aesthetics) is a symbolic capital, the value of which is increased and may acquire substantial economic significance in this situation. Gabor brokers involved in interethnic transactions are therefore also cultural brokers who strive to represent the interests of their employers in the most effective way by, among other things, analysing, interpreting, and manipulating the differences and similarities between the two prestige economies.

The economic significance of beakers and tankards thus remains decisive throughout the transactions examined, whereas which other object identity (political or cultural identity symbol) will also become dominant depends on the social context of the given bargaining process. The relationship between transactional identities associated with the concept of brokering is also context-sensitive; in the flow of these pieces, intermediaries participate at times as economic and political brokers, and at other times as economic and cultural brokers.

6

Political Face-Work and Transcultural Bricolage/Hybridity: Prestige Objects in Political Discourse

As discussed in the chapter on Roma politics, the Gabors often introduce political issues into conversations at various social gatherings such as weddings, betrothals, wakes, funerals, and the like, as well as into the more informal discussions that spontaneously emerge in market places, during intermissions in Adventist worship services, and so on. These political issues include, among others, the latest prestige-object transactions, recently formed marital alliances, and power relations between individuals, families, and patrilines. This chapter primarily analyses face-saving discursive strategies and techniques used to "frame" – that is, to mitigate the consequences of – the public mention of beakers and tankards in political discourse (including songs with political content), with a special focus on the linguistic indirectness frequently employed in political self-representation. These strategies and techniques are closely related to the Gabor Roma concepts of social person and success and to the constant search for equilibrium between the politics of difference and the ethics of sociability, and they reflect the value preferences underlying the latter categories.

Discursive Political Face-Work

As mentioned in chapter 1, political discourse is not limited to an unaltered representation of social and economic differences but also has a constitutive character. Prestige relations may be more or less affected by, among other things, (a) which individual or family is designated (repeatedly) as politically most successful in a local community or micro-region in public debates at the more significant wakes or weddings; (b) which beaker is placed on the top of the local or regional hierarchies of importance of prestige objects in the political discourse that takes place at social gatherings; and (c) the extent to which the public conversational contributions of a speaker are judged by his listeners to comply with the Gabor Roma ethics of political face-work. Participating in political discourse is therefore a significant means of shaping and managing political relations.

Most of my Gabor Roma acquaintances could be characterized by intense political face sensitivity, and they placed a huge emphasis on practicing discursive political face-work (Bull & Fetzer 2010; Bull 2012). In other words, when planning and performing their conversational contributions in public, they paid special attention to the effects those contributions would have on their own and their listeners' positive public image. (They monitored the conversational contributions of other participants with the same intensity and sensitivity.) What could explain the significance attributed to maintaining and saving a positive public image and to the related political relational work or face-work?[1] The explanation must be sought primarily in the Gabor Roma's intense dependence on each other in the processes of social authentication or ratification of their political achievements – that is, in the transformation of the latter into widely recognized successes. This interdependence, as mentioned in previous chapters is rooted in two factors.

First, the most important symbolic trophies of politics – prestige and renown – and the differences politics creates are essentially interactive; they can be constructed only in the context of social interactions and negotiations, and are qualities attributed to the individuals by other members of society as coauthors.

The second factor is the ethnicized character of Roma politics. As previously discussed, several of the symbolic arenas of politics – the prestige economy, the hierarchy of patrilines, and marriage politics – are highly ethnicized, and any successes achieved in them are rewarded with renown and social appreciation only by the Gabor Roma. For this reason, the Gabors may count only on each other's support and approval when converting their individual political performances into socially ratified successes and differences. One of the most efficient means of mobilizing this support and approval is earning respectability (i.e., *patjiv*), which can be achieved primarily by following the Gabor Roma ethics of sociability (i.e., by proper behaviour [*lašo phirajimo*]). These ethics emphatically call for intense face-work in public. In other words, proper behaviour, which includes the expectation of face-work, is an important condition for an individual to be regarded as a respectable person, and respectability in turn significantly contributes to the individual's political achievements being rewarded with appreciation and renown by other Gabor Roma, including competitors who have been outperformed by the individual.

The political performances of those who regularly neglect public face-work – the demonstration of respect for others' positive public image and the saving of their own face – in political discourses at wakes, weddings, and so on, will be met with less positive social response among the Gabors. This is clearly illustrated by the following comment, which appears in several different versions and is frequently addressed as a form of moral criticism to individuals who publicly mention their political achievements in a boastful and inconsiderate manner: "It's very well to be great or wealthy, but your behaviour must also be proper!" (*Lašo-j tjo barimo/barvalimo, ba te'l šukar vi tjo phirajimo!*) For this reason, the respectability or *patjiv* earned by following the ethics of sociability is one of the most important social values, and there is intense competition among the Gabors to accumulate and preserve it, given the strong influence this kind of respectability has on the dynamics of political relations between individuals, families, and patrilines.

The Ethics of Political (Self-)Representation

The ethics of managing social relations and interactions privilege the use of many discursive strategies and techniques in connection with public political face-work and (self-)representation. A large share of these are aimed at the avoidance of invidious comparison or the mitigation or counteraction of its negative effects – in other words, the simultaneous saving of the speaker's and the listeners' positive public image, and, ultimately, the prevention of conflict. Statements made with no regard to others' face sensitivity are considered to be morally inappropriate, even if no one doubts the truth of their content.

Invidious comparison can be avoided if the participants in a public discourse – at a wake, wedding, or other social event – refrain from mentioning other participants' characteristics and deeds that may threaten those individuals' positive public image, such as dubious business credibility, low patrilineal prestige, or the selling of prestige objects. A speaker, however, may also threaten the face of his conversational partners by extolling his own political successes in a conspicuous manner, openly and without any mitigating strategies and techniques. Someone who insults his conversational partners by enumerating his political achievements in an ostentatious and tactless manner or names the shameful political failures or deficiencies of those same conversational partners not only threatens their face but also, because of his impoliteness, risks his own. The ethics of sociability therefore privilege, and reward with appreciation, those means of political self-representation that clearly indicate the speaker's intention of respecting his audience's need to save their own positive public image.

The face-saving discursive strategies and techniques used in the course of public mention of one's own political achievements, such as owning valuable prestige objects or having influential co-fathers-in-law, mitigate – in a way that is immediately recognizable to the listeners – the symbolic damage (shame) that the speaker causes to the face of his interlocutors. The use of these strategies and techniques, of course, does not cancel or reduce the represented social or economic differences, nor – for those who know the cultural conventions applying to their interpretation – does it conceal them. Their importance lies in the unequivocal demonstration to the audience that the speaker is well aware of the fact that the public mention of his political successes threatens their face and makes them feel uncomfortable, and that when planning and delivering his conversational contribution he is therefore prepared to, and purposefully chooses to, make an effort to reduce his audience's loss of face. These face-saving strategies and techniques also have the function of advertising and enhancing the speaker's own positive public image (his respectability) through his display of voluntary self-restraint. Furthermore, in using these strategies and techniques the speaker not only demonstrates that he follows the ethics of sociability but also reveals his commitment to and dependence on his own Roma ethnic population. More precisely, the speaker's behaviour is a recognition of the fact that the social evaluation and impact of his individual political achievements depend to a significant extent on the opinions of the members of this ethnic population. This dependency – one that warns us of the limits of individualism – is one of the most important elements of the Gabor Roma concept of social person.

One of the major organizing principles of discursive political self-representation is therefore the disapproval, moral stigmatization, and preferably avoidance of ostentatious public self-praise ("boasting/showing off," *ašarimo/putjarimo*; "gives big words [says pretentious, boastful/proud words]," *bari duma del*). Many of my acquaintances contended that public "self-praise equals disgrace" (an impolite, shameful act), and some traced this moral judgment back to certain passages of the Bible. In an ideal case, therefore, political successes are introduced into public conversation not by the person who achieved them himself but by someone in his supportive social network – his co-father-in-law or brother-in-law, for instance – who starts praising ("elevating") him.[2] To cite only two commentaries:

[If you praise yourself,] you become a fool [will be regarded as a fool]! ... The Lord said that he will humble those who boast. If a man says before God, "I am a big man [baro fom]!" the Lord says to him, "Is that so?! Are you boasting of your wealth?" He takes it all away. He humbles him. But the Bible also says that the humble will be exalted by the Lord. That is how it is on earth too, because the Lord ordained that the laws are the same on earth as they are in Heaven. (31 July 2003)

When someone praises himself, that praise has no renown [the words have no effect, are not worth anything]. But if someone else praises him for his proper behaviour, good [valuable] prestige objects, [good] sons, that has renown. This [self-praise] is shameful. I must be praised by someone else. (27 March 2003)

The socially approved response to praise coming publicly from someone else is complete or partial rejection through various techniques. The latter include, among others, the "distribution" of agency in achieving individual political successes ("I'm not worth anything on my own, without the help of my father and my co-fathers-in-law"), the use of symbolic self-depreciating phrases ("We have a little bit of money, just what we need, and our grandfather left us a bit of patjiv"), and the sacralization of the origins of individual political achievements ("We're not [big men], brother, God is big! We're just unworthy people, the way God made us"). The "praise for someone/(partial) rejection of the praise" adjacency pair between individuals supporting each other's positive public image and political ambitions – such as co-fathers-in-law, brothers-in-law, or a new owner of a prestige-object and his broker – may be repeated several times in a row during a conversation, and it also often happens that at a later stage of the discourse the "praised" individual "praises back" the political achievements of the person who previously lauded him. (In the latter case, the exchange of praises is characterized by delayed reciprocity.) Leaving a public praise spoken by another person completely unanswered by the addressee or responding in a way that is not preferred socially (such as publicly agreeing with the speaker by saying, for example, "That's right!" or "My beaker certainly is the most valuable of them all!") are both to be avoided; both are held to be impolite and morally stigmatized choices that make the addressee a laughing stock and threaten his positive public image.

Face-Saving Techniques Used in Political Self-Representation

Several commonly known discursive means are available to a speaker who wishes to introduce his own political successes into a public conversation at a wake, wedding, or similar event in a face-saving manner. (See also the previous paragraph.) A common feature of these techniques is that they allow the speaker to mitigate at least partially the symbolic damage (shame) caused to others' positive public image by his self-praise and the resulting invidious comparison. Some of these techniques will now be discussed.

A speaker lauding himself or a close relative may "frame" his conversational contribution by apologizing to his audience or to God (or to both) either before or after voicing the praise, as in, for example, "There was no bigger Roma man [more successful in politics] in this village than my father-in-law, God forgive [what I'm saying]."

Another technique used to temper the negative effects of invidious comparison is the use of diminutives, which may be applied to grown sons and prestige objects in public political discourse. In the former case, the speaker refers to his own grown son with expressions such as the "little boy" or "sonny" (*šavořǎ*) instead of the usual term "son" (*šavo*). A similar naming practice can be observed for beakers: the speaker often refers to his own beaker as a "beakerette" (*taxtora*). The use of diminutives is a form of voluntary symbolic devaluation of the social significance attributed to the speaker's political successes (prestige objects or sons), and it is meant to underscore the speaker's modesty and demonstrate his sensitivity to the positive public image of others (i.e., his politeness). If, however, someone else were to refer to the speaker's beaker as a beakerette or his sons as little boys, that would be considered a political insult and would very likely lead to open conflict.

The most widespread and diversified face-saving technique used to introduce someone's own political successes into a public discourse is indirectness. Two ways frequently employed to achieve indirectness deserve special attention.

One way (see also above) is when someone's political successes are mentioned and advertised by other participants in a social gathering and not by himself, in line with the general requirement: "Let us be praised by others, not by ourselves." This manner of political self-representation is a case of voice-centred indirection (Brenneis 1986, 342) and closely connected to two practices discussed by Brenneis. The first of these is shared narration or co-performance (343), since the representation of political success is usually realized through conversational cooperation between two – or more – participants following some well-known patterns (the "praise for someone/[partial] rejection of the praise" adjacency pair, for instance). Second, since the initiator of the praise in effect talks in place of the addressee, this manner can be interpreted as a form of ventriloquism through spokesmen (343). Various types of praise coming from others are a popular means in (collaborative) political face-work because, although the message is unveiled and plain to hear, the words of praise attached to the person and his political achievements are not spoken by himself.

The other major way to achieve discursive indirectness by the speaker in political self-representation is the use of various metaphors, metonymies, allegories, and other figures of speech, which are examples of text-centred indirection (Brenneis 1986, 341). Their effectiveness resides in their being ambiguous; their meaning is left vague, with the result that there is no way to prove beyond reasonable doubt that the speaker has indeed committed the moral offence of public self-praise. The speaker, therefore, cannot be held clearly responsible for the message his audience attributes to his words, cannot be openly accused of self-praise and impoliteness, and cannot be morally criticized. The process of attributing meaning to metaphors and other figures of speech requires, as was noted by Brenneis (1986), the active cooperation of the audience; it is left to them to infer which of the possible meanings of the words uttered were actually intended by the speaker. The members of the audience, therefore, become co-authors of the message and co-owners of the responsibility borne for it. (Regarding the relationship between the politics of difference and linguistic indirectness in other social contexts see, for example, Brenneis 1984, 1986; Obeng 1997; Morgan 2010; Philips 2010. See also Tannen 1981; Kiesling & Ghosh Johnson 2010; Lempert 2012.)

Prestige-Object-Related Indirectness in Political Self-Representation

Linguistic indirectness – so popular in public political discourse and songs – is often applied to the theme of beakers and tankards. When referring to these pieces, the Gabors prefer to avoid using the words *taxtaj* or *kana* or the proper names of individual prestige objects. Since this practice requires continuous, conscious, and voluntary discursive manoeuvring and self-censorship and makes it obvious for the audience that the speaker is committed to protecting – at least partially – his listeners' positive public image, it is interpreted as a form of political politeness and an evident means of public face-work. That is, this practice is regarded as a suitable tool to mitigate the negative symbolic consequences of invidious comparison generated by public mention of the speaker's own beaker or tankard.[3]

As many of my interlocutors noted, "beakers [and tankards] are usually called horses" in political discourse and songs among the Gabors. That is, the words for the different classes of prestige objects – beaker and tankard – and the names of individual pieces are replaced by horse-related phrases such as "cart" (*vurdon*);[4] the "yellow cart" (*galbeno vurdon*; the adjective alludes to the gilding that can be seen on many prestige objects); "horse" (*grast*); the "dapple grey [horse]"; the "grey [horse]" (*suṙṙo [grast]*); the "greyish-blue [horse]" (*suṙṙo vuneto [grast]*); the "grey steed" (the latter four expressions allude to the colour of silver); or "yellow horse" (*galbeno grast*; the adjective refers to the gilding of the piece). Certain phrases apply specifically to one of the types of prestige objects: in political discourse "mare" (*grajni*) is synonymous with a tankard and "stallion" (*xărmăsari*) with a beaker. The words for the two classes of prestige objects and the pieces' proper names may also be replaced by the term "foal" (*khuri*). (The latter noun occasionally refers to the son of the prestige-object owner.) It is also a common technique for the speaker to talk about a "hussar upon a horse" or a "soldier in the cavalry." The latter phrases allude both to the speaker's prestige object (horse) and to the person who will inherit it, that is, his son (hussar, cavalryman). A few examples I observed in political discourses and songs are cited below:

> I get onto my cart, drive my two grey horses [the two prestige objects] and my sons are also sitting there behind me.[5]

> My grey horse [the prestige object] is such [so valuable] that it is known throughout the Seven Villages [the phrase "Seven Villages" is a synonym for the Gabor Roma ethnic population]!

> I mount my grey horse [prestige object], cross the border, and fear no one!

I have three horses [prestige objects] that I drive all the way to America!
With my three grey horses, and green cart, my chariot![6]

[The following is an excerpt from a song. Standing over the open coffin at
a wake in 2001, the singer summed up the life of the deceased with special
reference to his major political achievements. The text is in the first person,
as if the deceased himself were singing. Among these achievements, the
singer mentions the deceased's wealth and the purchase of his most
valuable beaker in the 1990s:]

> *Oh, the way I am, the way I was … ,*
> *Oh, I ate what I wanted,*
> *Oh, as much meat as I wanted … ,*
> *Brother, that I ate.*

[The representation of wealth.]

> *Oh, if a foal [prestige object] took my fancy … ,*
> *I just took the reins.*

[The deceased bought whatever prestige object he fancied.]

> *Oh, the Roma dispusssted with me,*

[Others had also competed for the beaker that he bought in the mid-1990s
and that became the most valuable piece in his collection – a reference to
the intense proprietary contest accompanying the transaction.]

> *Oh, I paid German marks for everything,*

[He paid the purchase price of the beaker in German marks instead of
old Romanian lei, which were of much lower prestige. German marks
therefore represent affluence.]

> *Oh, and I paid the Roma so they could eat and drink.*

[Here, the invitation to eat and drink is a synonym of *mita*-sharing.
In other words, the buyer gave many of his Roma acquaintances and
relatives a generous cash gift interpreted as "a representation of joy"
after purchasing the beaker.] …

Oh, so they wouldn't be angry with me.

[To temper their jealousy and show his commitment to the ethics of sociability.]

Several commentaries explicitly state that the substitution of the names of individual prestige objects with nouns such as "horse" or "cart" in political discourse and songs is a highly self-reflective practice related to the management of positive public image and the intraethnic politics of difference:

> We [the Gabors] substituted carts and horses for the beakers [in political discourse and songs]. When we say "cart," the other one [the listener] hears cart but knows that it's a *taxtaj* [beaker]. We talk about a "grey horse" but the other one [who hears it] understands that we are talking about a *taxtaj*. (19 July 2003)

> They [the prestige-object owners] didn't use the word *taxtaj* to refer to their beakers. Because they sang in the songs: "I've got two horses, dapple grey [two prestige objects]." They turned the *taxtaj* into a horse in the song. There was that Hungarian song: "The trumpet was blown in Târgu Mureş to call every horseman to saddle his horse." If I had a good *taxtaj*, I said [I continued the song]: "So I'll also saddle my golden-maned horse [prestige object]." The golden mane means that the piece is gilded inside and outside. This is how it's said, these boasting [competing] words ... "My grey horse, painted cart, I'm driving towards Oradea. The creaking of my cart is heard as far as Miercurea Ciuc."[7] But what does the creaking cart mean? It means that he [the singer]'s got a good [well-known, valuable] *taxtaj* ... If you sold your beaker or owed all over for it [that is, if the owner borrowed from several creditors, saying that he could repay the sums lent at any time from the sale of his beaker], you have no right to sing a song like that. (23 February 2001)

The source of the political effectiveness and popularity of these horse-related phrases is the already-noted fact that none of the listeners can prove beyond a doubt that when the speaker uses one of these expressions he is in fact praising a prestige object of his own or one belonging to one of his close relatives or political allies. In other words, since the precise identity of the beaker or tankard the speaker is referring to with these phrases remains vague and ambiguous, their use offers the possibility of evading (at least in part) political responsibility for his conversational contribution, and avoiding negative consequences, such as loss of face and moral criticism. Since in the case of these expressions it is essential for the listener to take an active part in creating the meanings associated with them (as co-author), the speaker called to account for presumed self-praise can at any time declare that he did not commit an act of self-praise – it was only a misinterpretation on the part of the listener, a figment of his imagination, because when the horse-related expression was used, speaker and listener had different meanings in mind. The performer's situation is even easier in the case of political songs; if he is called to account for the use of horse-related terms, he could even argue that the words "horse" and "cart" in the song didn't refer to his own beaker – he chose to use them at some point of the performance because certain formal features (the number of syllables, for instance) of these terms helped him to structure the flow of the song.

Linguistic indirectness is also widespread in political insults carried out through the symbolic devaluation of the addressee's prestige object. The main source of its popularity is that the already-mentioned ambiguity and vagueness it creates make any responsibility questionable and difficult to prove. This practice is excellently illustrated by some of the proverbs and aphorisms often voiced during public conversations at wakes, where the speaker addresses the entire audience of several dozen men. While he appears to be sharing with them some general wisdom, there is also an underlying political meaning behind these proverbs and aphorisms – in reality they are veiled insults aimed at one or more of the speaker's rivals present at the event. Let me briefly discuss two statements that may be interpreted as veiled insults. (a) "A horse that can't cope with the mountains should be kept in the stable" – meaning that if an individual's prestige object is not valuable enough (not strong enough "to cope with the mountains"), the owner had better not mention it at social gatherings ("keep it in the stable"). (b) "If you don't have a cavalryman that could ride it, your horse is only good for ploughing" – meaning that if a prestige-object owner's son is not successful in Roma politics (does not have "a good income," a proper behaviour, and so on), the value of the beaker or tankard he inherits will suffer. In the hands of an heir not suited to be a "cavalryman" or "hussar," the prestige object "fails to ring" (he can't mention it in conversation at social gatherings as often as his father did) and thus its significance may decrease – that is, it will be a "plough-horse" rather than a "stallion" in the hands of the person inheriting it. In these cases, it is impossible to prove unequivocally not only the speaker's intention but also precisely who among the listeners was the target of the political insult.

"My Stallion Is So Attractive / It Has No Match in the World" – Two Examples of Songs

The songs often sung by the Gabors fall into three major categories. The first comprises "slow songs" (*žalniko djili*), which were called "wake songs" by many of my interlocutors. These can typically be heard at wakes and commemorative events and occasionally during long car journeys or monotonous work activities. Slow songs are distinguished from other common types of songs mainly by their atmosphere, content, and tune. They are generally sung in either the Romani or Hungarian language, less often in Romanian. Typical features of slow songs are: (a) they are mainly composed of commonly used, well-known formulae and images of everyday life (including a wide range of linguistic representations – figures of speech, for instance – of political successes, social prestige, and patrilineal identity); and (b) during the performance the singer shapes the content and message to suit the given social context (such as the audience or the political achievements of the deceased) and his own political goals and interests.

"Table songs" (*meseljaki djili*) are associated with joyous social events, such as weddings or betrothal ceremonies, but may on occasion be heard at a wake (when, for instance, the deceased lived a long, full life and is therefore regarded as "not unfortunately dead" [*nemsajnos halott*]).[8] Most table songs are in either the Hungarian or Romani language and, like slow songs, tend to have political content. Many of them provide an opportunity for the singer to adapt certain content elements of the song to the given social context and occasion and to his own political purposes. As a rule, slow songs and table songs are led at any given moment by a single performer, while the others present may join in to sing certain lines or the ends of certain lines.

The so-called "holy songs" (*sento djili*), which are typically taken from the Adventist hymnal, have fixed words and tunes and are sung by those present as a group at worship services and at wakes, funerals, and commemorative events. The words of the "holy songs" are typically in Hungarian or Romanian, but we may occasionally come across some sung in Romani. The content of these songs is not determined by the Roma themselves, and they cannot modify them to suit their own mood or interests. For this reason, "holy songs" are unsuitable for adaptation by performers wishing to fill them with Roma political content.

As noted in the previous paragraphs, the Gabors often make mention of their prestige objects in songs other than the ones in Romani. Many Hungarian songs – originally learnt from Hungarian or other, non-Gabor Roma people – have become popular among the Gabors, because some of the motifs contained in them, such as horses, carts, or hussars, allow them to be used as effective means of representing successes achieved in the prestige economy – in other words, of political face-work.

In the following section, I present a passage from one song and the full text of another. Both are about prestige objects. They aptly illustrate how proper names of pieces and the words *taxtaj* and *kana* are replaced by tropes related to horses, carts, and so on, or how the objects are alluded to in some other manner.

(1) The first example is an excerpt from a song performed in Romani at a betrothal ceremony on 19 March 2002. The central participants of the event were Marko, a man in his early fifties from Mureş County (the paternal grandfather of the groom, who was one and a half years old at the time) and Bango, of a similar age from Cluj County (the paternal grandfather of the bride, who was four years old; see also chapter 12).

Marko was a member of one of the most influential families within the currently dominant patriline among the Gabors. He inherited two especially valuable prestige objects – a beaker and a tankard – from his father, who died in 1996. Although Marko was considered to be a "high-ranking Roma [coming from a patriline that had proved to be particularly successful in politics]," the evaluation of his own individual political performance was ambivalent – mostly as a result of his continuous financial difficulties (debts). Due to his political attractiveness, there was an intense competition among Gabor Roma men of low social prestige but substantial wealth and political ambition for a marital alliance with Marko. Bango, from Cluj County, who had accumulated his considerable wealth after the change of political regime – primarily through construction projects commissioned by state-owned companies – belonged to this group of Gabor individuals.

Following their negotiations about the betrothal and future wedding of their grandchildren, Marko and Bango agreed on a marriage payment of US$60,000, which was to be paid by Bango in two instalments; he would hand half of the total sum over to Marko at the time of the betrothal and pay the other half at the wedding of their grandchildren. Marko's sole reason to establish a marital alliance with someone ambitious but of low social prestige was to obtain the large marriage payment, so that he could use the money to redeem the extremely valuable beaker he had pawned around Christmastime in 2001. Bango, in contrast, was motivated by the prospect of a significant reputational profit and a higher social status.

The betrothal ceremony took place in a restaurant in a small town in Cluj County. The song excerpt below was performed by Marko, singing into a microphone. Thanks to the sound system, the performance was heard by every one of the more than 100 attendees.

[Accompanied by a Roma band employed for the occasion, Marko was singing in the name of his father, who died in 1996:]

My stallion is so attractive,

[Stallion = the beaker that Marko's father left Marko as his legacy.]

It has no match in the world.

[No Gabor Roma owns a prestige object more valuable than the beaker that Marko's father left Marko.]

And X also has one [another stallion],

[X = the Gabor Roma broker who arranged the marital alliance and the betrothal and who also owns a precious beaker.]

Let them be lucky to you!

[That is, may the beakers mentioned be lucky to Marko and the broker.] ...

[Marko sings in his own name from now on:]

I've just tied [acquired] *another brother,*
Bango and his son.

[Marko acquired another close political ally ("brother"[9]) in Bango by securing the betrothal between their grandchildren.]

He also has a stallion, an attractive one,

[Stallion = Bango's valuable beaker.]

That follows mine enticingly.

[Marko's beaker is more valuable than Bango's.]

And he has a good son,
May the Lord grant him good luck!
Because he also has only one [son],
Just as I was the only [son] *of my black father.*
And my father's black son hasn't died.

[Marko – the performer of the song – is still very much alive.]

Mine is now dancing!

[Mine = Marko's stallion, that is, beaker. Meaning Marko is at the peak of his political career, bathing in political glory.]

May the Lord be good,
And let good X,

[X = the Gabor Roma broker who arranged the marital alliance and the betrothal.]

And Bango be blessed,
Because they're luring my foal out,

[They're bringing Marko's "foal" back. As mentioned, Marko was planning to use the first installment of the marriage payment received from Bango on the day of the betrothal ceremony to redeem the beaker – "luring my foal out" – he had pawned around Christmastime in 2001.]

Making the three villages sparkle.

[Marko's foal – beaker – makes all "three villages"[10] sparkle = a synonym for the outstanding value and fame attributed to the piece in question.]

It was tied in the stable,

[Marko's foal being tied in the stable = Marko had pawned his beaker.]

At the side of F's famous [beaker],
At the side of the desired K.

[F = the father of the Gabor lender who took Marko's beaker as a security at Christmastime 2001. K = the proper name of the valuable beaker that belonged to F for a long time and was owned by one of F's sons – the lender's brother – at the time of the betrothal ceremony. Marko's foal being tied in F's stable, at the side of the beaker named K = Marko's beaker was taken as a security by F's family.]

But mine dances better,

[Marko's stallion dances better = his beaker is more famous and sought after than the beaker named K.]

Let five hundred Roma come.

[He is prepared to defend his opinion in public.]

After these two stallions,
After my black father's two stallions

[Marko is referring to his own beaker and tankard.[11]]

Comes X's,

[The broker's beaker.]

Because it's antique, it's old,
And then Bango's.

[Marko's last five lines arrange his own, the broker's and his future co-father-in-law's prestige objects in order of importance based on their social value and significance.]

The song excerpt above is an emblematic example of political self-representation accompanied by intense face-work. One of the main techniques of face-work employed here is text-centred indirection, and another – at the beginning of the song when it was sung in the name of the performer's father – is voice-centred indirection. As a result of the former, individual prestige objects appear in the song primarily in the form of horse-related expressions: "stallion" and "foal" stand for a beaker. Further elements that can be interpreted as political statements framed and blunted by means of linguistic indirectness include (a) mention of the outstandingly great social and emotional significance associated with the prestige objects inherited by the performer of the song ("My stallion is so attractive, / It has no match in the world" and so forth); (b) the fact that the performer publicly praises the broker's and his future co-father-in-law's beakers ("He [Bango] also has a stallion, an attractive one" and so forth); (c) the comparison of the importance attributed to the performer's beaker to that attributed to the beaker named K ("But mine dances better"); and (d) the ranking of the performer's, the broker's, and Bango's prestige objects according to their value. By using indirectness, the performer plainly demonstrates his commitment to the ethics of sociability and his sensitivity to the positive public image of his audience.

In addition, the song directly refers to the recent event of the performer pawning his own beaker as part of a loan transaction at Christmastime 2001 ("It [Marko's foal] was tied in the stable, / At the side of F's famous [beaker], / At the side of the desired K") and to his intention of redeeming the piece with the combined support of the broker and his future co-father-in-law – thanks to the US$30,000 instalment of the marriage payment he receives on the day of the betrothal ceremony ("they're luring my foal [beaker] out"). The special emotional, biographical, and economic value attributed by the performer to the beaker in question and his joy over the prospect of redeeming it largely explain why he keeps praising the broker and his new co-father-in-law and why he voluntarily chooses to make mention of a face-threatening and shameful event – the pawning of his beaker – in a song performed in front of a Roma audience of more than a hundred strong. (The debt was repaid, and the pawned object redeemed by Marko on the same day.)

This song excerpt is a convincing illustration of how a song performed at a social event, and therefore given great publicity, can be filled with hidden political content related to prestige objects and thus serve to promote the performer's political goals and interests.

(2) The second example is a song sung in Hungarian at a Gabor Roma wake in Mureş County on 15 March 2001. The deceased was a highly respected man – and regarded as "not unfortunately dead" – with outstanding achievements in several symbolic arenas of Roma politics (prestige economy, marriage politics, and proper behaviour) and five grown sons. His patriline was considered to be of "second rank" in his local Roma community. His political success is well-demonstrated by the fact that – alone or together with his sons – he bought six beakers and established marital alliances with many influential heads of family from patrilines of high social prestige. A key to his social and political success was his proper behaviour, manifested in practices such as his open admission of the modest prestige of his patriline in the course of public conversation with influential members of the dominant local patriline (at wakes, for instance) and his taking special care to appear polite and humble at times of public political self-representation.

The song was performed by one of the deceased's nephews. It was sung at the end of the second night of the wake, at about six o'clock in the morning, when the members of the dominant local patriline, who might have interpreted the enumeration of the political achievements of the deceased as a face-threatening act, had already left. By then only the deceased's close relatives and friends (almost thirty people) remained by the body laid out in the open coffin. The song was the "favourite song" of the deceased, which his nephew had frequently sung to him in the last five or six years of his life and which narrated the purchase of the beaker that came into the possession of his eldest son in the mid-1990s – thanks to the very substantial political and financial support received from the deceased. The object in question was the most precious of the six beakers bought by the deceased – alone or together with his sons – and my interlocutors considered it to be one of the three most valuable beakers currently in Gabor Roma ownership. At this relatively informal stage of the wake, when close relatives could voice their pain more freely and praise the political achievements of the deceased more openly, one of the central topics was the summing up, evaluation, and praising of his life and successes (in both conversations and songs). The song below – which remembers the most important political achievement of his immediate family, while respecting the ethics of political face-work – was a key element of these processes.

[The performer of the song sings in the name of the deceased:]

> *Oh, I go to the large market,*
> *Oh, I go to the large market,*

[Large market = the set of Gabor prestige objects for sale at the time.]

> *Because I see a grey one standing there,*
> *Oh, because I see a grey one standing there.*

[Grey one = the beaker they intended to purchase.]

[The performer sings in the name of the deceased addressing the seller of the "grey one" on the "large market":]

> *Tell me respected old man, how much?*
> *Oh, tell me respected old man, how much?*
> *How much is the grey one?*
> *Oh, how much is the grey one?*

[The seller replies to the deceased:]

> *Oh, three thousand and five hundred pengos,*[12]
> *Three thousand and five hundred pengos,*

[The purchase price of the beaker including the cash gifts interpreted as "representations of joy" distributed after the transaction came to 350,000 German marks. The reply "three thousand and five hundred pengos" refers to this sum.]

> *Oh, he's got the bell around his neck,*
> *He's got the bell around his neck.*

[Bell, ringing = reference to the renown of the object due to its exceptional value.]

[The performer sings in the name of the deceased, addressing the seller of the "grey one" on the "large market":]

> *Oh, listen respected old man, let it walk,*
> *Listen respected old man, let it walk.*

Let my big son see it,
Let my big son see it.

[Reference to the viewing of prestige objects before purchase and to the fact that the beaker was bought by the eldest son of the deceased – for himself – with his father's help.]

Oh, because if he likes its walking,
If he likes its walking,
We shall drink its libation,
We shall drink its libation!

[That is, they will buy it. The libation – which takes place after the completion of the sale transaction – is used here as a synonym for the distribution of cash gifts interpreted as "representations of joy."[13] The latter is a common practice following the purchase of a prestige object.]

[The performer sings in the name of the deceased, who has left the "large market" with his son, taking the "grey one" with him, and is on his way home:]

Oh, my grey horse, painted cart,
My grey horse, painted cart,

[My grey horse, painted cart = the beaker just purchased.]

I drive towards Miercurea Ciuc,
Oh, I drive towards Miercurea Ciuc.
The creaking of my cart,
The creaking of my cart,
It is heard all the way to Miercurea Ciuc,
Oh, in that luxury pub.

[The creaking of the cart is a synonym for the huge social interest in and response to the transaction among the Gabors.]

I walk into the pub,
I walk into the pub,
I ask for wine by the gallon,

[Again, the performer uses the practice of libation – wine – to refer to the handing out of the cash gifts interpreted as "representations of joy."

This type of *mita* handed out after the transaction in question amounted to approximately 50,000 German marks = US$32,836.]

Because I don't care about the price.

[Reference to the affluence of the deceased.]

[The performer is addressing his audience at the wake in his own name:]

God forgive my uncle and bless you all!

The singer learnt the song from his own father, who believes it is a song from Trei Scaune,[14] which the Gabors imported from the "(non-Gabor) Roma of Trei Scaune." The singer's father, who is one of the best-known Gabor Roma performers of songs in Romani and other languages at wakes and weddings, argued that in this song, the "Roma of Trei Scaune" (who do not own silver prestige objects but do own horses and carts) only

sang about horses [that is, the term "horse" actually referred to just horses]. Originally. Then we sang it politically [the Gabor Roma performers sang the same song in a politicized manner] to blow some dust into the other's eyes [to shame or insult their political rivals] ... Among us [the Gabors] it's turned into an imitation [the Gabors act as though they are only performing the original version again, while at the same time attaching a hidden political meaning to it]. This song is an imitation, I've shaped it to our own traditions. (15 August 2004)

That is, the Gabors filled this song, which has its own transcultural biography, with political content and adapted it to the given social context (among other things, the political interests and possibilities of the current performer).[15]

As mentioned above, the singer sang the song at the wake in the name of his influential paternal uncle and with the aim of evoking the story of his most important political achievement: the purchase of the most precious beaker in his family's possession. One strategy used in the song to depict the prestige object and the transaction is the imagery popular in political discourse – such as the "grey one," "my grey horse, painted cart" (the beaker); "He's got the bell around his neck" (the renown of the beaker due to its exceptional value); "Listen, respected old man, let it walk. / Let my big son see it" (viewing of the prestige object before the purchase); and

"I ask for wine by the gallon" (libation = *mita*-sharing). The interpretation of these tropes is assisted by widely known general background knowledge. On the other hand, the performer inserted into the song personal, specific pieces of information that functioned as useful contextualization cues and allowed his audience to infer which prestige-object transaction the song was about. These pieces of information include the total sum of the purchase price and the *mita* ("three thousand and five hundred pengos" – that is, 350,000 German marks) and the line "Let my big son see it," which makes clear that the item was bought by the eldest son of the deceased (with his father's help). Another informative contextualization cue is the well-known background information that – because of its political connotations – this was the "favourite song" of the deceased, which the performer had often sung to him in the past few years to alleviate the depression that accompanied his illness and to show his respect and admiration for him.

The purchase of this exceptionally valuable beaker increased not only the deceased and his eldest son's renown but also that of their entire patriline. This conclusion is supported by the fact that it was the deceased who mostly "did his brothers proud"; that is, it was primarily his political achievements – his more precious beakers, marital alliances, and proper behaviour – that his brothers invoked when attempts were made to insult them through allusions to their modest patrilineal prestige in public discourses at various social gatherings. The song is therefore also a means of collective patrilineal self-pantheonization or self-glorification; the singer himself was also interested in recalling the successful transaction. To quote the performer's father, this song

> is family history … My son is proud of his big [politically successful] cousin [who bought the beaker] … and the latter is proud of him, too [first of all because of his expertise in singing and political discourse] … And so one adds to [helps out] the other, you see? My son sings this song for Y [for – or more precisely, in place of – his cousin, who purchased the beaker], my son shows he's proud of him because he [Y] mustn't [publicly bring up his own political achievements]. Why? So that no one can say: "Y is boasting [publicly mentioning his own successes]." He's got someone to do his public praising! He's got someone to sing his file [political achievements], you see? (15 August 2004)

The above quote openly states that the performer is doing a favour to the beaker's owner because he is effectively singing in his place, as his mouthpiece. A song performed by a close relative instead of the owner allows the transaction in question and its accompanying reputational profit to receive further publicity without the possessor having to open his mouth. The latter's positive public image is thus saved, since he cannot be accused of morally stigmatized self-praise.

This song also aptly illustrates how the Gabors use various forms of linguistic indirectness in order to respect the ethics of political self-representation and to save their own and their interlocutors' positive public image. The song under discussion provides several examples of indirectness. These include (a) the choice of song itself (which was made possible by the fact that its original central motif was the purchase of a horse); (b) the phrases "grey one" and "my grey horse," used to refer to the beaker, and other figures of speech serving to describe the transaction; (c) the fact that the story of the purchase is performed not by the buyer himself but – as his mouthpiece – by one of his close relatives at the wake; and (d) the fact that the performer did not speak in the name of the buyer in the song but "puts the words into the mouth" of the deceased – that is, the buyer's father (and into the mouth of the seller of the "grey one"). Thanks to the latter two choices, the song is an excellent example of Brenneis' ventriloquism through spokesmen (Brenneis 1986, 343).

Transcultural Bricolage and Hybridity: Intellectual Import and Creative Recycling

Ethnographic and anthropological literature focusing on Transylvania often stereotypically characterizes the Roma ethnic populations as being disposed to adopt and preserve in unaltered form many creations of folklore (mostly folk songs and folk tales) of the Hungarian rural communities – primarily because of the "archaic lifestyle" and cultural and social "isolation" and "backwardness" frequently associated with the Roma. These essentializing and often tribalizing and exoticizing stereotypes tend to represent Roma communities as passive, "living archives" of the intellectual products crossing cultural and social boundaries, and to attribute a negligible role to conscious selection and creative recycling by the Roma themselves in the development and shaping of the set of these imported products. Let me cite just one example:

One thing is certain: during our fieldwork, we have all encountered Gypsy informants who have proved to be knowledgeable of the most archaic, rarest and most valuable Hungarian folklore pieces or even the sole preservers of these pieces in their environment ... In our times ... it is mostly Hungarian Gypsies throughout the Szekely Land [Ţinutul Secuiesc][16] who still know the classic ballads that disappeared from Szekely folklore one, two or sometimes even more generations ago ... We can only wish that Hungarian Gypsies keep on faithfully preserving more and more of the old Szekely ballad poetry. (Faragó 1994, 149, 151)

Some authors go even further; they suggest that the Roma communities of Transylvania never, or only to a modest extent, possessed cultural products of their own that were similar to those they adopted. Therefore, the adoption is supposed to fill in some sort of cultural gap (a deficit theory relying on the negative stereotype of "cultural backwardness"):

The claim that a Gypsy community settled at the edges of a village or town tenaciously preserves the traditions that the [non-Gypsy] inhabitants of that village (town) have mostly forgotten began to be quite widely accepted. It is well-known that Gypsies have hardly any folk culture of their own today. The bulk of their cultural knowledge has been borrowed from peoples living with them: Romanians, Hungarians, Germans, etc. (Ráduly 1978, 245)

These stereotypes suggest that the "archaic Roma lifestyle" usually equated with social marginalization and cultural "backwardness" favours the survival of "traditional creations of folklore" of the Hungarian rural communities, which would otherwise completely disappear as a result of the transformation and modernization of these rural communities. That is, the Roma ethnic populations – unwittingly – perform some sort of positively interpreted cultural mission; they "preserve" Hungarian "creations of folklore" for the benefit and in place of the Transylvanian Hungarian society.

The case of Hungarian-language songs being used as a means of intra-ethnic political self-representation focused on prestige objects demonstrates, however, that the borrowing and use of cultural products of the Transylvanian Hungarians by the Roma may follow a different logic than the one described above. That is, the import of intellectual goods crossing social and cultural boundaries is not necessarily a mechanical process lacking purposeful selection, and its goal is not necessarily the preservation of these goods in an unaltered form.[17]

The Gabors consciously and purposefully select Hungarian-language songs about horses, carts, and so on from the song repertoire of the Transylvanian Hungarians or other Roma ethnic populations – and it is not because of the stereotype of the "archaic way of life" often associated with the Roma or the frequently assumed "lack of similar cultural goods" that they regard them as attractive, worth learning and putting to further use. Their choice is not at all influenced by the meanings that the Transylvanian Hungarians usually associate with these songs (symbols of their disappearing rural communities and culture as well as authentic representations of their ethnic past viewed through the lens of romanticizing nostalgia). The Gabors are drawn to these songs precisely because they can be transformed into an effective means of Roma politics and political face-work; these songs allow them to represent at public gatherings the successes they have achieved in the prestige economy without the speaker significantly endangering his own and others' positive public image. As demonstrated in this chapter, the Gabors partially modify the imported Hungarian-language songs about horses, carts, hussars, and the like: the performer alters their content and meaning to suit the given occasion and social context – the audience, or the person of the deceased, for instance – and his own political plans and interests. Although it may appear to an observer unfamiliar with this process of intellectual recycling that in these songs the Gabors are singing about horses and carts – topics that are closely associated with the majority society's image of the Roma – this chapter has argued that the songs in question have in fact undergone a process of purposeful selection and creative recycling transforming them into reethnicized intellectual goods. They gain new social significance and meaning among the Gabor Roma as strategic tools in the politics of difference and are inseparable from the ethics of sociability and, in particular, from the practice of political face-work.

Photo 1. Gabor Roma family members at a commemorative event (*pomana*)
held six weeks after a funeral. Credit: Author, 2001.

Photo 2. Gabor Roma at the funeral of a prestige-object owner.
Credit: Author, 2010.

Photo 3. Gabor Roma at a funeral waiting for the ceremony to begin.
Credit: Author, 2014.

Photo 4. A Gabor Roma trader selling clothing items at a second-hand
market in Mureş County. Credit: Author, 2011.

Photo 5. Political discourse among Gabor Roma at a funeral.
Credit: Author, 2014.

Photo 6. Political discourse among Gabor Roma at a commemorative event
held six weeks after a funeral. Credit: Author, 2014.

Photo 7. Political discourse between two influential Gabor Roma prestige-object owners at a funeral. Credit: Author, 2010.

Photo 8. Wedding of a young Gabor Roma couple in the home of the husband's family. Credit: Andrea Szalai, 2010.

Photo 9. An exceptionally valuable Gabor Roma footed beaker decorated with – among other things – "unexplainable animals." Credit: Author, 2006.

Photo 10. A skillfully fire-gilt Gabor Roma footed beaker.
Credit: Author, 2014.

Photo 11. A Gabor Roma footed beaker with a hunting scene
below the girdle. Credit: Author, 2010.

Photo 12. A Gabor Roma *ščobo* beaker with two medallions and a finely
elaborated surface pattern similar to snakeskin. Credit: Author, 2010.

Photo 13. A Gabor Roma *burikato* beaker decorated with a rearing
horse and other animals. Credit: Author, 2012.

Photo 14. An exceptionally valuable, richly fire-gilt Gabor Roma roofed tankard decorated with vegetal motifs. Credit: Author, 2011.

Photo 15. An exceptionally valuable Gabor Roma roofed tankard decorated with biblical scenes (e.g., Daniel in the lions' den). Credit: Author, 2009.

Photo 16. The Gabor Roma owner holding the footed beaker
shown in photo 11. Credit: Author, 2013.

Photo 17. A richly fire-gilt Gabor Roma roofed tankard, held by the owner's son. Credit: Author, 2011.

Photo 18. The Gabor Roma owner and his grandson holding the roofed tankard shown in photo 14. Credit: Author, 2011.

Photo 19. A Gabor Roma footed beaker, held by the owner.
Credit: Author, 2011.

Photo 20. A silver coin with a portrait of emperor Franz Joseph I, used to cover a repair at the lip of a Gabor Roma beaker. Credit: Author, 2006.

Photo 21. Decorations identified by the Gabor Roma as "unexplainable animals." Credit: Author, 2006.

Photo 22. A Cărhar Roma prestige-object owner (possessing a
valuable *ščobo* beaker). Credit: Ágnes-Éva Varga, 2012.

Photo 23. A Cărhar Roma prestige-object owner (possessing five beakers).
Credit: Author, 2012.

Photo 24. Cărhar women and their children at a Cărhar Roma wedding in
the Olt River area. Credit: Author, 2011.

Photo 25. A Cărhar Roma man with a copper kettle for distilling the local brandy. Credit: Author, 2011.

Photo 26. A Cărhar Roma family looking at photos of beakers and roofed tankards in the catalogue of an American art collector. Credit: Author, 2012.

Photo 27. An exceptionally valuable, richly fire-gilt Cărhar Roma footed beaker with numerous antique coins with portraits. Credit: Author, 2010.

Photo 28. A richly fire-gilt Cărhar Roma *ščobo* beaker with a finely elaborated surface pattern similar to snakeskin and a medallion bearing a Hungarian personal name and a date: 1683. Credit: Author, 2010.

Photo 29. A Cărhar Roma owner with his two large footed beakers purchased earlier from the Gabors. Credit: Author, 2011.

Photo 30. A Cărhar Roma owner with his footed beaker (richly decorated with vegetal motifs) purchased from the Gabors. Credit: Author, 2011.

Photo 31. A footed beaker (decorated with portraits of elderly, bearded men and vegetal motifs) bought earlier from the Gabors and now in Cărhar Roma possession. Credit: Author, 2011.

Photo 32. The Cărhar Roma owner of the beaker shown in photo 31 measures the height of his prestige object. Credit: Author, 2011.

Photo 33. Kuna with his beaker, and the Cărhar Roma broker mentioned in the case study in chapter 8. Credit: Author, 2012.

Photo 34. A Cărhar Roma wearing a necklace decorated with numerous *galbi*s with a portrait of Austrian emperor Franz Joseph I. Credit: Author, 2011.

PART TWO

Contesting Consumer Subcultures: Interethnic Trade, Fake Authenticity, and Classification Struggles

7

Gabor Roma, Cărhar Roma, and the European Antiques Market: Contesting Consumer Subcultures

What other contemporary consumer subcultures – based on aesthetic tastes or ethnicity, for instance – outside the Gabor Roma are interested in "proper" silver beakers and tankards?

The European Antiques Market: Dealers, Collectors, and Museums

Since there is a fluctuating level of antiques-market interest in "proper" beakers and tankards in Europe, non-Roma art collectors and antiques dealers often attempt to buy these objects when they are put up for auction (or offered for sale in some other way) – mostly in Hungary, Romania, Germany, and Austria. In this context, their social meanings and economic significance are determined on the basis of the preferences belonging to the value regimes of the antiques market and art history. In these regimes, important sources of value include such components of the object's social career as the professional prestige, art-historical significance, or ethnic identity of the silversmith who made the given piece; the time and place of the item's creation; or the social status or ethnic belonging of the non-Roma individual who commissioned the work and of subsequent owners. In curatorial discourses relating to art history, museum exhibitions, and auction houses, these pieces tend to be interpreted as indexical representations of regionality, locality, and ethnic, national, family, or religious history, and they thus become integral parts of various identity projects. In the symbolic field of museum representation in Transylvania and Hungary, "proper" beakers and tankards often represent, according to the curatorial interpretations associated with them, the region where they were made in

greatest numbers – that is to say, Transylvania and Transylvanianness
("Transylvanian silversmithing") and historical Hungary ("Hungarian
silversmithing"); or they may appear as the materializations of an ethnic past ("Saxon silversmithing"; "Hungarian silversmithing"), family history (aristocratic commissioners and owners), church history, or
guild history.

The value regimes of the antiques market and art history – much like
that of the Gabors – attribute a substantial value- and price-forming
role to an object's material properties, such as decorations and shape,
and to related and highly esteemed rarity, uniqueness, or labour inten-
siveness. However, in many cases these regimes define the value and
importance of these properties differently than the Gabors' prestige-
object aesthetics does. For example, antiques-market participants
(antiques dealers, art collectors, and museum curators) do not attribute
special significance to the footed beaker shape, are unfamiliar with the
category of "unexplainable animals" as a type of decoration, do not
share Gabor Roma value preferences with regard to size measured in
capacity, and take a different attitude towards minor damages, such as
cracks at the lip or a thinning of the material just above the girdle. As
previously mentioned, the tankards and the types of beakers highly
esteemed by the Gabor Roma are not among the most wanted or most
valuable commodities on the antiques market. These beakers do not
usually sell there for more than US$9,000 to US$11,000, and interest
in or demand for them is generally both modest and limited to certain
regions of Europe.[1]

Since the Gabors buy "proper" objects coming from non-Roma
mainly on the antiques market, a few antiques dealers in Hungary and
Transylvania have established long-term business relationships with
them, some of which go back decades. Dealers in this small group are
quite familiar with the Gabors' prestige economy – their value preferences concerning material properties, the current conditions of the
Gabors' prestige-object market, and the most popular brokers – and
occasionally visit their Gabor Roma acquaintances with the aim of selling silver pieces that have recently appeared on the antiques market
and have the properties that the Gabors deem attractive. These dealers may also buy antiques from the Gabor Roma, such as paintings,
silver objects other than beakers and tankards, copper items, and folk
or other antique furniture, which they then try to sell in their antique
shops in Transylvania or Hungary. Very rarely, an antiques dealer may
buy a prestige object of complete value that has gradually lost almost

all its significance among the Gabors. This happened to a tankard, for instance, that was acquired by a dealer from Budapest for a mere 17,000 German marks (US$8,250) at the turn of the millennium.

The Transylvanian Cărhar Roma

The prestige economy built around silver beakers and tankards is a practice characteristic of not only the Gabors but also another Transylvanian Roma ethnic population known by the name of Cărhar or Cortu-rar (see Ries 2007; Tesăr 2012, 2016; see also colour plates: Photos 22–6, 29–30, 32–4.). Both ethnonyms are derived from the word for tent – *cărha* in Romani and *cort* in Romanian – and mean tent-dwelling. In the following section, I will give a short description of the Cărhar Roma ethnic population and their prestige economy and compare Gabor Roma and Cărhar Roma value preferences with regard to beakers and tankards.

The Cărhars mostly live in settlements in Sibiu and Braşov Counties, for instance in many villages and towns in the Olt River area. The vast majority of them are members of the Romanian Orthodox Church. While the Gabors usually speak Hungarian as their second language, in Cărhar communities, which are located in regions with a Romanian majority, the second language is Romanian.

The Cărhars live mainly from agriculture: breeding and raising livestock – horses, pigs, sheep, and cattle – and cultivating crops. The horses they raise are either offered for sale in local or regional markets – usually to Romanian or Hungarian farmers – or sold to clients from Italy, where their meat is used as an ingredient for the food industry. (A large share of the Cărhars' other livestock are also bought by non-Roma.) In some settlements, a number of the Cărhars earn their livelihood primarily by making copper objects to satisfy the demands of local and regional markets and the tourist industry, which has become more robust in recent decades. The large copper kettles made for distilling the local brandy or for other purposes are mostly purchased by farmers in their vicinity, while smaller copper objects – coffee pots, jugs, stew pots, vases, and decorative plates for tables and walls – are mainly sold to tourists. The Cărhars' copper products are occasionally also bought by intermediary traders from Hungary or from other parts of Romania who sell them to their own clients. (A copper kettle with a capacity of fifty litres takes five to seven days to make and in 2011 sold for between €250 and €300.) A considerable proportion of my Cărhar hosts who made copper pieces also took their products to fairs organized annually or more frequently in such centres as Sibiu, Ploieşti, and Bucharest. Some of these Roma specialize in collecting scrap metal – one entrepreneur operates an enormous wrecking yard in one of the settlements in the Olt River area, employing a number of workers. Others make some of their living through loan transactions or dealing in automobiles. A few of my hosts invested part of their cash reserves in apartments and houses, which they let out to tenants.

In recent years, these economic strategies for earning a livelihood have been supplemented, or in several cases replaced, by economic migration to certain Southern and Western European countries (for instance, Italy and France), where the Cărhars make their living primarily by begging. It is not unusual for dozens of adult members – of various ages and both genders – of a local community to set out in minivans operated by Romanian entrepreneurs who specialize in providing transport for economic migrants, among others, to spend months in one of the Southern or Western European cities (e.g., Milan, Naples, Florence, or Paris) begging in the street while living in extremely modest circumstances.[2] Many of my Cărhar acquaintances – especially the women – often used the strategy of begging in Romania as well.

There is a considerable social distance between the Gabors and the Cărhars; the members of both Roma ethnic populations employ the strategy of ethnic endogamy and very rarely participate in the social events of the other population (such as wakes or funerals). One such event – a funeral in Mureş County – took place on 11 January 2007. The deceased was an influential Gabor Roma broker who had played an important role in the prestige-object trade between the Gabors and the Cărhars. His funeral was attended by a few Cărhar men, including the brother-in-law of the creditor with whom the deceased had pawned his own footed beaker in 1998.

Contact between the two Roma ethnic populations is largely restricted to certain types of occasional economic cooperation. Most of these are prestige-economy-related transactions such as prestige-object sales, loans involving beakers and tankards as securities, or visits by affluent Cărhar men to the homes of Gabor owners who they believe will soon be forced to sell their silver pieces. The goal of these visits is to inspect the object potentially about to be offered for sale and sound out the purchase price the owner has in mind.

There is a further type of occasional gender-specific economic cooperation between the Gabors and the Cărhars. However, in contrast with prestige-object transactions, which almost exclusively involve men, this activity is engaged in only by women. Cărhar women occasionally hire a car with a driver in order to visit settlements in Mureş County, where a fairly large number of affluent Gabor Roma families live, to buy used clothes (skirts, aprons, and blouses) from Gabor women who no longer need them. The Cărhar women then sell these clothes either among their own acquaintances, or to other Roma women at second-hand markets near their homes.

Another case of occasional interethnic economic cooperation concerns the curse or, more precisely, the fact that my Cărhar hosts reacted much more sensitively to conditional self-curses spoken in public than my Gabor interlocutors; the former attributed a greater convincing power to these curses and believed their use carried a higher risk. My Cărhar acquaintances, like the Gabor Roma, often resorted to public swearings (*žal po trušula*) when trying to manage interpersonal conflicts – disagreements related to (among other things) economic transactions or marital alliances. This practice involves an oath-taker demonstrating the truth of what he or she is saying to everyone present by uttering conditional self-curses that threaten him- or herself and his or her family members with death and other misfortunes. (According to the ideology of public swearing, if an individual has sworn a false oath, the conditional self-curses will sooner or later strike him or her and his or her family members.) To increase the efficiency of the ritual, the curses are "uttered in advance" by one or more men asked to do so, and the individual wishing to prove his or her truthfulness repeats the curses in the first person singular. Many members of one of the largest Cărhar Roma local communities living in the north of Sibiu County (in Rupuno[3]) are, however, reluctant "to utter in advance" the conditional self-curses themselves and prefer to entrust Gabor Roma with the task – for a fee. Part of the explanation for their reluctance is the stronger agency they attribute to the curses – a more intense fear of their being fulfilled – and the other reason is their wish to avoid conflicts within their own local community. As many of them noted, if a local Cărhar man were "to utter in advance" the curses for another Cărhar individual also from Rupuno and some tragedy, such as death or serious illness, were to subsequently befall the latter or one of his or her close family members, many people would put some of the blame on the person who had "uttered the curses in advance" – irrespective of whether the individual swearing the oath had sworn a false oath or not – which could easily lead to a conflict.

Interactions between Gabor and Cărhar Roma may be more frequent in settlements situated at the meeting point of regions densely populated by the two Roma ethnic populations: the southern region of Mureş County and the northern region of Sibiu County. The same applies to the fairs and second-hand markets in Sibiu, Braşov, and Mureş Counties frequented by many Gabor and Cărhar Roma as traders or potential customers. These places provide excellent opportunities for increasing interethnic relational capital and exchanging information.

The Prestige Economy of the Cărhar Roma

Over the past hundred and fifty years, the Cărhar Roma have also developed a prestige economy involving the same types of silver objects that the Gabor Roma collect; that is, their prestige economy is also organized around tankards (*kana*) and the types of beakers (*taxtaj*[4]) discussed in chapter 4 (*kuštikasa*, *ščobo*, *burikato*, and *taxtaj andol pale*).[5] (See colour plates: Photos 27–8.) The Gabor and the Cărhar Roma prestige-object definitions specify the same material criteria: in addition to having one of the shapes listed above, an essential requirement for a silver beaker or tankard to become a prestige object is that it be made of antique silver; that is, it cannot have been manufactured in the recent past.

The beakers and tankards in Cărhar Roma ownership that have come to my attention were made in the workshops of non-Roma – mostly Transylvanian Saxon and Hungarian – silversmiths, and in the earlier periods of their social life they belonged to Transylvanian aristocrats, burghers, guilds, congregations of the Reformed Church, or Gabor Roma before being acquired by the Cărhars. The Cărhar individuals I met during my fieldwork neither made silver pieces nor had them made by Transylvanian silversmiths.[6] The only exception I know of was a man from Sibiu County who made and antiqued silver beakers that he attempted to sell to Cărhar and Gabor Roma and non-Roma customers – with modest success.

Within the Cărhar Roma ethnic population, beakers and tankards change hands for many times their antiques-market purchase price – just as in sales transactions among the Gabors or between Gabor sellers and Cărhar buyers. The purchase prices that the Cărhars pay for beakers and tankards (which, ideally, are passed down from father to son) are the highest they pay for any commodity; that is, the prices of the most valuable prestige objects are never exceeded by those of any other assets changing hands among them.

The accumulation of economic capital in the form of beakers and tankards as well as in cash is an integral part of the politics of difference characteristic of the Cărhars. In the words of one of my interlocutors, "There is big, big politics among us" (*Bari-j, bari-j e politika maškar amende*). Other symbolic arenas of Cărhar Roma politics – as among the Gabors – include the accumulation of relational capital (through, primarily, marriage politics – that is, the establishment of marital alliances with politically successful Cărhar families – and through the building of a social network consisting of consanguineous male relatives and co-fathers-in-law); behaviour (*phirajimo*) – in other words, adherence to the Cărhar Roma ethics of managing social relations and interactions and efforts to maintain a positive public image; and the accumulation of patrilineal prestige. In these symbolic arenas of politics the participants attempt to create, represent, and shape prestige differences between individuals, families, local communities, and patrilines. Like the Gabors, the Cărhar Roma also use the honorific title "big [Cărhar Roma] man" (*baro řom*) to refer to the men who are the most successful in politics in their own Roma ethnic population and therefore the most desirable – but, for many, inaccessible – targets in the search for co-fathers-in-law.

The Cărhars also tend to get involved in intense proprietary contests for valuable and sought-after beakers and tankards. The owners of the more precious pieces – just like the Gabor possessors – strive to keep them out of the circulation of commodities for as long as possible; that is, to keep them in their possession and pass them down to their sons. They only ever sell these objects, or pawn them as securities in loan transactions, as a last resort. The beakers and tankards are an important means of conceptualizing and materializing Cărhar Roma ethnic and patrilineal identity, past, and belonging, and are highly singularized; each has its own proper name and a unique composition of material properties. The Cărhars' prestige economy – like the Gabors' – is a translocal, ethnicized, informal, and gendered segment of the Romanian economy.

As we have seen, there is considerable similarity between the Gabor and the Cărhar prestige economies, and this is manifested primarily in the logic behind the attribution of meanings and values to the beakers and tankards. In both Roma ethnic populations, they are the most expensive commodities, highly esteemed political trophies, and symbols of both economic prosperity and ethnic and patrilineal identity and history. Moreover, the prestige-object aesthetics of the Gabor and the Cărhar Roma are very similar. It is, in part, this coincidence that ensures the inner dynamics of the interethnic prestige-object trade between the Gabors and the Cărhars that will be discussed in detail in chapter 8. There are, however, some striking differences between the two economies – these are summed up briefly as follows.

Material Patina

(1) *Value preferences concerning shape.* While the Gabors' and the Cărhars' prestige-object aesthetics agree in that the *burikato* and the octagonal/ *taxtaj andol pale* are the least valuable and least desirable types of beaker shape, they significantly diverge in their interpretation of the relationship between the *ščobo* and the footed shapes and in the importance attributed to them.

Unlike in the Gabor Roma ethnic population, where – as mentioned – the popularity and value of the *ščobo* shape and the number of these beakers have shown a decreasing trend since the decades preceding the 1989 political regime change, the *ščobo* beaker shape is still sought-after and highly esteemed in many Cărhar Roma local communities (a significant number of them are found in the Olt River area). In several Cărhar communities the number of *ščobo* objects exceeds the number of footed beakers.

Opinions voiced by my Cărhar hosts concerning the most sought-after beaker shape in their Roma ethnic population displayed surprising variation. While many of them maintained that the footed beaker shape was the most valuable, others claimed the same of the *ščobo* shape, and still others were of the opinion that both types of beaker shape were equally valuable and there was no significant difference between them. Opinions concerning the respective ranking of these beaker shapes were mixed not only at the level of individual value preferences – this is clearly shown by the regional variation discussed next. My interlocutors from Rupuno, who earn their living partially by making copper objects, for example, almost unanimously agreed that for them the most valuable shape is the footed beaker, while the great majority of my Cărhar acquaintances living in the Olt River area either saw little difference in value between the footed and the *ščobo* shapes or maintained that the most sought-after shape was the *ščobo*. (I observed no similar regional division of opinion among the Gabors.)

Many Cărhar individuals argued that the footed beakers were "Hungarian beakers" (*ungriko taxtaj*) – that is, objects of Hungarian origin, which "were mostly made by Hungarian silversmiths" and came to them "from Hungarian aristocrats" (and others). In contrast, they identified the pieces with a *ščobo* shape as "Romanian beakers [pieces having a Romanian origin]" (*vlašiko taxtaj*). The nationalization or ethnicization of beaker shapes is a remarkable practice, particularly because many of the Cărhar Roma assumed that the increased value and popularity of footed beakers among the Cărhars in Rupuno and in some other Cărhar Roma communities was in fact a phenomenon taken over from the Gabors. (The Cărhars regard the latter as "Hungarian Roma" because most of them live in regions of Romania with a Hungarian majority.)

The question of the difference in value between beakers and tankards is a further striking example of the differences between the two prestige-object aesthetics. Many of my Cărhar interlocutors saw no major difference between the social significance of the object classes of tankards and beakers, and several of them argued that the former were slightly more attractive and sought after than the latter. In contrast, the Gabor Roma I met thought without exception that – in their own Roma ethnic population – the tankards had much more modest significance than the beakers. The development of this discrepancy probably owes a great deal to the fact that the Cărhars own several times more tankards than the Gabors do; these objects are therefore much less frequently the topic of conversation or focus of social interest at Gabor Roma gatherings, and there are few intense proprietary contests for them.

(2) *Size expressed in capacity.* While the Gabors regard beakers with a capacity of about one litre to be an ideal size, the most sought-after beakers among the Cărhars have a capacity of about one-and-a-half litres – more precisely, thirteen decilitres or more. Many Cărhar Roma – most of them living in the Olt River area – argued that the value and significance attributed to an object's size increased in proportion to its capacity; "the larger [a beaker], the more valuable it is" (*te maj baro-j, maj valorime-j*). As noted in chapter 4, this in part explains why in the second half of the twentieth century the Cărhars were keen to buy the large and usually sparsely decorated beakers that, because of shifts in the Gabors' prestige-object aesthetics, had suffered a significant loss of value among the Gabor Roma. The Cărhars currently own many beakers with capacities approaching or exceeding two and a half litres – some of my Cărhar hosts, though, believed that a capacity much larger than that decreased rather than increased the value of a piece.

Some sort of regional variation can be observed not only in the popularity of beaker shapes but also in what is held to be an ideal size. In contrast with the Cărhars living in the Olt River area, my interlocutors from Rupuno considered markedly large beakers to be less attractive. Several of the Roma from Rupuno invoked the following stereotype to characterize this regional division: "The Olt Roma [the Cărhars living in the Olt River area], they pay for the big size [they want and value an object with a capacity as large as possible]! Even if the material [silver] of the piece is no good [not of good quality], as long as it's big! But we [the Cărhars from Rupuno] don't do that" (*Ol Voltaje, von den preco po barimo! Vi dakă o materialo na-j lašo andră leh, numa t'al baro! Ame na-j*). Consistent with what has been said so far, all of the Roma from Rupuno I talked to were agreed that the most valuable of all the prestige objects currently located in Rupuno is a footed beaker with a capacity approaching two litres that was bought from the Gabors in the late 1930s. (Similar regional variation with respect to size expressed in capacity is not found in the case of the Gabor Roma.)

Every single one of my Cărhar acquaintances defined a capacity of less than twelve or thirteen decilitres as less attractive and characterized it as too small (*pre cino*). (The 7.5-decilitre beaker that changed hands among the Gabors in 2009 for the highest-ever purchase price – US$1,200,000 – was considered disturbingly small by most of them.) Since a prestige-object sale is a rare occasion among the Cărhars, even a small-capacity piece quickly finds a new owner among them and – provided that they have desirable material properties – some of the Gabor beakers smaller than one litre also find a buyer in their Roma ethnic population. Many of my Cărhar hosts noted, however, that beakers with a capacity of less than one litre tend to be bought by "the poorer of the Roma" (*maj čoŕŕă ŕoma*), men "in the second class or third class" (*categorie a două, categorie a treia*). One of the explanations they gave for their preference for larger objects was that in the old days, the size of the beakers commissioned by Transylvanian aristocrats was the most effective way of demonstrating their wealth, since the larger a piece's capacity, the more silver was needed to make it; only genuinely affluent people could afford to buy such an object. This explanation, therefore, suggests that the greater a beaker's size and weight, the wealthier was the non-Roma person who had it made.

(3) *The quality and condition of the silver*. Both Roma prestige-object aesthetics attribute great significance to the quality and condition of the silver. The value-increasing properties of a piece with regard to its silver include, among others, (a) the purity of the silver – that is, the smaller the amount of other materials it contains, the better; (b) a dull,

dark tone unevenly distributed; and (c) numerous minor discolorations and damages on the surface (scratches, dents, and signs of wear). The members of both Roma ethnic populations were thus wary of conspicuously shiny objects with relatively undamaged surfaces, because they were convinced those had been made only recently and therefore represented a modest value. My Cărhar acquaintances, however, attributed greater significance to markers that served as evidence of the age of the silver and paid more careful attention to them than did the Gabors. The explanation for this difference is likely the fact that the Cărhars own a substantially greater number of modestly decorated and large *ščobo* and footed beakers, and the condition of the silver is practically the only guide that can be used to determine their age. Therefore, when perusing the catalogues of auction houses and museums, the vast majority of my Cărhar hosts regarded the silver pieces which had lost most of their natural patina due to restoration efforts and delicate handling as newly made, worthless objects in spite of the fact that these publications offered several pieces of evidence (the maker's mark, non-Roma ownership history, and so on) indicating that the beakers and tankards in question had been made hundreds of years before.

(4) *The abundance of decorations.* A striking difference between the two prestige-object aesthetics is that while the Gabors regard the richness of decorations as a value-increasing property and define the "whiteness" of the surface of a beaker or tankard – that is, the absence of decorations – as a value-decreasing attribute best avoided, most of the Cărhars I met felt that a richly decorated surface was distracting and unfavourable. For many of my Cărhar interlocutors, an ideal footed beaker is one with only a few decorative elements below the lip and the girdle and with an entirely undecorated band around the body where the beaker is held, since this allows a more reliable detection of signs of use – indicating age – and a closer inspection of the condition (and quality) of the silver. This quote sums it up: "One [object] that's simpler [more modestly decorated] is more authentic [old], more valuable" (*Savo maj simplu-j, kodo maj oridžinalo-j, maj valorime-j*). While viewing museum and auction house catalogues, when we came to a footed beaker with the central band covered in many plant or animal motifs several Cărhar Roma objected, "There are too many pictures [decorative elements] on it." Only a small group of them argued that the large number of the decorations was an unimportant feature that could be disregarded; that is, they contended that as long as "the silver was old" (*rup phurano*), the abundance of decorations did not make any difference.

The fact that most of my Cărhar hosts valued undecorated, "smooth" beaker surfaces more highly than an abundance of decorations can be explained largely by the importance attached to an object's embeddedness in history. More precisely, the explanation is to be found in a Cărhar ideology according to which the earliest-made pieces were entirely or almost entirely undecorated; decorations gradually proliferated and became more popular over the course of centuries. That is, the fewer decorations there are on a given item, the older and more valuable it is presumed to be. This ideology does not regard a relative sparseness of decorations – an object's being a "simple work [a surface having no or very few decorations]" (*simplavo butji*) – as a value-decreasing property. Rather, it is understood as evidence of the piece's embeddedness in history and is thus a value-increasing feature.

(5) *The types of decorations.* While many types of animal representations are sought-after, precious attributes according to the Gabors' prestige-object aesthetics, the vast majority of the Cărhars I talked to did not consider animal motifs (*animaluri*) to be desirable. On the contrary, they contended, "Animals [animal representations] are not valuable to us" (*Ol animaluri maškar amende na-j precome*). Browsing through museum and auction house catalogues or art historical publications, several of them commented that one or another piece we were looking at might be considered valuable among the Cărhars if only it had either no animals or fewer of them on it. Some of my Cărhar hosts consistently used the pejorative word "caricature" (*karikaturi*) when referring to the animal motifs, irrespective of their number and the quality of their workmanship. The representations of lions, horses, and bears, and the mythological or other creatures interpreted as "unexplainable animals" – held in high esteem by the Gabors – were not at all attractive to most of my Cărhar acquaintances.[7] Only a few of them, on seeing images of animals on the mantle of an object, said, "That's nothing [of no significance]" (*Na-j khanči*) or "It makes no difference. If the material [silver] of the piece is good, it makes no difference" (*Či kontil. Te o materialo lašo-j, či kontil*).

While the Gabors' prestige-object aesthetics regards animal representations as more valuable than plant motifs, my Cărhar hosts argued that although plant motifs were not particularly attractive, either, they were still more popular than animal representations. Most of them thought that a relatively small number of petite plant patterns "didn't do anything [caused no loss of value]" (*či kărăn khanči*) and "[were] not bad [did not have a value-decreasing effect]" (*na-j žungale*). A large number of conspicuous plant motifs (covering, for example, the handhold strip), however, would have an undesirable effect on the value of the object.

Another striking difference between the prestige-object aesthetics of the two Roma ethnic populations is that the Cărhars place less emphasis on the gender-based distinction of decorations and attribute less significance to the value difference between feminine and masculine decorative elements than the Gabor Roma do. For my Gabor interlocutors, motifs depicting men seen on the beakers and tankards – portraits of old, bearded men, soldiers, and so on – are substantially more valuable decorative elements than are portraits or full-figure representations of women. One reason is that the latter decorations provide an opportunity for the owner's political rivals to assign the adjective "feminine" (*žuvlikano/žuvlikani*) to the piece – which suggests that "the object is of only modest significance" and therefore has a negative effect on the value of the piece and the renown of its owner.

Many of the decorations regarded as desirable by the Cărhars are enumerated in a commentary by one of my Cărhar hosts from Sibiu County. To my question "Which are the most precious beakers?" he replied, "The ones with people on them, the heads [portraits] of emperors or old men, the ones showing bearded old men or saints, those are the old beakers, the good ones among us" (*Kaj sîn manuš, ol šără le împăracăngă, le manušhengă le phurăngă, kaj sîn phură le šorenca pre leh, ol sfînci, kodola-j ol taxtaja ol phurane, ol laśe maškar amende*). The more valuable decorative elements include representations of various human figures; portraits of, for example, elderly, bearded men, monarchs (identified by some of my acquaintances as historical figures such as Caesar or Maria Theresa), or other aristocrats; saints; rich firegilding; antique coins engraved in the mantle of the object, attached to its wall, or built into it; finely elaborated surface patterns of different shapes similar to snakeskin, fish scales, or beans (on *ščobo* beakers); and medallions (*pažga*) decorated with dates, coats of arms, names, or other inscriptions and figures.

Symbolic Patina

The Cărhars consider an esteemed, attractive ownership history developed within their own Roma ethnic population and excellent material properties as the ideal combination of features for a prestige object. They do not show interest in the non-Roma or other, non-Cărhar Roma phase of a piece's social life. My Cărhar hosts were all of the opinion that whether a piece came from a museum, an antiques dealer, or a congregation of the Reformed Church, neither its maker nor its former non-Roma or other, non-Cărhar Roma possessors made any difference in the significance they attributed to it. A typical comment relating to this question was, "No, it makes no difference to us where the beaker is from as long as it has good, old material" (*Na, či kontil amende kathar-i o taxtaj, numa te'l o materialo lašo, phurano*). According to their interpretation, previous non-Roma or other, non-Cărhar Roma owners are not part of the segment of ownership history that they define as valuable. This is why, when determining the price and estimating the importance of a beaker or tankard, my Cărhar acquintances took into account only previous possessors (and their renown and prestige) from their own Roma ethnic population; that is, they regarded these objects as precious materializations of their own Roma ethnic past and identity. The value of the ownership history of a beaker or tankard is estimated primarily on the basis of how successful its Cărhar Roma owners were in politics *within* their own Roma ethnic population.

However, in the case of prestige objects bought from the Gabors, a certain regional deviation can be observed – an exception to the rule. Several members of the Cărhar local community in Rupuno emphasized that in the case of some pieces bought from exceptionally influential Gabor men, the political prestige of the Gabor seller sometimes was remembered when the renown of the object purchased from him was evaluated among the Cărhars. (One of them argued that it is to the advantage of the piece coming from the Gabors if it is passed from one "big man" [*baro řom*] to another "big man," even if this involves its crossing the border between the two Roma ethnic populations.) They quickly added, though, that they would much rather buy beakers and tankards from members of their own Roma ethnic population than from a Gabor owner. This is partly because they attribute an incomparably greater value to a Cărhar Roma ownership history than to "big Gabor Roma men" and partly because they are much more familiar with the material properties of objects changing hands among themselves. By preferring to buy pieces within their own Roma ethnic population they can reduce the chance of accidentally buying a recently made, antiqued copy for the same high price usually paid for important Gabor prestige objects of complete value (see chapter 9).

The occasional modest interest in highly respectable former Gabor owners observed among the Cărhars living in Rupuno might be explained primarily by the fact that the contact and flow of information between the two Roma ethnic populations is the most intense in the region where Rupuno is located; in my experience, the Cărhars in Rupuno have the most detailed knowledge of the ownership histories and material properties of the more important Gabor beakers and tankards and of the memorable events, such as sales transactions or proprietary contests, connected to them. This intense relationship and exchange of information can be traced back to several factors. First, to spatial proximity – that is, to the circumstance that the Cărhars living in the north of Sibiu County are geographically the closest to Mureş County, which is densely populated by Gabor Roma. The Cărhars in Rupuno, for instance, frequently meet and talk to Gabor Roma when visiting the market in a nearby small town. Second, since the Gabors consider Rupuno to have the largest and wealthiest of the Cărhar Roma local communities, with outstanding purchasing power, they like to visit members of that community when they have a prestige object for sale; as a result, the Cărhars in Rupuno own quite a few beakers and tankards bought from the Gabors. Third, Rupuno is the place of residence of one of the most famous and successful Cărhar brokers, well-known to the Gabors, who often participates in the organization of interethnic prestige-object transactions.

In contrast, my Cărhar acquaintances living in places other than Rupuno unanimously considered a Gabor Roma ownership history to be equally or almost as unimportant to them as the non-Roma biography of an object; that is, there was no difference – or only a negligible difference – in their attitudes towards the social careers of beakers and tankards from museums or antiques dealers and those of prestige objects bought from the Gabors. To quote just two of them:

It makes no difference that it comes from the Gabors as long as its material is good. As long as it's a good beaker … It's the material that matters to us. We don't need the Gabors [as previous owners]. (24 September 2011)

The Gabors are not valuable to us [as the former possessors of the objects bought from them]. They are valuable to themselves! We're a different nation [different Roma ethnic population], they're a different nation. The Gabors. We are Roma, they are Hungarians, Hungarian Roma. They are Hungarian Roma. They speak Romani and Hungarian, too. (28 September 2011)

Their indifference towards the Gabor object biographies explains why
several of my Cărhar hosts living in settlements in the Olt River area
were unable to recall either the names of the Gabor Roma who had
sold their beakers to them a few decades previously or which Transylvanian settlements they were from. The few Cărhar individuals whom
Gabor owners looking for Cărhar buyers or creditors regularly entrust
with the task of brokering in prestige-object transactions were naturally
much better informed.

As previously discussed, the Cărhar Roma take two aspects into
account when assessing a piece's price and value: its material properties and the segment of its ownership history linked with their own
Roma ethnic population. However, unlike the Gabors, who regard
these two aspects of value as equally important, the majority of my
Cărhar interlocutors gave greater weight to *materialo* (material – that
is, to material properties) and attributed more modest significance to
ownership history (i.e., to symbolic patina). Typical comments were
"The material goes first [it's the more important]" (*O materialo žal angle*)
and "A beaker is valued highly because of its workmanship [material
properties]" (*O kărimo le taxtako thol o preco pre lehte*). Many of these
Cărhar Roma expressed the opinion that the Gabors attributed an
unjustifiable degree of significance to the *veste* – that is, to the renown
of former Gabor owners – and undervalued the importance of material
properties: "The renown [deriving from the ownership history] of the
object is the important thing [for the Gabors], yes! They [the Gabors]
say, 'X's beaker!!' It's not like that with us [with the Cărhars]. The material goes first for us [the material attributes are the most important]!"
(*E veste kontil, da! Von phenen: "Le X-ehko taxtaj!" Amende na-j. Amende
o materialo žal angle!*) In fact, some of my Cărhar acquaintances defined
even the Cărhar ownership histories of beakers and tankards offered
for sale in their own Roma ethnic population as of only marginal social
and economic significance.

Inheritance

One of the salient interethnic differences with respect to prestige objects
concerns inheritance. Among the Gabors, beakers and tankards can be
inherited by sons only. The most valuable item in the father's possession is passed down to the eldest son, the prestige object second in
the value ranking is inherited by the second-born son, and so on. The
Gabors very rarely deviate from this logic of inheritance; when they

do, it usually has something to do with a serious breach in the relationship between father and son or an heir's mental or other illness. As mentioned in chapter 2, during my fieldwork I learnt only of three exceptional cases in which the Gabor parents of a future wife gave a beaker in lieu of the marriage payment to the future husband's parents. In each case, the father had more prestige objects than he had sons and could not muster the marriage payment in time. The explanation for this choice was that substituting a prestige object for a marriage payment was less shameful than putting it up for sale, since in the former case the piece in question would, in a certain sense, "remain in the family" of the previous owner.

In the Cărhar Roma ethnic population, too, an ideal situation is when a father's prestige object is inherited by his son. In contrast with the Gabors, however, my Cărhar interlocutors did not define having no male child as an especially shameful or worrying state that would incur intense negative social or emotional consequences.[8] A strategy often used by Cărhar parents with only female children is to bring a son-in-law (žamutro) into the household – that is, to form a marital alliance with someone who has more than one son and does not object to one of them moving into the house of his co-father-in-law. In this situation, the property of the wife's father (prestige objects, house, and so on) is inherited by his daughter and son-in-law and then by their children. The Gabor Roma resort far less often to the strategy of bringing a son-in-law into the household – mainly in cases where a daughter of marriageable age is struggling with serious health problems and no fathers show any interest in seeking her hand in marriage for their sons. (In the majority of the Gabor Roma cases I documented, the son who moved in with the well-to-do family of his future wife was an orphan and lived in very modest circumstances; he accepted the marriage offer mainly in the hope that it would bring him financial security.)

Daughters, therefore, relatively often inherit prestige objects among the Cărhars. This is, in my opinion, best explained by the fact that they neither attribute as much significance to prestige difference between genders as the Gabors nor wish that a young couple have a male child at all costs. For my Cărhar acquaintances, an ideal family consists of two parents, a son, and a daughter, and a couple relatively rarely had more than two children.[9] The aim of this preference is twofold: it precludes the fragmentation of the paternal inheritance – more precisely, it avoids the son who inherits his father's prestige object having to pay compensation to his brother(s) – and it creates the possibility that the sums of the marriage payment the parents will give and receive can be more or less similar.

Among the Gabor Roma, the responsibility of taking care of parents falls on the youngest son; he lives with his parents until their death and takes on most of the responsibility of supporting them. In return, he will inherit the parents' house (regardless of whether or not his father has a prestige object – which would, as mentioned above, go to his eldest son). In contrast, in Cărhar families with a beaker or tankard, the parents share their home with the son who will inherit their prestige object (i.e., they live "where the beaker [or tankard] will remain" [*kaj te ašel o taxtaj*]). In the Cărhar Roma ethnic population, as among the Gabor Roma, it is (usually) the oldest son who inherits the most valuable prestige object (or the only prestige object if his father has only one beaker or tankard). In recent decades, however, a regional variation has emerged in connection with this logic of inheritance. In the Cărhar community of Rupuno the former tradition changed sometime in the past thirty or forty years; here, the only or the most valuable prestige object is inherited by the youngest son, and the parents share their home with him. As was noted by an elderly woman from Rupuno, "We had the same tradition before [as the other Cărhar local communities]. Thirty or forty years ago. The beaker was given to the elder son and they [the parents] stayed with him. But it's [the custom] changed" (*Maj anglal sa kade sah e tradicije. Tranda bărš, štarvardeš bărš. Dena o taxtaj le barăhkă, the le barăsa ašenah. Ba parudjilah*).

The gendered practice of *boldimo* (the meaning of which is best captured by the concept of compensation) can be observed in both Roma ethnic populations. It usually takes the form of cash and changes hands between two brothers.

A *boldimo* is given among the Gabor Roma (a) when a younger brother inherits from his father a more valuable beaker or tankard than is his due based on birth order; or (b) if the parents give a younger son their only prestige object, to which the elder son would normally be entitled, leaving the latter without a beaker or tankard. Departure from the general inheritance practice usually happens if the younger son is "much more open" (*maj puterdo*), a great deal cleverer and shrewder than his older brother, who is "foolish" (*dilo*), or if the older son is seriously ill; in either case, the older son is probably unsuited to keeping the more valuable or only piece in his possession in the long term. Another frequent reason would be a spectacular deterioration in relations between an elder son and his parents. The younger brother inheriting the more valuable piece (or the only one) is expected to give compensation to his elder brother, and payment of this compensation is a generally expected moral obligation. (c) A *boldimo* may occasionally also be given among the Gabors when inheritance follows the customary logic and a father has more than one son but only one prestige object – in this case, some heirs pay compensation (a symbolic sum) to their brother(s). The latter is a rare occurrence, however, and my interlocutors defined it as a discretionary gesture aimed at demonstrating and reproducing a harmonious relationship between the brothers.

My experiences suggest that *boldimo*s are paid considerably more frequently among the Cărhars, where it is a more intensely controlled and generally expected moral obligation in all three situation types mentioned above. That is, compensation is given not only when a younger son inherits a more precious beaker or tankard than is his due based on birth order, or if he inherits the father's only prestige object, but also when the order of inheritance is left undisturbed but the father has more sons than prestige objects; in the latter case, "the older [brother who inherits the beaker or tankard] gives a *boldimo* to the younger [brother who is left without a prestige object]"[10] (*boldel o maj baro le cinehkă*). The sum paid as compensation is a function of an agreement between the brothers. Several of my Cărhar acquaintances argued that the *boldimo* should ideally reach or approach half of the estimated value of the silver object bequeathed by the father.

Prestige Objects and Marriage Politics: "We Marry Our Daughters after the Beakers"

The most salient difference between the two Roma ethnic populations with respect to their prestige economies is connected to their marriage politics, which are based on arranged marriages. Patrilocal, endogamous arranged marriage (often of children) is a common practice both among the Gabors and the Cărhars; that is, the parents select their child's future spouse from among the members of their own respective Roma ethnic population, and the choice of partner, the betrothal, and the wedding are arranged, overseen, and controlled primarily by the parents and grandparents rather than by the young people. A marriage is accompanied by a marital alliance between the young couple's parents and is an important means and symbolic arena of the Roma politics equally characteristic of the Cărhars and the Gabors. In choosing a partner for their children, the primary consideration of a substantial proportion of parents is that the marital alliance should be made with a politically successful individual, which would increase their own and their family's social reputation. In both ethnic populations, any valuable prestige objects in the possession of potential co-fathers-in-law are important markers and proof of economic stability or prosperity, as well as sources of prestige and respectability, and therefore contribute greatly to enhancing the (marriage) political attractiveness of their owners.

While for the Gabor Roma the link between the prestige economy and marriage politics is essentially limited to the relationship discussed in the previous sentence, there is a substantially more intense and complex link among the Cărhars. It is worth emphasizing that the marriage payment changing hands during the wedding as a part of the dowry flows from the parents of the wife to the parents of the husband among both the Cărhars and the Gabors; that is, they "pay for the boy." This stands in contrast with common practice among the vast majority of Roma ethnic populations, where the direction of payment is reversed; the parents of the future husband pay a bride price to the parents of the future wife; that is, they "pay for the girl."

The Cărhars distinguish two types of marriage: one labelled *skimbo* (from the Romanian term *schimb*, meaning "exchange") and one called *separat* (from the Romanian term *separat*, meaning "separate") or *particular* (from the Romanian term *particular*, meaning "particular").

(1) *Wife exchange.* In *skimbo* marriages, the parents forming a marital alliance with each other exchange girls; that is, they each "give and receive a daughter-in-law." In this case, the dowry is limited to the clothing given with the girl, but no money changes hands between the families, and the prestige objects of the co-fathers-in-law remain at their pre-marriage locations – that is, with their owners. My hosts varied in their opinion of *skimbo* marriages. Some of them argued that this type of marriage is a marker of a low economic status, since a *skimbo* marriage is usually given preference by individuals with modest incomes who have no hope of putting together a substantial marriage payment as a part of the dowry. Others, however, thought that a *skimbo* marriage has the advantage that it allows the parents to exercise more intense control over what happens to their daughter in the family of her husband, due to the fact that any atrocities befalling her "can be directly and immediately revenged on their own daughter-in-law." A *skimbo* marriage is

a rare phenomenon between families with substantially different social and economic statuses.

(2) *The* separat *or* particular *marriage.* The common features of *separat* marriages are that only one marriage takes place, and that the parents of the future wife give a dowry with their daughter, which comprises a previously agreed-upon sum as marriage payment and some clothing for her personal use. The *separat* Cărhar marriages I observed and the remarks of my Cărhar acquaintances both suggest that a marriage payment of around 100,000 new Romanian lei (about US$28,700) or more counts as a large cash gift commanding respect. (Sometimes a marriage payment may considerably exceed that sum.) It is often handed over after the wedding, sometimes only when the first child has been born to the young couple, which contributes to the stabilization (*stabilizime*) of both the marriage and the marital alliance – that is, after the likelihood of their dissolution has substantially decreased. The sum of the marriage payment is decided through a process of bargaining in which the political successes of the future co-fathers-in-law and their families – with special regard to the values of their beakers and tankards – are among the most important factors. The sum of the marriage payment reflects first and foremost the value of the prestige object that will be bequeathed to the future husband by his father. In other words, the more valuable the prestige object that the future husband will inherit, the larger the sum of the marriage payment that his father can request from the father of his future daughter-in-law. This is clearly indicated by the following expressions often used by my interlocutors: "The marriage payment is paid after the prestige object" (*Pal e avere źal e zestre*) – that is, the sum of the former is decided primarily on the basis of the value attributed to the latter; and "We marry our daughters after the beakers [according to the value of the beakers]" (*Amen meritisarah le śejen pale taxtaja*). The following longer commentaries also corroborate this connection:

> The marriage payment goes after the *taxtaj* [the former is adjusted to the latter]. After the *taxtaj*. How good [valuable] the beaker is. If it's not too valuable [the prestige object], it's smaller [the sum of the marriage payment]. Smaller. 500 million [old Romanian lei, equivalent to new Romanian lei 50,000 = US$14,313], 300 million [old Romanian lei, equivalent to new Romanian lei 30,000 = US$8,588], 400 million [old Romanian lei, equivalent to new Romanian lei 40,000 = US$11,451]. How

the man is [how successful the future husband's father is in Roma politics] and [how valuable] the beaker is [that the future husband will inherit]. (25 November 2012)

A man [seeking a wife for his son] asks for a marriage payment on the basis of his prestige object [consistent with its value]. That his son will have [on the basis of the beaker or tankard the son will inherit from his father]. If he's got a good *taxtaj*, a big one, the marriage payment will also be bigger! But if his beaker is smaller, the marriage payment will also be smaller. (21 June 2012)

Besides the value of the prestige object(s) constituting part of the inheritance of the future husband, other factors may also affect the process of bargaining over the marriage payment. Since among the Cărhar Roma marriage politics is an important means of upward social mobility, men with low social prestige but substantial wealth often try to persuade an influential individual widely regarded as respected and attractive to choose them from among competing co-father-in-law candidates, by increasing the sum of the promised marriage payment and outbidding their competitors. For individuals with similar social and economic positions who are connected by harmonious and close kinship or friendship ties, the formation of the marital alliance is often a means of representing and reproducing solidarity, trust, and social closeness.[11] In the latter situation, the marriage payment may lose some of its political significance, a fact that is manifested primarily in the parties taking each other's financial constraints into greater consideration when making a decision on the sum or in their postponing the bargaining over the marriage payment until after the wedding.

Many Cărhar families have neither a beaker nor a tankard. My well-to-do acquaintances who owned prestige objects characterized most of these families as "poor" (*čořřo*), and tried to avoid forming marital alliances with them. Many of the men without a beaker or tankard are, however, themselves affluent, and their patrilineal forebears owned prestige objects (often for generations). The reason that these individuals do not currently own either a beaker or tankard is most often because the ones in the possession of their fathers were inherited by their brothers, and they have not had an opportunity to buy a prestige object even though they possess considerable cash reserves and political ambitions. Men with neither beaker nor tankard are no exception to the rule that political achievements and the degree of individual political ambition exert a powerful influence when it comes to bargaining over marriage payments. As suggested by the comments quoted above, the marriage payments that change hands in this situation are more modest than the sums that fathers (of sons) with valuable prestige objects can expect.

My interlocutors maintained that there were a number of advantages to a *separat* marriage: among other things, it may offer an occasion for fathers of daughters to represent their wealth (by making a large marriage payment) and achieve upward social mobility. In addition, it gives both co-fathers-in-law more opportunities to increase their intraethnic relational capital, since they can form marital alliances with more families than if they were to choose a wife exchange.

The Prestige Object as a Security Temporarily Handed Over to the Co-Father-in-Law Providing the Wife

It is worth distinguishing two types of *separat* marriages. One type comprises marriages in which the husband's father does not own a prestige object or, if he does, it remains under his supervision after the wedding; that is, he does not offer anything as a guarantee or security against the marriage payment received with his daughter-in-law. In this case "only his spoken pledge remains [as a security]" (*ašel numa [and]e vorba*) as part of the agreement concerning the marital alliance.

The other type of *separat* marriages are those in which, at the time of the wedding, the husband's father hands over his own prestige object – or one of his prestige objects – to his new co-father-in-law for temporary safekeeping. When referring to pieces looked after by the parents of a daughter-in-law, my Cărhar hosts used the words *amaneto* (from the Romanian term *amanet*, meaning "pledge") or *garancije* (from the Romanian term *garanție*, meaning "security"). The duration of safekeeping is a function of an agreement between the co-fathers-in-law; the beaker or tankard is usually returned after the birth of the first male child. If the future husband is to inherit more than one prestige object from his father, in addition to negotiating the duration of safekeeping, the parties also have to decide which of the pieces should be handed over to the future wife's father. The latter often makes a specific suggestion on the subject, which his future co-father-in-law may accept as a sign of trust, respect, social closeness, or political ambition. Alternately, he may reject the suggestion and offer another, less valuable, one of his prestige objects as a security.[12]

The future husband's father, however, is not obliged to temporarily hand over a beaker or tankard; this is an optional practice, and, using his best judgment, an owner may or may not comply with it. A reluctance to transfer a prestige object on a temporary basis is usually rooted in a lack of trust, a significant status difference between the parties (in favour of the future husband's parents), or the absence of an intense commitment to the formation of the marital alliance. Some of my Cărhar hosts categorically refused to part with their beakers or tankards, because they were afraid that their future co-father-in-law might keep the piece deposited as a security longer than agreed or even indefinitely (citing some fabricated reason if, for instance, a conflict developed between the two families in the future, or if the object in question became especially dear to him; see also the next section in this chapter). In one case, for example, a daughter-in-law's father repeatedly delayed showing the beaker, temporarily deposited with him as a security, to its owner – that is, his co-father-in-law – despite the latter's repeated requests, out of a wish for revenge when the relationship between the two families deteriorated after the wedding. This became a source of speculation and intense distress, with the owner and his family conjecturing that the co-father-in-law had perhaps sold the piece in question in secret or damaged it out of anger. The rejection of a request to hand over a security does not necessarily thwart the marriage – especially when the family providing the wife is less successful in politics and the marriage promises them substantial reputational profit.

It is of crucial importance that only the piece that the son being married will inherit from his father can be handed over to the co-father-in-law as a security at the time of the wedding. As was mentioned, if the father has fewer prestige objects than sons, he may ask his future co-father-in-law for a higher marriage payment for the son to whom he will bequeath a beaker or tankard than for the son of whom it is known that he will not inherit a prestige object.

The outcome of the negotiations about the temporary transfer – the choice of piece, for instance – depends first and foremost on the prestige relations between the parties, their personal attitudes and relationship, and their political ambitions. According to my Cărhar interlocutors, the social significance of temporary transfer derives from two sources.

(1) The process of bargaining over the transfer of supervision is an obvious means and arena of representing and shaping political relations between the families entering the marital alliance.

(2) Some of the significance of the temporary transfer of a prestige object comes from the fact that the wife's father can use this piece to exert a degree of influence on his daughter's treatment in her new family. It can preclude, for example, morally objectionable behaviour towards her, just as it can prevent her from being sent home by her father-in-law, who might dissolve the marriage and the marital alliance under the pretext of a fabricated reason – a "false reason" (*motivo xox-amno*) – if, for instance, he receives a new, more advantageous offer of marital alliance. In the words of one my acquaintances, having tempo-rary supervision of a beaker or tankard ensures for the father of a wife that "the husband won't beat her [his wife], won't send her home [to her parents], will stay with her ... and won't replace her with another wife" (*či mară la, či del lako drom, bešel lasa ... či lel aver ŕomnji te anel opral pre late*). By openly contemplating the temporary (or indefinite) withholding of the piece taken as a security, the parents of a wife can put some pressure on their co-father-in-law should the need arise to make sure that the latter acts in accordance with the Cărhar Roma eth-ics of managing social relations and interactions – that, for instance, he fulfils the promises he made when arranging the marital alliance and does not send their daughter home unless there is a socially acceptable reason for doing so.

Another situation in which a beaker or tankard deposited as a secu-rity may also play a crucial role is in the event of a divorce, especially when no unequivocal decision can be made as to who is to blame for the divorce or if one of the parties questions the validity of the rele-vant evidence, either of which could lead to a deepening of the con-flict between the two families. In this situation, too, the former wife's father can put pressure on his former co-father-in-law by withholding, or threatening to withhold, the beaker or tankard deposited with him as a security. Therefore, this piece can have a considerable effect on negotiations about the distribution of blame for the divorce (whether the former husband or the wife should primarily be held responsible) and, consequently, which family should be expected to pay symbolic damages (who should "pay for the shame") and what would be a mor-ally acceptable sum. If it is decided that the divorce is the former wife's fault – because she is medically proven not to be able to conceive a child or she suffers from a serious illness that was not discovered by the former husband and his family until after the wedding – her father is obligated to return the prestige object he took for safekeeping and to do so without recompense, and the former husband's father is entitled to request compensation for the shame he has had to endure (which is often subtracted from the marriage payment he has to return) and to be repaid the sum he spent on organizing the wedding. If the former husband bears the responsibility for the divorce, the former wife's father is obligated to return his former co-father-in-law's prestige object, but he has the right to request the return of the marriage payment in full and to have the former husband's father both pay his expenses in connection with the wedding and "pay for the shame befalling him and his family."

If there is a disagreement about who is to blame for the failure of the marriage, one of the families involved may call a *Romani kris*, where influential Cărhar men from various settlements come together to help the families reach a consensus acceptable to both of them, in accord with the Cărhar Roma ethics of sociability. Several of my hosts noted, however, that the justice administered by the *kris* is worth little if the father of the former wife is an influential person and insists that his daughter was not responsible for the divorce. In this case, the family of the former husband – even if he is blameless – has no choice but to "pay for the shame" – that is, to act as if they accepted responsibility for the events in order to get back (in effect buy back) the prestige object they handed over as a security.

The conflict is more difficult to manage if the couple already have one or more children when they divorce. My Cărhar acquaintances agreed that if a little girl stays with her mother, the prestige object kept as a security should be returned, but the family of the former husband is expected to offer a sum of money (depositing it in a bank account or paying it in cash) towards her future marriage payment. That is, the father supports his daughter's upbringing and future marriage. Opinions regarding the right course of action when a male child stays with the mother vary, however, and what happens in practice is also heterogeneous. Several of my Cărhar interlocutors maintained that people often followed the logic described above; the prestige object was returned to its owner, and the family of the former daughter-in-law received a given sum of money to cover some of the costs of bringing up the male child – which is exactly what happened in many of the cases I monitored. Others argued, however, that if the little boy stayed with his mother's parents and grew up under their supervision, the father of the former daughter-in-law might have a claim to the prestige object previously deposited with him by his former co-father-in-law as a security, and might wish to keep it in his family so that it could become the – paternal – inheritance of the boy.

To sum up: the temporary transfer of the prestige object owned by the husband's father is the materialization of his commitment to establishing the marital alliance, which may be motivated by considerations such as political ambitions, trust, respect, and social closeness (or often a combination of these). The efficacy of this strategy derives mostly from the fact that the husband's father voluntarily provides his co-father-in-law with a means of putting pressure on him and his family should he need to do so. A rejection of the transfer of a beaker or tankard is usually rooted in a lack of business trust or the absence of an intense desire to establish the marital alliance, or in an asymmetry of prestige relations between the future co-fathers-in-law; that is, it often reflects social and political differences.

It is unknown among the Gabors for the father of a husband to temporarily hand over his prestige object to the parents of his daughter-in-law as a security.

The Story of a Marriage Accompanied by the Transfer of a Beaker

The conflict story described below is an apt illustration of the dynamic and complex relationship between the Cărhar Roma prestige economy and marriage politics. The main character in the story is Anton, an outstandingly wealthy man who lives in one of the settlements in the Olt River area and owns more than half a dozen valuable prestige objects. Anton married off one of his granddaughters in the middle of the first decade of the twenty-first century. (Since his only son had died shortly after the turn of the millennium, Anton represented his granddaughter's interests during the marriage negotiations.) Anton formed a marital alliance with a similarly influential Cărhar family who also lived in one of the settlements in the Olt River area. His co-father-in-law – who belonged to the same generation as his deceased son – had only one son and owned two valuable prestige objects: a tankard and a beaker. The latter was a one-and-a-half-litre *ščobo* beaker with a snakeskin pattern and rich gilding on both the inside and outside. The outcome of the negotiations over the marital alliance was that the father of the husband would hand the above beaker over to Anton for temporary safekeeping, and that the beaker would stay with Anton until the birth of the first child to the young couple (the agreement was not recorded in writing). At the time of the wedding, Anton publically proclaimed that his granddaughter was both mentally and physically "healthy" (*sastevesti*) and that if her behaviour in her new family left something to be desired and her father-in-law were to send her home as a result, Anton – as dictated by the Cărhar Roma ethics of managing social relations and interactions – would return the prestige object taken as a security without a word. Anton contributed 50 million old Romanian lei to the organization of the wedding, the full costs of which exceeded 300 million old Romanian lei (US$10,955), and during the wedding gave his granddaughter 100 million old Romanian lei (US$3,652) as a *činste*.[13]

The marriage of the young couple, however, did not turn out as the parties involved had expected. Anton's granddaughter moved in with her husband's family but did not stay for long. She moved back with her grandfather from time to time, citing various reasons (according to some opinions, during the five years of their marriage, she spent no more than six months under the same roof as her husband); she did not give birth to a child; and her behaviour – excessive taciturnity, timidity, and similar signs – led her husband and his family to conclude that she was suffering from mental problems that rendered her unsuited to marriage. To quote just a few of the remarks on her behaviour: "The girl's sick, not right in the head" (*E śejori maj nasvali šărăhki*); "She's deranged" (*Dili*); and "She's not normal" (*Na-j normalo*). Her father-in-law finally sent her home to Anton for good, declaring that she bore the sole responsibility for the dissolution of the marriage and hoping that he would soon get back the beaker he had handed over as a security. (During these years, Anton had not given a marriage payment with his granddaughter.) Anton, however, stubbornly stuck to what he had claimed at the wedding, maintaining that his granddaughter was both physically and mentally healthy, and accused his former co-father-in-law of dissolving the marriage only because he had received a better offer of marital alliance. Anton took the sending home of his granddaughter as an overt face-threatening insult aimed at shaming him; he decided not to regard the marriage and marital alliance as dissolved and continued to keep his former co-father-in-law's beaker.

The divorce at the beginning of 2010 was followed by a deepening of the conflict between the two families. I witnessed one episode of this conflict when – in one of the settlements in the Olt River area in September 2011 – I attended a wedding to which both Anton and the supporters of his former co-father-in-law had been invited. A heated debate developed between Anton (who, aside from his wife, was accompanied by only one grandson in his early twenties) and his former co-father-in-law's supporters over who – the husband or Anton's granddaughter – had been responsible for the dissolution of their marriage, and whether Anton's decision to continue to hang onto the beaker deposited with him as a security was morally acceptable or not. (A vast majority of my interlocutors disapproved of Anton's behaviour.) Before the disagreement could turn into physical violence, and in an effort to protect Anton from further insults, the anxious father of the newly wed husband – our host – asked me to drive Anton to the home of the influential Cărhar man who was regarded as the *bulibaš* – that is, village leader – by the local Cărhar Roma. Anton spent more than three hours in the home of the *bulibaš* because he was afraid to go home before the last of the wedding guests dispersed. His worry was that his adversaries would wait for him on the way home so that they could continue the debate – and in that case he could not count on the support of anyone but his one grandson. (In the end, they did get home, and the conflict subsided, at least for that day.)

Over the course of the next few months, his former co-father-in-law repeatedly visited Anton and called on him to return his beaker, but these requests fell on deaf ears. After a while, he tried to involve the authorities in the management of the conflict by reporting Anton to them, but they did nothing to resolve the problem (partly because there was no written record of the agreement about the transfer of the prestige object as a security). Calling a *Ŕomani kris* did not appear to be a suitable way of obtaining a satisfactory resolution, since Anton – trusting his own affluence and relational capital – consistently ignored any criticism suggesting that his granddaughter was to blame for the divorce or that he no longer had the right to keep the prestige object.

Anton's former co-father-in-law then decided to try a different route in order to get his beaker back. He arranged a new marriage for his only son; this time, he brought a wife for him from another settlement in the Olt River area. His choice fell on an affluent family whose members – according to several of my Cărhar acquaintances – were especially effective in representing their interests during the management of economic and social conflicts, partly owing to their excellent non-Roma connections (with the police, for instance) and partly because, if the need arose, they did not shrink from threatening to use physical force.

The head of this family, Kalo, was in his early forties and had two daughters. He had inherited a total of four *ščobo* beakers from his father, three of which were considered to be valuable pieces in their Roma ethnic population but the fourth of which represented only a modest value; it had been made in 1887 using a material with a relatively low silver content, which was revealed in the series of brownish-green discolorations on its surface. Kalo's father had been given one of these beakers by his father-in-law in lieu of marriage payment at the time of his wedding (as Kalo's mother did not have any brothers), inherited two from his own father, and bought one from the Gabor Roma. He had purchased the latter *ščobo* beaker from a Gabor family living in a settlement in Mureş County in the mid-1980s. Since Kalo did not have a son, he had no choice but to bring a son-in-law into his family.[14]

The only son of Anton's former co-father-in-law and Kalo's younger daughter were married in May 2010 and have since had a son.[15] Their relationship is harmonious; "They get on well together." As had been decided during the negotiations over the marital alliance, Anton's former co-father-in-law handed his valuable tankard over to Kalo as a security, and they agreed that Kalo would return the object only when the first son was born to the young couple. (Kalo – like Anton – publically proclaimed at the wedding that if his daughter did not turn out to be "clever" [*godjaver*] and "healthy" and her father-in-law sent her home as a result, he would return the tankard taken as a security "within ten minutes.") Although Kalo – by his own admission – would have been prepared to pay as much as 200,000 new Romanian lei (approximately US$60,000) as marriage payment, his co-father-in-law did not insist on a concrete sum but instead proposed that Kalo pay only as much marriage payment as he would like over the next two or three years. However, the co-father-in-law's agreement to the marital alliance and the marriage was linked to one condition: that Kalo would get his beaker back from Anton, after which, like his tankard, it would be inherited by his only son – that is, Kalo's son-in-law. The agreement specified that all costs of getting the beaker back would be borne by Kalo. In Kalo's words, "What did he [Kalo's co-father-in-law] say? 'Give me as much marriage payment as you want, I'm not interested in the marriage payment. Give me as much as you want in the next two or three years ... But I have a condition: take my beaker from Anton and bring it back! I don't care how much it costs, just bring it back.'"

Since no other solution for putting an end to the conflict presented itself, at the time of our last conversation – in the summer of 2012 – Kalo and his co-father-in-law were planning to call a *Romani kris*. They were hoping to reach a public agreement on how much Kalo's co-father-in-law should pay Anton to return the beaker that had been deposited with him as a security – regardless of the fact that Kalo's co-father-in-law and his supporters still believed that Anton should feel morally obligated to return the object immediately and without recompense. Several of my interlocutors thought that the beaker had not been returned because of the shame befalling Anton and the "anger he felt" (*vaš o xoli*) as a consequence, and because Anton was still confident that he would be able to use the beaker to dissolve his former son-in-law's new marriage and persuade him to "take back" his granddaughter – that is, to continue their interrupted marriage. In the summer of 2012, Kalo offered €40,000 to compensate Anton for the shame he had suffered because of the divorce and to get his co-father-in-law's security beaker back from him. Anton, however, rejected the offer and continued to argue that his granddaughter was in immaculate mental and physical condition and that her marriage should be continued. The opposing views have not yet been reconciled.

8

Interethnic Trade of Prestige Objects

Although most prestige-object transactions occur within these Roma ethnic populations, Cărhar Roma often try to purchase beakers and tankards from the Gabors if they find the material characteristics of a piece attractive – offering the same high sums that are paid when these objects are bought and sold among the Gabors. (See colour plates: Photos 29–32.) It is also a common occurrence for Gabor owners to take out large loans from Cărhar creditors, leaving their beakers and tankards in pawn. However, it is extremely rare for the Gabors to buy Cărhar pieces, and during my field research I did not hear of any Cărhar owners leaving prestige objects in pawn with Gabor individuals. Thus, although the flow of objects between these Roma ethnic populations is bidirectional, it cannot be described as balanced.

The earliest data I have to indicate the existence of interethnic trade dates from the mid-twentieth century. According to my present knowledge, based on the oral history of my Gabor and Cărhar Roma hosts, since that time twenty-eight Gabor silver objects (twenty-four beakers and four tankards) have gone to the Cărhars: twenty-five pieces (twenty-two beakers and three tankards) were purchased by Cărhar Roma,[1] and on three occasions silver objects (two beakers and one tankard) were put in pawn with the Cărhars during loan transactions but were later redeemed by the Gabors.[2] Certainly, the actual number of objects going to the Cărhars in the last decades is greater than the number of cases I documented during my field research. In contrast, since the middle of the twentieth century, the Gabors have been able to acquire only four silver pieces (three beakers and one tankard) from the Cărhar Roma. Two of these were "exchange objects"; that is, the Cărhar buyer gave it as part of the purchase price – together with a sum of money – when he bought a much more valuable beaker from a Gabor owner.

A few of the interethnic transactions of the past few decades are described below – disregarding the several dozen failed or aborted attempts when Gabor owners tried without success to sell their prestige objects to Cărhar Roma or pawn such pieces with them.

(1) In 1986, a wealthy and influential Cărhar man bought a one-litre *ščobo* beaker from its Gabor owner, from Mureș County, for 500,000 old Romanian lei. This purchase price was worth about US$31,000, which was 150.7 times the gross average monthly salary in Romania at the time. The buyer, who lived in a settlement in the Olt River area, already had three beakers.

(2) In spring 2006, a Gabor owner in his early fifties sold his large – 3.1-litre – and modestly decorated beaker to a Cărhar buyer for US$200,000. (The purchase price was equivalent to 531.8 times the gross average monthly salary in March 2006 in Romania.) The reason the seller parted with his prestige object was to be able to buy another, more valuable Gabor beaker by adding his savings to the proceeds from the sale. However, his own co-father-in-law thwarted the latter transaction at the last minute, and in the end the beaker he had wanted to buy went to another Gabor Roma who had also shown an interest in it (see also chapter 12).

(3) In December 2006, to the great surprise of my Roma interlocutors, a Gabor man in his sixties from Mureș County paid €40,000 to redeem an extremely valuable Gabor tankard that had been pawned in the mid-1990s to the head of a Cărhar family living near Sibiu (see chapter 13). This sum was equivalent to 92.6 times the gross average monthly salary in Romania at the time.

(4) In 2007, one of my Cărhar acquaintances in his early forties from Sibiu County bought a meticulously fire-gilded footed beaker deco-rated with portraits of elderly bearded men and vegetal motifs, and with a capacity of about 0.8 litres, from its indebted Gabor Roma owner. The purchase price was €40,000. This sum was equivalent to 89.8 times the gross average monthly salary in 2007 in Romania.

(5) In summer 2012, an almost one-and-a-half-litre *ščobo* beaker with the sole decoration of a gilded band below the lip was bought by a wealthy Cărhar man from Sibiu County for 120,000 new Romanian lei (US$33,947). Several years before, the Gabor Roma owner had pawned the piece with a Gabor creditor living in one of the Romanian cities

near the Romanian-Hungarian border. Since the owner had not paid the interest throughout the duration of the loan, thereby clearly demonstrating that he could not afford to redeem his beaker, the Gabor creditor decided to sell the debt – with the help of his wife and unknown to the owner – among the Cărhar Roma. It is worth noting that the Cărhar buyer interpreted the transaction as the purchase of the beaker itself rather than the purchase of the debt and argued that he would have no obligation to return the object to its Gabor owner even if the latter could repay his debt in full in the future. The sum of 120,000 new Romanian lei was 56 times the gross average monthly salary in June 2012 in Romania.

Most of the prestige objects that passed into Cărhar ownership had been originally pawned by their Gabor owners; that is, they had been deposited with Cărhar creditors as securities against a loan of greater value, and the latter bought them after the loan period expired (or later). In most of the cases, when he could not pay the interest for years and the combined sum of the capital and interest approached or even exceeded the estimated market value of the pawn, the debtor made one last attempt to ask the Cărhar creditor for a small sum in exchange for ceding the ownership right. Some pawned Gabor prestige objects have, however, been under the supervision of a Cărhar creditor for fifteen or more years without the Gabor Roma debtors trying to formally close the credit deal. (Although it is very likely for the Cărhar creditors that the latter pawns will never be redeemed, as part of their business face-work most of them insisted during our conversations that the pawned beakers and tankards were not their property, and that if the capital and accrued interest were repaid in full they would return the objects to their Gabor owners.) This was precisely the case in the loan agreements discussed below:

(1) In 1994, a modestly decorated, 1.4-litre footed beaker was pawned by its Gabor Roma owner from Mureş County with a Cărhar man who lived in a settlement in the Olt River area. At the time the agreement was struck, the latter had two beakers of his own. As part of the agreement, the borrower received 35,000 German marks (US$22,287), which – like the interest – he has still not repaid because of his financial difficulties.

(2) A footed beaker richly decorated with plant motifs was pawned in 1998 by its Gabor possessor with a Cărhar creditor from Sibiu County, who himself owned three beakers at the time the loan agreement was entered into. The capital of 200 million old Romanian lei was equivalent to US$22,920 at the time. To this day, neither the capital nor the interest has been repaid.

(3) A 1.3-litre footed beaker was pawned in 2004 by its Gabor owner, from the region of Târgu Mureş, with an affluent Cărhar individual who lived in the Olt River area. The loan sum was 600 million old Romanian lei (approximately US$18,000). Not long after the debtor died, his widow visited the Cărhar creditor offering to renounce all rights to the beaker in exchange for another substantial sum. The creditor, however, rejected the widow's offer, arguing that he had not yet received a single dollar of interest from them and he did not have enough cash anyway. His decision was motivated by the assumption that if the widow was prepared to relinquish possession of the beaker, she would be unable to repay the interest and capital and so redeem the pawn, and thus he would eventually become the owner of the beaker in any case – without the need for any further expenditure.

During my fieldwork, I witnessed (as a driver or as an acquaintance who had friendly relations with the owner) many unsuccessful attempts by Gabor prestige-object owners to take out a loan from one of the wealthy Cărhar individuals with a beaker or tankard as a security, or to sell a piece to them. In most of these cases, the rejection was motivated either by the size of the object – as, for instance, in the case of a barely four-decilitre tankard decorated with a snakeskin pattern and rich gilding, or a five-decilitre *ščobo* beaker with two medallions on it – or by its saliently bright colour and injury-free surface. The latter properties suggested to the potential Cărhar creditors or buyers that the piece on offer must have been manufactured recently in a European silversmith workshop and was therefore almost worthless.

On the morning of 15 June 2012, I accompanied the owner of a nine-decilitre *burikato* beaker – Kuna from Mureş County – as his driver and friend on a trip to Sibiu County, where he intended to sell or pawn his prestige object. The piece was meticulously decorated with rich fire-gilding and many plant and animal motifs; it had two horses and a lion elaborately worked on its mantle. Kuna had inherited the object from his father and was trying to make money out of it because of his financial difficulties: his son's debts and the approaching foreclosure of his own house by the bank.[3]

Kuna made no attempt to sell his beaker among the Gabors. The primary reasons for this were his "soft," conflict-avoiding nature, his modest ability to assert his interests (in the absence of significant cash reserves and influential supporters), and his advanced age (he was seventy years old at the time). Kuna was afraid that if he put his beaker up for sale among the Gabors, influential uninvited brokers would interfere in the transaction in his support, simply in order to demand a substantial success fee after the transaction had been made. This could easily lead to a conflict and substantially reduce the profit he hoped to make on the sale.

Besides me, Kuna was accompanied on the nearly one-and-a-half-hour journey by a Gabor acquaintance and one of his brothers-in-law. The son of the latter lived in Sibiu County and was thus more familiar than most Gabor Roma with the Cărhars. He recommended an influential Cărhar individual who could perhaps help Kuna as a broker during the planned transaction.

Kuna brought his beaker to this Cărhar broker's home, and the broker thoroughly examined its nominal authenticity by, for instance, scraping its gilding with his nails to ensure it would not come off easily and pressing the lip of the beaker to check the flexibility of its silver material. Confirming the conclusion of previous experiences that the Cărhar Roma take into consideration nothing but material properties in their evaluation of prestige objects coming from the Gabors (see also chapter 7), the Cărhar broker we visited did not ask for any information about either the ownership history of Kuna's beaker or Kuna's home and patriline; that is, he did not show the least bit of interest in the Gabor Roma social career of the object.

Kuna, with the help of his brother-in-law, spoke at length to the broker about his financial difficulties, and asked his help in finding a wealthy Cărhar man who would be willing to pay him at least €25,000 to €30,000 "in return" for the purchase or pawn of his beaker. Although the broker acknowledged that Kuna's beaker was "not a fake" (*na-j xoxamno*), and he admitted that he knew a wealthy Cărhar individual living in one of the neighbouring settlements who not only would be pleased to buy a beaker any time but also had the necessary cash, he refused to take Kuna to this potential buyer. In order not to offend him, the broker simply said his acquaintance "wasn't looking for that kind of beaker" because he wanted to buy one of a much larger size. Kuna tried to persuade the broker to help him, saying with evident exaggeration that "the Gabors have barely any beakers with the material properties most valued by the Cărhars," so they should be satisfied with objects of a less ideal shape and size. But the broker would not budge. (See colour plates: Photo 33.) As we were leaving, he politely noted Kuna's telephone number and promised to let him know if he found a potential buyer or creditor.

Leaving the broker's home, we stopped in another settlement so that Kuna could show his brother-in-law an exceptionally valuable, richly gilded tankard that had full-figure "musical angels" on its mantle and was owned by one of Kuna's Cărhar acquaintances. At Kuna's request, the Cărhar host took the object out of the lockable drawer of an old dining table, where it was kept together with a *sčobo* beaker that had been pawned with him and a smaller footed beaker. Our host said we were lucky to arrive just then; he was storing the tankard in an easily accessible place because his grandson was to be married in the near future and on that occasion he wanted it to be placed with the future wife's family as a security. Kuna did not consider our host or his family as a potential buyer or lender; a year before our visit, the host (and his brother, who lived next door) had already had a look at Kuna's beaker and – for reasons mentioned below – had not shown special interest in it.

On our way home, we stopped in two further Sibiu County settlements where Kuna's two other Cărhar acquaintances lived. He hoped that one of them would offer – for a considerable success fee – to perform the broker's task. He was unlucky, however, as one of his acquaintances was in Italy trying to earn an income through begging, and the other was in hospital in Sibiu and Kuna could only speak with his daughter-in-law. So in the late afternoon hours, we returned to Kuna's home in Mureş County, having arranged neither a broker nor a buyer or creditor.

Weeks later, when the two of us talked between ourselves, the Cărhar broker explained that he did not see a viable way of selling or pawning Kuna's beaker, because several of its decisive material properties were considered to be of only modest value among the Cărhar Roma. These properties were the following: (a) Kuna's beaker had a smaller capacity than that generally wanted among the Cărhars; (b) the mantle of the beaker had a worryingly large number of decorations (most of my Cărhar interlocutors concluded from this fact that the piece had been made more recently than large beakers with hardly any decoration); and (c) the broker found the (silver) material of the beaker too thin.

Why do the Gabors sell some of their prestige objects to the Cărhars rather than selling them within their own Roma ethnic population?

One reason is to be found in the discrepancy between the prestige-object aesthetics of the Gabors and the Cărhars. More precisely, certain material properties of some of the Gabor beakers for sale turn out to be more valuable among the Cărhars, so it is more profitable for the Gabor seller to find a Cărhar buyer. For example, a large share of the Cărhars highly value and are keen to buy large-capacity beakers, some even with a volume of several litres, in which the Gabors now show very little interest (see chapter 4).

However, there is yet another reason why a seller may choose a Cărhar individual to do business with. As discussed in previous chapters, the more valuable prestige objects are means of materializing economic stability or prosperity and are endowed with multiple identity values in both Roma ethnic populations, and their sale is therefore a face-threatening practice, an event that brings shame to the seller. A frequent consequence of a sale is that the seller's political rivals publicly bring up the transaction at social gatherings such as wakes or funerals, thereby insulting the seller and exacerbating the reputational damage he has suffered. (This may happen years or, occasionally, even decades after the object has changed owner.) The most effective verbal insults are those coming from the buyer himself or from someone in his immediate family.[4] Hence, many Gabor Roma prefer to sell to Cărhars – even if this means accepting, in some cases, a lower price for the piece – since communication between the two Roma ethnic populations is limited to occasional economic cooperation. For this reason, the seller does not have to worry about bumping into the new owner (or his close relatives) at every Gabor Roma social gathering he attends. In this way, he will be able to reduce somewhat the frequency of political insults that threaten his positive public image. One cause behind the flow of Gabor prestige objects to the Cărhars is, therefore, to be found in Roma politics and related face-sensitivity.

Selling a beaker or tankard within his own Roma ethnic population may also constitute a problem for a Gabor owner if he is considered an influential individual but his business reputation is significantly damaged – that is, if he is known as a person who tends to put his own economic interests before Roma business ethics, ignoring the latter. In such a situation, many Gabor men interested in buying the prestige object for sale may be concerned that the seller will use his relational capital and influence to demand further payments from the buyer after the sale has been completed, claiming that the purchase price was lower than the actual market value of the piece. The risk of conflicts surrounding such a demand and of the extra expenditure deters a substantial share of potential buyers. Cărhar individuals wishing to buy beakers or tankards from the Gabors, however, avoid this risk altogether, since a Gabor seller cannot use his prestige or the relational capital accumulated in his own Roma ethnic population to pressure the Cărhar buyer into paying additional cash after the sale.

Another factor that plays a significant role in the flow of Gabor silver objects to the Cărhars is the post-socialist consumer revolution – the rapid spread of new consumer goods (such as costly Western cars and minivans, mobile phones, and colour televisions), practices, and ideologies that appeared after 1989. As a result, the Gabor Roma concepts of what constitutes a good/normal/ideal life and an average standard of living, as well as the dominant patterns of income distribution characteristic of the Gabors, underwent a major transformation – especially among young people socialized in the 1990s. As part of this process, the number of expensive commodities that became classified as necessary to an average standard of living increased dramatically following the change of political regime. Consequently, the cost of the goods belonging to the dominant interpretation of an average standard of living now consumes a much higher share of Gabor Roma household incomes than it did in the decades before 1989.

The position of valuable prestige objects did not change in the classification system of commodities after 1989; they continue to be categorized as luxury goods in the positive sense of the term, and the Gabors still regard them as the most expensive commodities, those that promise the greatest reputational profit within their Roma ethnic population. However, after the change of political regime not only the position of precious prestige objects but also one of the main organizing principles of consumption stayed the same: namely, that commodities commonly associated with an average standard of living should be acquired *before* pieces assigned to the class of luxury goods – that is, before (among other things) beakers and tankards. The post-socialist consumer revolution has had a strong impact on the Gabors' prestige economy. The transformation of the concepts of a good/normal/ideal life and an average standard of living has had the effect that saving the cash – sometimes hundreds of thousands of US dollars – needed to buy one of the more valuable beakers or tankards has become a greater challenge than it once was. Also, many owners who are struggling with a long-term shortage of cash will – in an effort to raise enough money to buy the costly commodities now considered part of an average standard of living – decide to sell their prestige objects sooner than their forebears would have done had they found themselves in similar situations before the change of political regime. The social evaluation of the prestige economy is changing among the Gabors, or at least among members of the younger generations; many individuals believe that its political popularity and people's willingness to take economic risks in order to participate in it are somewhat on the decline. This process itself contributes to the flow of prestige objects to the Cărhars (see also the conclusion).

Finally, Gabor owners may occasionally choose to sell their beakers and tankards to the Cărhars because (as exemplified in Kuna's case above) they feel that their modest social prestige and relational capital provide them with insufficient bargaining power to effectively represent their business interests in a sales transaction within their own Roma ethnic population. There are the risks, for instance, that in the Gabors' prestige-object market the prospective seller might be forced to accept a purchase price offer substantially below the actual value of his beaker or tankard, or that he would be unable to resist pressure from influential brokers wishing to be employed in his service for unjustifiably high success fees. If these worries proved to be well founded, the owner would profit much less than he had hoped from the sale.

Why do the Cărhars buy beakers and tankards that come from outside their own Roma ethnic population, and why do they often choose Gabor prestige objects rather than purchasing pieces for considerably lower prices on the antiques market?

The most important reason is that, although the Cărhars own many more silver objects than the Gabors, they very rarely offer their beakers or tankards for sale,[5] and the demand for them in their own Roma ethnic population is far too intense to be satisfied by the very modest supply within their own prestige-object market. Many of the Cărhar individuals who would like to invest their money in silver objects are therefore forced to turn to alternative markets beyond their own Roma ethnic population. Pieces with the material properties highly appreciated by the Cărhars, however, also constitute a scarce resource on the European antiques market and are only sporadically available. (My experience also suggests that the Cărhars have significantly fewer opportunities to make contact with the various participants in the antiques market – such as auction houses, non-Roma antiques dealers, and touts – than do the Gabors, who are often in a position to do so in Hungary or many other European countries.) Many potential Cărhar buyers who wish to acquire beakers and tankards, therefore, have no choice but to do business with Gabor owners who live nearby and decide to sell their silver objects.

To save space, I will discuss just one of the transactions that have taken place among the Cărhar Roma in the past few decades. The piece changing hands was an almost one-and-a-half-litre *ščobo* beaker decorated with a snakeskin pattern, a wide gilded band beneath the lip, and a gilded medallion, which was sold in 1998 by its Cărhar owner from Sibiu County because of his debts. The transaction was assisted by a Cărhar broker, who was a member of the seller's own local community. The beaker was bought by the head of a family living in a settlement in the Olt River area for 300 million old Romanian lei (US$34,380). The business opportunity had taken the buyer by surprise, and he could not muster the entire purchase price in cash in the short time available to him. (Although other Cărhar Roma in the seller's local community were also interested in the beaker, they finally relinquished their plans primarily because they thought the spatial closeness and daily interactions between the seller's and their own family members might lead to serious conflicts in the future.) The buyer paid some of the 300 million old Romanian lei in goods; he gave the seller two horses (valued at 30 million old Romanian lei), ten pigs (valued at 20 million old Romanian lei), an automobile (valued at 60 million old Romanian lei), a small *ščobo* beaker of very modest value (valued at 50 million old Romanian lei), and 140 million old Romanian lei in cash. Although the seller and the buyer were planning to distribute 25 million old Romanian lei each as a cash gift interpreted as "a representation of joy" (to the broker commissioned by the seller and to other Roma supporting them), the buyer did not give a single Romanian leu as a gift – in the absence of any cash – while the seller did as they had planned.

The rarity of prestige-object sales and the intensity of the demand for silver beakers and tankards among the Cărhar Roma explain why it is an exceptional event when the Gabors manage to buy a prestige object from them – that is, why almost all of the pieces sold by Cărhars end up in the ownership of other Cărhar Roma. This explanation is supported by the fact that I am not aware of a single case in which a Gabor prestige object was successfully bought back by the Gabors after it had been purchased by a Cărhar buyer in accordance with business ethics.

As previously discussed, when the Cărhars buy beakers and tankards from the Gabors, they do not consider the objects' Gabor Roma social career as a source of value. Rather, when they estimate the value of pieces arriving from outside their own Roma ethnic population, it is only the "material properties" (*o materialo*) that count (see also the discussion of the Cărhar community in Rupuno in chapter 7). This is aptly illustrated by the following comment, made by one of the best-known Cărhar prestige-object brokers in connection with silver beakers and tankards coming from external sources: "If it's brought by a dog in its mouth [if the piece does not have any non-Roma or Gabor Roma social career] but it's good [has the material properties highly valued by the Cărhars], it doesn't matter where it's from." The primary reason the Cărhars may occasionally show some level of interest in the social careers of Gabor beakers and tankards offered to them for sale is that a long and authentic Gabor ownership history is taken as evidence of the pieces not having been made recently.

Cărhar buyers pay Gabor sellers many times the antiques-market price, because they know that the Gabors will not bargain with them below a certain threshold, since that would mean an unacceptably large financial loss to them and – notwithstanding the risk of more political insults – they would probably decide to sell their objects within their own Roma ethnic population instead. The Cărhar buyer purchases a Gabor beaker or tankard primarily because of shortages on the supply side – that is, the scarcity or inaccessibility of opportunities of purchase in his own Roma ethnic population or on the European antiques market – and he pays for its ethnicized symbolic patina (Gabor ownership history) in order to acquire the object itself and then integrate it into the history of his own Roma ethnic population and transform it into a symbol of patrilineal identity. Thus, from the Cărhars' perspective, making use of the Gabor prestige economy as an alternative market is best interpreted as a case of forced substitution (Kornai 1992) related to the supply side.[6]

The prestige-object trade between the Gabors and the Cărhars can be defined as a "proprietary contest" (Harrison 1995) in which the Gabors – especially the older generations – aim to retain their more valuable silver objects within their own Roma ethnic population, while the Cărhar Roma try to purchase many of them. The primary reason for the development of this proprietary contest is to be found in the economic interdependence between the Gabors and the Cărhars, which derives in part from the outstandingly high economic value attributed to beakers and tankards (characteristic exclusively of these two Roma ethnic populations) and in part from the scarcity of these objects: in other words, from the facts that the Gabor Roma cannot sell their prestige objects for the prices they are used to (which are well above the antiques-market prices) anywhere but within their own Roma ethnic population or among the Cărhars, and that many of those Cărhar Roma who wish to invest their savings in beakers or tankards can count above all on Gabor sellers.

9

Constructing, Commodifying, and Consuming Fake Authenticity

The Politics of Object Authenticity

Reisinger and Steiner (2006), following Wang (1999), have associated various interpretations of object authenticity with the modernist/realist, constructivist, and postmodernist approaches. According to the modernist/realist approach, "There is a discernible objective basis for the authenticity of artifacts ... generally underpinned by a fixed and knowable reality" (Reisinger & Steiner 2006, 66). From a constructivist perspective, authenticity is a social and personal quality; it is "a socially constructed interpretation of the genuineness of observable things" rather than "a real and objective phenomenon discernible empirically" (Reisinger & Steiner 2006, 69) and, consequently, it is inevitably "unfixed, subjective and variable." However, postmodernists argue that the problem of authenticity has become marginal in several contexts – for example, for tourists who "either do not value it, are suspicious of it, are complicit in its cynical construction for commercial purposes, or are aware that it is merely a marketing device" (Reisinger & Steiner 2006, 66).

Although we have no reason to doubt that the question of authenticity is of little importance for many people, in the case of certain social, cultural, and economic goods and practices it still holds considerable significance. For participants in the globalized art market, auctions, and the antiques trade or visitors to museums, as well as the producers, distributors, and consumers of branded commodities, the origin and nominal authenticity of things are a significant source of value, and great attention is paid to their control (see, for instance, Steiner 1994; Myers 1998, 2002, 2004b, 2006b; Kingston 1999; Geismar 2001; Graburn

2004; Velthuis 2005; Wood 2005; Price 2007; Colwell 2015). The question of authenticity – as in, for example, many consumer subcultures – also often acquires special importance in the course of the creation, performance, and materialization of social and cultural belonging, otherness, and differences (see Lemon 2000; Myers 2002, 2004a, 2006b; Jenß 2004; Elliott & Davies 2006).

This chapter adopts the constructivist approach in arguing that authenticity is not an inherent and static property but a socially constructed – and often contested – ideology attached to objects, practices, and identities by interpretive communities. This approach asserts that interpretations of object authenticity are, first, often closely connected to the politics of identity and value; they are, in many cases, strategic tools of identity marketing and management. Secondly, they can often be characterized by economic utility.

(1) The differentiation of authentic from non-authentic objects is a practice of classification that often plays a decisive role in the construction, materialization, and representation of social and cultural identities. Therefore, I partially agree with Spooner (1986, 226), who defines authenticity as "a form of cultural discrimination projected into objects" or systems of objects. This is the case, for example, with national consumer tastes or sensitivities that aim to create and reproduce a sense of national belonging and identity through the preference for consumer goods, practices, values, and patterns defined as icons of the consumer's own nation (see Caldwell 2002; Morris 2007; Fox & Miller-Idriss 2008). The regular consumption of national(ized) commodities and the preference for national ways of consumption are often defined as preconditions for, or social markers of, the authentic performance of national identity.

(2) Canonized interpretations of object authenticity are also often used as economic resources, as they are able to spotlight and increase the biographical value attributed to the objects and, through this, to raise market demand for them. The label "authentic" centres and verifies the provenance or social career of goods and makes them more attractive to consumers who purchase such commodities primarily for the identity values attached to them – that is, because they regard them as iconic representations of certain social populations, cultures, geographical regions, or historical periods. This is the case, for example, in the globalized market of authentic tribal art – that is, in the subcultures of art collectors and galleries specializing in, among other things, African masks and figural statues (Steiner 1994, 111–20).

Because of its multifarious usefulness, the category of "authentic" often becomes a contested field, the subject of conflicts of values and interests. The essence of these symbolic conflicts is that each of the rival groups striving for exclusive control over the definition of the meaning of authenticity attempts to normalize the interpretation of authenticity that represents its own values and interests. Such proprietary contests are of great significance: products labelled as "authentic" can give the producers and the social populations that these goods represent easier access to often scarce resources, such as opportunities for identity representation or monetary profit deriving from the commodification of "authentic products." (Consider, for example, public and professional debates on which products – such as certain artisanal handicrafts or local foods – are to become the distinguishing markers or representations of a given settlement or microregion, the icons of the local or regional cultural identity.)

The term "politics of object authenticity" can be applied in at least two ways. First, it refers to symbolic conflicts and contests between various interest groups that focus on where the boundaries between authentic and non-authentic should be drawn – that is, which things should be included in the category of "authentic representations" of an ethnic population, social class, or nation, and which should be excluded from it (see Bourdieu 1984; Myers 1991, 2002, 2004b, 2006a; Steiner 1994, 1995, 1996, 2001, 2002; Fox & Miller-Idriss 2008). Second, the politics of object authenticity may refer to strategies and techniques that focus on the manipulation of a piece's nominal authenticity. In this case, the aim is to represent an object as belonging to a certain class of objects to which it does not, or as being identical to a particular piece which it is not, or even to a piece which does not exist. Examples of this include art forgery (Dutton 1983, 2003; Jones 1990, 1992; Moffitt 1995; Radnóti 1999; Myers 2002, 2004b; Hay 2008), brand falsification (Jamieson 1999), or certain marketing strategies used in the globalized art market (Steiner 1994, 1995). Several local African dealers, Steiner argues, shape their marketing strategies based, in part, on their assumptions of how foreign buyers interpret the concept of authentic African art, and, in doing so, manipulate the ethnic identity and provenance of certain art objects:

Many of the art objects traded in the market places [of the Ivory Coast] are classified according to their ethnic style: *Dan* masks, *Senufo* figures, *Baule* combs, et cetera. In most cases, it is ethnicity alone which is the most intrinsic element in the definition and classification of art objects.

When tourists buy art in the market place, one of the first questions they ask the trader is, "What tribe is this from?" Some traders are able to recognize, with great accuracy, the ethnic attribution of an art object. Others, however, have not the slightest clue where an object may be from. Whether or not a trader knows in which ethnic style an object is carved, he will *always* provide the buyer with an attribution – i.e., failure to do so might jeopardize the sale. For those who are unable to recognize ethnic attributions, the tendency is to identify *everything* as Baule: "It's Baule, just like the President." (Steiner 1994, 91–2)

In Steiner's example, sellers create or modify the ethnic origin or biography of commodities to bring them into line with what they assume are the buyers' value preferences and thus increase the chances of a sale.

The examples presented in the following – like those provided by Steiner – are related to the second interpretation of the politics of object authenticity: the manipulation of nominal authenticity.

Types of Fraud Involving Gabor Roma

The term "fraud" as used here refers to those techniques and strategies by which some Gabor individuals attempt to manipulate the symbolic patina (ownership history) and, if necessary, material properties of a silver object.[1] There are a number of motivations for fraud.

In the first type of fraud, the fraudsters are motivated by monetary profit (*money-oriented fraud*). The second type of fraud involves cases that can be traced back to political motives. In such cases, the fraudster manipulates the nominal authenticity of a beaker that a rival Gabor Roma wishes to buy, claiming that the piece concerned is just a fake. The aim of this practice is to make the potential buyer uncertain and to thwart the planned transaction – that is, to prevent the current difference in prestige between the potential buyer and the fraudster from shifting to the detriment of the latter (*political fraud*; see chapter 12). Finally, the common feature of cases constituting the third type of fraud is that they are aimed at providing ad hoc entertainment for the Gabor Roma present (*fraud as a teasing technique*).

Fraud that can be interpreted as money-oriented or teasing occurs in interethnic encounters, while politically motivated fraud is linked to transactions organized between Gabor Roma. With the exception of teasing, fraud is viewed with moral disapproval and criticism.

In the following, I deal only with money-oriented fraud; in the great majority of cases Cărhar Roma and, less often, non-Roma individuals are the targets of such fraud.

Money-Oriented Fraud and the Cărhar Roma

The money-oriented attempts at fraud that were intended to mislead Cărhar creditors or buyers and that I observed typically followed this scenario:

(1) One of the Gabor individuals bought a beaker on the European antiques market that he thought the Cărhars might like.

(2) Then, and in all cases, to ensure that the Cărhar creditor or buyer would not express the value of the object in prices typical of the antiques market but would instead take into account the prices customary among the Gabors, the fraudster supplemented the ethnicized symbolic patina that the beaker lacked. In other words, he created an invented Gabor Roma biography for it and, if necessary, manipulated its material properties; he attempted to create the impression that the object offered for sale was in fact a highly esteemed beaker of complete value that had been passed from owner to owner among the Gabors for a long time.

(3) Finally – taking advantage of the interethnic trade of authentic prestige objects – the fraudster either tried to sell the fake or offered it as a security in exchange for the loan of a large sum among the Cărhars. Throughout the whole process (although this was always kept secret during negotiations with potential creditors and buyers), the fraudster regarded the piece as a commodity, seeing it exclusively as a means of earning income.

If successful, this strategy can generate substantial profits; in the deals that I have documented since the change of political regime in 1989, the greatest difference between the sum paid to the non-Roma seller and the selling price received from the Cărhar buyer exceeded 85,000 German marks (US$47,000). Most of my Gabor interlocutors regarded this type of fraud as a promising means of earning a quick profit and of recovering from a situation of economic crisis. Despite this, they rarely resort to this practice, above all because the silver objects they look for on the antiques market – as well as the interethnic relational capital and experience in brokering required to do business with the Cărhars – are scarce resources; they are not available for everyone.

In the hopes of finding a silver beaker to purchase at a reasonable price and resell to the Cărhar Roma, several Gabor traders regularly visit the antique shops in Budapest and seek the company of touts who earn their living on the local antiques market. In the autumn of 2006, for example, Rupi, a middle-aged Gabor trader who regularly monitored the offers of the better-known Budapest antique shops on Váci and Falk Miksa streets, found an auction catalogue that included a photo of a trumpet-shaped, footed beaker made of antique silver. Since Rupi was not familiar with how auctions worked, he asked me to help him buy the piece. The beaker was a parcel-gilt object from approximately the end of the sixteenth century, with a starting price of 1,200,000 Hungarian forints (US$5,700). Rupi worked out a detailed plan, which included an invented Gabor ownership history, to persuade potential Cărhar buyers that the piece was really an authentic Gabor prestige object, as well as a list of close relatives who would cooperate in the scheme. However, in the end, Rupi was unable to come up with the necessary funds to purchase the beaker. (In the end it was auctioned for HUF1,500,000 [US$7,126].) Such schemes frequently arose among the Gabor Roma.

Secrecy is crucial at every stage – from the acquisition of the silver objects on the antiques market to their sale to the Cărhars. It is crucial vis-à-vis other Gabor Roma, because if the source of the piece were to become known, they would probably attempt to buy similar pieces from the same antiques dealer (thus creating competition for the fraudster), and also because of the possibility that Gabor rivals might reveal the planned fraud. Secrecy is also crucial during negotiations with the Cărhars, because if the potential buyers were to find out the real social career of the manipulated object, they would not pay more than approximately the fraudster's initial purchasing sum, thus rendering the whole effort unprofitable. But why is secrecy vis-à-vis non-Roma antiques dealers important? This is in order to keep the purchase price low, an essential condition for achieving the profit the fraudsters hope to gain from the deception. It is definitely in the interest of the Gabor fraudsters that, as far as possible, antiques dealers do not learn that the commodities they are selling are intended to enter an ethnicized consumer subculture, where similar pieces regularly change hands for many times more than their purchase price on the antiques market. If the majority of antiques dealers were to become aware of the existence of the Gabors' prestige economy, it is highly probable that they would set a specific price range for the Gabors, based on ethnic identity, that would be much higher than the customary prices for non-Roma collectors. This is the reason why my acquaintances who went to check out what the Budapest antiques dealers had for sale tried to conceal their ethnic identity and the real importance they attribute to the beakers and tankards. The techniques they frequently used in the antique shops included not using Romani language or even any words borrowed from that language, not wearing their wide-brimmed black hats and dark jackets, not taking their wives with them (the colourful clothes the women wear are much harder to hide from the eyes of non-Roma), and in some cases asking a local Hungarian individual, such as the driver they had employed or their landlord, to make enquiries from the dealer for them. One of my interlocutors, for example, explained his obvious interest in footed beakers with the fabricated explanation that he was a member of a congregation of the Reformed Church in Romania and had come to Budapest to buy a communion beaker for the congregation. However, such secrecy about the later fate of the objects that come into the possession of the Gabors is obviously quite useless vis-à-vis the small group of antiques dealers and touts who have been doing business with them for a long time. The pieces and services they offer are generally more expensive than those offered by non-Roma who know nothing about the Gabor Roma ethnic population.

Between 1998 and 2015, I was able to document in detail seven attempts at money-oriented fraud.[2] In five cases, the targets of the fraud were Cărhar Roma, and on two occasions, non-Roma persons. Two of the attempts directed at Cărhars, and both of those directed at non-Roma, were successful. In addition, I witnessed many sessions in which detailed plans for fraud were drawn up that were, in the end, not put into practice. I also succeeded in reconstructing quite a few successful or failed fraud attempts made in the decades before the start of my fieldwork.

Of course, the opportunity for money-oriented fraud would not arise if the Cărhars did not occasionally buy Gabor beakers and tankards of complete value – that is, with a perfect symbolic and material patina – at the high prices customary in the case of deals organized among the Gabors. As the interethnic trade of prestige objects serves as the wider economic context for the sporadic cases of money-oriented scams focused on the Cărhars, the Gabor fraudsters take great pains to ensure that the sale or pawn of a manipulated beaker does not differ in any way from typical transactions between Gabor sellers/debtors and Cărhar buyers/creditors. The more these deals resemble those of authentic Gabor objects, the less likely the Cărhar buyer is to suspect that anything is untoward.

(1) *Artificial material patina: aging.* Gabor individuals may purchase from non-Roma sellers beakers made of antique silver, or ones recently produced in a Hungarian or Transylvanian silversmith's workshop. Because the latter are made of newer materials, they cannot become prestige objects of complete value among the Gabors. Therefore, to give the impression of centuries-long use, the owner must artificially create a material patina. Techniques used to artificially age beakers are referred to by the Hungarian term *megöregítés* (aging). They can be applied by a non-Roma specialist (a silversmith or restorer), a well-known Gabor broker with a vast knowledge of aging techniques and silver beakers, or the Gabor fraudster himself. The owner who is planning fraud is often wary of the specialist commissioned to do the job, partly because if the specialist leaks information about the order, others can easily upset his plans, and partly out of fear that the object may be accidentally "spoiled" (damaged), or even misappropriated. To prevent such "spoiling," a number of my acquaintances asked the specialist to demonstrate, in their presence, the effectiveness of his recommended procedure on a smaller silver piece. But the only way to prevent misappropriation is for the owner to be present throughout the process of aging and not let the object out of his sight for a minute. During my fieldwork, two attempts at finding a specialist to fake the age of a piece – one planned with the involvement of an antiques dealer in Târgu Mureş and the other with a museum restorer in Braşov – failed because the beaker concerned would have had to be left with the specialist for at least a few days. The owner found this too risky and instead tried to do the aging himself.

What procedures do the Gabors use themselves to give silver an antique look, that is, to make a strikingly even colour "blotchy" and uneven, and to change the shiny surface of the beaker to a darker shade (or "blacken" it)? (a) One often-employed technique is burying the object in the hopes that the earth's sulphur content will change its colour; (b) also because of the presence of sulphur, my hosts thought it advisable for the owner to keep the piece wrapped up in a cloth soaked in red wine for a while, or to bury it in the ground wrapped in the same way; (c) another well-known method of aging among Gabor Roma is to put the object in dung; or (d) to smear it with sulphuric acid (according to my interlocutors, the application of sulphuric acid also gives the piece a darker tone, "making it brown"); aging can also be helped and hastened (e) by smoking a beaker with a piece of sulphate; or (f) by smearing it with sulphuric shampoo (a comparatively recent and more rarely used technique); (g) I once observed a Gabor man dilute hypo-chlorite with water and spread it over the beaker's surface with a soft cloth – the achieved "patina" could easily be removed with toothpaste, and after a few failed attempts he gave up the experiment. Techniques (a), (b), (e), (f), and (g) were each used in the course at least of one of the fraud attempts I observed in detail, while I learnt about the procedures mentioned in points (c) and (d) from recollections on this subject.

Aging also included adding signs that indicate use over a long period. Such signs may include dents, scratches, abrasions, and discolouration on the body of the beaker, and partial deformation of the lip or the base.

(2) *The addition of artificial symbolic patina.* The fraudster makes up for the lack of a Gabor Roma social career by fabricating an ethnicized object biography. Thus, in the course of bargaining with the potential Cărhar creditors or buyers, he presents the piece recently purchased from the antiques market as a beaker that has changed owners among the Gabors over the course of many years. In the cases I documented, the fraudsters generally specified their own patrilineal predecessors (their fathers, grandfathers, and so on) as the earlier owners. In this way, they not only defined the beaker for sale as a representation of *Gaborness* (a symbol of ethnic identity) but also attributed to it another invented social identity – a symbol of patrilineal identity.

(3) *Manipulation of the context of the transaction.* Besides the added material patina and the invented object biography, the fraudster's bargaining position may also be improved if he manipulates the context of the transaction. He can enhance his own business credibility and build trust in the object biography if he has ready-made answers to several questions that the potential Cărhar buyers may ask – if they think it necessary – to verify that the piece being offered is really a Gabor Roma prestige object of complete value. The most common techniques used to manipulate the context of the transaction are described below:

- Embedding the invented object biography into the histories of the interethnic prestige-object trade and the Gabors' prestige economy. A useful strategy for building trust is for the fraudster, before raising the real purpose of his visit, to recall a few memorable events of the interethnic prestige-object trade that are also known to the potential Cărhar buyer – with particular regard to earlier deals between the fraudster's patrilineal forebears and Cărhar individuals. The fraudster may also try to gain the buyer's trust by mentioning his father's or grandfather's prestige objects to

demonstrate that he "grew up among beakers" (*dendol taxta barjila*).
By framing the object's invented biography with these and similar
verifiable pieces of information, the false provenance becomes more
credible and convincing.

- Describing, in detail, the economic circumstances compelling the
  seller to part with the piece.
- Demonstrating to the potential buyer that the beaker has
  inestimable emotional and biographical value for him (it is, for
  instance, a precious identity symbol of his patriline). Here, the seller
  may emphasize how painful and difficult it is for him to part with
  the object, a cherished family heirloom for the possession of which
  his family made huge economic sacrifices, and, as proof of its high
  emotional value, he may argue that he does not want to sell the
  piece but only to put it in pawn. This performance also reinforces
  and authenticates the invented biography of the object for sale.
- Explaining why he does not want to sell the beaker to another
  Gabor Roma individual even though it is really so valuable among
  the Gabors. The fraudster may use the most frequently given
  explanation, namely that, although he did receive favourable price
  offers from numerous Gabor acquaintances, he has decided to offer
  the object for sale to the Cărhars, because in this way he will suffer
  fewer verbal insults after the transaction.
- Putting forward convincing arguments to explain why the fame of
  the piece has not reached the Cărhars. (Naturally such explanations
  are not needed if the fraudster claims that the fake offered for sale is
  identical to an important Gabor beaker of complete value.)
- Commissioning a broker. This is an important means of
  manipulating the participant framework of the business
  negotiation. In the course of price bargaining, it is mainly the
  broker who represents the owner's interests, authenticating the
  invented object biography with his business reputation, expertise,
  and capacity for persuasion, and thereby increasing the potential
  buyer's willingness to purchase. According to my interlocutors,
  the broker is often aware of the real biography of the manipulated
  object, or at least suspects it, but if he thinks that the potential
  Cărhar buyers will not become suspicious, the success fee offered
  usually persuades him to accept the task. In some cases that
  I documented, it was in fact the broker himself who gave the
  fraudster detailed information on how to achieve the aging of the
  piece to be sold.

To illustrate, I will provide the story of one successful fraud attempt. The deal examined took place in the summer of 2010. Tamas, a Gabor Roma living in one of the Romanian cities along the Hungarian-Romanian border, had secretly had a silver-plated alpaca copy made of the eight-decilitre beaker he inherited from his father. The work was done by a non-Roma silversmith, who also aged the object and gilded it inside and out.

Since the copy turned out very well, Tamas hastened to contact a Gabor acquaintance in Mureş County who had earlier taken part in coordinating a number of interethnic transactions, and asked for his help as a broker in selling the fake among the Cărhar Roma. Because the acquaintance did not have up-to-date information on who among the Cărhars had the necessary cash reserves and political ambitions for the purchase, he took Tamas and his wife to visit one of the wealthy Cărhar men living in the Olt River area and asked him to broker the deal. The Cărhar host owned numerous prestige objects (some pieces had earlier come into his family from the Gabors), and he frequently participated as a broker in prestige-object transactions between the two Roma ethnic populations.

Since he counted on being paid a substantial success fee, the Cărhar host immediately accepted the request and took Tamas and his companions to an acquaintance, a man in his mid-sixties who also lived in Sibiu County with two sons, both of whom had long wanted to buy a precious beaker. Although the acquaintance was not at home (he was in France begging, together with his wife), his younger son, Viktor, found the beaker very attractive and began to bargain with Tamas.

Tamas talked at length about his hopeless financial situation, the result on the one hand of a series of family tragedies (among other things, the illness and death of one of his daughters) and on the other of the global economic crisis of 2008, and supported his statement that the nominal authenticity of the beaker was unimpeachable with conditional self-curses.[3] He also spoke in detail about some of the influential Gabor individuals who had owned the object in the past and of the great biographical and emotional value he attached to it. Finally, he also gave reasons why he had not tried to sell it within his own Roma ethnic population.

Through the coordination of the Gabor and the Cărhar brokers, Tamas and Viktor finally agreed on a purchase price of €35,000. Viktor managed to muster the sum in two days, borrowing part of it from some friends. The seller and buyer together paid the two brokers €5,000 each, a cash gift defined as a success fee. On the day the purchase price was paid, the participants in the transaction and their close relatives were received in Viktor's home with food and drink. On that occasion, Tamas and Viktor publicly distributed among those present €1,000 that they put up in equal proportions, as a cash gift interpreted as "a representation of joy."

When, not long after the deal was concluded, Viktor's father returned from France and examined the newly purchased beaker, he was shocked, and informed his son that he had made a "bad bargain": he had bought a "foolish [an almost worthless] beaker" (*dilo taxtaj*), because the piece was not made of antique silver but of silver-plated alpaca. In the words of Viktor's mother, "It's not valid [proper]. It's a new [recently made] beaker, made of alpaca" (*Na-j valabilo. Njevo taxtaj-i, alpakkaš-i*).

Because he was afraid people would learn that he had not recognized the object as a copy, Viktor did not show the recent purchase to anyone after that, although when they heard the news of the transaction many of his relatives and acquaintances visited him in his home to see it. Accordingly, he and his family treated the fact that the beaker was a fake as a secret. If Viktor's mistake became known, he would be in danger of serious loss of face, and he and his close relatives would be the butt of sarcasm and ridicule.

When I asked why they did not personally visit the Gabor fraudster and, with the help of the Cărhar broker who had assisted in the deal, ask him to pay back the purchase price or at least a part of it, Viktor's parents replied that this would have led to the fraud being revealed. In spite of the considerable financial loss, it seemed to them more favourable to keep their failure a secret and try to postpone as long as possible the shame it would bring.

Their great concern that the failure would become known also meant that they did not report the fraud to the police. Since no written contract had been drawn up for the transaction, the identity of the parties concerned, the sum paid, and other details could be proven only through witnesses, and this would inevitably lead to the secret of the fraud becoming revealed. In addition, during the bargaining, Viktor had not asked where exactly in the border city Tamas was living at the time, nor did he enquire from which village in Mureş County Tamas's patrilineal forebears had come. This meant that it would not have been possible to establish Tamas's precise address without going public, or at least involving a few Cărhar and Gabor Roma individuals. Nor had Viktor attributed significance, during the bargaining with Tamas, to checking the authenticity of the Gabor ownership history of the beaker, because he was interested solely in its material properties.

Viktor and his parents made efforts to sell some of their valuables for cash to repay as soon as possible the debts incurred from the transaction examined here, as well as in connection with a marriage conflict. In April 2011, a German antiques dealer visited their village, guided by a Romanian acquaintance of his from Sibiu County, and went from house to house buying antiques from the local residents. When the antiques dealer was called in to Viktor's home, the latter's parents showed him numerous old implements and decorative objects, most of which the dealer was happy to buy – among them the silver-plated alpaca beaker bought from Tamas in the summer of 2010. The dealer paid slightly more than €10,000 for the antiques selected. Victor and his family tried to keep the sale of the beaker secret. If people would have learnt that they had sold it for scarcely more than €10,000 – together with numerous other antiques! – and moreover to a non-Roma antiques dealer, it would have become obvious to all their Cărhar acquaintances that the object had been only a fake.

As Viktor's parents put it, they wanted at all costs to avoid the Roma "mocking us and laughing at us" (*te prasan ame the asan amendar*), and for this they were prepared to accept the substantial monetary loss; that is, they renounced all hope of recovering the greater part of the price paid, rather than "eating shame" (*xan o lažavo*, being shamed publicly). This explains why, in their case, selling the fake within their own Roma ethnic population was out of the question.[4] The only sanction applied towards the fraudster was that Viktor and his parents often cursed him and all those who had hastened to help him in the course of the transaction.

Viktor's case is a striking example of how the Cărhar Roma, like the Gabors, often attach greater importance to public loss of face suffered in the prestige economy than to the financial losses caused by avoiding, postponing, or moderating such symbolic loss. This can be clearly seen from the following remarks made by Viktor's mother:

> We sold it [the beaker] for less than half the earlier purchase price, so that the Cărhar Roma would not know about it. Because they would have made fun of us, they would have said, "Look, the fools spent a lot of money on it, and now they're giving it away for free. Just to be rid of the shame!" ... It was a beaker that had been made specially [to order, recently]. Somebody, somewhere made it in a factory, who knows? It was made to order, not

good ... It was new [made recently]. Perhaps it was made after another beaker [as a copy] ... We [Viktor's parents] could see that it was silver-plated alpaca ... We bought it [their younger son, Viktor, bought it], but we don't know who we bought it from. We sold it, but we don't know who we sold it to. That's how it was. (21 August 2011)

Money-Oriented Fraud and the Non-Roma

However, it is not only Cărhar Roma who can be the targets of money-oriented fraud; although much less often, the Gabor Roma also use this livelihood strategy in dealings with non-Roma. This phenomenon needs to be explained. Earlier, I argued that non-Roma extremely rarely buy silver objects from the Gabors. If this really is the case, when do the Gabors have the opportunity to apply their fraud strategy in deals with Hungarians or Romanians?

(1) Fraud attempts involving non-Roma are directed in part at non-Roma entrepreneurs who have been living adjacent to the Gabors for many years and have sufficient cash reserves to lend smaller or larger sums to Roma and non-Roma who turn to them for financial help. Both fraud attempts focusing on non-Roma that I observed in detail fall into this category, with the fraudsters aiming to pawn a fake disguised as a prestige object of complete value. Both attempts were successful.

This type of fraud is made possible by two circumstances. On the one hand, many Hungarians and Romanians living in proximity to the Gabors know that beakers and tankards have special social and economic significance for them, and that in larger loan transactions between Gabor Roma the lender often holds the borrower's prestige object as a security. Some Hungarian or Romanian creditors who lend significant sums to Gabor Roma also resort to this strategy, thereby creating the framework within which fakes can reach them. Fraud is also facilitated by the circumstance that the great majority of non-Roma have no knowledge of the unique material properties of the Gabor beakers and tankards that would enable them to check the nominal authenticity of the objects concerned. The fraudster exploits precisely this lack of knowledge. The more superficial and inadequate the non-Roma creditor's knowledge of prestige objects is, the smaller the chance that the fraud will be discovered in time.

In the successfully concluded fraud attempts that I observed in detail, the fraudster manipulated both the symbolic and material patina. While the creation of an invented object biography followed the same pattern as in the frauds involving Cărhar Roma, a special logic was applied in the artificial creation of material patina; the latter was an exclusively discursive practice. That is, the fraudsters did not bother with various procedures to age the object offered as a security; they simply trusted that the creditor would be incapable of distinguishing between the material of the fake and antique silver.

One of these successful frauds involved Laji, a man in his fifties from Bigvillage in Mureș County. Laji had gradually become indebted following the change of political regime, and therefore decided in 1999 to pawn his *ščobo* beaker to a Gabor Roma acquaintance. Laji's choice fell on the grandson of one of the earlier owners of the object, who lent him 30,000 German marks (US$15,670) and took control of the beaker as a security. The creditor hoped that if the beaker "sank in the debt," he would buy it, and so remedy the reputational damage suffered when his grandfather had been forced to sell it earlier. Laji's financial problems were not eased even after the loan; he reached the stage where he was no longer able to pay his utility bills and his creditors were becoming more and more insistent in demanding that he settle his debts. Finally, in the autumn of 2002, he and his family moved to one of the Romanian towns along the Romanian-Hungarian border, in the hope that they could begin a new life there, put their financial situation in order, and eventually repay their debts.

As it was commonly known among the Gabors that Laji had already pawned his beaker, in order to raise more funds before moving away he visited a local Hungarian entrepreneur from whom he had regularly bought various household articles. In the entrepreneur's home, he pulled out a small beaker that he had recently bought on the flea market of the nearby county seat; it resembled in shape the *ščobo* beakers but was made of silver-plated alpaca, not silver. Laji described this piece to the Hungarian host as his own prestige object, inherited from his father. After speaking at great length about his financial difficulties, he asked the entrepreneur to lend him a small sum for a high interest rate and accept the object as a security. The entrepreneur finally gave him a loan of US$5,000, after they had agreed on the interest rate and the duration of the loan. Laji then disappeared without a trace and did not pay the interest either. When the creditor began to enquire about his whereabouts, it soon became clear to him that Laji had not been living in Bigvillage for a considerable time. Then he secretly showed the pawned object to one of the local Gabor men, asking whether it was really worth US$5,000 and also trying to find out whether, if necessary, he would be able to find someone who could redeem it in place of Laji. However, the Gabor individual gave an evasive reply to both questions, as he did not want to later come into conflict with Laji for confirming the entrepreneur's suspicion of fraud. (In December 2009, Laji redeemed his prestige object of complete value that he had pawned in 1999 to the Gabor Roma creditor mentioned, paying him US$30,000, which represented the capital and interest.)

Non-Roma creditors who accept Gabor prestige objects as securities are motivated exclusively by monetary profit, just like the Gabor men who resort to fraud in such transactions. It never occurs to the Hungarian or Romanian creditors, but it is the unspoken desire of most of the Gabor individuals who keep one of the valuable beakers or tankards with them as a security, that – if the debtor is unable ever to make repayments on the loan – in time they themselves can acquire the right of ownership of the pawned object.

(2) Other attempts at fraud were directed at me – the anthropologist interested in the Gabors' prestige economy. It occurred on several occasions during my fieldwork that an individual with whom I had only a passing acquaintance secretly showed me a piece that he said was an important prestige object of complete value, inherited in his own patriline over a long period, and, citing his financial difficulties, asked me to help as a broker in selling the object on the antiques market in Budapest or to a museum in Hungary. The pieces produced on such occasions were generally made not of silver but of silver-plated alpaca. The majority of the "clients" hoped to make a very substantial profit from the invented Gabor Roma social career attributed to the object and trusted that I would be unable to identify the material of which the piece was made.[5]

The Politics of Ethnic Provenance Attributed to Objects

The ethnic character or identity attributed to certain commodities often plays a significant role in determining their price and emotional value and in monitoring their nominal authenticity, and can be based on various criteria or certain combinations thereof. For example, tribal art products may be defined by various interpretive communities – local producers, tourists, traders, collectors, and art historians – as ethnically marked commodities according to ethno-aesthetics, ethno-technologies of production, or the ethnic identity of the producers or previous possessors (Steiner 1994, 1996; Myers 2002, 2006a, 2006b). Steiner (1994, 91) argues that "at the demand end of the African art market, ethnicity functions as a form of commodity – which can be packaged, marketed, and sold to foreign buyers." The Gabor Roma who engage in money-oriented fraud also transform the invented ethnic identity and provenance attributed to the fakes into a commodity, in the hope that they will be able to sell these objects for far more than their antiques-market purchase price. To achieve significant financial gain through the manipulation of nominal authenticity, the fraudsters must – among other things – practise the politics of ethnicity attributed to economic actors and commodities.

On the one hand it is essential for fraudsters that the value and price of the objects they wish to buy and later manipulate should be determined on the basis of the antiques market's value regime by non-Roma sellers. They thus obtain these pieces at prices significantly lower than those fetched by prestige objects of complete value that change hands among the Gabors or between the Gabor and the Cărhar Roma ethnic populations. Therefore, as mentioned before, when scouting antiques markets and in bargaining with antiques dealers, these Gabor individuals try to hide their ethnic identity so that dealers will not adjust their prices to those of the Gabors' prestige economy. In other words, Gabor Roma fraudsters adopt the strategy of *ethnic invisibility* when purchasing silver pieces of a non-Roma provenance.

On the other hand the politics of ethnicity connected to economic actors and commodities also plays an important role when, in the course of negotiations with potential Cărhar buyers and creditors and with non-Roma creditors, the fraudster presents the fake as being an authentic Gabor Roma prestige object, while his own ethnic identity also acquires a special economic significance, framing and authenticating the beaker's invented Gabor social career. In such cases, the fraudster resorts to the strategy of *conspicuous ethnicity* – with respect to both his own ethnic identity and the ethnic provenance constructed for the manipulated piece. This practice aims to increase the symbolic distance between the manipulated object and the antiques market and to unilaterally define the limits of price bargaining. That is, by using this strategy, the fraudster can declare more convincingly that he is prepared to negotiate with Cărhar and non-Roma enquirers only on the basis of the value preferences and price domain characteristic of the Gabors' prestige economy.

10

The Politics of Consumption:
Classification Struggles, Moral
Criticism, and Stereotyping

Dimensions and Strategies

Ever since the rapid growth of interest in consumption shown by social scientists in the 1980s (Miller 1995), many anthropological or sociological analyses published on the topic have devoted attention to the relationship between politics and consumption. As several authors (Bourdieu 1984; McCracken 1988; Fox 2006; Fox & Miller-Idriss 2008) have pointed out, this relationship is both dynamic and dialectical in nature. Consumption is a highly contested and politicized field; it is a strategic means and symbolic arena not only for constructing and representing social relations, values, and identities, but also for qualifying, classifying, and hierarchizing them. We can agree with Hilton and Daunton (2001, 9) that "consumption has never existed outside of politics."

Following the interpretations of Sassatelli (2007, 113–15) and Hilton and Daunton (2001, 1), it is worth distinguishing at least three of the dimensions of the politics of consumption: the politics of identity and public image, the politics of normalization, and the politics of fairness.

(1) *The politics of identity and public image.* Community-specific – nationalized, ethnicized, gendered, and so on – commodities, consumer practices, and preferences constitute a symbolic repertoire (Elliott 2004, 129) that offers consumers the possibility to perform and experience various types and levels of groupness "as an *event*, as something that 'happens'" (Brubaker 2004, 12). Utilization of this symbolic repertoire is usually defined as an identity practice. For example, consumption provides consumers with a way of creating a sense and experience of national, ethnic, or class belonging and of materializing their loyalty and commitment to certain communities (positive identity practice).

The politics of consumption is often also an important means of managing inequalities and symbolic conflicts between communities – nations, ethnic populations, religious denominations, or classes, for instance. The dominant communities participating in these relationships can employ some strategies of the politics of consumption, among other things, to represent, authenticate, or reproduce the existing relations of dominance (see Bourdieu 1984; McCracken 1988), while the members of the subordinated communities often utilize the same or similar strategies to counterbalance and rationalize their social, economic, or power vulnerability and the related symbolic loss of positive public image or prestige. For example, several Roma and Traveller populations attempt to compensate for political, social, and economic inequalities by – among other things – associating the concepts of impurity and immorality with certain of the dominant majority society's consumer practices (such as forms of eating and dressing) and morally stigmatizing both these practices and the ethnic others who utilize them (see Okely 1983; Stewart 1997). That is, consumers can also formulate negative identity messages by symbolically devaluing and consciously avoiding those commodities, consumer practices, and preferences, that are interpreted as icons of the negatively defined ethnic or national other (negative identity practice). See, for example, the cases of spontaneous or organized consumer boycott of ethnic(ized) or national(ized) goods (Friedman 1999; Chavis & Leslie 2009).

Consumption, therefore, often plays a significant role in the creation and materialization of social closeness and distance, as well as of belonging and difference. As Wilk (1995) and Miller (1997) have pointed out, however, the relation to the meanings of commodities is not limited to the practices of identification and rejection; it can also take other forms – such as creative recycling (see the interpretation of bricolage in Hebdige 1979). For this reason, consumption should be understood much more as an interaction based on continuous and creative interplay between producers and distributors, commodities, the meanings attached to the latter, and consumers, rather than as a mechanical, uniformized process that subordinates consumers to the intentions of producers and distributors and the meanings they associate with the goods. However, as Fox and Miller-Idriss (2008) have noticed, from the consumer's point of view, the consumption of socially marked commodities is not necessarily an intentional identity practice. It may happen that it is only a group of observers who interpret the consumer's choice as an intentional identity message. Campbell (1997) also draws attention to the dangers of overgeneralizing the "consumption as communication" thesis and to the limits of its applicability.

(2) *The politics of normalization.* Through normalization, wants are transformed into needs; certain goods, services, and consumer ideologies – tastes, styles, or sensitivities – come to be seen as "normal" and taken for granted by a certain group of consumers. As the normalization of commodities and consumer practices and preferences is not only an "ongoing" (Hand & Shove 2007, 95) but often also a contested process, it has a political dimension as well. Slater's analysis (1997a, 1997b) of the politics of need serves as a good example of this. Basic need, Slater argues (1997a, 2; see also Slater 1997b, 2000; Campbell 1998), is often assumed to be "natural and self-evident" or, on the contrary, "arbitrary and subjective" – both approaches, however, "obscure the fundamentally social nature" and politics of need. According to Slater, the contesting interpretations focusing on the concept of need include at least two types of demands. On the one hand they refer to assumptions connected with values, ideals, and identities "about how people would, could or should live in their society" (Slater 1997a, 3). On the other hand they also formulate demands with regard to the distribution of political, social, and economic resources – demands which represent the values and interests of certain communities. Any interpretation of need becoming dominant in a certain social context can play a significant role in how people interpret the concept of a good/normal/ideal life, which models of lifestyle they regard as desirable, or how they think about the order of importance of available goods. Thus, needs "are not only social but also political, in that they involve statements about social interests and projects" (Slater 1997a, 3).

(3) *The politics of fairness.* The third dimension of the politics of consumption, ethical or moral consumption (Hilton & Daunton 2001, 1; Sassatelli 2004, 2006, 2007; Harrison, Newholm, & Shaw 2005), is linked to the demand to counteract and eliminate economic and political exploitation, a demand in which discourses of justice and fairness play a central role.

While the literature on the politics of consumption often examines strategies such as moral boycott, value-based shopping, or positive buying ("buycott"; see Friedman 1999; Caldwell 2002; Fischer 2007), relatively little attention is devoted to analysing discursive strategies – although, as Sassatelli (2004, 178) points out, they are particularly worthy of study: "When considering consumer practices ... where social order is constantly produced, reproduced and modified, we should acknowledge discourses about consumption as an important part of the field."

Agreeing with Sassatelli, in this chapter I describe a Romanian case of the politics of consumption through an analysis of the contesting discourses that serve to explain and "frame" the interethnic trade in silver beakers and tankards carried out between the Gabors and the Cărhars. Although there are several reasons why this interethnic trade – which can be described in somewhat simplified terms as the flow of some of the Gabors' prestige objects towards the Cărhars – developed, both my Gabor and Cărhar Roma interlocutors pointed to each other's consumer behaviour as the dominant reason, and either marginalized or erased several other significant motivations behind this trade. The examined discourses focus mainly on negatively defined consumer practices and value preferences attributed to the ethnic other, and assign a central role to strategies such as stereotyping, moral criticism, and classification (or definition) struggle (Bourdieu 1984, 479).

Through these discourses, the members of both Roma ethnic populations aim primarily to counteract the negative, symbolic consequences – the partial loss of positive public image and prestige – deriving from the asymmetric prestige-object trade. The Gabor Roma, who participate in this trade mainly as sellers, strive to ease the shame and reputational damage that arise from the forced sale of some of their prestige objects, endowed with (multiple) identity values. The Cărhars, who buy these pieces, use the discursive strategies mentioned and the ideology of ethnic identity pollution (Harrison 1999, 10–11) to rationalize and "frame" their passion for silver objects and to counteract certain negative ethnic stereotypes that are associated with their own Roma ethnic population (among others, by the Gabor Roma).

The chapter shows how these Roma, when explaining their consumer choices, construct and attach partially different meanings to the concept of a good/normal/ideal life and to such dichotomies as an average standard of living versus luxuries, morally acceptable versus morally stigmatized patterns of consumption and consumer value preferences, and consumer modernism versus conservatism. The analysis furthermore demonstrates how the Gabor and the Cărhar Roma create their rival ethnic interpretations of consumer moral superiority.

As already noted, in addition to constructing stereotypes, the members of both Roma ethnic populations frequently use the following interconnected discursive strategies:

(1) *Context-sensitive and audience-designed moralizing* primarily involves negative moral criticism of the consumer decisions of the ethnic other, and aims to rationalize and verify the consumer choices of the members of the interlocutor's own Roma ethnic population. As a key part of moralizing, participants attach qualifying labels to consumer practices and value preferences, such as "morally approved," "proper," "rational," or "justified" versus "morally questionable," "inappropriate," "irrational," or "unnecessary." As several authors have pointed out, consumption is "in essence a moral matter" (Wilk 2001, 246), and what is more, a "contested moral field" (Sassatelli 2004, 176) that is inseparable from politics. According to Wilk (2001, 246), moralizing about consumption is a widespread phenomenon that "can be strategically deployed during class conflict, inter-ethnic strife, nationalist or fundamentalist agitation, religious anti-secularism, and even trade negotiations." That is why moral criticism that focuses on the consumer practices and value preferences of the rival national, ethnic, or religious other "is and should be an important object of study for those who want to understand consumer practices and culture" (Sassatelli 2004, 178).

(2) Another dominant strategy in the discourses of both the Gabors and the Cărhars is interethnic *classification (or definition) struggle*, concentrating on categories such as an average standard of living, waste, luxury, or a good/normal/ideal life, which have a significant impact on consumer behaviour and its social evaluation. These Roma ethnic populations elaborated partly differing interpretations when it comes to which of these categories certain commodities and services should fall into, positioning themselves as contesting interpretive communities with the aim of normalizing their respective interpretations and, in this way, facilitating the management of the values and interests manifested in them. As the analysis of the process of classification (or definition) struggle will show, categories such as morally respectable consumption, waste, an average standard of living, or luxury often become contested symbolic fields because their control is a means of rationalizing, reproducing, or questioning social, economic, or power relations (Bourdieu 1984; McCracken 1988; Slater 1997a, 1997b).

Post-Socialism, Consumer Revolution, and Romanian Roma

The Gabor Roma have shown more intense social sensitivity to new consumer goods, value preferences, and practices coming from non-Roma in the past few decades than have the Cărhar Roma.[1] This was particularly true in the period following the collapse of socialism, when hitherto unknown or – to a large segment of consumers – unavailable goods, services, and consumption patterns appeared en masse and were accompanied by the spread of new places of consumption (supermarket chains, fast food restaurants, shopping malls, and the like) as well as new techniques for managing consumer desires. I refer to these phenomena as the post-socialist consumer revolution.

The openness of the Gabors to the consumer revolution following 1989 was mainly inspired not by the desire for Westernization – as could be observed in some segments of the Romanian majority society – but by the possibility that this revolution offered for the representation of wealth and well-being. The appearance of costly and conspicuous new commodities and services, often identified with the West, created a new post-socialist symbolic repertoire of representing economic prosperity that became a popular tool in the politics of difference among the Gabor Roma.

As economic migration acquired an international dimension, it also favoured the openness of the Gabors to new techniques of demonstrating wealth. Up until the change of political regime, the dominant form of trade characteristic of this Roma ethnic population had been intermediary trade between Romanian regions at different levels of economic development. After 1990, several Gabor traders also extended their activities to Hungary and Turkey, and later many of them began to show an interest in other European countries as well. Thus, in post-1989 interethnic encounters, Gabor traders more frequently found themselves constrained to convincingly demonstrate their solvency to their potential foreign buyers – who knew nothing about them – without the favourable economic effects of the positive ethnic stereotypes associated with their own Roma ethnic population in Romania (they are the "aristocracy of Romanian Roma," and so on). Constructing the image of a wealthy and successful merchant was one of their most important trust-building strategies in trading outside Romania, and the conspicuous possession of costly new Western consumer goods proved to be an effective means of achieving this aspiration.

The new, post-socialist commodities and spaces of consumption that quickly became popular among the Gabor Roma included – among other things – Western cars and minivans (particularly Opels, Mercedeses, and Volkswagens); modern multi-room family homes with indoor bathrooms, comfortable furnishings, and expensive household appliances; the latest models of mobile phones and colour televisions; and fast-food restaurants and shopping malls.

Unlike the Gabors, who have been purchasing cars more and more frequently ever since the 1970s (up to the change of political regime, these were mostly Dacias – the "icons" of the socialist Romania[2]), most of the Cărhar families I know have only relatively recently, since around the time of the regime change, begun to own cars. Several of my well-to-do Cărhar interlocutors still do not possess a car and continue to rely upon horse-drawn carts for local transport and agricultural work. The housing situation of the two populations is similar. Until the 1920s and 1930s, most Gabors migrated periodically or throughout the year, and lived in tents. In subsequent decades, they began to build small, one- or two-room adobe houses, most of which have, since the 1970s, gradually been replaced with more comfortable and spacious brick houses. In contrast, many Cărhar Roma known to me lived a nomadic life in tents until the 1960s, when the Romanian authorities attempted, more or less successfully, to settle them (Achim 1998). The majority of them began to build or purchase brick houses around the time of the collapse of socialism. However, in part because of the 2008 global economic crisis, many of the houses the Cărhars have built in recent years are still unfinished (the exterior walls are unplastered, windows and doors are missing), and they are almost – or even entirely – uninhabitable. (It is not unusual for the owners of these houses to use some of the ground-floor rooms for storing animal fodder.) Similarly, the majority of my Cărhar Roma interlocutors did not use mobile phones and colour televisions until very recently. Furthermore, there is a significant difference in household expenditures between the Gabor and the Cărhar Roma families with whom I developed contacts during my fieldwork; most of these Gabor families now spend much more on food, clothing, and other consumer durables (such as fabrics for women's clothing, which they have sewn by local tailors) and on maintaining mobility than do Cărhar Roma families.

In the Gabor communities known to me, not only has the group of commodities suitable for representing economic prosperity grown spectacularly under the influence of the economic transformation accompanying the political regime change, but the meaning of many concepts determining consumption and its social evaluation – such as luxury, an average standard of living, or a good/normal/ideal life – have also changed. Certain commodities have been recontextualized within the classification system of consumer goods; they have shifted from the luxury category and are now associated with an average standard of living. Other goods (such as Western cars) that were unattainable before 1989 became integrated, almost as soon as they appeared, into the notion of an average standard of living.

In the case of the new post-socialist commodities mentioned above, the process of normalization[3] can be regarded as well advanced among the Gabors. These commodities have now become – mainly among those socialized after 1989 – significant elements in the dominant concepts of an average standard of living and a good/normal/ideal life. Among my Cărhar Roma acquaintances, however, while the process of normalization of some post-socialist consumer goods (new brick houses, cars, and so on) also began around the change of political regime, it has been proceeding at a much slower pace than in the Gabor Roma ethnic population. A similarly striking difference is that only a small proportion of my Cărhar interlocutors enthusiastically supported the process of normalization mentioned; that is, it appears that the integration of post-socialist commodities and services into the above concepts enjoys less social consensus and approval among the Cărhars.

It is worth noting that the members of both Roma ethnic populations consume only a portion of the post-socialist goods and services that have become popular among non-Roma living in Romania. For example, they do not spend their money on "conspicuous commodities" (Miller 1995, 265) and services such as (Western) cultural heritage tourism, fashionable women's clothing brands imported from the West, or luxurious weekend houses.[4]

Stereotyping, Moral Criticism, and Classification (Definitional) Struggles

In what follows, I will focus on Roma discourses (of consumption) serving to explain and "frame" the interethnic trade in silver beakers and tankards in order to answer two questions: How do the Gabors try to rationalize the distressing asymmetry of this trade and mitigate their symbolic loss – of prestige and positive public image – arising from it? And how do the Cărhar Roma counterbalance the negative ethnic stereotypes associated with them – among others – by the Gabors, partly as a face-saving response to the outflow of their silver objects? While the central question of the Gabors' discourse is why the Cărhars can buy beakers and tankards from them, the Cărhars primarily seek to answer why the Gabors are unable to keep these objects.

"The Cărhars Are Prepared to Die for Their Beakers" – The Discourse of the Gabor Roma

(1) One group of explanations given by my Gabor hosts criticizes the attitude of the Cărhars towards beakers and tankards. They argued that the Cărhar Roma attach an "unreasonable" emotional importance to these pieces and designate their place within the value hierarchy of subjects and objects in a morally questionable manner. Moreover, several of my Gabor interlocutors asserted that the Cărhars misinterpret the concept of the morality of spending or, more precisely, the morality of saving.

Many of the Gabors claimed that the Cărhar Roma are extremely committed to their beakers and tankards and that they are prepared to make greater financial, political, and emotional sacrifices than the Gabor Roma in order to purchase and retain them. As a Gabor individual in his fifties, whose grandfather had sold two valuable beakers to Cărhar buyers, noted:

> The Cărhars are even crazier about the beakers than we Gabors are. They [beakers and tankards] are the universe for them [for the Cărhars]. They are important to us, too, but not that much. Let us have the house and the family first, and then, if we can afford, we also buy beakers. Someone who has no means to buy a beaker or tankard for himself, can live without it. (21 June 2010)

Several of my Gabor interlocutors asserted that these pieces are not just valuable prestige objects for the Cărhars, but "gods" and "fetishes" (*balvanjure/idolure*). The Gabors' discourse rationalizing the interethnic trade also implies that some Cărhar owners attribute greater emotional importance to these objects than to their own family members – the risks they are prepared to take to buy or hold onto these pieces could even endanger the lives of their family members. To quote a Gabor individual who owns five beakers, "These [beakers and tankards] have a great, a very great value for them [the Cărhars]. God forbid, they would let a twenty-year-old man die rather than sell a beaker. They would rather let a man die!" One of my Gabor acquaintances from Cluj County, who does not possess any beakers or tankards but whose paternal grandfather had twelve silver prestige objects, put it this way:

> They [the Cărhars] will even give ten lives for it, burn their own house for it, but they do not give [away] the beaker. Not like us, the Gabors. When faced with financial difficulties we quickly say, "Well, I sell it [the beaker or tankard]." Or should I or my family rather die?! There [among the Cărhars] even if ten family members die, they do not sell a single beaker![5] But why should you give your life for a beaker?! It would be a crazy thing! When your son is in serious need, what wouldn't you do for him? But for them [the Cărhars] the beaker is more important than life! Ask anybody. They are like this. There you don't hear anybody speaking about selling a beaker ... Well, I, so not to lose you [turning to his son, sitting in the room], would give all twelve of my grandfather's silver pieces away! Who can see one family member perishing and not give his wealth [the beaker] away? Who? Well, they [the Cărhars] can do it. (18 June 2010)

In the above quotation, my interlocutor was referring to an interethnic transaction (the Cărhars "burn their own house for it [a beaker or tankard]") in which a Gabor owner, around the time of the political regime change, borrowed a significant amount from a Cărhar creditor, giving his beaker as a security for it. Several years later, when the debtor wanted to pay back the capital and its interest, the Cărhar creditor received him with the news that his house had, in the meantime, burned down, and the beaker serving as a security had perished. The debtor – as well as all of my Gabor acquaintances – thought that the Cărhar creditor burned down his own house in order to avoid returning the beaker that he "had fallen in love with" and had moved it to a safe place before the fire. Although the Gabor debtor filed a complaint with the police against the Cărhar creditor, they could not prove that the latter had intentionally burned down the house, and the debtor had to relinquish his hopes of getting his beaker back. This case has often been referred to by the Gabors to demonstrate the extremes to which some Cărhar Roma can go in order to keep the beakers and tankards they consider attractive – suggesting that for them these pieces have an "inestimable value" and are objects of "fanatic adoration." In order to underscore the same stereotypes, my Gabor interlocutors also liked to recall the story of the Cărhar creditor in Sibiu County who in 2001 (at least in their interpretation) paid with the life of his only son for contravening business ethics; without the consent of a Gabor debtor, he had bought the latter's debt and received the security, an exceptionally valuable beaker – for which the debtor's wife had repeatedly cursed him and his family. (This case is described in more detail in chapter 13.) The story of this Cărhar creditor was frequently mentioned as illustrative proof of the Cărhars' silver-object fetishism and of the dramatic consequences of someone taking control of a silver beaker or tankard without the permission of its owner.

The stereotype of the Cărhars having an extreme passion for collecting is a suitable ground for moral criticism mainly because it implicitly claims that some Cărhar Roma ignore the business ethics of prestige-object transactions and the resulting negative consequences (such as the curses of a cheated owner), and in so doing also disregard the principle of the primacy and irreplaceability of human life. Although rare, there are also examples within the Gabor Roma ethnic population in which a death has been regarded as the consequence of excessive attachment to a prestige object. However, in the Gabors' explanations rationalizing the interethnic prestige-object trade, such cases are consistently deleted; they are never referred to.

The ethnic stereotypes mentioned suggest that the Gabors are unable to stop the partial outflow of their prestige objects because the Cărhar Roma represent an immoral consumer ideology with which they cannot, and do not even want to, identify themselves: namely, the unacceptably high social and emotional significance attached to these pieces, and their occasional placement at the top of a value hierarchy of subjects and objects. In other words, the Gabor Roma position themselves in their own discourse as victims of the Cărhars' morally inappropriate consumer patterns and value preferences; as moderate, rational, and responsible consumers; and as defenders of the moral hierarchy of values that appreciates human life over commodities. This strategy of moral dichotomization focusing on consumption aims to counterbalance, on an ethical level, the Gabors' symbolic loss arising from the interethnic trade of beakers and tankards.

(2) The second group of explanations used by the Gabors to rationalize and "frame" the outflow of their prestige objects focuses on the lifestyle of the Cărhar Roma and their relation to new consumer goods, practices, and patterns. In these explanations, the Cărhars are often stereotypically characterized with such remarks as "They are less civilized [less interested in the development of technology]," "They do not know modern things," and "They stick too much to

traditions." Moreover, their way of life is frequently described as "too behind the times," "backward," and "withdrawn." According to the Gabors' discourse (which my own experiences partially confirm), most of the Cărhar Roma are less attracted than the Gabors to expensive and conspicuous post-socialist consumer goods and services regarded today as fashionable by the Romanian non-Roma (such as expensive Western cars, or big, new family houses). This discourse suggests that the lifestyle and consumer attitude of the majority of the Cărhars has remained largely unchanged since 1989, and – in contrast to the Gabors – post-socialist consumer sensitivity has had a negligible impact on them, despite the fact that many of them could afford the new costly commodities that have become widespread in the last two decades or so. The Gabors' discourse also associates with the Cărhars the stereotypes of rigid saving and self-restriction in household consumption, habits that in this discourse are regarded as synonymous with meaningless and morally reproachable deprivation. My Gabor hosts argued that these practices are inevitable consequences of the Cărhars' extreme passion for collecting silver objects. In describing the latter attitude they often used the essentializing stereotype that the Cărhar Roma "are prepared to spend their last Romanian leu" on buying or keeping these pieces, to the detriment of their other needs. Finally, in the Gabors' discourse, the Cărhars are often characterized as resorting to low-prestige and frequently stigmatized strategies of subsistence, such as begging, fortune-telling, and collecting garbage for recycling. (This discourse conceals the fact that, mainly before the fall of socialism, Gabor Roma, primarily women, also widely employed these strategies.)

These negative ethnic stereotypes are often dichotomized with statements that the Gabors are more open to global changes and processes, more travelled and mobile, and more familiar with the social practices and value preferences of the non-Roma majority society than the Cărhars. In their discourse serving to explain the interethnic prestige-object trade, the Gabors attribute positive characteristics to themselves; in the context of comparison with the Cărhars, they represent modernity, "civilization," "openness to the world," and Westernization, and are sensitive to new trends of consumer culture and the development of technology. In contrast, this discourse represents the Cărhars as people who are "tied to a place"[6] and associated in their consumer attitude and lifestyle with an exaggerated and negatively interpreted traditionalism and conservatism, who reject modernity and could be labelled as backward.

This is well illustrated by the following comment made by one of my Gabor hosts in his fifties. His father, regarded by the Gabor Roma as one of the most influential prestige-object brokers before his death in 2007, had in 1998 borrowed 200 million old Romanian lei (approximately US$23,000) from a Cărhar creditor in a village in the Olt River area, leaving his only beaker as a security. Although it is regarded as a valuable piece among the Gabors, to this day my interlocutor and his four brothers have been unable to redeem the object, because of the family conflicts between them and their financial difficulties – despite the fact that the capital borrowed against it in 1998 does not qualify as an exceptionally large sum, at least when compared to similar deals.

> They [the Cărhars] spend or eat as they earn. Do you understand? They do not sell the beakers, their wealth, under any circumstances! ... They have started to become civilized only now, since democracy [that is, since 1989], because earlier they all lived in tents. My grandfather lived in a house, we all built houses. But they still lived in tents, even in wintertime ... Well, I say, they were backward even before democracy. They did not know what a bathroom was ... But in the meantime they collected money! ... Regarding culture, they are very backward in comparison with us, you see? Our kind of Roma [the Gabors] have always been more civilized, always. Because we have known what a bathroom is for a long time, we have always needed this or that, you see? We follow the [non-Roma majority] society. (8 September 2008)

According to the explanations above, the "open" (*puterde*) and "civilized" (*čivilizature*) Gabors cannot stop their beakers and tankards being bought by the "closed" (*phandade*), "less civilized," and "old-fashioned" Cărhar Roma precisely because the Gabors are modern; they "go with the times" and are sensitive to new trends in the consumer culture of Romanian majority society. In other words, the Gabors spend at least as much of their income on the consumption of modernity as they spend on ethnicized goods that materialize their ethnic past and intraethnic social differences (silver beakers and tankards).

The quotations above illustrate how strategies such as the construction of essentializing, homogenizing, and often stigmatizing ethnic stereotypes; moral criticism focusing on consumption; and the classification (or definition) struggle connected with the concepts of a good/normal/ideal life and an average standard of living are exploited in interethnic symbolic conflicts – how they can become tools to restore a positive public image.

"The Gabors Spend a Lot on Luxury Goods ... and They Do Not Mind If They Lose Their Beakers!" – The Discourse of the Cărhar Roma

The Cărhars themselves are familiar with the negative stereotypes that the Gabors' discourse associates with them. They attempt to protect their positive public image through moralizing on the growing popularity of post-socialist consumer patterns among the Gabors and their changing relation to prestige objects; classification (or definition) struggles connected with the concepts of positive versus negative luxury and an average standard of living; and the ideology of ethnic purism (Herzfeld 2003).

As many of my Cărhar interlocutors argued, the solvent demand for beakers and tankards is primarily decreasing among the Gabors because the young Gabor people socialized after the collapse of socialism spend an increasing part of their income on commodities such as new family homes equipped with expensive furniture, fashionable Western cars, and other types of costly durable consumer goods. In contrast to this, the Cărhar Roma represent themselves in their own discourse serving to explain the interethnic prestige-object trade as a people who still cling to their silver pieces with the same, or almost the same, intensity as before the political transformation of 1989. This is well illustrated by this statement – from a man in his fifties, the son of a Cărhar Roma prestige-object owner – on the order of importance of beakers and tankards versus houses:

> We value beakers [and tankards] more than they [the Gabors] do ... If I had ten houses like this one, I would not value them more than this [his father's beaker]. I do not appreciate houses; I am not rich because I have a house ... Among us [the Cărhars], that [the beakers and tankards] means wealth. Not land, not houses; only beakers [and tankards] are our wealth. (27 June 2010)

To quote another Cărhar Roma commentary:

> God forbid that this should actually happen, but I would rather sell my house and make a little hut for myself, than sell my beaker ... We

[the Cărhar Roma] are not rich because of this house ... [It is only important so that] the children could live somewhere. A house? What is it?! Only mud and stone! That's it. You will find it anywhere. But a beaker [or tankard], my brother, you will not find so easily. Isn't it true? (18 June 2010)

In contrast to the opinion of a significant number of my Gabor Roma acquaintances, the Cărhars' discourse does not regard post-socialist consumer goods and practices as irresistibly attractive or indispensable, and does not classify them in the category of an ideal life. On the contrary, their discourse describes them with negative Romani terms such as *luxuri* (useless luxury goods), *cifrasăguri* (flashy goods), or *putjarimo* (morally reproachable ostentation). In other words, the Cărhars' discourse defines these commodities and consumer practices as superfluous, associates them with negative luxury (waste) and excessive comfort-seeking, and therefore regards them as morally stigmatized. While it is obvious that the comfortable new brick houses and cars are also becoming more popular among the young Cărhar Roma – although not to the same extent as among the Gabors – I met only two isolated cases in which my Cărhar interlocutors asserted that it was worth even going into debt, or undergoing the shame and loss of prestige that results from selling silver pieces, in order to buy post-socialist goods. These were, however, the exception to the rule. Several Cărhar individuals who owned new houses – often unfinished and unplastered, with only one or two modestly furnished rooms – emphasized that these had not been built with money they had made by selling their beakers or tankards, and that they built only at a pace and extent that did not require them to pawn or sell these objects.

Many of my Cărhar hosts stated that, since the political transformation of 1989, the Gabors borrow from each other, or from other Roma or non-Roma, more often and at high interest rates to buy new consumer goods, and that many were unable to repay these loans. As a consequence, the debtors were often forced to put in pawn or sell their last reserves: their silver objects (or, lacking these, their house or other assets). Using analytical categories, the Cărhars' discourse argues that the demand for beakers and tankards has declined somewhat among the members of the Gabor generations socialized after 1989, mainly due to the rapid spread of post-socialist commodities and consumer sensitivity, and this is why the Cărhars are able to buy some of the Gabors' silver objects. (This argumentation, however, ignores the fact that other important factors have also contributed to the outflow of the latter pieces.) As a middle-aged Cărhar man, whose father owns a beaker and is also one of the brokers often employed in interethnic prestige-object transactions, said:

> The Gabors spend a lot on luxury goods, Mercedes cars ... and they do not mind if they lose their beakers [if they have to sell their beakers]! They become lords; they began to resemble non-Roma. Our men [the Cărhars] do not live like this. We do not seek luxury, those things. We work, we collect money, and we collect beakers as well! ... Among the Gabors life is more lord-like; they have already bought cars, luxury goods, big houses, and then they get into debt and sell the beakers [and tankards]. Our Roma do not do that. Ours buy from them! (23 June 2010)

While most Gabor Roma socialized after the change of political regime do not define the partial replacement of their beakers and tankards with post-socialist goods as a threatening anomaly, my Cărhar interlocutors – regardless of age – asserted, almost without exception, that this practice was superfluous and meaningless: an "irresponsible waste." Moreover, in the Cărhars' discourse, this process is linked to the question of Roma ethnic identity, and has a disquieting moral dimension.[7] The Cărhars' discourse interprets the rapid spread of post-socialist consumer sensitivity among the Gabors – which contributes to the fact that they are forced to part with some of their silver objects – as a process that threatens and pollutes (Harrison 1999, 10–11) the Gabors' Roma ethnic identity. In other words, this discourse argues that because of their excessive attachment to new consumer practices and value preferences, the Gabors are gradually "becoming non-Roma"; that is, they have set out on the path of ethnic identity loss – by selling some of their beakers and tankards they are losing part of their *Gaborness*. The pejorative term "become lords" (*rajisejle*; the noun "lords" is a synonym of non-Roma people) in the above quotation refers to this process. My Cărhar interlocutors often expressed their disapproval of the diminishing interest of the younger Gabor generations in silver objects by referring to them as "not true," "not original" Roma, that is – using analytical categories – by questioning the authenticity of their ethnic identity as Gabor Roma. In Romania today, according to the Cărhars' discourse serving to explain the interethnic prestige-object trade, it is only their own Roma ethnic population that continues the "ancient Roma tradition" of collecting beakers and tankards, at least in its pre-democracy form. It is partly for this reason, argued my Cărhar acquaintances, that, unlike the Gabors, the Cărhar Roma have remained "true" (*ćaće*), "original" (*oridźinaluri*) Roma. The fact that the Cărhars associate them with the above negative ethnic stereotypes is not unknown to the Gabors either. This is well illustrated by the following comment by a Gabor individual from Cluj County: "They [the Cărhars] say that we [the Gabors] are *gaźos* [non-Roma]! [Laughing.] That we are no proper [true] Roma! Only they are well-to-do, true Roma!"

In the Cărhars' discourse, the Gabors are associated with the consumer modernity coming from the non-Roma, which is considered destructive and is thus morally stigmatized; with the outflow of silver objects explained by this modernity; and with the loss of tradition and ethnic identity attributed to the latter process. (As one of my Cărhar interlocutors stated, "The Gabors have forgotten their traditions.") At the same time, the Cărhars attribute to their own Roma ethnic population such positively defined practices as creating a distance from the non-Roma and the exaggerated consumption of post-socialist commodities ("luxury"), upholding conscious consumer traditionalism and conservatism, and a respect for traditions. These practices appear in the Cărhars' discourse as indispensable conditions for the survival of their prestige economy and the authenticity of their Roma ethnic identity. In this context, the significant consumer self-restraint and thrift undertaken in the interest of retaining beakers and tankards (which now appears unacceptable to many Gabor Roma) are also characterized positively. To quote a proud Cărhar woman in her forties, "The Gabors go and sell them [their silver objects]. But we do not sell them! We would rather not eat to retain our beakers and tankards! To leave them to our kids."

The moral criticism focusing on the Gabors' consumer practices and value preferences can also be used to rationalize (destigmatize) the low-prestige strategies of subsistence usually associated with the Cărhars, such as begging. As previously mentioned, before the political transformation of 1989, begging was a frequent means of subsistence within both Roma ethnic populations. Today, while very few Gabor women beg, many Cărhar Roma men and women earn an income through begging, mostly in Italy and France. The Cărhars try to counterbalance the moral stigma associated with begging by asserting that it is less shameful for them to earn money by begging than by selling their silver objects. Thus, in their discourse, begging is a necessary evil that enables them to achieve important social goals: to retain their prestige objects and remain "true Roma." This is well illustrated by

.the following – exaggerated – comment a Cărhar woman made to a Gabor woman of the same age at a Sibiu County flea market: "You are ashamed to beg, but we have all our beakers [and tankards], while you have sold them all! Your nation [the Gabor Roma] has sold them all! You have sold your beakers [and tankards] for food!" With the often used negative stereotype that the Gabors "have been exchanging their beakers and tankards for food and drink," the Cărhars argue that, due to the growing popularity of the morally stigmatized, post-socialist commodities and services, the amounts spent for the goods that now fall into the category of an average standard of living have increased so much among the Gabors that many prestige-object owners can procure them only by selling their silver pieces. That is, in the Cărhars' interpretation, the Gabors who sell their precious beakers and tankards in order to buy "food and drink" (in other words, to achieve a post-socialist average standard of living) make an irrational and senseless consumer decision: "They don't know how to handle money."

Constructing Contesting Interpretations of Consumer Moral Superiority

This chapter has presented a Romanian example of the politics of consumption by analysing discourses that explain and "frame" the prestige-object trade between the Gabor and the Cărhar Roma. Although there are several important reasons for this trade, in the discourses of both Roma ethnic populations negative stereotypes focusing on certain consumer practices and value preferences attributed to the ethnic other, and such related discursive strategies as dichotomization, hyperbolization, essentialization, and homogenization, play a dominant role (see Table 10.1, at the end of this chapter). While the negative stereotypes associated with the ethnic other are accompanied by moral criticism and stigmatization, the qualifying labels attached to the consumer decisions of one's own population are used as a means of moral self-justification and self-glorification.

Among the dimensions of the politics of consumption outlined in the first section of this chapter, the examined discourses are more closely linked to, first, the politics of identity and public image and, second, the politics of normalization.

(1) As previously mentioned, the members of both Roma ethnic populations use these discourses primarily to explain and reduce the negative symbolic consequences of the interethnic prestige-object trade. On the one hand, the Gabor Roma try to compensate for the loss of positive

public image and prestige resulting from the sale of some of their ethnicized silver objects, which are imbued with identity and emotional
value. On the other hand, the Cărhar Roma resort to the politics of consumption to blunt the face-threatening, negative ethnic stereotypes that
are attached to them by the Gabors who are forced to part with some of
their beakers and tankards.

(2) The role of the politics of normalization in these discourses
becomes apparent when we examine one of the dominant strategies
employed by the Gabors and the Cărhars: the interethnic classification
(or definition) struggle related to some key concepts that have a significant impact on consumer behaviour and its social evaluation. In the
case of the comments examined, such symbolic struggles developed
between the Gabor and the Cărhar Roma in connection with the following issues (among others):

- Which consumer goods and practices should be classified in the
  categories of an average standard of living, positive luxury, waste
  (negative luxury), and essential to a good/normal/ideal life – and
  which should be excluded from them?
- Into which of these categories do the new, post-socialist consumer
  goods and practices fall? Should they be considered as integral to
  an average standard of living (as most Gabor Roma socialized after
  the collapse of socialism suggest), or are they negative luxuries (as
  most Cărhar Roma I know argue)?
- How should one interpret consumer modernity and consumer
  traditionalism and conservatism, and what kind of value judgments
  should be associated with them?
- What role does consumption (of silver prestige objects) play in the
  construction and representation of ethnic identity or – using the
  ideology of ethnic purism characteristic of the Cărhars' discourse –
  in preserving "true Roma" identity?

Classification (or definitional) struggles, defined as one possible type
of symbolic conflict between contesting communities, are often practices imbued with strategic significance in the process and politics of
normalization. To put it in other words, classification (or definitional)
struggles are frequently directed at determining which consumer
goods, practices, and patterns should be defined as "normal," "ordinary," and dominant in a particular social context, and which should

be marginalized; that is, these struggles can often be interpreted as normalization contests.

The politics of consumption, however, not only contributes to the rationalization of the symbolic consequences of the interethnic prestige-object trade, but also has further-reaching social implications. By means of negative stereotypes and moral criticism focusing on the ethnic other, as well as contesting interpretations of what constitutes a good/normal/ideal life and consumption, the members of both Roma ethnic populations try to construct and monopolize a position of consumer moral superiority. The ideology of consumer moral superiority plays a decisive role in the construction, representation, and authentication of ethnic identity and social closeness within these Roma ethnic populations, and of social distance and difference between them. In other words, it is an important element in creating a sense and everyday experience of ethnic belonging and in managing ethnic otherness for these Roma.

Hence, this chapter argues that a deeper understanding of "who makes moral arguments" in relation to consumption, and of "how these arguments are deployed, what kinds of effects they have on others, and how inequality is justified and rationalized" (Wilk 2001, 250; see also Sassatelli 2004, 178), is not only essential in the analysis of the examined, competing discourses, but is also useful for anthropologists and sociologists interested in the discursive repertoire of symbolic conflicts between religious denominations, genders, or nations.

Table 10.1. Stereotypes of consumer patterns/value preferences and lifestyles in the discourses analysed

Auto-Stereotypes of the Gabors	*Hetero-Stereotypes Attributed to the Cărhars by the Gabors*	*Auto-Stereotypes of the Cărhars*	*Hetero-Stereotypes Attributed to the Gabors by the Cărhars*
• "civilized and cultured" • "open to the [non-Roma] world" • "keep abreast of the times" • "modern" • deny that it would be worth it "to die for a beaker" (rational, responsible, and morally approved consumption: familiarity with the non-Roma majority society; positively defined Westernization and sensitivity to new trends of consumer culture and the development of technology; consumers of modernity; mobility and	• "less civilized," • "socially and culturally backward and withdrawn" • "closed to the [non-Roma] world" • "too behind the times," • "old-fashioned in their lifestyle [their living conditions have not really changed since the fall of socialism]" • "not modern," "stick too much to their traditions" • "prepared to die for the beakers" • "spend or eat as they earn" (irrational, irresponsible, and morally inappropriate consumer patterns and value preferences: rejecting Westernization and new	• "usually avoid dangerous *luxuri* ('luxury' [expensive post-socialist consumer goods and services])" • "preserve and respect their [consumer] traditions: stick to their prestige objects" "they have remained true, original Roma" (rational, responsible, and morally approved consumption: positively defined, conscious consumer traditionalism and conservatism, self-restraint, and thrift; creating distance from the non-Roma society and the	• "spend a lot on *luxuri* ('luxury' [expensive post-socialist consumer goods and services])," which often leads to running into debt and to the fact that "the Gabors have been exchanging their beakers and tankards for food and drink." This practice (a) is a meaningless and irresponsible waste; (b) threatens the Gabors' ethnic identity: "they become non-Roma," "become lords" (*rajsejle*), "not true, not original Roma" • "have forgotten their traditions" • "don't know how to handle money" (irrational, irresponsible, and morally inappropriate consumer patterns and value preferences:

[international] migration; defenders of the dominance of the moral order that appreciates human life above objects)

trends of consumer culture; morally stigmatized, extreme consumer traditionalism and conservatism, self-restraint, and thrift; consumers of the past; immobility; prestige-object fetishism)

post-socialist consumer goods, services, and sensitivity [the "luxury"])

morally stigmatized and criticized fetishism of consumer modernity and Westernization; extreme sensitivity and affinity to expensive post-socialist consumer goods and services [the "luxury"]; identity pollution and loss of tradition)

PART THREE

Multi-Sited Commodity Ethnographies

11

Things-in-Motion: Methodological Fetishism, Multi-Sitedness, and the Biographical Method

Monitoring the spatial movement of things – objects, technologies, tastes, and so on – has long been a part of anthropological research focusing on how economic practices are embedded in social relations. The investigation of things-in-motion, especially things crossing the boundaries of social or cultural contexts and value regimes, however, played only a marginal role in anthropological research until the 1980s, when its methodological advantages and explanatory power gained widespread recognition.

Arjun Appadurai's classic study, "Introduction: Commodities and the Politics of Value" (1986), made a significant contribution to recognizing the intellectual importance of analysing the impacts caused, influenced, and suffered by things-in-motion as an anthropological perspective.[1] His work focuses, among other things, on shifts in the relations of things to commodity status, with particular regard to the processes of commodification as well as of de- and recommodification. He argues that the study of the "paths" along which things migrate, often crossing social and cultural boundaries, can significantly contribute to a deeper understanding of the complex nature – inner dynamics, context dependency, and variability – of processes such as colonialization, globalization, or the spread of capitalism.

Appadurai attempts to rethink the dominant perspective within the social sciences that prefers the examination of subjects while questioning and depreciating the social significance and agency of things – that is, their capacity to construct contexts, subjects, and identities. With this view in mind, he introduces the concept of "methodological fetishism":

Even if our own approach to things is conditioned necessarily by the view that things have no meanings apart from those that human transactions, attributions, and motivations endow them with, the anthropological problem is that this formal truth does not illuminate the concrete, historical circulations of things. For that we have to follow the things themselves, for their meanings are inscribed in their forms, their uses, their trajectories. It is only through the analysis of these trajectories that we can interpret the human transactions and calculations that enliven things. Thus, even though from a theoretical point of view human actors encode things with significance, from a methodological point of view it is the things-in-motion that illuminate their human and social context. No social analysis of things (whether the analyst is an economist, an art historian, or an anthropologist) can avoid a minimum level of what might be called methodological fetishism. This methodological fetishism, returning our attention to the things themselves, is in part a corrective to the tendency to excessively sociologize transactions in things, a tendency we owe to Mauss, as Firth has recently noted. (Appadurai 1986, 5)

Although the construction of this term was inspired by Marx's "commodity fetishism," fetishism does not have a negative connotation in this context. On the contrary, according to Appadurai's interpretation, it is a useful and necessary methodological turn for social scientists to increasingly focus on analysis of the complex systems of relations among things themselves, as well as between things and subjects (see Pels 1998, 95; Brown 2001, 7). Methodological fetishism is a research perspective that includes the recognition of and conscious concentration on the significance of things. According to Pels (1998, 94), "'methodological fetishism' is a reversal of the commonly accepted hierarchy of facts and values in social and cultural theory, which says that things don't talk back." Instead of Appadurai's methodological fetishism, Pels proposes the alternative term "methodological animism" (Pels 1998, 94). In his study of globalization, Foster (2006, 286) uses the term "critical fetishism" to refer to the need for the social sciences to place greater emphasis on analysing the social, cultural, and economic impacts produced by things migrating between contexts and value regimes (such as nations or ethnic populations), because in this way the nature of interactions between global tendencies and local worlds can be investigated and understood from a new, promising perspective.

Appadurai demonstrates unambiguously that monitoring the careers and biographies of things-in-motion is crucial to a more nuanced understanding of the social and cultural contexts, relations, and processes surrounding them. In doing so, he primarily asserts that not only do subjects shape migrating things, but migrating things also have a significant impact on how subjects perceive themselves and construct their identities and their social, cultural, and economic relations. In other words, things possess a material agency (Hoskins 2006; Knappett & Malafouris 2008). Agency, however, is not an exclusive attribute of the world of either things or subjects – these two spheres are created and acquire social meanings and significance in the context of the inter-actions arising between them, and therefore things and subjects are simultaneously products and producers of these interactions, as well as of each other. The relation between things and subjects is characterized by constant interplay and interdependence.

The study of things-in-motion usually results in "object ethnog-raphies" (Fowles 2006, n.p.), which challenge the widespread notion that the analysis of social processes and relations is possible primar-ily "through the thoughts, experiences and actions of human agents" (Fowles 2006, n.p.). In these object ethnographies, the "ethnographic gaze should be upon an object individual, a class of objects, or a discrete community of objects" (Fowles 2006, n.p.), and should create distance from the longstanding anthropological perspective that focuses on "how people make things." Object ethnographies – like new material culture studies as a whole – aim to investigate primarily "how 'things make people,' how objects mediate social relationships – ultimately how inanimate objects can be read as having a form of agency of their own" (Fowles 2006, n.p.).

Several things-in-motion studies follow commodities crossing one or more cultural, social, or political boundaries in the course of their social lives. The analyses of these "transnational commodities" (MacDougall 2003) or "transcultural commodities" (Maynard 2004, 103) primarily focus on the influence that commodity migration has on the new contexts in which the commodities have become embedded, as well as the altera-tions of their material and symbolic properties (their meanings, values, or functions) after they have crossed boundaries. The group of commodi-ties – that anthropologists, sociologists, and human geographers have examined – moving between various social, cultural, and political con-texts and value regimes includes used clothes (Hansen 2000), Barbie dolls (MacDougall 2003; Magee 2005), human organs for transplant (Scheper-Hughes 2000), copper kettles (Turgeon 1997), Coca-Cola (Miller 1997; Foster 2008), coffee (Weiss 1996), pearls (Saunders 1999; Straight 2002), and guns (Hugh-Jones 1992). Objects, designs, and technologies usu-ally categorized as tribal, Aboriginal, or Indigenous art when they enter

Western museums, galleries, auction houses, and private collections have also been frequently studied (Myers 1991, 1998, 2002, 2006a, 2006b, 2006c, 2013; Thomas 1991; Levi 1992; Steiner 1994, 1995, 2002; Marcus & Myers 1995; Fenn 1996; Phillips & Steiner 1999; Geismar 2001, 2008).

In documenting and interpreting the movement of transnational and transcultural commodities and their interactions with various contexts, several researchers have either explicitly or implicitly adopted the biographical method. (In addition to the works mentioned in the previous paragraph, see also Gosden & Marshall 1999; Hoskins 2006.) This method became especially popular among anthropologists, sociologists, archaeologists, and human geographers interested in new material culture studies following the publication of Igor Kopytoff's (1986) study. It starts from the assumption that things – from the first stages of production to final rollout – not only are capable of materializing the life and experiences of their owners by functioning as souvenirs or other types of "biographical objects" (Hoskins 1998), but may also acquire their own socially constructed biographies. The latter may include various aspects of the piece's career: the producer and the conditions of production; the piece's ownership history; its movement between various contexts of use; modifications related to its meaning, value, and function; and the categories – commodity, art, identity symbol, and so on – into which the given piece was classified in the course of its social life (see also Schamberger, Sear, Wehner, & Wilson 2008). The biography-constructing processes most often studied by social scientists interested in object ethnographies are undoubtedly change in ownership and pawning, migration between value regimes (de- and recontextualization), and the transformation of the symbolic (meaning and value) and material properties of commodities.

The novelty and explanatory power of the biographical method lies primarily in the fact that it offers an analytical perspective that (a) can be used to track the movement of things within and between contexts; (b) can help trace the metamorphoses of their symbolic and material features; and (c) contributes to a deeper understanding of the practices, ideologies, processes, and emotions developing around, or caused and influenced, by things. That is, the effectiveness of this method lies primarily in the fact that it is capable of capturing the agency of things as well as their dynamic and complex relationships with various subjects and contexts.

As the biographical method frequently requires tracking migrating things, it often prefers multi-sited ethnography to the principle of "one

research: one locality" (Foster 2006, 285). As mentioned in the introduction, one of the techniques of multi-sited fieldwork described by
Marcus is "following the thing" (Marcus 1995, 106). This technique
"involves tracing the circulation through different contexts of a mani-
festly material object of study (at least as initially conceived), such as
commodities, gifts, money, works of art, and intellectual property"
(Marcus 1995, 106–7). As Marcus also points out, the study of things-in-
motion through multi-sited fieldwork has become especially popular
among researchers interested in objects that are interpreted as works
of art or museum objects, and the globalizing markets for these pieces.

Combining the interpretations of Marcus (1995) and Fowles (2006), I
argue that analyses based on multi-sited research that focus on tracking
commodities-in-motion and on their – often transnational and transcultural – biographies or social lives, should be defined as *multi-sited commodity ethnographies*. Some of these deal with things that migrate within
a single cultural or social context (see chapter 12), while others focus on
things that cross cultural or social boundaries (see chapter 13).

The following two chapters will trace the post-socialist careers of a
beaker and a tankard by applying the "methodological fetishism" proposed by Appadurai, as well as the perspective of things-in-motion and
the biographical method. These multi-sited commodity ethnographies
can contribute, for example, to a more nuanced understanding of how
the Gabors' prestige economy participates in shaping social differences,
and how it is intertwined with other symbolic arenas of politics (such as
marriage politics or the competition to achieve and maintain a positive
public image). In addition, these ethnographies show in a more contextually embedded way (a) the inner dynamics of the prestige economy
(e.g. by throwing light on the diversity of discursive and other means
used in the proprietary contests occurring there); (b) such tools of conflict management as convening an "assembly" and public swearing;
(c) the Gabor Roma concepts of morality, business ethics, and social
prosperity; and (d) the techniques (such as sharing *mita* interpreted as
"a representation of joy" or public business face-work) used to facili-
tate the transformation of the achievements realized in the symbolic
arenas of politics into successes accompanied by social appreciation
and approval. These multi-sited commodity ethnographies also clearly
demonstrate the significant differences between the value regime
(related to silver objects) of the Gabor Roma and those of the antiques
market and art history.

12

Prestige Objects, Marriage Politics, and the Manipulation of Nominal Authenticity: The Biography of a Beaker, 2000–2007

Value Aspects

The object in question is a seven-decilitre, richly gilded, trumpet-shaped, footed silver beaker. It is decorated with a series of elaborated floral motifs, the richness of which was characterized by one of my interlocutors in the following way: the surface of this piece "is so richly decorated that there is no place on it where one could put down a needle" (i.e., there is no unadorned part of the surface that is larger than a needle).

In addition to its attractive material properties, this beaker is also considered a valuable object because of its Gabor Roma social career. In the words of an influential Gabor man's son, who often participated in prestige-object transactions as a broker, the piece in question is

> Old. An antique. It used to belong to our [Gabor Roma] forebears, it's our heritage from our forebears! It belonged to important people, famous [Gabor] Roma! In the case of beakers, it's the coat of arms [the fame of the former Gabor owners] that counts; we pay for the coat of arms, not the material. A gilded silver beaker, that's where our wealth is. (16 June 2006)

A number of successful, influential, and widely known people are to be found among the eight recorded Gabor owners in the biography of the piece in question. The fame arising from its ownership history is due primarily to the second and fourth possessors, whose wealth and social prestige contributed significantly to making this object especially valuable in the eyes of the Gabor Roma. Most of my interlocutors were of the opinion that the piece was somewhere in the middle of the ranking of the ten most valuable Gabor beakers.

Its first known Gabor owner sold this beaker in the 1930s to the head of a Gabor family living in a small settlement in Mureş County. Up until his death during the Second World War, this second owner acquired an especially valuable collection of prestige objects; he owned seven silver pieces. Because his three sons were still minors at the time of his death, the objects passed into the care of his widow, who thus became the third owner of the beaker.[1] In the mid-1950s, plagued with constant financial difficulties, the widow was constrained to pawn the beaker to a Gabor Roma creditor, also from Mureş County. During the seven years of the loan, the total sum owed – including the capital and the interest – was more than 55,000 old Romanian lei.[2] In the seventh year, the creditor, whose principal aim was to acquire ownership of the beaker, claimed that he was in urgent need of cash and forced the widow to make a decision: either pay off her debt or sell the pawned object to him so that he could then sell it himself. (He did not seriously intend to sell it, but made this statement only in order to disguise his real aim, namely, to purchase the beaker.) But the creditor did not succeed because, although the widow decided to sell the beaker,[3] she sold it not to him but to a respected and wealthy Gabor man in Cluj County, who thus, in 1961 and for 105,000 old Romanian lei, became the fourth owner.[4] After the death of the Cluj County owner in the mid-1970s, the beaker became the property of his eldest son, the fifth owner, who – to settle his debts – sold it in 1982 to one of his sons-in-law, Janko, for 1,700,000 old Romanian lei.[5] For close to two decades, as the sixth owner, Janko retained full possession of the beaker, but in 1998 he was sentenced to two years of imprisonment for smuggling. In his absence, his family accumulated considerable debt by sending him money regularly and taking out loans to make up for the loss of his earnings.

Bango (the Seventh Owner) Buys the Beaker

Shortly after his release in November 2000, Janko, faced with the impatience of his family's creditors, decided to sell his prestige object and settle their debts from the proceeds. He called Kalo, a prestigious Gabor individual living in Mureş County, who had experience in prestige-object brokerage, and asked him to sell his beaker.

Kalo, who also owned a silver beaker bequeathed to him by his father, had not acquired his wealth primarily as a trader or a building contractor, as the majority of Gabor men usually do, but as a manager of Gabor Roma social and economic relations. A significant part of Kalo's income came from the following sources: (a) success fees received for his participation in organizing marital alliances as well as for his activity as a prestige-object broker; (b) marriage payments and other cash gifts received in the course of marrying off his grandchildren; and (c) interest earned on money he lent out.

Kalo thus hurried, together with his two sons, to Janko's Cluj Napoca home, expecting to acquire a significant success fee from the deal. Having accepted the commission, Kalo made a formal "request to view" Janko's beaker to check its nominal authenticity – that is, to verify that it was truly identical with the piece known to the Gabor Roma as Janko's beaker. Then he enquired about the amount of Janko's debt as well as the price the latter expected to receive for the beaker, and Kalo himself estimated its value. Finally, they agreed on the amount of the success fee due to the broker: 20,000 German marks (US$9,063). According to the terms of their agreement, this amount was independent of the final purchase price.

Kalo then visited several of his Gabor Roma acquaintances in Mureş County who he thought had both the political ambitions and cash reserves to buy Janko's beaker. Although the piece was regarded as one of the ten most valuable Gabor beakers, none of the individuals Kalo visited wanted to participate in the deal. Their reason was obvious: none of them dared to do business with a seller of bad moral reputation and to accept the attendant risks. Most of them feared that after the sale Janko would demand additional sums beyond the purchase price, and that he would not shrink even from conflict to achieve his aim. One of the main reasons why Janko commissioned a widely respected and influential broker was precisely because he had correctly presumed that a number of Roma individuals would be unwilling to do business directly with him. The broker's presence thus served – among other things – to reduce the distrust stemming from Janko's bad moral reputation and was to be interpreted as a guarantee of the deal's fairness.

After the unsuccessful attempts in Mureş County, the broker went to Bango, a hitherto overlooked acquaintance of his from Cluj County. Bango, who had relatively low social prestige, did not own any prestige objects. He had acquired most of his wealth after the 1989 political regime change, mostly through commissions received from state-owned construction companies, and had made significant efforts to convert his economic capital into personal fame in the prestige economy and in the competition for marital alliances with Gabor families of high social status. Like most Roma, Bango regarded success achieved in these symbolic arenas as a popular and effective means of accumulating political capital, catalyzing upward social mobility, and reformulating prestige relations. As "Bango was very eager to buy a good beaker," he was willing to risk potential conflicts with the seller.

According to his own recollections, the broker described to Bango the value and social significance of the beaker as follows:

> It is an important and famous piece which is worth buying! ... It is a richly decorated and gilded footed beaker, a very valuable object! It has great fame, because it belonged to the big X [the second owner of the beaker] who lived in the village of Y. So you don't have to be afraid to spend your money on it ... It is a beaker that will bring great renown to you. You can mention it and boast with it everywhere among the Gabor Roma! (14 August 2003)

Bango, who was not experienced in estimating the value of prestige objects, completely trusted the broker. Bango's reply to the above was "I will pay as much as you say for it, Kalo! If you say it is valuable and worth being purchased, then I will buy it!" Bango promised Kalo 20,000 German marks (US$9,063) as a success fee if "he would stand on his side" and help him to purchase the beaker.

After negotiating with both parties separately, Kalo organized a meeting for them at Janko's home. Here, in November 2000, after a brief bargaining session, they agreed to a purchase price of 300,000 German marks (US$135,954).[6] Bango, however, did not have enough cash at his disposal and needed to borrow more than 100,000 German marks (US$45,318). He paid for the beaker in early December in the presence of the broker and his sons, as well as some close family members of both parties.

In addition to the purchase of this prestige object, Bango also wanted to increase his renown in the politics of marriage. Therefore, in 2002, he arranged a marriage for his granddaughter with the grandson of Marko, a Gabor man who was extremely influential and widely honoured in their Roma ethnic population. Marko possessed two outstandingly valuable prestige objects – a beaker and a tankard – but his own contribution to the fame of his patriline was rather modest, primarily because he was a man of "poor income." He tried to ease his constant financial difficulties due to debts by, among other things, commodifying the renown of his patriline (especially of his father and paternal grandfather). This involved asking for high marriage payments when marrying off his children and grandchildren, and accepting cash gifts of great value from aspiring and wealthy Gabor individuals of low social prestige in exchange for entering into marital alliances with them.

They agreed that as soon as their grandchildren reached the necessary age (at the time, Marko's grandson was one and a half and Bango's granddaughter four years old), they would have them married and create a marital alliance between themselves. A lengthy bargaining process began regarding the amount of the marriage payment Bango would pay Marko. Marko referred primarily to his and his family's social fame and influence and the outstanding value of his prestige objects. At first he asked Bango for US$80,000, but in the end they agreed on US$60,000, to be paid in two instalments: half on the occasion of their grandchildren's betrothal and half at their wedding.

The betrothal was held on 19 March 2002 in a restaurant in Bango's town in Cluj County. In accordance with the gendered patterns of space usage characteristic of public events among the Gabor Roma, the men and the women sat at separate tables. After several hours of Roma political discourse between the invited Gabor men, they ate, and Bango publicly counted half (US$30,000) of the marriage payment he had promised Marko on the table. Bango then publicly shared *mita* interpreted as "a representation of joy," from himself and Marko, among the Gabor men present. (In addition to his share of the publicly distributed *mita* regarded as "a representation of joy," the broker who coordinated the establishment of the marital alliance received a secret *mita* payment of US$5,000, interpreted as a success fee, from both parties.)

Bango Puts His Beaker in Pawn

Bango, however, did not enjoy his increased renown for long. Indeed, from the beginning of the autumn of 2002, he fell further into debt, and by the winter of 2003–4, he was forced to put his beaker in pawn for a significant loan – US$90,000 – with a Gabor individual living in one of the Romanian cities along the Romanian-Hungarian border. Although Bango periodically sent small amounts of money to the lender to pay off at least part of the interest, by the end of 2005 it became clear to him that he would never redeem his beaker, and he hurried to find a buyer for it.

The Prospective Buyer: Laji (the Eighth Owner)

One of the potential buyers very interested in Bango's beaker was Laji, a 36-year-old Gabor man of modest social prestige living in Cluj County. He had acquired considerable wealth as a merchant, but had not inherited or bought any prestige objects. Laji and his father, like Bango, had strong Roma political ambitions and placed great emphasis on converting part of their disposable income into a marital alliance or a valuable beaker/tankard that would significantly increase their renown, or both.

As one of Laji's daughters had reached the age considered ideal for marriage, Laji and his father took stock of the Gabor Roma families with sons of similar age in order to find an influential co-father-in-law with considerable success in Roma politics. Laji, due to the modest social prestige of his family, was primarily attractive as a co-father-in-law because of the high marriage payment he could offer with his daughter.

Laji established a marital alliance with one of the sons of an extremely prestigious Gabor man in his sixties, who lived in Mureş County. The father of his co-father-in-law (hereinafter, old co-father-in-law)[7] was known in his own Gabor Roma local community as a village leader. He was also one of the most influential brokers who regularly took part in the management of prestige-object transactions between the Gabors, and between the Gabor and the Cărhar Roma. Furthermore, the old co-father-in-law had five sons and four brothers; in other words, he had a substantial stock of intraethnic relational capital.

Laji gave his new co-father-in-law (the third son of the old co-father-in-law) US$100,000 as a marriage payment during the wedding in the winter of 2002–3.[8] At the wedding and afterwards, Laji distributed among his relatives, friends, and acquaintances more than US$30,000 as cash gifts (interpreted in part as "representations of joy"). US$10,000 out of this sum was given in secret to his old co-father-in-law as thanks for supporting the marriage of the young couple and the marital alliance between the families.

The Price Bargaining

By the winter of 2005–6, everyone surmised that Bango's beaker would soon change hands. So speculation began over who would be able to raise the money necessary to buy it, and within this circle, which individuals would have the necessary political ambitions (who were eager to "put their money into a precious beaker"). Over time, the group of competing potential buyers was narrowed down to two Gabor men.

Laji was one of these, and in late 2005, after a number of phone calls, he and his father went to Bango to agree on the purchase price. Bango, however, asked a very high price for the beaker – US$800,000, and later US$500,000 – which Laji did not want to pay. Yet, a month later, Bango – who had gone into hiding in Mureş County to evade his impatient creditors and was being pressured by them through messages sent via some of his relatives – called Laji to continue the price bargaining. Bango said that they could continue on the condition that no one else attend the negotiations except Laji, his father, and one of his uncles on his father's side, and that these people should contact him in secret. According to the recollection of Laji's uncle, who participated in the transaction as a broker, he warned Laji's father as they were approaching Bango's hiding place: "The beaker is worth three [US$300,000]. I'm telling you so you know. But you and your son must give fifty [US$50,000] or a hundred [US$100,000] more to purchase it; Bango doesn't want to sell it to you because you're on bad terms, since you loved his wife." (The conflict between Laji's and Bango's families dated back to the 1980s. It was started by a secret love affair between Laji's father and Bango's wife, which was discovered after a while, and led to the souring of the relations between the two families. This conflict and the shame that accompanied it were the main reasons why Bango was so reluctant to sell his beaker to Laji.)

Bango – referring to the shame he had had to endure back then – opened the negotiations by again asking for US$500,000. Laji and his father considered this to be too much and made a final offer of US$400,000. Finally, Bango agreed to the US$400,000 because Laji's uncle convinced him that no Gabor Roma would offer more than this for the beaker and that the pressure of his creditors would leave him no time to wait for another serious buyer. In the words of Laji's uncle to Bango:

You know, if you have any sense, forget the love [reference to the former love affair between Bango's wife and Laji's father] now when your life's on the line [reference to the impatient lenders and the threats coming from them]. The love of your wife. You already got US$100,000 extra from us [as I have mentioned, Laji's uncle estimated the beaker to be worth US$300,000]. You have no reason to be angry, not for the rest of your life! Bring me water [a soft drink] and a brandy whenever we meet in the future because I, X [he mentions his own first name], have made you this hundred thousand extra [that is, he convinced Laji and his father that they should pay US$100,000 more than the estimated value of the beaker]! (4 August 2008)

Laji's family had to face another challenge, however, apart from the collection of the purchase price. Laji had to ensure that his old co-father-in-law, considered one of the most experienced prestige-object brokers among the Gabors, would not be insulted by the fact that he had not been allowed to participate in the bargaining. To avoid publicly humiliating the old co-father-in-law and later conflicts, Laji and his relatives immediately went to him and told him the details of the bargaining. When the old co-father-in-law heard about the negotiation, he angrily said to Laji, "Did you make a fair [transaction]? You are a snotty-nosed kid! Without me?!" Laji and his father promised him and his sons a significant cash gift as a kind of compensation. At the same time, those present agreed that after paying the purchase price, they would tell anyone curious about the details that the old co-father-in-law had been present during the price bargaining, and that it had, in fact, been primarily directed by him.

Laji's jubilation, however, did not last long. One of his political rivals found out about the impending beaker purchase and "pulled up" (provoked) Bango by referring to the secret love affair that had developed in the 1980s between Bango's wife and Laji's father and had ended with a severe conflict between the two families. The rival tried to "ruin the fair" by arguing that if Laji purchased the beaker, it would erect an "eternal monument" to Bango's wife's adultery and drag their shame back into the limelight. That is, Bango's Roma political competitors would ironically mention that he had sold his beaker to the son of the man who had "loved away his wife." Thus, Bango – out of anger and fear of being publicly shamed – terminated the oral contract he had established with Laji.

The Emergence of a Rival Buyer and the Manipulation of Nominal Authenticity

In early 2006, another ambitious Gabor Roma attempted to buy Bango's beaker. Tibor, who lived in Mureş County, began to negotiate with Bango and offered him US$375,000 for the beaker. Despite the fact that his offer was US$25,000 less than Laji's, due to the aggravated conflict with Laji's family Bango decided to sell his beaker to Tibor. Tibor did not have enough cash to purchase Bango's beaker and hastily sold his own prestige object – a large and modestly ornamented footed beaker his father had purchased in 1985 for 700,000 old Romanian lei[9] from a Gabor owner. The sale wasn't difficult for Tibor, as a wealthy Cărhar Roma man in Sibiu County – for whom this piece was especially attractive for its large capacity – had already tried several times to acquire it. Tibor visited this Cărhar man and received US$200,000[10] for his beaker. He used this, along with the money he had borrowed from several sources and the cash he had at his disposal, to make a large down payment on the desired piece. Furthermore, he planned to take over two of Bango's debts, worth more than US$70,000.

Finally, on 29 May 2006, Tibor went see the Gabor Roma creditor who had held Bango's beaker in pawn for two and a half years, and who lived in a Romanian city close to the Romanian-Hungarian border. Tibor took more than US$300,000 with him, as well as Bango and a number of other Gabor men – whom he expected to help him in the deal as supporters and witnesses. To his misfortune, Tibor also asked his father-in-law to assist him during the purchase. His father-in-law, considered a businessman "capable of everything," had accumulated a large debt and was not happy to hear about the prospective success of his son-in-law. He had entirely different plans with Tibor: since he knew that he would soon be forced to sell his own extremely valuable beaker, which he had inherited from his father, in order to pay off his debts, he wanted Tibor to buy or take this beaker in pawn from him, to "keep it in the family." Tibor, however, refused the request, fearing it was only Roma political "trickery." He suspected that if he took his father-in-law's beaker in pawn the latter would exploit their age and status difference to "play a trick" and take it back before repaying the loan. Or, if he did buy it, his father-in-law would continue to ask for more money years after the initial transaction, claiming that the beaker had been sold below its real market value. Another reason why Tibor's father-in-law was unhappy with the impending transaction was his envy and Roma political ambition; he feared that the status distance between him and his son-in-law would decrease significantly if Tibor bought Bango's beaker and he had to part with his own.

When they arrived in the city on the Romanian-Hungarian border and were examining Bango's beaker, the father-in-law – much to Tibor's astonishment – shouted at the creditor, feigning outrage, "Don't blind me [do not try to deceive me]! Bring forth the other beaker [Bango's real beaker]! That beaker is larger!" The creditor, however, consistently asserted that they were looking at Bango's beaker, and that he had not received any other prestige object in pawn. Bango and several of the Gabor men accompanying Tibor also argued that this was the beaker Tibor wanted. To quote one of the witnesses, "It was not copied and replaced [that is, the beaker they saw was not a much less valuable copy of the original]." The doubt his father-in-law cast, however, was sufficient to make Tibor uncertain and "quit the fair" (to withdraw from the deal). As many of my interlocutors later pointed out, Tibor did not believe at the time of the transaction that his father-in-law would knowingly deceive him and cause him, his daughter, and grandsons such a great financial and symbolic loss by thwarting the deal. (Apart from the public shame he suffered from the failure of the transaction, Tibor also had to pay interest on the sums he had borrowed and was left without any prestige object.)

Laji Pays the Purchase Price

On the day that he failed to complete the transaction with Tibor, Bango called Laji and offered him the beaker. Laji seized the opportunity, and, on 30 May 2006, he travelled together with his family and a number of Gabor men supporting him to the city on the Romanian-Hungarian border where Bango's creditor lived. (The leader of the almost fifty-member group was Laji's old co-father-in-law, who had previously complained because he could not be present at the bargaining between Laji and Bango.) Although Laji could have offered to pay only US$375,000, the amount Tibor had offered, he insisted on paying his initial offer price, US$400,000.[11] This decision was motivated, on the one hand, by his political ambition. On the other hand, he was afraid that if he lowered his previous offer, it – along with their earlier conflict (the adultery) – could lead Bango to cancel the deal again. As one of the men who witnessed the transaction later formulated:

> Bango would have preferred to sell his beaker to Tibor for US$300,000, than to that one [Laji] for US$500,000. But the trouble was already hot for him [Bango]. He badly needed the money because he was in debt with other [non-Gabor] Roma [who did not shy away from threats to enforce the repayment of their outstanding debts], so he had to pay the money back. (24 June 2010)

Laji had only a few hours to prepare for the deal, but he succeeded in borrowing a substantial amount of money to supplement the cash he had at his disposal. He brought the euro equivalent of US$250,000 with him. (This was converted to US dollars in the aforementioned city.)

Because of the failure of the negotiations on the previous day, Laji and his relatives placed special emphasis on verifying the nominal authenticity of the pawned object as a first step of the transaction at the creditor's house; they picked up the beaker a few times and thoroughly examined it before making the deal. The key figure in the examination was Laji's uncle, who had led the secret negotiations with Bango and had previously had opportunities to hold the object in his hands; he had even drunk from it as a young man. After checking its nominal authenticity, the uncle verified that the piece presented by the creditor was without doubt the beaker that Bango owned, and Laji could safely buy it.

Bango's beaker had remained in pawn for nearly two and a half years. As stipulated in the loan agreement, Bango had received US$90,000 from the Gabor Roma creditor, and by May 2006, he had accumulated a total debt of US$220,000. Although Bango could have repaid this loan in its entirety from the sum that Laji had brought with him, this solution proved unacceptable for Bango. In fact, news of Tibor's unsuccessful transaction the previous day had rapidly spread among the Gabor Roma, so that by 30 May 2006, some of Bango's other influential creditors had rushed to the city on the border and were impatiently waiting in front of the home of the creditor who held Bango's beaker in pawn, in hopes of getting back at least part of the money they had lent.

Therefore, the parties made the following agreement: Laji gave the US$250,000 to Bango, who then gave US$85,000 as a partial repayment of his debt to the creditor holding his beaker in pawn. The remaining US$165,000 Bango distributed at his discretion among some of his other impatient creditors who had gathered in the city. At the same time, Laji took over Bango's remaining debt of US$135,000, with the creditor holding Bango's beaker in pawn on the condition that he would pay it within three months, at the latest. In addition, Laji agreed to pay back one of Bango's smaller debts (US$15,000). Thus, besides the US$250,000 paid on that day, Laji had to raise another US$150,000 before he could take possession of the desired prestige object. It was agreed that the beaker would remain with the creditor until the full repayment of the debt.

Returning to his home in Cluj County, Laji tried to repay the loans he had taken out on the previous day for the beaker's purchase – in order to pay the least amount of interest he could – and to secure the still missing US$150,000 as soon as possible. Therefore, he put two houses he owned up for sale. One sold for €285,000 and the other for €120,000.

Three months later, in August 2006, Laji returned to the creditor with several witnesses, gave him the agreed-upon US$135,000, and received the beaker. He also paid back the other, smaller debt to ensure that the piece became his in terms of both non-Roma law and Gabor Roma business ethics.

Sharing *Mita*

In late August 2006, upon hearing the news of the beaker's purchase, several relatives, acquaintances, and friends came to see Laji and his father to share their joy, congratulate them on the transaction, express their good wishes, and take a look at the newly purchased prestige object. They also hoped to receive a cash gift – that is, *mita* defined as "a representation of joy" – as is customary among the Gabor Roma in such cases. (In this section I use the term *mita* to mean a cash gift interpreted as "a representation of joy." Where this is not the case will be clear from the context.) Laji, however, tried to dodge the moral expectation to give *mita*. He suspected that, due to his youth and his family's modest social prestige, the more influential Gabor men would be more encouraged to ask him for *mita*, and that many would not be satisfied with the amount he would willingly give them. His decision was motivated on the one hand by parsimony, and on the other by a desire to avoid conflict. Laji refused the requests to share *mita* and tried to cover his motivations by arguing that he had used all of his cash during the transaction, and was, in fact, in debt.

He planned to start distributing *mita* only months after the transaction, when public interest related to the purchase would have somewhat declined and asking for *mita* would largely lose its timeliness – at least for most of his friends and acquaintances. Laji wanted to give a cash gift primarily to those who had offered him valuable assistance during the purchase of the beaker.

Before listing a few of the cash gifts that were given, it is worth noting that the old co-father-in-law had called Laji and his father in July 2006, warning them that they would "owe him and his sons a total of US$30,000 *mita*" if they gained definite ownership of the beaker. This sum included the cash gift defined as "a representation of joy" that was "due to them" and payment for their assistance, as well as "payment for the shame" caused to them when Laji and his father had left the old co-father-in-law out of the price bargaining. Laji and his father – although they regarded the demand of US$30,000 as excessive and unjustified – promised to visit him in September 2006 at the latest with his *mita*. Let us not forget that, at the time, the great majority of the Gabor Roma thought that the old co-father-in-law had directed and controlled the whole transaction. Therefore, in order to avoid conflict, it was also in Laji's interests to keep the old co-father-in-law's absence secret.

In November 2006, more than two and a half months after taking the beaker into his possession, one of the first persons Laji gave *mita* to was his old co-father-in-law, who had played, along with his sons, a key role in managing the 30 May 2006 transaction (by calming Bango's impatient creditors, for instance). The delay further deepened their conflict. In fact, most Roma interpreted Laji's delay as a lack of respect and appreciation for the old co-father-in-law – an act of symbolic devaluation and humiliation. Furthermore, Laji's stalling only gave strength to the widespread suspicion that the old co-father-in-law had not played as important a role in the transaction as those involved would want outsiders to believe. The old co-father-in-law was so enraged by Laji's procrastination that he swore he would not take a single dollar as *mita*. According to the recollection of one of Laji's relatives, the old co-father-in-law commented on Laji's procrastination with the following words: "Has Laji been mocking us for two or three months? Should I go for my *mita*? Am I such a person? Should I go to beg? Should I go there, begging at his gate? That's what he wants?!" In fact, the old co-father-in-law, to demonstrate his own outstanding social prestige and influence, expected most of his friends and relatives to bring his *mita* personally to his home. However, the general practice among the Gabors is for the person wishing to receive *mita* to approach the person having the "great joy" (the purchaser of a beaker or tankard or the individual who has secured a marital alliance, for example), or to congratulate him at a chance encounter and ask for *mita*. The fact that the old co-father-in-law referred to this general practice as "begging" symbolically devalued it while emphasizing his own distinguished social prestige. Laji and his father finally distributed *mita* of only US$12,000, not US$30,000, in the home of the old co-father-in-law.

Not long after, Laji and his father contacted a smaller group of Gabor men in Mureş County, who – accompanied by other witnesses – had gone with them to the town on the Romanian-Hungarian border on May 30. Since these individuals in part "live on cash gifts" (sometimes extorted) from other Gabor Roma, Laji and his father distributed almost US$20,000 among them, as payment for their work as witnesses and as cash gifts interpreted as "representations of joy" – not least of all to preclude a future conflict with them because of the omission of *mita* sharing or the inadequacy of the cash gift.

Laji's uncle, who had played a key role as a broker in organizing the transaction, was given only US$2,000 as *mita*, and even for this payment he had to wait until a year after the closing of the deal. Also, only half of this sum was given to him in cash. The rest was paid in "goods" – US$1,000 worth of clothing (such as suits and trousers) – which he then had to sell himself on the markets of Cluj County to "turn them into money."

The highly respectable and successful Gabor man who is now considered to be the village leader in Bigvillage visited Laji's home in Cluj County in late 2008. He was then – more than two years after the sale – given *mita* (3,000 new Romanian lei [US$993]). As a representation of friendship, the influential guest gave 500 new Romanian lei to Laji's uncle, who had participated in the transaction as a broker and was present at the time of the visit. (It is common practice for the recipient of the *mita* to pass on some of his or her cash gift to a favourite grandchild, close friend, or other such person.)

According to their estimates, Laji and his father distributed more than US$50,000 of *mita* (defined as "a representation of joy," wage, or compensation) following the transaction. However, one of their close relatives once remarked that even so, not all of the deserving, influential Gabor men received *mita* – although "if you do not give *mita*, your fair will not resonate [the transaction will not bring the desired amount of social renown]." This phrase refers to the fact that the distribution of *mita* is an important means of fame management. This is primarily because according to Gabor Roma business ethics, it is the moral duty of a person accepting *mita* to "raise" the value and fame of the newly purchased object in public discourse and thereby contribute to the increase of the new owner's prestige. Or, if the recipient is not willing to do so, he or she should at least refrain from symbolic devaluation of the deal.

The cost of the entire transaction (purchase price, interest paid on loans, distributed cash gifts, food and drink, and so on) was about US$500,000, according to Laji's estimate. In the words of Laji's father,

"It was a difficult sale, difficult all the way till it was closed. Six months, seven months, almost a year till it was closed [from the beginning of price negotiations to taking the beaker home]."

The Aftermath: The Impact of the Beaker Transaction on the Politics of Marriage

Although Laji, his old co-father-in-law, and their family members tried to keep the old co-father-in-law's lack of involvement in the price bargaining secret, soon after the transaction was closed Bango let others know. His motivation was clear: the desire to generate conflict between Laji and his old co-father-in-law, in order to take revenge on Laji's father for making a cuckold of him and for the shame that had come from it, as well as his anger over losing his beaker. The old co-father-in-law was publicly humiliated and his social prestige damaged when it became well-known that his services as a broker had not been used in the price bargaining, and that any rumours to the contrary had been only attempts at face-saving. The conflict between Laji and his old co-father-in-law was only worsened by the disagreement mentioned earlier over the *mita* – that is, that Laji gave him and his family a smaller cash gift than they expected, and even this was taken to them much later than promised. These three factors became a source of serious conflict because they were interpreted as questioning the social reputation and prestige of the old co-father-in-law and his expertise as a broker.

The conflict relating to the purchase of the beaker greatly contributed to the fact that Laji's daughter, married to one of the old co-father-in-law's grandchildren in the winter of 2002–3, was sent home in early 2007; this ended the marriage, and with it the marital alliance with Laji. (The US$100,000 marriage payment was also returned to Laji some months after the divorce.) In order to avoid even greater shame, the family of the old co-father-in-law publicly justified sending the young wife home not by the reputational damage suffered as a consequence of the prestige-object transaction, but by the fact that in the years of the young couple's marriage no child had been born to them. As mentioned in chapter 1, this is a worrying fact according to the Gabor Roma ideology of marriage and biological reproduction, and usually reason enough for divorce.

13

Proprietary Contest, Business Ethics, and Conflict Management: The Biography of a Roofed Tankard, 1992–2012

Value Aspects

The social significance and value the Gabors associate with the tankard in question – ranked among the three most precious tankards currently in Gabor ownership by most of my interlocutors – come from two sources.

First, this piece has several of the material properties that are regarded as valuable in the prestige-object aesthetics of the Gabors. The tankard's surface has been finely fire-gilt both inside and out. The exterior bears many meticulously crafted – mainly floral – decorations. It has a unique handle in the shape of a female figure which, according to some Roma interpretations, can be associated "with the Egyptian Pharaohs." The latter feature, along with the blackening of the silver, several scratches, dents, and small punctures, has led my Roma acquaintances to claim that the object was produced many centuries ago.

Second, the tankard's social popularity and fame come from the fact that its former Gabor owners were successful, wealthy, and influential individuals. The prestige they enjoyed within their own Roma ethnic population has significantly contributed to the reputation and attractiveness of this piece.

A prosperous and highly respected man from Mureş County is considered to have been the first, well-known Gabor owner of the tankard. He bequeathed the object to his son, who, like him, was successful in Roma politics and in turn passed it down to his son, Pista, born in the 1940s. Pista, the third owner of the tankard, had by the 1980s amassed considerable wealth as a merchant and was ambitious in Roma politics. Thus, he tried to increase his social reputation by purchasing other prestige objects. In the early 1980s, he bought a beaker of middling value from a Gabor owner in Mureş County. "During the revolution" in December 1989, he purchased another piece, which, according to my interlocutors, is one of the three most valuable beakers in Gabor Roma ownership today: a richly gilded, 7.5-decilitre, footed beaker decorated with several antique coins. (The portraits on the coins – in the words of many of my Roma acquaintances – are of "emperors, rulers" ["imperial heads," *šără împărăticka*] "who lived in ancient Rome.") Pista paid 6 million old Romanian lei (US$402,145) for the beaker, 1,696 times the gross average monthly salary in Romania in 1989. He paid over 3.5 million old Romanian lei in cash (part of which he raised through large loans), and offered the beaker he had purchased in the early 1980s in exchange for the remaining 2.5 million old Romanian lei.[1] This transaction was considered a particularly significant and resounding event in Roma politics, and remained a key topic of conversation among men for quite some time. Thus, by January 1990, Pista owned a beaker and a tankard, the combined value of which could be compared to that of the prestige objects of only one of his Gabor Roma contemporaries.

The First (1992) and Second (1993) Pawn of the Tankard

The reputational profit that Pista enjoyed from the acquisition of this extremely valuable beaker did not last long, partly due to the significant sums he had borrowed to make the purchase, and partly due to the fall of Caritas.

Caritas was a Romanian pyramid scheme organized by Ioan Stoica in November 1991 as an "action of mutual assistance" (Verdery 1995, 1996). In the uncertain and confusing labyrinth of post-socialist economic transformation, when hyperinflation was 210.4 per cent in 1992, and 256.1 per cent in 1993, Caritas attracted many Romanians with its promise to offer an eightfold return on initial investments within three months.[2] For more than a year, the Caritas staff gained the confidence of new investors; earlier investors therefore received their promised benefits, and Caritas earned the reputation of a reliable defence against hyperinflation. According to the estimates most frequently published in Romanian newspapers, in its golden age Caritas had more than four million investors (Verdery 1996, 171).

Like many other Transylvanian Gabor Roma, Pista became involved in Caritas. Hearing that the initial investors had fully obtained their expected profits, Pista put his cash into the scheme and continually reinvested his eightfold return. In 1992, he pawned the beaker he had purchased in December 1989 to a Roma creditor in Cluj County in order to have more cash to invest in Caritas. As a precaution, he deliberately chose a creditor whose Roma ethnic population did not define and collect silver beakers and tankards as prestige objects. In fact, in contrast to most of the Gabor and Cărhar creditors who primarily hope to acquire ownership of the pledge, this Roma creditor aimed to obtain only the interest expected from the transaction.

That same year, in order to repay his previous loans, Pista borrowed 40,000 German marks (US$26,410) from his wife's cousin and offered the tankard he had inherited from his father as a security on the loan. The cousin himself took out loans in order to provide Pista with the cash, and by the spring of 1993 he urgently needed to get back his capital, plus interest from Pista. Pista, however, didn't have the money and – in accordance with his political ambitions – was willing to sell neither his tankard nor his beaker. So, in March 1993, Pista and his wife's cousin sought out Rupi, another Gabor man living in Mureş County, in the hope that he could lend Pista money from which Pista could repay the loan from his wife's cousin.

Rupi, who was in his forties at the time, had inherited from his father a nine-decilitre beaker of lesser value. He earned his living from intermediary trade and often worked with Pista. They bought – among other things – cotton, yarn, and thread in bulk from the Tălmaciu thread factory, and transported it by truck to a city along the Romanian-Serbian border, where Pista sold it primarily to Serbian wholesalers and retailers "for hard currency." Rupi recalled their business relationship as harmonious and mutually profitable, which is why Pista was so confident that Rupi would willingly give him a loan, and why Rupi had no reason to question Pista's credibility. As Rupi later explained, "I trusted him [Pista] as the good God."

Pista considered Rupi an ideal creditor not only because of their well-balanced business partnership, but also because he thought of him as "soft" – a withdrawn person who avoided disputes and could count on little support from his consanguineous male relatives and co-fathers-in-law in the event of social or economic conflicts. Furthermore, Rupi was known as a man who placed great emphasis on preserving his business reputation and living according to the principles of the Adventist lifestyle. (He had joined the Seventh-Day Adventist Church in the mid-1970s.) In order to demonstrate the latter fact, several of my interlocutors referred to the unusual practice that Rupi, with reference to the

Bible, refused to collect interest on loans, an otherwise general practice among the Gabors.

In March 1993, Pista borrowed 152,000 German marks (US$91,479) from Rupi, offering as a security the tankard that he had inherited from his father and that his wife's cousin had returned.[3] Rupi agreed to the loan on the condition that Pista either (a) repay the full amount of the loan within three weeks, or (b) "make a bargain with him" and sell him his beaker. Rupi insisted on these conditions, first for moral reasons, because he did not want to earn income from getting interest (he did not charge a single German mark of interest for these three weeks), and second, because what he really wanted was ownership of the beaker that Pista had purchased in 1989, which was considered more valuable than the tankard, but was at that time – as previously mentioned – in pawn in Cluj County.[4] Pista verbally promised Rupi that, if he violated the agreement, he would take responsibility for any financial damages Rupi might accrue because of the loan. Rupi, who had not been informed of the massive debts Pista had already accumulated in several Transylvanian counties, accepted the tankard as a security and did not ask to put the loan contract in writing.

As a creditor, Rupi did not have enough cash to conduct the transaction. Nevertheless, in the hopes of eventually buying Pista's beaker, he borrowed 100,000 German marks (US$60,183) from a Hungarian creditor in Mureş County. Rupi signed a written contract stating that if he could not repay this loan within a year, the Hungarian creditor would take ownership of his most valuable assets. Thus, as a security on the 100,000 German marks, Rupi "had his house written on the creditor's name." This house consisted of four rooms, two kitchens, a bathroom, and a large workshop. Rupi did the same with a 75-by-75-metre plot of land (where two buildings stand today) on which he wanted to build a gas station for his elder son. He also gave the creditor 550 quintals of Russian 0.5-millimetre zinc plates.

Pista, however, never returned to Rupi's home, and his beaker remained in pawn with the Roma creditor in Cluj County. Rupi was unable to repay the 100,000 German marks by the following year, and in April 1994 he lost everything he had offered as security in the contract to the Hungarian creditor; his family was forced to move in with his adult daughter for more than a year until he managed to buy a small house. Although Pista's tankard was with Rupi, and selling Pista's loan would have solved his financial problems, he refrained from doing so because in terms of Gabor Roma business ethics the sale of a loan and the handover of a pledge cannot be done without the knowledge and consent of the debtor. Rupi, however, was unable to contact Pista for a long while, either by phone or in person.

It was not only the sums he had borrowed earlier that made Pista's financial situation increasingly untenable but also the decline and eventual collapse of Caritas. Beginning in early 1993, profits promised to Caritas investors were paid either with delays, only in part, or not at all, and in May 1994 the termination of Caritas activities was officially announced. Pista was one of the large group of investors who had to give up all hope of recovering the significant sums they had invested only recently.

The Death of Pista (1995)

Pista, having pawned his tankard with Rupi in 1993 and unable to repay his creditors, was forced into hiding in a Romanian city near the Romanian-Serbian border, where – according to many of my interlocutors – a local Orthodox priest was sheltering him. To make matters worse, in the winter of 1994 news spread that the Cluj County Roma creditor who had Pista's beaker in pawn wanted his money back, with interest, and was planning to sell Pista's loan to one of the Cărhar Roma. Rupi, hearing this news, quickly travelled to the city where Pista was said to be hiding. Although Rupi finally managed to meet Pista in secret, the latter did not explain why he had broken their agreement, nor did he offer to compensate Rupi for the financial losses he and his family had suffered as a result.[5]

In December 1994, the Roma creditor sold Pista's loan to a wealthy and influential Cărhar man in Sibiu County for 300 million old Romanian lei (US$169,119) – 1,147 times more than the gross average monthly salary in Romania in December 1994 – and three horses. He also handed over Pista's beaker to this Cărhar man. Shortly thereafter, the Gabor Roma were astonished to hear that Pista had died. Many believed that he had committed suicide. Several of my acquaintances argued that "he had died because of his hopeless indebtedness," as well as the shame and depression that came after the Cărhar creditor had gained control of his extremely valuable beaker. As Rupi put it, "Pista died for that, for the sorrow for that beaker. Because he knew he would never bring it back from there [from the Cărhar creditor]." In other words, although Pista retained ownership of his prestige object in terms of Gabor Roma business ethics even after it went to the Cărhar creditor, the bleakness of his financial situation, and the well-known fact that pieces pawned to Cărhar Roma were very rarely redeemed by the Gabors, led him to believe that it was very likely he would have to give up all hope of recovering his beaker.

Following Pista's death, his wife and three sons took on his massive, interest-accruing debt, which they were unable to settle.

"In Return for My Goodness I Was Made a Fool": The Third Pawn of the Tankard (1995)

In early 1995, Rupi was visited by one of his nephews, the eldest son of his late brother, who, finding himself in financial difficulties, wanted to take out a loan from a Djurdjovaje Roma creditor[6] living in Mureş County and asked to use Pista's tankard as a security. Rupi decided to assist him, because his nephew claimed that he intend to borrow only a smaller amount (15 million old Romanian lei [US$8,446]), and Rupi believed that he and his two sons would be able to help if his nephew was unable to repay the loan. Therefore, Rupi gave him Pista's tankard.

Among brothers who are on good terms with each other, it occasionally happens that the owner of a prestige object may lend it to a brother, so that the latter can use it as a security to gain access to credit that is especially important to him. (This generally happens – as a kind of compensation – if only the older son inherits a prestige object from the father and the younger son does not.) However, Rupi's case cannot be classified in this group of rare deals, since he "lent" his nephew a piece that was not his own property but had only been placed with him as a security. This ran counter to Gabor Roma business ethics and was therefore morally questionable. While Rupi may have acted as he did primarily in response to the expectation that he should provide help to close relatives, his decision was probably also motivated by anger over the financial and emotional loss caused by Pista's breach of contract.

Rupi later learned that his nephew had misled him; at the time he had asked for the tankard, he already owed the Djurdjovaje Roma creditor more than 40 million old Romanian lei (US$22,522) and wanted to use the piece to borrow yet more money from him. The Djurdjovaje Roma creditor, for his part, was not interested in owning the tankard; he was motivated simply by the interest expected from the transaction. His nephew's total debt, as Rupi recalled, was finally around 40,000 to 45,000 German marks (US$25,715 to 28,930). This amount, however, was much higher than Rupi and his sons – who at that time were busy with their own repayments and their efforts to buy a house – could ever repay. To quote Rupi in his resignation, "In return for my goodness I was made a fool … At that time [when the amount of his nephew's real debt was known] I already could not get to the tankard [that is, to redeem it], as we had no place to live! We had to repay our own debts."

The Fourth Pawn of the Tankard (Winter 1996–7)

Neither the nephew nor Rupi could repay the loan from the Djurdjovaje Roma in the following two years. So, in the winter of 1996–7, once the Djurdjovaje Roma creditor realized he was waiting in vain, he and his wife secretly visited one of the wealthy Cărhar Roma men living in the Olt River area to make a bargain without the knowledge of Rupi, his nephew, or Pista's widow. The Cărhar man purchased Rupi's nephew's debt for 150 million old Romanian lei along with fifty Austrian four-ducat coins made of 986 parts per thousand of fine gold (more than twenty-two carats) minted in 1915. The coins bore a portrait of Franz Joseph I – emperor of the Austro-Hungarian Monarchy – and weighed 13.9 grams each[7] (see colour plates: Photo 34). They were included in the purchase price at 3 million old Romanian lei per coin.[8] Furthermore, the tankard serving as a security was given to this Cărhar creditor.

Redeeming the Tankard (2006)

The tankard remained with the Cărhar creditor in the Olt River area from the winter of 1996–7 until December 2006. Neither Rupi nor Pista's widow made any attempt to redeem it or to pay off the interest. The fate of the pawned object took a new turn at Christmas 2006, when Rupi was informed by a relative, who lived in the same city along the Romanian-Serbian border as Pista's widow and sons, that the widow, under pressure from her creditors, was planning to visit the Cărhar creditor within a few days to sell him the tankard and repay at least a portion of her debts.

Rupi had not received a single Romanian leu from Pista, his widow, or his sons since March 1993. He knew that if the widow sold the tankard to the Cărhar creditor, he would never see his 152,000 German marks[9] again, since he would have no means to pressure the widow to repay the money Pista had borrowed in 1993 and to compensate him for the losses he attributed to Pista's violation of their agreement. In terms of Gabor Roma business ethics, Pista's sons and widow still owned the tankard and were entitled to sell it. For this reason, Rupi could not raise any objections to the transaction, especially as it was his fault that the tankard had been passed in secret to the Cărhar creditor in the first place. He therefore decided to redeem the tankard from the Cărhar creditor before the widow could reach him. Rupi's wife supported the plan because by retrieving the pawned object, Rupi could have mitigated the reputational damage of having irresponsibly handed it over to his nephew.[10]

In the last week of December 2006, Rupi secretly visited the Djurdjovaje Roma man who, in the winter of 1996–7, had sold his nephew's debt to the Cărhar creditor who lived in the Olt River area. Rupi asked the Djurdjovaje creditor – who admitted that he had acted in a manner contrary to business ethics and thus felt morally obliged to support the idea of recovery – to go to the Cărhar creditor and find out how much the latter wanted for the redemption of the tankard. The Djurdjovaje Roma man did so, and called Rupi that very afternoon to tell him that the Cărhar creditor wanted roughly €30,000 as compensation for the 150 million old Romanian lei and fifty gold ducats, plus ten years' worth of interest.

Rupi did not tell anyone that he was planning to redeem the tankard, because he knew that a number of influential Gabor individuals among his acquaintances were unable to redeem their own pawned prestige objects from the Cărhars and would therefore, out of mere jealousy, try to prevent the deal. There was another reason for Rupi's secrecy: he did not want any of the Gabor Roma who often brokered interethnic prestige-object transactions to visit him and offer their services, which would have involved substantial additional expenditure.

Rupi departed in secret that evening with his wife, elder son, and only grandson for the tankard. They arrived at the Cărhar creditor's house late at night. There, after a short negotiation, Rupi redeemed the tankard for €40,000 – 92.6 times the gross average monthly salary in December 2006 in Romania. They left for home at two o'clock in the morning.

The Cărhar creditor's behaviour struck Rupi and many other of my Roma interlocutors as highly unusual; he showed much less resistance than expected during the redeeming of the tankard.

Taking into consideration that the creditor hadn't received a single Romanian leu during the ten years in which the piece had remained with him as a pledge, he charged a remarkably modest amount of interest. As previously mentioned, the vast majority of Gabor beakers and tankards pawned with Cărhar Roma "remain forever among the Cărhars"; the Gabors are very rarely able to redeem them. The most obvious means to prevent the redemption of a pawned object – especially in cases where loan repayment is delayed several years – is for the creditor, in the final negotiation, to demand such a high amount of interest that the debtor is unable to pay. Although the Cărhar creditor had grounds to do just this and to ensure that Rupi, in the words of the latter, would "not have enough force to lift [bring away, that is, redeem] the tankard," he did not act that way. According to Rupi, the creditor could have demanded between €150,000 and €200,000 without being accused of making an immoral profit. Yet, he remitted both the tankard and a significant chunk of the interest.

The creditor's decision may not appear logical at first, especially considering that during the ten years the pawned tankard had become very dear to him. He claimed that, due to its extremely valuable material properties, among the five silver beakers in his possession it was surpassed only by a beaker decorated with more than thirty antique coins. Why, then, had he demanded only €40,000 from Rupi?

The Circumstances of Redemption: Prestige Objects, Business Ethics, and Curses

The fact that Pista's beaker and tankard went to Cărhar Roma creditors had significantly worsened his widow's bargaining position with Gabor lenders, who considered it highly unlikely that she could redeem and sell the beaker or the tankard to cover her debts. Due to her desperate financial situation and mounting threats from creditors, the widow often publicly cursed the individuals who had ever intervened in the fate of her husband's debts in a manner contrary to Gabor Roma business ethics (i.e., without the knowledge and consent of her husband or his heirs). She especially cursed the Cărhar individuals into whose hands her husband's beaker and tankard had finally fallen.

It should be noted that both the Cărhar Roma and the Gabor Roma assume a close relationship between business ethics, the prestige economy, and cursing as a kind of moral sanction. They regard curses uttered by an injured party in a prestige-object deal as "more effective"; that is, the violation of business ethics in transactions of this kind can have more serious consequences (curses of death or illness are much more likely to be fulfilled in connection with beakers and tankards). Furthermore, the members of both Roma ethnic populations consider that curses in which more vulnerable and defenceless persons – for example, orphans and widows – express their grievances are more potent than those of others. As Rupi put it, "The files of widows and orphans are put aside separately [they are handled with special attention] by the good God."

In November 2001, the fate of Pista's beaker took a significant turn when the Cărhar creditor who had purchased one of Pista's debts in December 1994 and taken the beaker as a security lost his only son. Both my Gabor and Cărhar interlocutors attributed the son's death to the open violation of business ethics related to prestige objects (the secret purchase of Pista's debt), and the widow's morally justified curses. The Gabor Roma often referred to this case publicly as a clear example of the dramatic consequences one should consider when illegitimately (i.e., without the owner's knowledge and consent) taking over someone else's silver pieces. Four years later, in 2005, the Cărhar creditor, fearing that the widow's curses might lead to more deaths in his family (his son left behind a son and three daughters), sold Pista's debt to a Gabor man in Mureş County and gave him the "cursed" beaker serving as a security.

My interlocutors in both Roma ethnic populations argued that the return of Pista's beaker to the Gabors and the fact that the other Cărhar creditor did not prevent the redemption of the tankard in December 2006 could primarily be attributed to intense fear that the widow's curses would be fulfilled again. The circumstance that the Cărhar creditor who had acquired the tankard and the related debt in the winter of 1996–7 had only one son, and one daughter, also made it easier for Rupi to redeem the tankard. As Rupi put it:

> The only son [of the Cărhar creditor who had purchased one of Pista's debts in December 1994] died for the beaker. Because of the widow's curses … His son died, because the widow threatened him and told him, "I will put your son into the earth so that your wealth is inherited by the dogs!" And indeed his son died. And then this one [that is, the other Cărhar creditor who had taken Pista's tankard as a security without the knowledge and permission of Pista's heirs] was also afraid of the same. (27 June 2010)

The Assembly Following the Redemption of the Tankard

On the morning of the tankard's redemption, at Rupi's request, his elder son phoned several influential Gabor acquaintances and relatives to inform them of the transaction and invite them to come and have a look at the object. When Rupi and his family arrived back at their Mureş County home at seven o'clock that morning, a number of Gabor men were impatiently waiting for them – or, more precisely, waiting to verify the return of the tankard after its ten-year hiatus along the Olt River. Rupi showed the object to many of the individuals present, giving them a chance to check its nominal authenticity, in order to increase the publicity accompanying the act of repatriation.[11]

That same morning, news of the redemption reached the city along the Romanian-Serbian border where Pista's widow resided, and by early afternoon one of her sons had phoned Rupi to verify that he had indeed redeemed his father's tankard. Receiving confirmation from Rupi, the widow and her eldest son immediately departed by car for Rupi's home in Mureş County. Rupi, for his part, convened another assembly in his home, inviting – or, had they already visited him that morning, calling back – a considerable number of prestigious Gabor men who supported him to be present during his negotiations with Pista's widow.

The widespread publicity of the tankard's redemption, considered a "historic event" endowed with great political significance by the Gabor Roma, was important to Rupi for several reasons.

First, it allowed him to effectively counterbalance the reputational damage that had occurred when he let the tankard slip out of his hands via his nephew.

Second, Rupi was aware that if the fact of the redemption became widely known, some of Pista's and his heirs' creditors would come to him and – on the grounds that the value of the tankard would abundantly cover their outstanding debts – demand compensation for their financial losses. Therefore, it was very much in Rupi's interest to invite politically successful and respectable Gabor men who could stand in solidarity with him and to seek their support for his own position: that no one had the right to claim the debts of Pista and his heirs from him. That is, Rupi used the unusually high interest that accompanied the tankard's redemption to establish a social consensus, via the opinion of influential Gabor individuals, to discourage creditors who might want to recover their outstanding loans from his family.

Third, Rupi wanted the backing of prestigious Gabor men on another issue: as he had not received a single Romanian leu of repayment from Pista or his heirs, Rupi considered that the combined value of his financial losses was nearly equal to the tankard's current market value. Hence, Rupi expected that the individuals invited to his home would confirm his right to demand the final, contractually stipulated cession of the ownership right of the tankard from the widow and her sons (either freely or for a small purchase price). He needed considerable social pressure to persuade the widow and her sons, and his only morally acceptable means of doing so was the establishment of a wide consensus based on the opinion of successful and honoured Gabor individuals "whose words are listened to by many."

Pista's widow and sons, however, had absolutely no interest in ceding the right of ownership of the tankard to Rupi, as he would have simply deducted his financial losses from its estimated market value, which would have left them – even in the best of cases – with only a small amount of profit on it. It is worth noting that Pista's widow and his sons still owned his prestige objects according to Gabor Roma business ethics, and the only way they could hold the impatient creditors at bay was to promise that they would redeem the beaker and tankard soon and repay their debts by selling them. As the widow told me in March 2007 (months after the assembly in question), she considered that her only chance was to redeem the tankard from Rupi "for pennies," and sell it to someone else for a huge profit. Her plan was based on the assumption that Rupi was a "soft" person, unable to resist the pressure of her powerful creditors. The widow's own interests thus dictated that she exaggerate the current market value of the tankard and acknowledge the least amount of debt so that she would have to pay the smallest amount possible to redeem the tankard from Rupi.

In order to establish whether the tankard was really "sunk in the debt" or not, a number of questions remained, to which Rupi and Pista's widow developed very different answers, according to their respective interests: (a) What would the current worth of the tankard be if it was offered for sale among the Gabors? (b) What was the current euro equivalent of the 152,000 German marks Rupi had lent Pista in 1993? (c) What was the value, in euros, of Rupi's other losses (e.g., his house, the plot of land, and the zinc plates) caused by Pista's violation of the loan agreement? (d) And finally: How much interest could Rupi rightfully claim for the nearly fourteen years since he had made the loan agreement with Pista?[12]

The significance of the social consensus based on the opinions of politically successful and influential Gabor men in disputes over prestige-object ownership can be better understood if we recall that the Gabors determine the value of these pieces in an ethnicized way (i.e., on the basis of the renown of their earlier Gabor owners and the value preferences of their prestige-object aesthetics). Therefore, in negotiations and conflict management concerning the price and value of beakers and tankards, the Gabors cannot turn to non-Roma antiques dealers, museum experts, and the like for their estimates, but rely exclusively on the members of their own Roma ethnic population.

Over the course of a several-hours-long discussion in the presence of more than forty Gabor men, the widow acknowledged her husband's financial responsibility. Yet she offered Rupi a much smaller sum (US$100,000) than the one (approximately US$270,000) suggested by the most influential Gabor individual in the assembly for the redemption of the tankard. However, it was obvious to Rupi, whose purpose was to acquire the right of ownership of the tankard, that the widow did not have so much as a fraction of the promised sum; even if he accepted her offer, he would not receive a penny. Thus, he first asked her for €500,000 to compensate his losses. He gradually decreased this to €450,000. He knew very well that the widow could not meet his demands; no one would lend her such a high sum without an asset for security. Rupi wanted to use these demands to pressure the widow into the realization that it was time to cede the ownership right of the tankard to him. Finally, Rupi pretended to be interested in a compromise and asked her to pay back only the US-dollar equivalent of the 152,000 German marks, and to buy back everything (the securities) he had lost due to her husband's violation of the loan agreement.

When he saw that, despite his best efforts, he could not "make a bargain" with the widow, Rupi in despair threatened that if she could not settle her husband's debt within thirty days, he would take the tankard back to one of the Cărhar Roma in the Olt River area and use it as a pledge to take out the biggest loan he could receive. This was merely another pressure tactic intended to force the widow into an agreement. In fact, Rupi was under almost as much pressure as the widow; while the latter was under the pressure of her impatient creditors, Rupi felt the pressure of advancing age (he was sixty-three at the time). Rupi feared that if he did not buy the tankard "in a Gabor Roma way" – in a manner preferred by Gabor Roma business ethics (with the widow's knowledge and consent) – as soon as possible, then the most influential of the widow's creditors would demand repayment of their outstanding loans from his elder son after his (i.e., Rupi's) death. And if his son refused to pay them, they – by conflict or violence – would "wangle the tankard out" of his hand without compensation for the losses his family had suffered due to Pista's breach of agreement. Rupi therefore strove to clarify the ownership of the tankard and to "strike a bargain" with the widow in order to not only advance his political ambitions but also avoid further conflicts.

A Means of Conflict Management: The Public Swearing

The reputational profit the tankard's redemption brought Rupi could not distract him from his most pressing challenge: how to protect his family from Pista's and his heirs' creditors and ensure that the tankard would remain safely with his elder son after his death. The most obvious way to achieve this would have been to convince the widow and her sons to cede or sell the rights of ownership to him, but they refused to do so out of fear of their creditors.

Rupi was finally prompted to action by news that spread in mid-January 2007. According to this, one of Pista's desperate and influential Gabor Roma creditors had publicly announced at a wedding party that he would soon "swear an oath" (žal po trušul); he would commit himself through the utterance of conditional self-curses (threatening himself and his family members with death and other losses) to collecting from Rupi the amount (US$50,000) he had demanded in vain from Pista's widow. The purpose of such public swearing is to exert pressure and demonstrate the individual's determination through committing him- or herself (as oath-taker) to a future action – for example, threatening to report the other person in an argument to the police. In such cases, the oath-taker generally sets a deadline for the threatened individual to settle the dispute. This type of public swearing primarily serves to prevent the conflict from escalating.

One of Rupi's co-fathers-in-law informed him of the desperate creditor's plan and advised Rupi to publicly swear an oath announcing that he did not owe this creditor a single Romanian leu – and that, therefore, the creditor had no right to demand he repay Pista's loan – before the creditor could go through with his plan.

Rupi's public swearing took place in a suburban park in Târgu Mureş at the end of January 2007. The event was organized by Rupi and his sons. First, they visited ten influential Gabor Roma men whom they thought would stand in solidarity with them in the dispute and asked these individuals to participate at the swearing as more than mere audience members. Rupi asked these men to swear an oath with him, committing themselves through conditional self-curses on themselves and their families to protect him and his sons if the creditors of Pista and his heirs demanded their outstanding debts from his family in the future. As is the custom, Rupi promised each man a cash gift – interpreted as a wage – to swear an oath with him. His elder son borrowed US$10,000 in order to present each man with US$1,000. Next, Rupi went to see some of the officers working at the local police station, and – again in return for a cash gift defined as a wage – asked them to take part at the swearing as witnesses whose presence would give his words even more weight. The policemen's presence made it clear that Rupi had large relational capital even with the local police, which could be mobilized at any time. It also demonstrated his conviction in the rectitude of his position and the fact that, if necessary, he would not hesitate to turn to the authorities for help.

During the first part of the public swearing, Rupi briefly summarized the story of the conflict in the Romani language for the more than fifty assembled Roma, and then retold it in Romanian for the policemen. He recounted Pista's visit to him in 1993, their agreement, the large sum he had lent to him, the financial and emotional losses he had suffered since, and how he had managed to redeem the tankard a few weeks earlier from the Cărhar Roma creditor living in the Olt River area. He then proceeded to explain what exactly had triggered him to swear an oath: the threat of one of Pista's creditors against him and his family. With regard to the desperate creditor, Rupi announced that because he had not taken part in the loan transaction between Pista and the creditor, the latter had no right to demand Pista's debt from him, even if Pista's tankard had once again come under his supervision.

Then, as is customary on such occasions, for the benefit of those present, Rupi explained exactly what he was going to swear to. He declared that he would denounce to the police any of the creditors of Pista or his heirs if they were to come and demand repayment of their outstanding debts from him. As he put it, "Whether he be a man from X settlement, from Y settlement, or from Z settlement, the one who comes against me to demand the debt of Pista or his heirs to him, I will be obliged to give him up at the anticorruption [the group of the local police responsible for corruption issues] and the militia! If I do not do it, all of the curses I am about to utter threatening myself and my family members with death and other losses will be fulfilled!" He translated this for the sake of the Romanian-speaking policemen as well.

Then Rupi, hatless, with the Bible in his left hand, knelt on the coat of one of the invited witnesses and swore, uttering many conditional self-curses. For this part of the proceedings, five Gabor Roma came forward individually and "gave the curses" to Rupi by publicly uttering curses that Rupi then repeated in the first person.[13]

Next, the ten influential Gabor Roma supporters stood and swore, left hands raised in the air, that they would immediately come to the aid of Rupi's family members if, despite Rupi's present swearing, any creditor should harass his family. And, should they fail to do as promised, Rupi's conditional self-curses would be fulfilled on them and their families. In Rupi's words, "If from now on anyone demands anything, they are with me through thick and thin to give them up at the militia and the prosecutor's office."

Rupi's plan worked well; after this public demonstration of force carried out with many influential Gabor individuals, the desperate creditor waived his intention to demand repayment of Pista's loan from Rupi and his family.

February 2007 to the Present

At the time of writing, the situation remained stagnant; Rupi repeatedly called Pista's widow and sons, urging them to either pay their debt or legally sell him the tankard. He told me in an interview recorded in August 2010, "It has been two or three months since I called upon the eldest son [of the widow]. I last told him, 'Look for someone; either sell [the tankard] or put it in pawn [with another creditor]. Come. Bring me my money, and then I will accept less than what you owe me. But let us draw a line [let us make a decision]. Because I do not want to leave this affair in abeyance to my children after my death.' He did not even come to the town where I live." As Pista's widow and sons have no money with which to redeem the tankard, and they do not dare to cede the right of ownership to Rupi for a smaller amount, it seems that for the time being there is no chance of relief for Rupi's impatience and anxiety.

Conclusion
The Post-Socialist Consumer Revolution and the Shifting Meanings of Prestige Goods

Post-Socialist versus Conservative-Traditionalist Interpretations of the Significance of Beakers and Tankards

Just as they did in the decades of socialism, the Gabor Roma continue to pay the highest purchase prices for the more valuable silver prestige objects.[1] Within their local communities, as discussed in chapters 2, 8, and 10, the post-socialist consumer revolution that involved the mass appearance of Western consumer goods, practices, and ideologies led to the emergence of a new, post-socialist consumer taste or sensitivity, which became especially popular with generations socialized around 1989 or soon after. This new taste or sensitivity had a strong influence on consumer patterns and value preferences, significantly changing the dominant interpretations of what constituted an average standard of living, which luxuries could be morally encouraged and which ones morally stigmatized, and what represented a good/normal/ideal life.

As part of this process, the number of commodities and services the Gabor Roma classify as necessary to an average standard of living and a good/normal/ideal life has dramatically increased. Moreover, many of these are costly. In the eyes of most of my Gabor hosts, many post-socialist goods – such as large new houses, quality Western cars, and other durable goods that represent the latest trends in technological development – as well as the habit of frequenting fast-food restaurants and shopping centres, are considered to fall into these categories.[2] In other words, their normalization can be regarded as well advanced. As a consequence, the structure of household consumption expenditure is also changing; today the Gabors spend a much larger proportion of their income on maintaining what they consider an average standard of living than their fathers and grandfathers did during the socialist era.

Since goods and services classified as necessary to an average standard of living take priority over those commodities interpreted as luxuries – a category into which silver beakers and tankards also fall – the spread of post-socialist consumer taste or sensitivity, and the resulting changes, have had a substantial impact on the Gabors' prestige economy. First, it has become a greater challenge for those individuals who long for important beakers and tankards to save up the sums, which often amount to hundreds of thousands of US dollars, needed to buy one of these pieces. As a consequence, fewer and fewer individuals are able to join in the proprietary contests for precious prestige objects. Second, in order to obtain the amounts of money necessary to purchase the costly commodities and services preferred by the new interpretation of an average standard of living, many Gabor prestige-object owners struggling with a shortage of cash show greater readiness than they would have before the change of political regime to sell their beakers and tankards. As a result of these factors, the social popularity and attractiveness of the prestige economy now shows a declining trend, primarily among members of younger generations. This is well demonstrated by the fact that many owners who find themselves in economic crisis are less keen now than they would have been before 1989 to accept risks and sacrifices – such as taking out large loans or renouncing new "conspicuous commodities" (Miller 1995, 265) – in an effort to save their beakers and tankards, and that the demand for pieces of modest value is gradually falling. In this way, the post-socialist consumer revolution is one of the major factors leading the Gabors to part with some of their prestige objects, which, with only a few exceptions, are bought by wealthy Cărhar Roma.

As already noted, the Gabors are now markedly divided in their opinions regarding the social significance and desirability of silver beakers and tankards, holding two contrasting views. One, which I call a conservative-traditionalist attitude towards prestige objects, is represented mostly by men from older generations. The great majority of owners belong to this group. This attitude regards the unaltered preservation of the social popularity and economic significance of beakers and tankards that existed before the change of political regime as the ideal, desired state. The other attitude, which can be defined as post-socialist, is popular primarily among young people socialized after 1989, who have become the most committed proponents of the post-socialist consumer taste or sensitivity. According to the latter attitude, the post-socialist political, social, and economic transformation is a progressive and beneficial phenomenon that has radically modified the system of Gabor Roma consumer values and preferences, and this process in turn has inevitably and understandably had an unfavourable impact on the social and economic evaluation of the prestige economy. During my conversations with representatives of the post-socialist attitude, several of them expressed criticism of their fathers and grandfathers for occasionally failing to take into account the moral hierarchy of basic human needs and the prestige economy – the primacy of the former over the latter – when attempting to buy or keep in their possession a precious beaker or tankard. This choice was typically interpreted by them as an irrational and morally questionable consumer decision or at times even as a form of gambling ("The old [Gabor Roma] people give everything for a beaker. They even run into debt").

The following comment relevantly compares the social attractiveness and significance of houses and automobiles versus those of silver prestige objects during the decades before the political regime change:

> The Gabors bought beakers when they made money. That's what they made money for, not for cars. When somebody bought a car, here among the Gabors, he was laughed at, saying "This one's gone crazy, he's bought a car!" When someone had a large house built, they said "This man is crazy, did he have that big house built because he's nuts? Why didn't he use that money to buy a beaker instead?!" This is how it was. If you'd built a castle out of diamonds, the Gabors would still have said, "The Lord would have given you mud and stone! Why didn't you buy a silver beaker instead?!" (23 February 2001)

By way of contrast, the following three quotations aptly illustrate the inclusion of post-socialist consumer goods and services in the concepts of an average standard of living and a good/normal/ideal life ("Roma eyes have opened") and the consequences of this process: the post-1989 decrease in cash reserves available to buy prestige objects and the partial decline in the popularity of the economy surrounding them:

> The world's changed because today you have to have a valuable beaker that can be quickly converted into cash. Things have changed! Not just because of the crisis [the global economic crisis of 2008] … Forty years ago, if there was a two-deciliter beaker, it got bought. Or a three-deciliter

or a four-deciliter one. But now, Roma eyes have opened so much that if a young man has €100,000 ... you know what he does? "You want me to buy that tiny beaker?! I'll build a new house for myself instead, buy a car and live happily." (29 June 2010)

Young people don't need this history any more [ethnic history, which here is synonymous with prestige objects]. Young people say, "Where shall I get the money for it [a valuable beaker or tankard]? When I have US$100,000, I'll buy a house and a good car." So these [post-socialist consumer goods] run better. But before [1989], the Gabor Roma lived in tiny huts and gave all their money for beakers and tankards. And they had their meals down on the floor. (27 June 2010)

This [the post-regime change world] is not the same world as at the time of socialism, when you sold your house for a beaker, went to live in a rented place just to be able to buy the beaker. The beaker was the Gabors' life. If you wanted to become someone in life ... It was the [Gabor] Roma rank, the beaker. If you didn't form a marital alliance with a big Gabor Roma man, and if you didn't buy a beaker, you were left out [of political success]. But now it's the great palaces [new family homes equipped with expensive furniture], beautiful [elegantly dressed] people [that are important]. Young Roma today don't die so much for the beakers. (4 September 2008)

The opinion of one of my acquaintances in his late twenties is an exact illustration of the diminishing appetite for taking risks or making sacrifices for prestige objects among (younger) Gabor Roma since the change of regime:

When would I buy a beaker? If I had a comfortable house, if it was well-furnished, if I had a car and everything that a family needs to live. And if for instance a beaker was for sale for US$100,000 and I knew I had US$200,000, then I would buy it. But to spend all of my US$200,000 and start over from nil, that [is not a good idea] ... I'd rather not buy a beaker, I'd invest the money I have and wait so I don't get the family into trouble ... We need cash reserves. My family and I shouldn't suffer because of a beaker. (25 March 2005)

When talking about the long-term future of the prestige economy, the same young man claimed that it will slowly go out [the prestige economy will gradually disappear] because of the great modern world. Because there's a great, a very great [consumer] desire among us. And we have also found the taste of life [just like the non-Roma majority society]. That I should have a good house, my child should have what he needs, the house should be well-furnished, things like that. (25 March 2005)

The "great modern world" and the "taste of life" for which an increasing number of Gabor Roma have "a very great desire" are synonyms for the new commodities, consumer ideologies, and lifestyle models that have been appearing since 1989.

The spread of new, post-socialist consumer taste or sensitivity and the resulting social and economic consequences are not, however, solely responsible for the declining interest in the prestige economy. There are also other significant causes behind this phenomenon. Before discussing them, let us briefly summarize the motivations that inspired the Gabor Roma to participate in the prestige economy before the change of political regime.

Causes behind the Popularity of the Prestige Economy before 1989

Informality as a Means of Evading State Intervention Aimed at Limiting Private Property

As noted in chapter 2, the Gabors' prestige economy is one of several informal economies in Romania: apart from, for instance, a few anthropologists and antiques dealers, members of the Romanian majority society have no detailed knowledge of its fundamental value ideologies, participant framework, and major events. (On the crucial role of informality in other socialist and post-socialist contexts, see, for example, Ledeneva 1998, 2006; Morris 2012, 2016; Morris & Polese 2013, 2015; Kovács, Morris, Polese, & Imami 2017.)

This informal character can be traced back in part to the nature of the social life of prestige objects (*discursive conspicuous possession*) – that is, to the fact that the dominant arena of representation and invidious comparison focused on them is intraethnic political discourse. The owners of these pieces typically keep them in hiding places and rarely take them out to show them to Roma (and even more rarely to non-Roma) visitors.

Another reason for informality is the ethnicized nature of the prestige economy. That is, the values and meanings associated with the beakers and tankards – such as Gabor Roma ownership histories, the preferences of the Gabors' prestige-object aesthetics, and the price range characteristic of these pieces – constitute an ethnicized regime of value that differs in many respects from the value discourses of the European antiques market and art history. As a result of these silver objects being ethnicized, there is a relative lack of value consensus between the Gabor Roma and the members of the Romanian majority society regarding their social significance and market value. That is, the ethnicized character of these pieces is primarily responsible for why the antiques market and art history relate to them in a fundamentally different way than the Gabors do, and why the purchase price of these objects on the antiques market is only a fraction of the prices that the Gabor Roma are prepared to pay each other for the more important beakers and tankards of complete value. As a consequence, the Gabors never use the services of non-Roma experts and brokers in organizing their sales transactions and credit deals. The relative lack of an interethnic value consensus obviously limits the opportunities of even those non-Roma individuals most interested in the prestige economy – such as antiques dealers – who are very rarely able to buy a Gabor Roma beaker or tankard.[3]

For these reasons, the Gabors' prestige economy is an informal segment of the Romanian economy that is largely "invisible" and unknown to members of the majority society and to government bodies: a kind of terra incognita. Occasional encounters between authorities such as the police, judges, or prosecutors and the prestige economy – for example, when ownership disputes between Gabor individuals are brought before the courts – tend to evoke reactions of incredulity, indignation, and rejection on the part of non-Roma.

The fact that the authorities of the socialist Romanian state did not have detailed knowledge of the Gabors' beakers and tankards and that, even if some of those pieces appeared in their field of vision, they were thought to be commodities of little or no economic significance, allowed their Roma owners to accumulate wealth informally while at the same time eluding the possible negative consequences of state monitoring, such as wealth confiscation, taxes on purchase prices, or investigations into the amassing of personal wealth.[4] That is, during the decades of socialism, due to the informal nature of the prestige economy, investing cash reserves in silver beakers and tankards proved to be an effective means of protection and "everyday resistance" against state control and the appropriation of private property.[5]

The Meagre Choice of State-Approved Forms of Wealth Accumulation and Representation

The fact that the forms of wealth accumulation and representation legally available to citizens were considerably more limited prior to the 1989 regime change than after it – primarily because of state-imposed restrictions on and strict control of private property – undoubtedly contributed to the popularity of the prestige economy. The citizens of the socialist Romanian state were not allowed to own more than a certain area of land, freely set up privately owned enterprises, or accumulate large sums of foreign currency. Moreover, the old Romanian leu often suffered substantial devaluation; it was not a reliable, predictable means of payment because its value was not stable. Whenever expensive commodities came to the knowledge of the authorities, their owners could expect investigations into the origin of their wealth and sometimes even confiscation of their property. The small choice of legally available and reasonably secure forms of investment also encouraged the Gabor Roma to invest their cash reserves in their informal prestige economy, "invisible" to the Romanian majority society, rather than in the kinds of conspicuous goods, such as cars or houses, that would easily attract the attention of the authorities. In the words of one of my hosts remembering these times,

> Under communism I couldn't just set up a [privately owned] laundry or start up a business for myself or open a bar; everything was state-owned. There were only state-owned laundries, bars, shops, hotels. Nothing was privately owned. And we didn't have any other possibility: if someone had money, all they wished was to buy a beaker. This was the best investment. They [the Gabors] didn't invest their money in houses – but in beakers! Because during the communism, the way it was was that if I had two houses under my name, for one year there was no problem. The first year passed and two weeks or three weeks and then we got a notice from the people's council: "Mr. X. We live in a communist world, you can't have two houses. Which one shall we take? And how did you get two houses anyway?" … They [the authorities] were suspicious. We couldn't possess two houses, but for a year. There was no land for sale, everything was the property of the state. (26 June 2010)

Mobile and Easily Concealable Assets

Another feature of prestige objects that contributed to their popularity as a form of investment during the decades of socialism also relates to the state's restriction and control of private property. Beakers and tankards, being generally small in size and, therefore, mobile assets, are easy to hide and, if necessary, easy to carry without detection. Their owners can take them wherever they go, carried in the inside pocket of a jacket or hidden in personal luggage – unlike houses or cars, for instance. The comment below not only highlights the significance of mobility but also discusses how the relative lack of an interethnic value consensus regarding beakers and tankards is exploited as an economic resource:

> This [the group of beakers and tankards] is the kind of wealth that there can be a war, there can be anything, other laws ... a Romanian man looks at it, a Hungarian man, any nation, even if a policeman [looks at it] by chance ... [all of them say,] "It's not a gold beaker. I don't want it!" He gives it back. If there's a war, I can put it in my bag and take it with me anywhere. But I can't carry a hundred kilos of gold! That would be taken, stolen. With this [the prestige object] I can go where I want! (2 July 2011)

Symbols Endowed with Multiple Identity Values

Another factor that contributed greatly to the attractiveness of the prestige economy was its constitutive role in various – ethnic, patrilineal, gender, and so on – identity projects. As mentioned earlier, this economy is interpreted, among other things, as an important symbolic arena of the intraethnic politics of difference, in which the prestige relations between individuals, families, patrilines, and local communities can be conceptualized, materialized, and recreated. As a consequence, the more precious beakers and tankards are symbols endowed with political meanings, values, and significance, and the proprietary contests for them are essential means of (re)negotiating hierarchies and differences among the Gabors.

Form of Investment of Stable Value

Finally, as confirmed by all of my Gabor Roma interlocutors, the pre-1989 social and economic popularity of beakers and tankards can also be traced back to the fact that the majority of them preserved their market value throughout the decades of socialism; if forced to sell them, their owners could recover at least the previously paid purchase price or a sum approaching it. My Roma acquaintances often noted that if they had stored their surplus in cash instead, they would have suffered considerable losses because of the repeated, unexpected, and substantial devaluation of the Romanian leu. As mentioned in chapter 4, however, changes in some value preferences of the prestige-object aesthetics had a significant effect on the value-preserving capacity of certain pieces. For instance, conspicuously large beakers as well as almost completely undecorated ones lost a (substantial) part of their value in the decades before 1989. The following comment aptly illustrates the significance of buying prestige objects as a form of value-preserving investment:

> They [the Gabor Roma before the change of political regime] were very much attached to their beakers ... The old men were crazy about the beakers, they found their wealth, their greatness, their nobility, and their rank in them ... And they preferred to keep their money in beakers. Because the money spent on them preserved its value ... The money loses some value every day. You will touch your money all the time and it will go. But this [the group of beakers and tankards] remains a value. There's value in it. Whatever currency came [however much the Romanian leu lost its value], that was value. (19 March 2005)

The Symbolic Conflict between Post-Socialist and Traditional Prestige Goods after 1989

The previous section described the five major reasons for the prestige economy's attractiveness before the change of political regime. Which of these have changed and in what ways?

The political turn of 1989 and the ensuing economic and social transformation led to a fundamental shift in the attitude of the state towards private property and the accumulation of individual wealth. Private individuals were now in a position to, among other things, possess unlimited sums of foreign currency, land, and houses, and to start their own businesses. As a consequence, the Gabor Roma had less cause to fear state control over their financial situation and all its possible negative consequences, thus essentially eliminating one of the major pre-regime-change motivations for the purchase of traditional prestige objects: informal collecting of these pieces had been an effective means of protection from state restrictions on private property, since it rendered cash reserves "invisible." With respect to the method and intensity of the state's collection of information on private property, the status of beakers and tankards is no different today from that of commodities such as works of art, gold, or quality cars.

The legalization of foreign currency possession became a powerful antidote to fears of a rapid devaluation of the Romanian leu, and following the regime change, most Gabor Roma kept a substantial part of their savings in such currencies as German marks and US dollars (and later, also in euros), which they also used to calculate the prices of beakers and tankards and pay for them. After the collapse of socialism, therefore, a potential hyperinflation of the Romanian leu was no longer an incentive to buy traditional prestige goods.

After 1989, the mass availability of expensive post-socialist consumer goods and services and the liberalization of spending also ended the shortage of legally available conspicuous forms of wealth accumulation; anyone could now freely spend his/her savings on the wide range of consumer goods (flashy cars, new houses, and so on) that effectively represented the extent of their owner's economic capital.[6]

It also follows from the shift in the state's position on private property that beakers and tankards lost some of their pre-regime-change significance as mobile objects that could be easily concealed and transferred.

Because of the processes described above, the prestige economy has lost some of the popularity it enjoyed prior to the regime change, and, as a consequence, people now place less firm trust in the ability of beakers and tankards to keep their economic value without loss. The decline in the readiness to purchase these silver items is, however, limited primarily to pieces of moderate significance – the social interest in and demand for prestige objects of higher value have not (or have only slightly) diminished in intensity. This is aptly demonstrated by the considerable number of outstandingly high purchase prices paid in recent years (US$400,000 in 2006; US$300,000 in 2008; US$600,000 in 2009; US$250,000 in 2009; US$1,000,000 in 2010; and US$220,000 in 2011), topped by the most remarkable transaction in the history of the Gabors' prestige economy (described in chapter 2): the 2009 sale of a beaker for US$1,200,000.

In addition to the changes mentioned in the previous paragraphs, why have costly post-socialist commodities and services became serious competitors of beakers and tankards in the distribution of incomes? The explanation in short is that the former have given rise to a new, post-socialist, symbolic repertoire of wealth accumulation and representation, which offers an attractive alternative to the patina-based consumption of generally very expensive beakers and tankards of limited and unpredictable availability. The rise in the demand for post-socialist prestige goods was driven by a number of their characteristics:

(1) They are not ethnicized. The conspicuous consumption or possession of such goods is a strategy of public representation of purchasing power that every Romanian citizen can understand in the same way.
(2) They are more visible and therefore a more efficient means for invidious comparison and the demonstration of economic prosperity.
(3) They can (almost) always be purchased.
(4) As they are (considerably) cheaper to buy than precious beakers and tankards, they are also suitable for representing even more modest cash reserves. For this reason, far more Gabor Roma are able to participate in the conspicuous consumption of post-socialist prestige goods; unlike a more valuable beaker, a barely used Western car is within the reach of many people.
(5) Several of them, such as houses located in more sought-after parts of settlements, allow the possessor to invest his/her income with more or less assurance of preserving value.
(6) They are easier to sell than beakers or tankards, whose ethnicized nature and high prices limit market size. While traditional prestige objects can be sold only to the Gabor Roma (or the Cărhars) for the high prices expected by the Gabors, post-socialist prestige goods are also in demand among non-Roma buyers. In other words, the potential market for the latter is substantially larger.[7]

Internal Factors Threatening the Prestige Economy: Ethnicized Character, Gerontocracy, and Elitism

I have so far been concerned with the *external* causes of the declining popularity of the prestige economy, causes that can be tied to its broader economic and social environment and the 1989 political regime change. This process, however, also has its *internal* driving forces: features that can be interpreted as intrinsic to the prestige economy and are independent of the Romanian majority society and the post-socialist transformation.

One of these internal causes is the ethnicized nature of the meanings and values associated with the beakers and tankards, and of the prices paid for them. Under socialism, the ethnicized nature of prestige objects played a key role in rendering the incomes invested in them "invisible" to the authorities; that is, their being ethnicized was a positive property, an economic resource. Since 1989, however, when the post-socialist consumer revolution and its consequences (the rapid increase in the number of conspicuous forms of wealth accumulation and representation, for example) have posed a more and more serious challenge to the prestige economy, the importance of the economic risk arising from the ethnicized character of beakers and tankards has significantly increased. The two major sources of this risk were mentioned in the previous two sections of this chapter – the ethnicized nature of beakers and tankards (a) prevents them from being seen by members of the Romanian majority society as representations of social and economic success, wealth, and purchasing power; and (b) essentially limits market demand for these objects. That is, while their ethnicized character restricts the political agency of beakers and tankards to the Gabors exclusively, it limits the market demand for them mainly to the Gabor and Cărhar Roma ethnic populations. The increased importance of these risk factors in the post-socialist era has undoubtedly contributed to the decreased attraction of purchasing prestige objects.

The popularity of this economy with young people is further endangered by its gerontocratic nature. Most young and middle-aged individuals who cannot afford to buy a prestige object themselves are able to take possession of their father's beaker or tankard only shortly before or after his death – assuming that the father owned such a piece. It is thus typically a long time before they have an opportunity to actively participate in the prestige economy as owners.

The attractiveness of this economy is also threatened by its characteristic elitism, the most important sources of which are the relatively small number of beakers and tankards and the high purchase prices associated with the more precious pieces. Prestige-object owners constitute a vanishingly small minority among the Gabors, most of whom are merely passive participants, members of the "audience" following the events of this economy from a distance. Since the prestige economy is an important symbolic arena of the intraethnic politics of difference, and achievements in it can be transformed into social successes only if they are ratified and approved by many other influential Gabor Roma (i.e., fame and prestige are goods "on loan ... from society" [Goffman 1967, 10]), owners therefore have a vested interest in maintaining "audience" members' interest in and commitment to this economy. Given the considerable shifts in consumer value preferences, practices, and patterns that the past decades have brought, this is an ongoing and ever-greater challenge.

Types of Loss that May Accompany the Decline in
Popularity of the Prestige Economy

For those with the strongest incentive to maintain the popularity of this economy – the owners and their immediate family members – a possible negative consequence of the waning social attractiveness of beakers and tankards is a further decline in their value-preserving capacity. In other words, if forced to sell them, possessors – having likely spent substantial sums on precious pieces and accepted considerable economic risk to keep them – would find it increasingly difficult to recover the purchase prices they previously paid for them (or a sum of comparable magnitude). Their situation would be made even more complicated by the absence of alternative markets; apart from the Cărhar Roma, there is no other consumer subculture that assigns a similarly high price range to beakers and tankards as the Gabors do. The owners, therefore, interpret the post-regime change decrease in the social interest in and market demand for prestige objects as an undesirable process that goes against their economic interests and calls into question the sense and significance of the financial sacrifices many of them once made in order to acquire and maintain possession of these pieces.

As I have already indicated several times, the important beakers and tankards are endowed with multiple identity values, and their possession is a multi-level practice of identity. They are a highly esteemed means of conceptualizing and materializing political success and economic prosperity, as well as ethnic and patrilineal identity, past, and belonging. This partly explains why owners attach special emotional and social value to more precious pieces. Many of my hosts referred to the purchase of their (most important) prestige object as the peak of their political career and the achievement of their lifetime – an honourable act constituting one of the most important sources of their self-esteem, reputation, and success. With the marginalization of the prestige economy, the political and social sacrifices and emotional and identity values associated with it would also gradually lose most of their significance.

Discursive Strategies Characteristic of the
Conservative-Traditionalist Attitude

The dominant discursive strategies used by those who espouse a conservative-traditionalist attitude towards prestige objects – first and foremost, owners – to counteract the post-regime change decrease in the social attractiveness of these pieces are in part the same as those we encountered in the examination of the discursive framing of the interethnic prestige-object trade between the Gabors and the Cărhars in chapter 10.

"This Luxo [Luxury] Is Consuming Us": The Strategy of Moral Criticism and Scaremongering

One of the frequently used strategies in this discourse is moral criticism of post-socialist consumer taste or sensitivity and the expensive commodities and services that became widespread after 1989 – that is, post-socialist prestige goods. This discourse defines these goods – in a homogenizing and essentializing way – as meaningless and unnecessary, and synonymous with waste. Moreover, these goods are labelled as morally destructive, risky, and dangerous. According to the conservative-traditionalist discourse, the use of these negative labels is supported by the argument that selling beakers and tankards – which are endowed with multiple identity values – in order to acquire non-ethnicized (or at least non-Gabor Roma) costly post-socialist commodities is an open rejection and symbolic devaluation of Gabor Roma ethnic identity (i.e., *Gaborness*). In other words, this consumer choice is defined as a negative identity practice, a disturbing and morally stigmatized type of symbolic pollution and loss of ethnic identity (Harrison 1999, 10–11). Emblematic of the moral criticism and scaremongering that is applied to the growing popularity of post-socialist consumer taste or sensitivity is the often-repeated statement, "This *luxo* [luxury = the set of expensive post-socialist prestige goods] is consuming us." Here the concept of luxury is laden with negative connotations in the same way as when it is used by the Cărhar Roma to criticize the Gabors' openness to post-socialist consumer taste or sensitivity ("The Gabors spend a lot on luxury goods ... and they do not mind if they lose their beakers!" etc.). In the sentence mentioned, the verb "consume" is a metaphor for the pollution and loss of ethnic identity: the partial marginalization of beakers and tankards, attributed primarily to the mass appearance of the morally condemned post-socialist prestige goods, is interpreted as a process of "devouring" Gabor Roma ethnic identity, of questioning and eventually eliminating it. The Gabor Roma proponents of the conservative-traditionalist attitude towards beakers and tankards draw on the same ideology of pollution and loss of ethnic identity, and the strategy of moral scaremongering concerning consumption, as the Cărhar Roma do when they discuss what the Gabors lose by letting some of their traditional prestige goods flow out of their own Roma ethnic population.

"They Were Very Good Times, the Communist Times": The Strategy of Structural Nostalgia

The discourse of the conservative-traditionalist attitude is also characterized by the frequent use of structural nostalgia (Herzfeld 1990).[8] The core of this strategy is the depiction of the decades of socialism as a past golden age that represented an ideal world order, a time when post-socialist commodities were nowhere to be seen, and beakers and tankards were unquestionably the dominant and most sought-after forms of accumulating and representing wealth and preserving the value of cash reserves. (On the politics of nostalgia for the socialist past, see also, for example, Berdahl 1999, 2000; Boym 2001; Morris 2005, 2007, 2014; Klumbytė 2010; Ghodsee 2011; Light & Young 2015.) The following quotation is an eloquent example of the nostalgia for the decades before 1989 and the way in which this period is often homogenized and idealized:

> The Gabor Roma accumulated debts during the democracy [after the change of political regime]. That was when you started hearing, "That one's so much in debt. That one is … That one is …" Since [we have had] luxury [the mass spread of expensive post-socialist prestige goods]. Believe me, it was a very good world during communism. We weren't used to having a lot of money … or to foreign countries [foreign travel], we didn't have these luxuries, we didn't have the big Real or Selgros stores [the names of two hypermarket chains that appeared in Romania after 1989]. There weren't any at all … We did coppersmithing and tinsmithing. The Lord knows that we did the handiwork … we got a bushel of grain, a bushel or two of potatoes … We had a little money and, believe me, we didn't need this big luxury … that there is now. (26 June 2010)

"They [the Cărhar Roma] Invest [Their Money] in Their Own Traditional Valuables!": The Strategy of Displaced Meaning

Another means used to both rationalize and counterbalance the decrease in the prestige economy's popularity is the strategy of "displaced meaning" (McCracken 1988, 14), which also often appears in the discourse of the conservative-traditionalist attitude towards beakers and tankards.

As McCracken (1988) notes, members of groups that are deprived of the realization of the ideal order – moral or other – in their own culture or society often find that ideal order in another culture or society and, as a consequence, idealize and fetishize the latter. In the discourse of Gabor owners who fear the devaluation of their traditional prestige goods, that other consumer culture or social context – where silver beakers and tankards are granted the social appreciation, popularity, and demand they regard as ideal – is that of the Cărhar Roma. In this case, the Cărhars – who in the Gabors' discourse serving to explain the interethnic trade of prestige objects are otherwise assigned such negative ethnic stereotypes as culturally "backward," "uncivilized," and excessively attached to consumer traditionalism and conservatism – appear as a positive model worthy of emulation and respect. In other words, while many Gabor Roma comments representing the conservative-traditionalist view criticize the younger Gabor generations for underestimating the social significance of beakers and tankards, they depict the Cărhar Roma as embodying the ideal attitude towards the prestige economy – as persons who display the expected respect for their own cultural and political heritage and consumer traditions, and properly guard their "traditional valuables" and Roma ethnic identity.

As this concluding chapter has clearly demonstrated, the Gabors' prestige economy depends on many economic, social, cultural, and political factors and the continuous interplay between them – making the future very difficult to predict. But, in the optimistic opinion of one of my Gabor Roma interlocutors, a man in his sixties from Cluj County:

> This will never die, this fire [the passion for collecting beakers and tankards] among us! … No matter how many houses you buy, it doesn't have the same resonance [it doesn't result in as much social prestige, appreciation and renown] as buying a beaker. That is heard in the whole world wherever Gabor Roma live [the Gabors will talk about it everywhere], "X bought the beaker of that one [that individual]!!" (11 July 2009)

Notes

Introduction: Translocal Communities of Practice and Multi-Sited Ethnographies

1 In this monograph, the terms "prestige object(s)" and "prestige economy" denote exclusively silver beakers and roofed tankards. Where this is not the case will be clear from the context.

2 The adjectives "Roma" and "Romani" are used synonymously. The term "Roma" (plural) is also used as a noun referring to a group – large or small – of Roma people. The comprehensive phrases "the Gabor Roma" and "the Gabors" denote the Gabor Roma ethnic population. The nouns "non-Roma" or *gaźos* refer to all people except ethnic populations of Roma. The term "other, non-Gabor Roma" denotes one or more ethnic populations of Roma that are not identical with the Gabor Roma ethnic population. *Řom* = Roma man, *řomnji* = Roma woman. In terms of origin and meaning, the adjectives "Romani" (from the Romani noun "Roma") and "Romanian" (from the country name "Romania") are completely independent of each other.

3 The only estimate known to me of the number of Gabor Roma is found in the study by Gardner and Gardner (2008, 155). In their opinion, there are around 14,000 Gabor Roma living in Romania.

4 As I will discuss in detail later in this book, the Cărhar Roma of Transylvania are just as passionate about collecting silver beakers and roofed tankards as the Gabor Roma, and their prestige economy specializing in those objects is very similar to that of the Gabors.

5 See also the "extended network of practice model" proposed by Morris (2012) and Warde's analysis of the relationship and interplay between consumption studies and theories of practice (Warde 2005).

6 The phrases "ethics of sociability" and "ethics of managing social relations and interactions" are used synonymously.

7 For the sake of simplicity, I will henceforth often refer to roofed tankards simply as tankards.

8 I identify the concept of "symbolic patina" with ownership history in places, and elsewhere with the political renown accumulated by the previous Gabor Roma owners of a beaker or roofed tankard. For the sake of simplicity, I treat these two interpretations as synonyms (despite the obvious fact that the political renown of previous possessors is only one component of the ownership history).

1. Symbolic Arenas and Trophies of the Politics of Difference

1 For the sake of simplicity, in place of "Roma politics," "Roma political," etc. I will often use the terms "politics," "political," etc. The latter terms refer exclusively to Roma politics in this monograph. Where this is not the case will be clear from the context.

2 Roma politics characteristic of the Gabors is a larger, ethnicized, and translocal community of practice comprising four smaller communities of practice – namely, the participants in the four symbolic arenas of politics mentioned.

3 The word "file" (*dosszár*) is used in the Gabors' political discourse in the sense of personal files kept by authorities. That is, it – metaphorically – denotes documents recording all important information about an individual's political performance.

4 To save space, I will not give the Romani-language originals of longer quotations.

5 The term "meeting" (*djîleši* or *kris*) denotes the social gatherings organized on the occasion of wakes, funerals, weddings, betrothals, and so on.

6 My knowledge of political discourse comes from the following sources: (a) Regular observations and documentation of public discourses at social gatherings. During my fieldwork, I attended mortuary rituals on thirty-nine occasions, and was a guest at several weddings and christening ceremonies, where one of the most important activities of men was having conversations, in groups of different sizes, that were often centred around Roma politics. With one exception, I had the opportunity to record the mortuary rituals mentioned on video. (b) I watched a good few of these videos subsequently in the company of my Roma interlocutors and we analysed what we saw. (c) I conducted several semi-structured interviews about the ideologies, strategies, and techniques of political discourse.

(d) Finally, I witnessed (and occasionally participated, in a marginal role, in) several conversations about political topics; these conversations were not linked to any social event but emerged spontaneously in, for instance, second-hand markets, coffee shops, or shopping centres.

7 A wake is usually held for two nights: from eight or nine in the evening until sunrise the next morning (unrelated people and distant relatives usually leave the home of the deceased at about one or two in the morning). Like the wake, the day of the funeral also provides an opportunity for several hours of political discourse with those present. The same can be said of the six-week memorial ritual and the social gathering organized for the day after the funeral. To the latter of these, the family of the deceased invites, in addition to the closest relatives, mostly the men who gave active support during the wake and the funeral (by supervising death rituals, distributing drinks, and so on). The purpose of the gathering held the day after the funeral is to console the family, to publicly go over the costs related to the death (wake and funeral expenses, for instance), to qualify the behaviour of the persons participating in the rites, and to express thanks to unrelated Roma for their help in organizing the death rites.

8 The word *vica* (literally, "rope") signifies, among other things, the concept of patriline in the Gabors' Romani dialect.

9 In the Gabors' discourse, *baro řom* is an ethnicized and gendered category; it refers exclusively to certain Gabor Roma men. This honorific title is in many respects similar to that of the "big man" found in classic anthropological literature (see, for example, Godelier & Strathern 1991).

10 See also Engebrigtsen 2007, 117–24.

11 A marriage payment (*juššo*) is a sum of money forming part of the dowry paid by the parents of the future wife to the parents of the future husband during (or, if the wife's family have financial difficulties or other obstacles, after) the wedding.

12 The dominant principle of conceptualizing descent among the Gabors is patrilineality. Patrilineal forebears in our case is a category comprising primarily male members of the patriline. The women belonging to a patriline only rarely become a part of long-term political memory; this generally occurs in cases where their marriage brings with it a marital alliance later regarded as the beginning of a long-term and close political cooperation between the two patrilines or families involved.

13 The local, regional, or ethnic-population-level prestige hierarchies of patrilines are based on the combined successes achieved in the arenas of politics, similar to prestige relations between individuals.

14 The main factors determining the intensity of interest in the ethnic past
and genealogical memory include the degree of personal political ambition
and the level of activity and success an individual's patriline achieves in
politics.

15 A particular "rank" or "class" may comprise more than one patriline.

16 My Gabor interlocutors and I agree in our interpretations of the tropes
"first/second/third ranks" that they have nothing to do with the concept
of caste or with the notion of "Indian origin" often associated with the
Roma. The spread in this Roma ethnic population of the word "rank" as a
political category serving to represent differences in prestige can probably
be traced back to the military ranks of Romanian armed forces (the police,
the army, etc.). This explanation is supported by the fact that, when they
said the word "rank," several Roma touched a shoulder with one hand
where insignias showing military ranks are worn.

17 The great-grandfathers, great-great-grandfathers, and so on of the
generation currently in their forties or fifties.

18 Among the Gabor Roma, *mita* is a sum of money that, depending on the
context, can be interpreted as a wage (for example, to a broker), a success
fee, a compensation, a gift as "an expression of gratitude," a gift for
persuasion (bribe), or a gift as "a representation of joy." (On the politics
of gift-giving in other post-socialist social contexts, see, for example,
Ledeneva 1998, 2006; Patico 2002, 2008.)

19 English-language anthropological and sociological analyses of the Roma
ethnic populations living in Romania have so far paid very little attention
to the social, cultural, and economic factors determining a marriage (choice
of partner, for instance). The most detailed investigation of the arranged
marriages (often of children) characteristic of some Romanian Roma ethnic
populations – using a combination of sociological, legal, and social policy
perspectives – is undoubtedly the work by Bitu and Morteanu (2010). See
also Oprea's analysis (2005), as well as certain sections of the following
publications: Troc 2002; Engebrigtsen 2007, 78–90; Fosztó 2009; Pantea
2009; Olivera 2012; Plainer 2012; Tesăr 2012.

20 The choice from among co-father-in-law candidates is limited not only
because the ideal age range for the marriage of young people is only a
few years, and only a limited number of Gabor parents have children of
similar ages. Fathers/paternal grandfathers planning a *xanamikimo* usually
also need to exclude individuals who are much more successful than
themselves in Roma politics.

21 The grandparents of the married couple use the phrases "old-co-father-in-
law" (*phuro xanamik*) and "old-co-mother-in-law" (*phuri xanamik*) for each

other. The parents of the young couple often refer to them in the same way, too.

22 The most common causes of divorce are the following: the young people "do not match" (they do not take a liking to each other and have a lot of conflicts); the co-father-in-law giving the wife cannot pay the promised marriage payment in time; no children are born to the young couple within the first few years of their marriage.

23 As for the Roma living in Romania, see, for example, Engebrigtsen 2007, 80; Bitu and Morteanu 2010, 111. Salo and Salo noticed among the "Kalderaš in Eastern Canada" that the amount of bride price seemed to remain constant during their fieldwork (Can$5,750) while earlier it had fluctuated between Can$2,000 and Can$8,000 (Salo & Salo 1977, 147). Sutherland (1975, 220) reported that in the Roma ethnic population she examined, the bride price was generally between US$400 and US$5,500, and Miller (1975, 54) mentioned a sum of US$5,000 in one of her writings.

24 The Romanian leu (plural Romanian lei) is the currency of Romania.

25 These motivations may appear in various combinations.

26 Marriage between close consanguineous relatives is not at all characteristic of the Gabor Roma.

27 Among the cases that can be classified here, sending home a daughter-in-law is usually justified with a morally acceptable explanation meant to disguise the real motives of the young husband's parents. A common pretext is the failure of a young couple to produce offspring in the first few years of their marriage, as this gives the parents reason for concern and raises the possibility that the daughter-in-law is infertile. Although infertility may affect either member of the young couple, in accordance with the Gabor Roma ideology of gender differences (the higher prestige associated with masculinity), it is primarily the woman who is held responsible – at least in public – for childlessness.

28 For the ethics of sociability in a Masari Roma community in Hungary in the second half of the 1980s, see Stewart 1994, 1997.

29 The concept of *patjiv* may be associated not only with individuals but also with families and patrilines.

30 This value preference is probably not independent of the fact that while few people can be really successful in marriage politics or in the prestige economy, *patjiv* is accessible to all.

31 Also, the *patjiv* lent to the individual by society may acquire considerable political significance and become the basis of distinction when the goal is to compare the political success of two individuals or families having similar economic and social status.

2. The Gabors' Prestige Economy: A Translocal, Ethnicized, Informal, and Gendered Consumer Subculture

1 According to Matras (2002, 28), the Romani term "*taxtaj*" is of Persian origin.
2 I discovered the criteria and markers of authenticity gradually during
  fieldwork through activities such as conversations I initiated on this
  subject, participation in Roma viewings of beakers and tankards, and
  prestige-object transactions and discourses, as well as by leafing through
  and discussing art history books and auction and museum catalogues
  containing photographs of silver objects with my Roma acquaintances.
3 For the sake of simplicity, let us disregard those very few silver objects that
  came to the Gabors from the Cărhar Roma. These will be discussed later.
4 In some cases, it may not be so easy to identify the material. This is
  especially true for objects made of silver-plated alpaca.
5 The classic anthropological definition of a prestige economy usually
  includes complex non-market exchange systems extended in space and
  time, such as the Kula, Potlach, and Moka.
6 In connection with the Gawa island kula shells, Munn gives an excellent
  analysis of why fame can be regarded as a social construction that cannot
  exist without publicity and social interactions – that is, without the active
  cooperation of individuals. In the case examined by Munn, the category
  of these individuals includes: the participants in the individual shell
  transactions; the persons to whom the owners lend their kula shells to
  wear and thereby spread the fame of those objects and their possessors
  (see notes 8 and 10 to chapter 5 in this book); as well as "the virtual
  third party," that is, "the distant other who hears about, rather than
  directly observes the transaction" (Munn 1986, 116). "In sum, fame can be
  understood as a coding of influence – an iconic model that reconstitutes
  immediate influence at the level of a discourse by significant others about
  it … Without fame, a man's influence would, as it were, go nowhere;
  successful acts would in effect remain locked within themselves in
  given times and places of their occurrence or be limited to immediate
  transactors. The circulation of names frees them, detaching them from
  these particularities and making them the topic of discourse through
  which they become available in other times and places … fame is the
  circulation of persons via their names in the realm of other minds (or in the
  oral realm of the speech of others)" (Munn 1986, 117).
7 Pengo is a former Hungarian currency that was in circulation between
  1927 and 1946.

8 In the Hungarian- and German-language historical and other reports published by non-Roma authors that I have perused, the first mention of silver beakers in the possession of Transylvanian Roma dates from 1831. Between 1831 and 1917 several dozen in-text mentions, separate studies, or newspaper items report on the intense passion for collecting silver beakers – earlier made and owned by non-Roma – in certain Transylvanian Roma communities. Several hundred beakers in Roma possession appear in these reports, which pay special attention to the social, economic, and emotional significance attributed to them by the Roma and to the related rituals. (See, for example, the writings of István Téglás: Téglás 1899, 1912a, 1912b, 1912c, 1913.) The authors of some of the reports specifically call on their readers to try to buy back from the Roma as many as possible of the silver beakers that once belonged to the non-Roma Transylvanian aristocracy or bourgeoisie so that these pieces can find their place in the Transylvanian Hungarian or Saxon museums set up in the second half of the nineteenth century, principally as indexical representations of Hungarian and Saxon national/ethnic identity and history. Although it is not possible to establish a direct connection between the "Gypsy treasures" and their owners described in non-Roma reports of that period and the Gabor and Cărhar Roma prestige objects and their possessors that came to my knowledge in the course of my fieldwork, the large number of these reports is nevertheless clear proof of the intense interest shown by certain Transylvanian Roma communities in silver objects in the nineteenth and early twentieth centuries.

9 All names are pseudonyms. Where this is not the case will be clear from the context.

10 As will soon be explained, the discourses of the antiques market and art history determine the value and meaning of these objects in a fundamentally different way.

11 In some cases, the Gabors consider the Cărhar Roma to be ideal buyers. See chapters 7 and 8.

12 The buyer estimated that the total costs of the transaction approached US$1,400,000. In addition to the purchase price, this amount included the interest paid on the loan taken to buy the beaker, the cash gifts (interpreted as "representations of joy") distributed since 2009 (US$110,000), and other subsidiary costs (food and drinks, solicitor's fee in connection with the transaction, etc.: US$15,000).

13 In table 2.4, the calculations are based on the purchase prices paid converted into Hungarian forints.

The purchase prices shown do not include the auxiliary costs of buying something at an auction (e.g., the auction house fee) and the auxiliary costs of prestige-object sales transactions (such as the cash gifts distributed after the purchase or the success fee of the broker).

In reality, the price listed in second place in the section "Purchase price of the beaker" is qualified as the highest on the basis of the value calculated in Hungarian forints. However, my Gabor interlocutors took the price paid in US dollars as the basis and regarded the US$1,200,000 transaction as the deal involving the largest sum of money. For this reason, I also accept their interpretation.

14 The size of the purchase price paid is only one of the possible sources of the reputational profit arising from the purchase of a prestige object (see chapter 4).

15 The intensity of efforts made to maintain inalienability depends to a considerable extent on the magnitude of the economic, emotional, and identity values associated with the given object. If these values are not especially significant, it is very likely that the owner will show less resistance and part with the piece more readily.

16 As previously mentioned in chapter 1, the Gabors are characterized by the dominance of "soft" hierarchies. In accordance with this, the competition in the symbolic arenas of politics aims at the accumulation of fame and appropriation of certain honorific titles. Individuals who have been successful in these arenas and have gained considerable renown can influence social and economic processes solely by using the strategy of persuasion, at least if they want to respect the Gabor Roma ethics of sociability.

17 Let us disregard for now objects of modest value, for which there is no proprietary contest and the sale of which constitutes only moderate relief in the event of a personal economic crisis. The lengthy "immobility" of these pieces – that is, the absence of change in their ownership situation – is a marker and consequence primarily of their modest value.

3. From Antiques to Prestige Objects: De- and Recontextualizing Commodities from the European Antiques Market

1 Although – as I will soon discuss – some of the beakers and tankards coming into the possession of the Gabors do not originate from the antiques market, for the sake of simplicity I will usually refer to the objects acquired from non-Roma or other, non-Gabor Roma as pieces from the antiques market. This practice is explained by two factors. The first is

that the vast majority of the Gabors' beakers and tankards come from the antiques market (antiques dealers, collectors, auction houses, and so on). The second factor is that all non-Roma sources of object acquisition – antiques market, museums, congregations of the Reformed Church, etc. – used by the Gabors are based primarily on the value regimes of the antiques market and art history.

2 Regarding the practices of de- and recontextualization used in other social and cultural contexts, see, for example, Appadurai 1986; Kopytoff 1986; Myers 1991, 1998, 2001, 2002, 2006b, 2006c, 2013; Thomas 1991, 2001; Marcus & Myers 1995; Phillips & Steiner 1999.

3 I use the word "pedigree" as a synonym for ownership history.

4 The claim that the Gabors are not interested in the non-Roma pedigree of their beakers and tankards is only seemingly contradicted by the fact that several households own books and catalogues of auctions or museum exhibitions that include photographs of "proper" objects. These publications were mostly used by my hosts to enhance their knowledge of the material properties of silver pieces.

5 On such occasions, they often refer to their prestige objects as "baron beakers [pieces that were once the property of barons and other aristocrats]."

6 The partial removal of non-Roma meanings and values created by the earlier non-Roma possessors – that is, the practice of symbolic emptying or divestment – can also be observed in the case of houses. The Gabors do not usually leave houses bought from non-Roma untouched but rather rebuild and redecorate them to fit their needs. One element of this process is enlarging the kitchen area or creating a new kitchen, since this room is the centre of social life. Another frequent strategy is the complete redecoration of the bathroom (new tiles, for instance) and replacement of its furnishings. If there is a toilet inside the newly purchased house, the Gabors tend to dismantle it and build another one in an inconspicuous part of the courtyard not visible to guests entering the house (for example, behind the house or garage). The latter practices are usually justified by the Roma ideology that the non-Roma's relationship to the body and its purity is dubious and sometimes threatening since they – unlike the Roma – do not make a careful distinction between the parts of the body regarded as "pure" and "impure." The Gabors therefore maintain that the purity of not only the non-Roma's body but also the tools and rooms used to clean the body is questionable.

7 It occasionally happens that two objects are given the same proper name. See later in this section.

8 In this and the following five paragraphs, in a departure from the author's practice of anonymization, the actual names the Gabor Roma gave their prestige objects are used.

9 A spoken curse usually applies not only to the new owner unfairly obtaining the piece but also to his potential heirs: his son, grandson, and so on.

4. Creating Symbolic and Material Patina

1 According to Dawdy's interpretation (2016, 4), "the word *patina* summons a triangular relationship between time, materiality, and the social imaginary." For a brief history of patina see Dawdy 2016, chapter 1.

2 Ownership history is, of course, not the only factor here; other elements of its biography may also add to the singularity and desirability of a second-hand commodity.

3 Family heirlooms typically change hands through inheritance, and their value is therefore only rarely expressed in monetary terms.

4 Using another perspective, patina-based commodities are often not merely the property of individuals or groups, but – thanks to the fact that they make their possessors an inalienable part of their biographies and ownership histories – also possess their owners in a metaphorical sense.

5 The term *kuštik* refers to the girdle articulating the beaker's body. *Taxtaj kuštikasa* therefore means "a (footed) beaker articulated with a girdle."

6 Chalices on thin solid stems (frequently used in Catholic churches) were not regarded as prestige objects by my acquaintances.

7 The size of a footed beaker is calculated by adding up the capacity of the upper vessel and the capacity of the hollow foot. The weight and height of an object measured in centimeters are disregarded and generally ignored. The same two measures are usually important features of value estimates characteristic of the antiques market.

8 *Ščobo* beakers have a surface with, at most, a dotted or other pattern; a band beneath the lip with etched motifs; one or more medallions with inscriptions, coats of arms, dates, and so on; and gilding. Animal representations and other figural motifs as decorative features are mostly found on footed and *burikato* beakers.

9 Encompassing, for instance, the names of composers or writers and the titles of specific works preferred by the group.

10 It is worth noting that my hosts never questioned the authenticity of the *Gaborness* of any of their Gabor Roma acquaintances simply because they were found to be inexperienced in prestige-object aesthetics.

5. The Politics of Brokerage: Bazaar-Style
Trade and Risk Management

1 For the rest of this chapter, the words "broker" and "intermediary" are used as synonyms of *cenzar* unless specified otherwise. The *cenzar*s are always male.

2 The Gabors may also occasionally use the services of an intermediary similar to a *cenzar* when they buy a silver piece from the European antiques market in the hope that it will become a prestige object of complete value after a period of time in their possession, or when they try to sell pieces that have lost their value in their own Roma ethnic population to a non-Roma antiques dealer (which is a vanishingly rare occurrence). This intermediary may be either Roma or non-Roma. Since in transactions with the non-Roma the intermediary's job is usually limited to finding potential buyers and sellers, it is worth distinguishing these economic actors from *cenzar*s, who commonly have a more complex set of responsibilities. I shall not discuss transactions involving non-Roma in the current chapter.

3 The rest of this chapter deals with brokers coordinating sales transactions. Where this is not the case will be clear from the context.

4 It is often possible to buy or pawn the more valuable beakers or tankards only with the joint efforts of family members. This may involve brothers or co-fathers-in-law lending a substantial sum of money with favourable interest conditions to the buyer or to the individual who has consented to give a loan, in return requiring that the debtor's prestige object be handed over as a security.

5 There may be other reasons for the absence of intermediaries. These include, for instance, a lack of trust in available brokers or a decision by the buyer or seller to avoid spending the sum that would have to be paid to an intermediary.

6 In connection with singularization, see also the naming practices described in chapter 3.

7 This sum is equivalent to 264.5 times the gross average salary in Romania in December 2004.

8 Munn (1986, 112–14) also stresses the significance of the "visual channel" and the "material mode of self-display" based on it in fame creation and management. Men living on Gawa island often lend the shells they own to others so that they can wear them in public. The essence of this practice is that "the media of influence a man acquires are demonstrated ... in his beautification of another person. When shells are lent out to be worn by

someone else, the owner's self-decoration is, in effect, detached from him and made public by another. The shell refers back to the owner, adorning him through his capacity to physically adorn another. In this respect, the wearer becomes the publicist of the donor's influence, as if she or he were mentioning his name" (Munn 1986, 113).

9 These motivations often appear in various combinations.

10 Munn reports a similar practice on Gawa island involving kula shells. She argues that "verbal publication" (Munn 1986, 113) is one of the most important local techniques for the creation of fame; it is linked to the practice already mentioned where owners lend their necklaces to women among their close kin "to wear on a daily basis or for ceremonies" (Munn 1986, 112). These women usually "compose fame chants called *butura* that celebrate a man's kula acquisitions, telling of the journey in which he obtained the shells, and other related events" (Munn 1986, 112). These public chants "spread the fame of men who have honored (-*kaves*) them, 'naming' the men by naming the kula shells and canoes identified with them. In these contexts, women are the others who transform the selves of the male actors by converting the latters' particular acts and material acquisitions into a verbal discourse that circulates apart from them, the artifacts, and the relevant momentary events. At the same time that their chants are about fame and its processes, they also make famous what they chant about" (Munn 1986, 112–13).

11 Limited visual accessibility also explains why many of my acquaintances possessed a collection of publications (museum and auction catalogues and art historical publications) showing, among other things, "proper" beakers and tankards. These publications were usually supplemented by colour photocopies and a series of digital photographs (stored on mobile phones) of Gabor Roma and antiques-market silver objects. My interlocutors often spent time browsing these publications and photos, and during my fieldwork they sometimes turned to these sources in conversations about material properties to help me understand which properties are considered valuable in their own Roma ethnic population. These publications and photos are an important means of acquiring knowledge of the material features of beakers and tankards and also help the Gabors gather information about the European antiques market.

12 In contrast to the buyer, the seller knows very well whether the beaker or tankard he calls by proper name X is indeed the object known as X.

13 These are only a few of the frequently used conditional self-curses: "May all the curses in the Bible come down upon me [on the oath-taker]," "May my sons and grandchildren die, may they all suffer a fatal road accident,"

"May I buy coffins for them [the oath-taker's sons and grandchildren] within six weeks" [if, for instance, this beaker or tankard is not worth at least this or that sum of money].

14 If both parties engage an intermediary, the brokers try to come to an agreement, consulting sometimes with their own employers and sometimes with each other or directly with their employer's prospective transaction partner.

15 If the object for sale is not especially sought after, the broker exercises caution in citing the prestige hoped to be gained from the purchase. If the buyer is a young man, a common strategy is to describe the transaction as a big success for someone of his age; that is, the broker may argue that the buyer "is still young; a less important beaker will be just right for him as a start."

6. Political Face-Work and Transcultural Bricolage/Hybridity: Prestige Objects in Political Discourse

1 "Face-work or relational work, which is an ingredient of every interaction, 'refers to the "work" individuals invest in negotiating relationships with others,' i.e., relational work is a means and arena of negotiations about interpersonal relationships and meanings" (Szalai 2013, 469).

2 It is also regarded as an ideal solution if the speaker praises himself but does so in a polite manner, applying various face-saving strategies and techniques. See the next section.

3 Making an invidious comparison does not necessarily require the speaker praising himself to explicitly use both structural elements of the comparison – what is compared with what. The words of self-praise spoken are in themselves sufficient for the hearers to compare their own political achievements with the content of the self-praise, and for many of them to feel they have been shamed.

4 Before cars came into general use, the Gabors travelled in horse-drawn carts that were also used for agricultural and other work. These carts were often decorated with colorful painted motifs and functioned as assets.

5 A speaker often mentions both a cart and one or two horses pulling it. In this case, the audience must decide for themselves which part of the scene (cart, horse, or perhaps both) refers to the prestige object(s).

6 The ability of the "grey horse" to cover a large distance or cross the mountains is a representation of the high quality and value of the prestige object in question. The image of a "lame horse," in contrast, alludes to the modest significance of a beaker or tankard.

7 Oradea and Miercurea Ciuc are county seats in Romania.

8 The categories "unfortunately dead" versus "not unfortunately dead" have nothing to do with the intense personal loss experienced by the bereaved. These categories are intended to express whether, taking into account the social definition of the Gabor Roma concept of "ideal life," the deceased lived a full life or not.

9 Marko had sisters but no brothers.

10 "Three villages" refers to a microregion in Mureş County with three large and wealthy Gabor Roma local communities. Marko is a member of one of them.

11 Departing from the customary practice (to make it easier for him to organize the song), Marko here uses the term "stallion" to refer also to his tankard.

12 As previously mentioned, the pengo was a Hungarian currency in circulation between 1927 and 1946.

13 While the *mita* regarded as "a representation of joy" always takes the form of cash, a libation is typically an invitation for a drink. The latter is usually a catalyst in triggering the hoped-for social acknowledgement of minor individual successes (buying a car, for instance). Following the purchase of a prestige object, the new owner gives a libation primarily to those at a considerable social distance from him and who are thus not important enough to him to "merit receiving *mita* [interpreted as 'a representation of joy']," which is reserved for relatives, friends, supporters, allies, etc. more significant to him.

14 Trei Scaune is a region in Central Romania.

15 Very few of the analyses dealing with the relationship between the Roma and transcultural bricolage/hybridity have looked at how certain Roma ethnic populations or local communities imported and recycled some cultural products of the ethnic populations living around them (see, for example, Kertész-Wilkinson 1992). Most investigations focused on the borrowing and intellectual recycling of certain elements of Roma music in global contexts (for example in the "world music" industry); that is, they analysed how Roma music is recontextualized and reinterpreted in non-Roma musical markets and subcultures. In connection with the latter investigations, see for example Brown 2000; Silverman 2007, 2011, 2012, 2014, 2015a, 2015b; see also Okely 2013; Tremlett 2009.

16 Ţinutul Secuiesc is a historical region in Romania, inhabited primarily by Hungarians, Romanians, and Roma. The Szekelys (*Secui*) are an ethnic population of the Hungarian people who live mainly in this region.

17 As for material culture, a parallel example in support of this claim is the
case of the collecting of beakers and tankards (i.e., the adoption of this
practice in the nineteenth century from non-Roma aristocrats, burghers,
and so on) and the ethnicized reconceptualization of numerous properties
of these objects by the Gabors.

7. Gabor Roma, Cărhar Roma, and the European Antiques Market: Contesting Consumer Subcultures

1 On the antiques market, tankards are often sold for higher sums than
beakers belonging to the types of shape wanted by the Gabors.
2 The recent wave of economic migration of Romanian Roma to Italy and
France is the subject of many studies (see, for example, Sigona 2008;
Pesarini 2010; Solimene 2011; Matras & Leggio 2017).
3 Due to the large number of Cărhar Roma families in Rupuno, many of
whom are affluent, and to the intense Romanian and international media
interest shown in them, my Cărhar interlocutors often referred to the
Cărhar community of Rupuno as the "capital" of their own Roma ethnic
population.
4 While in the Gabors' dialect, the plural of the noun *taxtaj* is *taxta*, in the
Cărhars' dialect, it is *taxtaja*.
5 The Cărhar Roma term for the beaker shape called octagonal (*njolcsegîvo*)
by the Gabors is "a beaker consisting of sides [literally meaning planes]"
(*taxtaj andol pale*). We may also occasionally come across a piece of modest
value among the Cărhars that cannot be classified under any of the shape
types mentioned above.
6 In the mid-nineteenth century, many Roma individuals in Transylvania
owned *sčobo*-shaped, generally large, silver beakers with simple
ornamentation made for them by Transylvanian silversmiths. While
several of these pieces are now in the possession of Cărhar Roma, I did
not find a single beaker of this type among the Gabors. It is not possible to
determine whether the nineteenth-century Roma individuals who ordered
these beakers are related to the Roma known today as Gabors and Cărhars.
7 In the Cărhar Roma dialect, the equivalent of the phrase "unexplainable
animals" is "unknown animals" (*animaluri necunoscute*).
8 It is not a rare occurrence among the Cărhars that when the parents have
two daughters, they stop having more children even though there are no
health obstacles to having a bigger family. I did not hear of similar cases
among the Gabors. With only a few exceptions, as mentioned in chapter 1,

Gabor Roma marriages in which no male child is born tend to be dissolved so that the husband can remarry and ensure the continuity of his patriline.

9　Just as among the Gabor Roma, it is also cause for concern among the Cărhars if a young couple do not have any children within the first few years of their marriage. The usual reaction is to solicit medical assistance to find out what could be the cause of the couple's childlessness and whether there is a chance of their having children in the future.

10　In the case of the Cărhars living in Rupuno, the meaning of the marked quotation is, "The younger [brother] gives a *boldimo* to the older [brother]."

11　Just as in the Gabor Roma ethnic population, there are also occasionally fathers with sons among the Cărhars who see the establishment of a marital alliance primarily as a temporary source of income, and the choice of co-father-in-law may also be motivated by a need to find a political supporter.

12　Several of my interlocutors noted that the more precious the beaker or tankard deposited with the co-father-in-law as a security, the higher the "respect" shown by the husband's father towards him. When a marital alliance is formed between individuals in similar economic and social positions and the husband's father has only one son but owns more than one prestige object, the wife's father usually requests the most valuable piece.

13　A *činste* (in Romanian *cinste*) is a cash gift made up of sums contributed by the relatives of the young couple and intended for the couple's personal use. The *činste* is not part of the dowry. (See also Verdery 1983, 61–2; Engebrigtsen 2007, 165–8; Vasile 2015.) Many of my Cărhar hosts defined the *činste* as some sort of cash gift that primarily "represents love from the parents."

14　Kalo brought a son-in-law into his family in 2009 as his elder daughter's husband; the couple would inherit his house and prestige objects. This was the second marriage for the son-in-law. He had first married into the family of another Cărhar man who also had two daughters, and had moved in with them, together with the prestige object that was his paternal inheritance. (This piece is a slightly more than one-and-a-half-liter *sčobo* beaker with a medallion and a gilded lip.) His first marriage was, however, soon ruined because of conflicts between him and his father-in-law. Finally, despite having a son with his first wife, he and his wife divorced and he moved in with Kalo as a son-in-law. He left his beaker with the family of his former wife as his son's paternal inheritance.

15　Kalo gave his daughter €3,000 as a *činste* at the time of her wedding.

8. Interethnic Trade of Prestige Objects

1 I consider cases in which a Gabor owner pawns his prestige object with a Cărhar creditor who later purchases the pledge without the Gabor possessor being able to redeem it as a single (sales) transaction.

2 The remark I heard from many of my Gabor interlocutors is thus fully justified; namely, that the great majority of Gabor prestige objects pawned to the Cărhars "remain there forever in the Olt River area," meaning that there are only very rarely opportunities to redeem them. The "Olt River area" here is used as a synonym for the Cărhar Roma ethnic population.

3 Kuna's father bought three beakers and a tankard in his lifetime: the *burikato* beaker bequeathed to Kuna, two footed beakers, and a 3.5-deciliter, richly gilded tankard. The tankard and one of the footed beakers were later bought by Cărhar Roma. During the last few years, Kuna made several unsuccessful attempts to sell or pawn his beaker to the Cărhars.

4 The degree of symbolic loss caused by verbal insults also depends on the value of the object sold: the former increases proportionally with the latter.

5 The rarity of sales among the Cărhars is best explained on the one hand by the unique social significance attached to silver prestige objects (a significance somewhat surpassing that found among the Gabors) and on the other hand by the Cărhars' consumer conservatism and self-restraint shown towards new commodities, services, and consumer value preferences that come from the non-Roma majority society. See also chapter 10.

6 Many of my Cărhar interlocutors gave the following explanation for the fact that several Cărhar Roma plunged into the construction of unusually large, ostentatious family homes (many of which remained unfinished) with many rooms over several storeys: while their owners would much rather have invested their cash reserves in beakers and tankards, they did not know of any prestige objects for sale and thus – for lack of a better solution – chose this spectacular form of prestige consumption. The son of the owner of one of these "palaces" in Sibiu County argued that he and his father would sell their house at any time if they had the opportunity to buy a valuable beaker or tankard, and they "would be happy to move into a tiny hut." See also Tesăr 2016. Regarding the relationship between prestige consumption and houses in other – non-Gabor and non-Cărhar – Roma ethnic populations living in Romania, see, for example, Calzi, Corno, & Gianferro 2007; Nemeth & Gianferro 2009, 2010; Nemeth 2010.

9. Constructing, Commodifying, and Consuming
Fake Authenticity

1 All attempts at fraud that I followed were related to beakers, and all the fraudsters were men.
2 Not including the cases when the fraud attempt was directed at me, the anthropologist, as described later.
3 If the speaker making a conditional self-curse and his listener do not have detailed knowledge about each other's families, the impending misfortunes outlined in the conditional self-curse can be easily evaded – for example, through the choice of reference. If, for example, the speaker uses the following conditional self-curse, "May my Rupi die if I am not telling the truth!" it has to be taken as a serious threat only if he really has a son called Rupi.
4 Nonetheless, by the summer of 2011, the fact of the fraud and its details were already commonly known among the Cărhars.
5 I did not come across any signs that money-oriented fraud also existed within the Gabor Roma ethnic population – no doubt because, in such a case, the potential buyer could not count on his relatives, friends, or brokers to certify that the invented Gabor history of ownership of the fake offered for sale was genuine, and in the absence of social consensus and ratification the fraud would be revealed immediately.

10. The Politics of Consumption: Classification Struggles,
Moral Criticism, and Stereotyping

1 According to the recollections of my Gabor and Cărhar Roma interlocutors, the situation was the same in the 1950s and 1960s.
2 On the politics of national iconization focusing on cars in socialist and post-socialist contexts, see, for example, Berdahl 1999, 2000; Merkel 2006; Siegelbaum 2011.
3 For many, normalization is a process that occurs only in the symbolic field of consumer desires and value preferences. In other words, although a growing number of Gabor Roma think that a prestigious-brand Western car is an indispensable part of a good/normal/ideal life, this does not necessarily mean that they are all capable of buying one. On the logic and techniques of normalization in socialist and post-socialist social settings, see Fehérváry 2002, 2013.
4 On the politics of leisure and luxury in socialist contexts, see, for example, Crowley & Reid 2010; Massino 2012; Miklóssy & Ilic 2015.

5 My interlocutor used this homogenizing and undoubtedly exaggerated statement to refer to the already-mentioned fact that prestige objects change hands much less often in the Cărhar Roma ethnic population than among the Gabors.

6 It was only after 2000 that transnational economic migration – begging in Italy, France, and elsewhere – became an increasingly popular livelihood strategy among the Cărhars. In contrast, many of the Gabor Roma had specialized in transregional intermediary trade in Romania from the 1970s, and after the change of political regime a large number of these individuals travelled to Hungary and Turkey, and later to various other countries of Europe to trade there.

7 As already mentioned, beakers and tankards are ethnicized goods for both the Gabors and the Cărhars – a means of creating and materializing ethnic history, identity, and belonging – and members of both populations refer to them, although with varying frequency, as evidence of the "genuineness" of their respective Roma ethnic identity. Analytically speaking, they define these objects and the prestige economy organized around them as markers of the authenticity of their Roma ethnic identity, which distinguish them from Romanian non-Roma and other Transylvanian Roma ethnic populations. Furthermore, both the Gabors and the Cărhars consider the prestige economy to be one of their "most ancient traditions."

11. Things-in-Motion: Methodological Fetishism, Multi-Sitedness, and the Biographical Method

1 Appadurai's chapter is one of the major works published in the 1980s that contributed to a great extent to the culmination of the "material turn" in the social sciences (Edwards 2002, 69; Kitzmann 2005) – or in other words the "reinvention" of material culture studies, the "rehabilitation of things" (Olsen 2004, 89), or the "rematerialization of social sciences" (Woodward 2007, 28) – that began from the late 1960s, and became increasingly popular in disciplines such as anthropology, sociology, cultural studies, and art history.

12. Prestige Objects, Marriage Politics, and the Manipulation of Nominal Authenticity: The Biography of a Beaker, 2000–2007

1 Although I argued earlier that a widow is not regarded as owner of her deceased husband's prestige objects, there are occasional exceptions. After the widow sold the beaker or tankard entrusted to her care, most of my

interlocutors spoke of her as "the previous owner." In this chapter I accept that interpretation.

2 This sum was equal to 61.2 times the gross average monthly salary in Romania in 1961.

3 The widow eventually sold all seven objects. Four of those pieces – three beakers and a tankard – are still possessed by Gabor Roma, while the remaining three were purchased by Cărhar Roma buyers.

4 This purchase price was equal to 116.9 times the gross average monthly salary in Romania in 1961.

5 This purchase price was equal to 579 times the gross average monthly salary in Romania in 1982.

6 This purchase price was equal to 1,215 times the gross average monthly salary in Romania in 2000.

7 As mentioned before, the term "old co-father-in-law" is used by – among others – the young couple's fathers to refer to each other's father.

8 This sum was equal to 513.6 times the gross average salary in Romania in December 2002.

9 This purchase price was equal to 213.2 times the gross average monthly salary in Romania in 1985.

10 This purchase price was equal to 531.8 times the gross average salary in Romania in March 2006.

11 This purchase price was equal to 961 times the gross average monthly salary in Romania in 2006.

13. Proprietary Contest, Business Ethics, and Conflict Management: The Biography of a Roofed Tankard, 1992–2012

1 The reason the seller insisted that Pista should not only pay cash for his beaker but also give him a prestige object of lesser value was so that the seller would not "be left without a beaker" – that is, to mitigate the loss of prestige suffered by him and his family as a result of the sale.

2 Caritas initially imposed limits on the sum an individual could deposit at one time, but this restriction was later removed.

3 Pista returned the amount that he owed to his wife's cousin from the 152,000 German marks he borrowed from Rupi.

4 Rupi hoped that Pista would not be able to scrape together 152,000 German marks in the three weeks and that he would therefore visit him with his beaker and an offer to sell.

5 Although Rupi consistently argued before the Roma and in his conversations with me that Pista's breach of contract was the cause of his

losses, the majority of my acquaintances were of the opinion that Rupi's credulity and excessive good faith, as well as his political ambition – his desire to take possession of Pista's beaker – were also major factors contributing to the present situation.

6 The Djurdjovaje Roma are a Transylvanian Roma ethnic population. Today, they live mostly in Harghita County, and their dominant strategy of subsistence – like that of the Gabors – is intermediary trade. According to the recollections of my Roma interlocutors, several Djurdjovaje Roma also owned silver beakers and tankards interpreted as prestige objects at the turn of the nineteenth to twentieth century, but have since sold almost all of them.

7 The members of certain Transylvanian Roma ethnic populations – including the Cǎrhars, and in contrast to the Gabors – prefer to invest part of their money in gold coins (*galbi*) minted at the turn of the nineteenth to twentieth centuries. Of these, the four-ducat gold coins dated 1915 with the portrait of Franz Joseph I are the most popular.

It is a widespread practice among the Cǎrhars for parents to give their daughters one or more *galbi*s as part of their dowry. At joyful social events, such as weddings, girls often wear necklaces with *galbi*s, interpreted as representations of wealth.

The four-ducat gold coins are sold at auctions in Hungary today for around 140,000 to 150,000 Hungarian forints (US$479–513). In contrast to the beakers and tankards, gold coins are not singularized in any of the Transylvanian Roma ethnic populations known to me; they have neither proper names nor a unique composition of material properties, and their value – taking into account primarily their weight – is calculated on the basis of the prices of precious metals valid among the non-Roma.

8 The total purchase price of 300 million old Romanian lei (US$72,534) was 565 times the gross average salary in Romania in January 1997.

9 More precisely, the equivalent of this sum in euros or US dollars.

10 Rupi's comment below clearly indicates the great emotional value attached to the tankard: "Most of the Gabor Roma, including my brothers-in-law, envy me for that piece. And what's the situation among our Roma [the Gabors]? Any object that is not so outstanding, important [valuable] they run down, belittle. But this tankard is such a piece … that no one, even if they are angry with me, even if they wish me ill, can say that it is bad [not valuable]. It was in the first place [among the Gabor Roma tankards]! … Its handle alone is worth a *taxtaj* [the value of a beaker]! … When my mother-in-law saw it [the tankard], she kissed it. She said, 'This is the tankard of tankards [the most valuable tankard among the Gabors]!'" (29 June 2010)

11 News of the redemption spread very quickly among the Gabor Roma. In the weeks following the transaction, many individuals visited Rupi to view the object and ask about the details and circumstances of its return. For months, it remained one of the most important topics in formal and informal conversations among Gabor men living in and outside of Transylvania.

12 Although Rupi had in 1993 rejected the idea of asking Pista to pay interest, the nearly fourteen years that had passed since the tankard was pawned were such a long period that he could not ask Pista's widow to repay simply the capital and the value of his goods that had passed into the ownership of the Hungarian creditor. This is why he also demanded a sum equivalent to what was customarily defined in similar deals as interest.

13 In the following I cite part of another oath-taking ritual to give an idea of the nature of the dialogue between the oath-taker and the person uttering in advance the curses:

– THE INDIVIDUAL WHO "UTTERS IN ADVANCE" THE CURSES: May God strike you!
– OATH-TAKER: May God strike me!
– THE INDIVIDUAL ... : All the oath-takings that have taken place since the beginning of time at this bridge [at one of the bridges in Bigvillage]!
– OATH-TAKER: All the oath-takings that have taken place at this bridge!
– THE INDIVIDUAL ... : May they all [that is, all the curses uttered at the oath-takings mentioned] fall on your head!
– OATH-TAKER: May they fall on my head!
– THE INDIVIDUAL ... : And on your son's head, and on your wife's head!
– OATH-TAKER: May they fall on my son's head and my wife's head! ...
– THE INDIVIDUAL ... : If you said of your co-father-in-law that ...
– OATH-TAKER: If I said of my co-father-in-law that ...

Conclusion: The Post-Socialist Consumer Revolution and the Shifting Meanings of Prestige Goods

1 In this chapter I use the terms "traditional prestige objects" and "traditional prestige goods" to refer exclusively to silver beakers and roofed tankards. "Post-socialist prestige goods" and "post-socialist commodities" are used synonymously – both phrases refer to certain costly commodities and services widely available since 1989.

2 On the post-socialist relationship between fast-food restaurants and prestige, see Czeglédy 2002.

3 Maintaining informality is in the vested interest of antiques dealers as
  well, since their transactions tend to be carried out "under the counter,"
  outside the authorities' field of vision, whether they are selling silver
  objects to the Gabors or (in very rare cases) buying such pieces from them.
4 Many of my Gabor interlocutors expressed their sympathy for the
  members of Roma ethnic populations in Romania who invested a share
  of their incomes in gold coins – four-ducat coins with a portrait of Franz
  Joseph I on them, for instance – or other gold objects, many of which they
  had to surrender to the state during the decades preceding 1989 because
  of the existence of an interethnic value consensus. See, for instance, the
  case of Rudi Varga, who according to his own recollection, had a total of
  almost fourteen kilograms of gold (409 gold ducats, among other things)
  confiscated by the state in repeated house searches between 1976 and 1988.
  See Tibori Szabó 2001.
5 For an argument interpreting "informality as a 'normal' response to
  uncertainty and contingency," see Morris 2016, 87–121.
6 On the politics of shortage in socialist and post-socialist contexts, see, for
  example, Shafir 1985; Crowther 1988; Verdery 1991, 77–79, 209–213, 1996,
  27–28; Kideckel 1993; Kligman 1998, 67–68; Chelcea 2002. See also Beck
  1991; Latham 2002.
7 Several factors accounting for the attractiveness of post-socialist
  commodities and services also apply to the foreign currencies that spread
  after 1989: the German mark, the US dollar, and the euro. These currencies
  can, therefore, also be regarded as post-socialist rivals of the beakers and
  tankards.
8 Compare this to Boym's concepts of "restorative" and "reflective"
  nostalgia (Boym 2001, 41–56); Dawdy's interpretation of "critical
  nostalgia" (Dawdy 2016); and Morris's definitions of "utopian" and
  "ironic" nostalgia (Morris 2005).

References

Achim, V. (1998). *The Roma in Romanian History*. Budapest, Hungary: Central European University Press.

Alexander, C., & Reno, J. (Eds.). (2012). *Economies of Recycling: The Global Transformation of Materials, Values and Social Relations*. London, United Kingdom: Zed Books.

Alexander, P. (1992). What's in a Price? Trading Practices in Peasant (and Other) Markets. In R. Dilley (Ed.), *Contesting Markets: Analyses of Ideology, Discourse and Practice* (pp. 79–96). Edinburgh, United Kingdom: Edinburgh University Press.

Anderson, B. (1991). *Imagined Communities: Reflections on the Origin and Spread of Nationalism*. London, United Kingdom: Verso.

Ang, I. (2014). Beyond Chinese Groupism: Chinese Australians between Assimilation, Multiculturalism and Diaspora. *Ethnic and Racial Studies, 37*(7), 1184–96. https://doi.org/10.1080/01419870.2014.859287

Appadurai, A. (1986). Introduction: Commodities and the Politics of Value. In A. Appadurai (Ed.), *The Social Life of Things: Commodities in Cultural Perspective* (pp. 3–63). Cambridge, United Kingdom: Cambridge University Press. https://doi.org/10.1017/CBO9780511819582.003

Argo, J.J., Dahl, D.W., & Morales, A.C. (2006). Consumer Contamination: How Consumers React to Products Touched by Others. *Journal of Marketing, 70*(2), 81–94. https://doi.org/10.1509/jmkg.70.2.81

Bagwell, L.S., & Bernheim, B.D. (1996). Veblen Effects in a Theory of Conspicuous Consumption. *The American Economic Review 86*(3), 349–73.

Barany, Z. (2001). *The East European Gypsies: Regime Change, Marginality, and Ethnopolitics*. Cambridge, United Kingdom: Cambridge University Press. https://doi.org/10.1017/CBO9780511817373

Beck, S. (1991). What Brought Romanians to Revolt. *Critique of Anthropology,* *11*(1), 7–31. https://doi.org/10.1177/0308275X9101100102

Belk, R. (1988). Possessions and the Extended Self. *Journal of Consumer Research, 15*(2), 139–68. https://doi.org/10.1086/209154

Belk, R. (1995). *Collecting in a Consumer Society.* London, United Kingdom: Routledge.

Belk, R. (2013). The Extended Self in a Digital World. *Journal of Consumer Research, 40*(3), 477–500. https://doi.org/10.1086/671052

Belk, R. (2014a). The Extended Self Unbound. *Journal of Marketing Theory and Practice, 22*(2), 133–4. https://doi.org/10.2753/MTP1069-6679220202

Belk, R. (2014b). Alternative Conceptualizations of the Extended Self. In J. Cotte & S. Wood (Eds.), *Advances in Consumer Research 42* (pp. 251–4). Duluth, MN: Association for Consumer Research.

Berdahl, D. (1999). "N(O)stalgie" for the Present: Memory, Longing, and East German Things. *Ethnos, 64*(2), 192–211. https://doi.org/10.1080/00141844.1999.9981598

Berdahl, D. (2000). "Go, Trabi, Go!": Reflections on a Car and its Symbolization over Time. *Anthropology and Humanism, 25*(2), 131–41. https://doi.org/10.1525/ahu.2000.25.2.131

Billig, M.S. (2002). *Barons, Brokers, and Buyers: The Institutions and Cultures of Philippine Sugar.* Honolulu: University of Hawai'i Press.

Bitu, N., & Morteanu, C. (2010). *Are the Rights of the Child Negotiable? The Case of Early Marriages within Roma Communities in Romania.* Bucharest, Romania: Centrul Romilor Pentru Intervenţie Socială şi Studii.

Blackmore, P., & Kandiko, C.B. (2011). Motivation in Academic Life: A Prestige Economy. *Research in Post-Compulsory Education, 16*(4), 399–411. https://doi.org/10.1080/13596748.2011.626971

Blasco, P.G.Y. (1999). *Gypsies in Madrid: Sex, Gender and the Performance of Identity.* Oxford, United Kingdom: Berg.

Blasco, P.G.Y. (2001). "We Don't Know Our Descent": How the Gitanos of Jarana Manage the Past. *Journal of the Royal Anthropological Institute, 7*(4), 631–47. https://doi.org/10.1111/1467-9655.00081

Boissevain, J. (1974). *Friends of Friends: Networks, Manipulators and Coalitions.* Oxford, United Kingdom: Basil Blackwell.

Bourdieu, P. (1977). *Outline of a Theory of Practice.* Cambridge, United Kingdom: Cambridge University Press. https://doi.org/10.1017/CBO9780511812507

Bourdieu, P. (1984). *Distinction: A Social Critique of the Judgement of Taste.* Cambridge, MA: Harvard University Press.

Bourdieu, P. (1998). The Economy of Symbolic Goods. In *Practical Reason: On the Theory of Action* (pp. 92–123). Cambridge, United Kingdom: Polity.

Boym, S. (2001). *The Future of Nostalgia*. New York, NY: Basic Books.

Brenneis, D. (1984). Straight Talk and Sweet Talk: Political Discourse in an Occasionally Egalitarian Community. In D.L. Brenneis & F.R. Myers (Eds.) *Dangerous Words: Language and Politics in the Pacific* (pp. 69–84). New York, NY: New York University Press.

Brenneis, D. (1986). Shared Territory: Audience, Indirection and Meaning. *Text, 6*(3), 339–47. https://doi.org/10.1515/text.1.1986.6.3.339

Brown, B. (2001). Thing Theory. *Critical Inquiry, 28*(1), 1–22. https://doi.org/10.1086/449030

Brown, J. (2000). Bartók, the Gypsies, and Hybridity in Music. In G. Born & D. Hesmondhalgh (Eds.), *Western Music and Its Others: Difference, Representation, and Appropriation in Music* (pp. 119–42). Berkeley: University of California Press.

Brubaker, R. (1998). Myths and Misconceptions in the Study of Nationalism. In J. Hall (Ed.), *The State of the Nation: Ernest Gellner and the Theory of Nationalism* (pp. 272–306). Cambridge, United Kingdom: Cambridge University Press. https://doi.org/10.1017/CBO9780511897559.013

Brubaker, R. (2002). Ethnicity Without Groups. *European Journal of Sociology/ Archives Européennes de Sociologie, 43*(2), 163–89. https://doi.org/10.1017/S0003975602001066

Brubaker, R. (2004). *Ethnicity without Groups*. Cambridge, MA: Harvard University Press.

Brubaker, R. (2009). Ethnicity, Race, and Nationalism. *Annual Review of Sociology, 35*(1), 21–42. https://doi.org/10.1146/annurev-soc-070308-115916

Bucholtz, M. (1999). "Why Be Normal?": Language and Identity Practices in a Community of Nerd Girls. *Language in Society, 28*(2), 203–23. https://doi.org/10.1017/S0047404599002043

Bull, P. (2012). The Microanalysis of Political Discourse. *Philologia Hispalensis, 26*(1–2), 79–93.

Bull, P., & Fetzer, A. (2010). Face, Facework and Political Discourse. *International Review of Social Psychology 23*(2–3), 155–85.

Caldwell, M. (2002). The Taste of Nationalism: Food Politics in Postsocialist Moscow. *Ethnos, 67*(3), 295–319. https://doi.org/10.1080/0014184022000031185

Calzi, R., Corno, P., & Gianferro, C. (2007). *Gypsy Architecture: Houses of the Roma in Eastern Europe*. Stuttgart, Germany: Axel Menges.

Campbell, C. (1995). Conspicuous Confusion? A Critique of Veblen's Theory of Conspicuous Consumption. *Sociological Theory, 13*(1), 37–47. https://doi.org/10.2307/202004

Campbell, C. (1997). When the Meaning Is Not a Message: A Critique of the Consumption as Communication Thesis. In M. Nava, A. Blake, I. MacRury,

& B. Richards (Eds.), *Buy This Book: Studies in Advertising and Consumption* (pp. 340–51). London, United Kingdom: Routledge.

Campbell, C. (1998). Consumption and the Rhetorics of Need and Want. *Journal of Design History, 11*(3), 235–46. https://doi.org/10.1093/jdh/11.3.235

Chavis, L., & Leslie, P. (2009). Consumer Boycotts: The Impact of the Iraq War on French Wine Sales in the US. *Quantitative Marketing and Economics, 7*(1), 37–67. https://doi.org/10.1007/s11129-008-9043-y

Cheetham, F. (2009). Out of Control? An Ethnographic Analysis of the Disposal of Collectable Objects through Auction. *Journal of Consumer Behaviour, 8*(6), 316–26. https://doi.org/10.1002/cb.296

Chelcea, L. (2002). The Culture of Shortage During State-Socialism: Consumption Practices in a Romanian Village in the 1980s. *Cultural Studies, 16*(1), 16–43. https://doi.org/10.1080/09502380110075243

Coleman, S., & Hellermann, P. von (Eds.). (2011). *Multi-Sited Ethnography: Problems and Possibilities in the Translocation of Research Methods.* New York, NY: Routledge.

Colwell, C. (2014). The Sacred and the Museum: Repatriation and the Trajectories of Inalienable Possessions. *Museum Worlds, 2*(1), 10–24. https://doi.org/10.3167/armw.2014.020102

Colwell, C. (2015). Curating Secrets: Repatriation, Knowledge Flows, and Museum Power Structures. *Current Anthropology, 56*(S12), S263–75. https://doi.org/10.1086/683429

Crowley, D., & Reid, S.E. (Eds.). (2010). *Pleasures in Socialism: Leisure and Luxury in the Eastern Bloc.* Evanston, IL: Northwestern University Press.

Crowther, W.E. (1988). *The Political Economy of Romanian Socialism.* New York: Praeger.

Curasi, C.F., Price, L.L., & Arnould, E.J. (2004). How Individuals' Cherished Possessions Become Families' Inalienable Wealth. *Journal of Consumer Research, 31*(3), 609–22. https://doi.org/10.1086/425096

Czeglédy, A.P. (2002). Manufacturing the New Consumerism: Fast-Food Restaurants in Postsocialist Hungary. In R. Mandel & C. Humphrey (Eds.), *Markets and Moralities: Ethnographies of Postsocialism* (pp. 143–66). London, United Kingdom: Bloomsbury Academic.

Damon, F.H. (2002). Kula Valuables. The Problem of Value and the Production of Names. *L'Homme, 162*, 107–36. https://doi.org/10.4000/lhomme.158

Dant, T. (1999). *Material Culture in the Social World: Values, Activities, Lifestyles.* Buckingham, United Kingdom: Open University Press.

Dawdy, S. (2016). *Patina: A Profane Archaeology.* Chicago, IL: The University of Chicago Press. https://doi.org/10.7208/chicago/9780226351223.001.0001

Denegri-Knott, J., Molesworth, M. (2009). "I'll Sell This and I'll Buy Them That": eBay and the Management of Possessions as Stock. *Journal of Consumer Behaviour, 8*(6), 305–15. https://doi.org/10.1002/cb.295

Dutton, D. (Ed.). (1983). *The Forger's Art: Forgery and the Philosophy of Art.* Berkeley: University of California Press.

Dutton, D. (2003). Authenticity in Art. In J. Levinson (Ed.), *The Oxford Handbook of Aesthetics* (pp. 258–74). New York, NY: Oxford University Press.

Eckert, P. (2009). Communities of Practice. In J.L. Mey (Ed.), *Concise Encyclopedia of Pragmatics* (pp. 109–12). Amsterdam, The Netherlands: Elsevier.

Eckert, P., & McConnell-Ginet, S. (1992a). Think Practically and Look Locally: Language and Gender as Community-Based Practice. *Annual Review of Anthropology, 21*(1), 461–90. https://doi.org/10.1146/annurev.an.21.100192.002333

Eckert, P., & McConnell-Ginet, S. (1992b). Communities of Practice: Where Language, Gender, and Power All Live. In K. Hall, M. Bucholtz, & B. Moonwomon (Eds.), *Locating Power: Proceedings of the Second Berkeley Women and Language Conference* (pp. 89–99). Berkeley, CA: Berkeley Women and Language Group.

Eckert, P., & Wenger, E. (2005). Communities of Practice in Sociolinguistics: What Is the Role of Power in Sociolinguistic Variation? *Journal of Sociolinguistics, 9*(4), 582–9. https://doi.org/10.1111/j.1360-6441.2005.00307.x

Edwards, E. (2002). Material Beings: Objecthood and Ethnographic Photographs. *Visual Studies, 17*(1), 67–75. https://doi.org/10.1080/14725860220137336

Elliott, R. (2004). Making Up People: Consumption as a Symbolic Vocabulary for the Construction of Identity. In K.M. Ekström & H. Brembeck (Eds.), *Elusive Consumption* (pp. 129–43). Oxford, United Kingdom: Berg.

Elliott, R., & Davies, A. (2006). Symbolic Brands and Authenticity of Identity Performance. In J.E. Schroeder & M. Salzer-Mörling (Eds.), *Brand Culture* (pp. 155–70). London, United Kingdom: Routledge.

Engebrigtsen, A.I. (2007). *Exploring Gypsiness: Power, Exchange and Interdependence in a Transylvanian Village.* Oxford, United Kingdom: Berghahn.

Falzon, M.-A. (Ed.). (2009). *Multi-Sited Ethnography: Theory, Praxis and Locality in Contemporary Research.* Farnham, United Kingdom: Ashgate.

Falzon, M.-A. (2015). Multisited Field Studies. In J.D. Wright (Ed.), *International Encyclopedia of the Social & Behavioral Sciences* (pp. 103–8). Oxford, United Kingdom: Elsevier. https://doi.org/10.1016/B978-0-08-097086-8.12211-1

Fanselow, F.S. (1990). The Bazaar Economy or How Bizarre Is the Bazaar Really? *Man, 25*(2), 250–65. https://doi.org/10.2307/2804563

Faragó, J. (1994). Régi székely népballadák a magyar cigányok örökében [Old Szekely Folk Ballads Preserved by Hungarian Roma]. In Zs. Bódi (Ed.), *Az I. nemzetközi cigány néprajzi, történeti, nyelvészeti és kulturális konferencia előadásai. Budapest, 1993. március 16–20* (pp. 148–51). Salgótarján, Hungary: Mikszáth Kálmán Emlékbizottság.

Featherstone, M. (1991). *Consumer Culture and Postmodernism.* London, United Kingdom: Sage.

Fehérváry, K. (2002). American Kitchens, Luxury Bathrooms, and the Search for a "Normal" Life in Postsocialist Hungary. *Ethnos, 67*(3), 369–400. https://doi.org/10.1080/0014184022000031211

Fehérváry, K. (2013). *Politics in Color and Concrete: Socialist Materialities and the Middle Class in Hungary.* Bloomington: Indiana University Press.

Fenn, C.J. (1996). Life History of a Collection: The Tahltan Materials Collected by James A. Teit. *Museum Anthropology, 20*(3), 72–91. https://doi.org/10.1525/mua.1996.20.3.72

Fischer, J. (2007). Boycott or Buycott? Malay Middle-Class Consumption Post-9/11. *Ethnos, 72*(1), 29–50. https://doi.org/10.1080/00141840701219510

Foster, R.J. (2006). Tracking Globalization: Commodities and Value in Motion. In C. Tilley, W. Keane, S. Küchler, M. Rowlands, & P. Spyer (Eds.), *Handbook of Material Culture* (pp. 285–302). London, United Kingdom: Sage. https://doi.org/10.4135/9781848607972.n19

Foster, R.J. (2008). *Coca-Globalization: Following Soft Drinks from New York to New Guinea.* New York, NY: Palgrave Macmillan. https://doi.org/10.1057/9780230610170

Fosztó, L. (2007). Királyok, papok, újságírók és az angol bárónő: romániai romák a posztszocialista nyilvánosságban [Kings, Priests, Journalists, and the English Baroness: Romanian Roma in Post-Socialist Publicity]. *Regio, 18*(1), 25–50.

Fosztó, L. (2009). *Ritual Revitalisation after Socialism: Community, Personhood, and Conversion among the Roma in a Transylvanian Village.* Münster, Germany: LIT Verlag.

Fowles, S. (2006). *Thing Theory* [Syllabus]. New York, NY: Department of Anthropology, Columbia University. http://www.columbia.edu/~sf2220/Thing/web-content/Pages/Syllabus.html

Fox, J.E. (2006). Consuming the Nation: Holidays, Sports, and the Production of Collective Belonging. *Ethnic and Racial Studies, 29*(2), 217–36. https://doi.org/10.1080/01419870500465207

Fox, J.E., & Miller-Idriss, C. (2008). Everyday Nationhood. *Ethnicities, 8*(4), 536–63. https://doi.org/10.1177/1468796808088925

Friedman, M. (1999). *Consumer Boycotts: Effecting Change through the Marketplace and the Media.* London, United Kingdom: Routledge.

Frijters, P., & Leigh, A.K. (2008). Materialism on the March: From Conspicuous Leisure to Conspicuous Consumption? *Journal of Socio-Economics, 37*(5), 1937–45. https://doi.org/10.1016/j.socec.2008.07.004

Fuh, D. (2012). The Prestige Economy: Veteran Clubs and Youngmen's Competition in Bamenda, Cameroon. *Urban Forum, 23*(4), 501–26. https://doi.org/10.1007/s12132-012-9157-x

Gardner, D.J., & Gardner, S.A. (2008). A Provisional Phonology of Gabor Romani. *Romani Studies, 18*(2), 155–99. https://doi.org/10.3828/rs.2008.7

Geertz, C. (1963). *Peddlers and Princes: Social Change and Economic Modernization in Two Indonesian Towns.* Chicago, IL: University of Chicago Press.

Geertz, C. (1978). The Bazaar Economy: Information and Search in Peasant Marketing. *American Economic Review, 68*(2), 28–32.

Geertz, C. (1979). Suq: The Bazaar Economy in Sefrou. In C. Geertz, H. Geertz, & L. Rosen, *Meaning and Order in Moroccan Society. Three Essays in Cultural Analysis* (pp. 123–44). Cambridge, United Kingdom: Cambridge University Press.

Geismar, H. (2001). What's in a Price? An Ethnography of Tribal Art at Auction. *Journal of Material Culture, 6*(1), 25–47. https://doi.org/10.1177/135918350100600102

Geismar, H. (2008). Alternative Market Values? Interventions into Auctions in Aotearoa/New Zealand. *Contemporary Pacific, 20*(2), 291–327. https://doi.org/10.1353/cp.0.0024

Gell, A. (1998). *Art and Agency: An Anthropological Theory.* Oxford, United Kingdom: Clarendon.

Ghodsee, K. (2011). *Lost in Transition: Ethnographies of Everyday Life after Communism.* Durham, NC: Duke University Press. https://doi.org/10.1215/9780822394617

Giloi, E. (2011). *Monarchy, Myth, and Material Culture in Germany, 1750–1950.* Cambridge, United Kingdom: Cambridge University Press.

Godelier, M., & Strathern, M. (Eds.). (1991). *Big Men and Great Men: Personifications of Power in Melanesia.* Cambridge, United Kingdom: Cambridge University Press.

Goffman, E. (1967). *Interaction Ritual: Essays on Face-to-Face Behavior.* New York, NY: Anchor.

Gosden, C., & Marshall, Y. (1999). The Cultural Biography of Objects. *World Archaeology, 31*(2), 169–78. https://doi.org/10.1080/00438243.1999.9980439

Graburn, N.H.H. (2004). Authentic Inuit Art: Creation and Exclusion in the Canadian North. *Journal of Material Culture, 9*(2), 141–59. https://doi.org/10.1177/1359183504044369

Gregson, N. (2011). Performativity, Corporeality and the Politics of Ship Disposal. *Journal of Cultural Economics, 4*(2), 137–56. https://doi.org/10.1080/17530350.2011.563067

Gregson, N., Crang, M., Ahamed, F., Akhter, N., & Ferdous, R. (2010). Following Things of Rubbish Value: End-of-Life Ships, "Chock-Chocky" Furniture and the Bangladeshi Middle Class Consumer. *Geoforum, 41*(6), 846–54. https://doi.org/10.1016/j.geoforum.2010.05.007

Gregson, N., & Crewe, L. (2003). *Second-Hand Cultures.* Oxford, United Kingdom: Berg. https://doi.org/10.2752/9781847888853

Gregson, N., Metcalfe, A., & Crewe, L. (2007). Moving Things Along: The Conduits and Practices of Divestment in Consumption. *Transactions of the Institute of British Geographers, 32*(2), 187–200. https://doi.org/10.1111/j.1475-5661.2007.00253.x

Gupta, K.D. (2009). Changing Paradigms of Luxury Consumption in India: A Conceptual Model. *South Asian Journal of Management, 16*(4), 29–43.

Han, Y.J., Nunes, J.C., & Drèze, X. (2010). Signaling Status with Luxury Goods: The Role of Brand Prominence. *Journal of Marketing, 74*(4), 15–30. https://doi.org/10.1509/jmkg.74.4.15

Hand, M., & Shove, E. (2007). Condensing Practices: Ways of Living with a Freezer. *Journal of Consumer Culture, 7*(1), 79–104. https://doi.org/10.1177/1469540507073509

Hansen, K.T. (2000). *Salaula: The World of Secondhand Clothing and Zambia.* Chicago, IL: University of Chicago Press.

Harrison, S. (1995). Four Types of Symbolic Conflict. *Journal of the Royal Anthropological Institute, 1*(2), 255–72. https://doi.org/10.2307/3034688

Harrison, S. (1999). Cultural Boundaries. *Anthropology Today, 15*(5), 10–13. https://doi.org/10.2307/2678369

Harrison, R., Newholm, T., & Shaw, D. (Eds.). (2005). *The Ethical Consumer.* London, United Kingdom: Sage.

Hay, J. (2008). The Value of Forgery. *RES: Journal of Anthropology and Aesthetics, 53–54*, 5–19.

Hebdige, D. (1979). *Subculture: The Meaning of Style.* London, United Kingdom: Routledge.

Herrmann, G.M. (1997). Gift or Commodity: What Changes Hands in the US Garage Sale? *American Ethnologist, 24*(4), 910–30. https://doi.org/10.1525/ae.1997.24.4.910

Herrmann, G.M. (2004). Haggling Spoken Here: Gender, Class, and Style in US Garage Sale Bargaining. *Journal of Popular Culture, 38*(1), 55–81. https://doi.org/10.1111/j.0022-3840.2004.00100.x

Herzfeld, M. (1990). Pride and Perjury: Time and the Oath in the Mountain Villages of Crete. *Man, 25*(2), 305–22. https://doi.org/10.2307/2804566

Herzfeld, M. (2003). Localism and the Logic of Nationalistic Folklore: Cretan Reflections. *Comparative Studies in Society and History, 45*(2), 281–310. https://doi.org/10.1017/S0010417503000148

Hilton, M., & Daunton, M. (2001). Material Politics: An Introduction. In M. Hilton & M. Daunton (Eds.), *The Politics of Consumption: Material Culture and Citizenship in Europe and America* (pp. 1–32). Oxford, United Kingdom: Berg. https://doi.org/10.5040/9781350048928-ch-001

Holmes, J., & Meyerhoff, M. (1999). The Community of Practice: Theories and Methodologies in Language and Gender Research. *Language in Society, 28*(2), 173–83. https://doi.org/10.1017/S004740459900202X

Hoskins, J. (1998). *Biographical Objects: How Things Tell the Stories of People's Lives.* New York, NY: Routledge.

Hoskins, J. (2006). Agency, Biography and Objects. In C. Tilley, W. Keane, S. Küchler, M. Rowlands, & P. Spyer (Eds.), *Handbook of Material Culture* (pp. 74–84). London, United Kingdom: Sage. https://doi.org/10.4135/9781848607972.n6

Hugh-Jones, S. (1992). Yesterday's Luxuries, Tomorrow's Necessities: Business and Barter in Northwest Amazonia. In C. Humphrey & S. Hugh-Jones (Eds.), *Barter, Exchange, and Value: An Anthropological Approach* (pp. 42–74). Cambridge, United Kingdom: Cambridge University Press. https://doi.org/10.1017/CBO9780511607677.003

Ichinosawa, J. (2007). Economic Anthropology of Bangkok Go-Go Bars: Risk and Opportunity in a Bazaar-Type Market for Interpersonally Embedded Services. In D.C. Wood (Ed.), *Choice in Economic Contexts: Ethnographic and Theoretical Enquiries* (pp. 125–50). Amsterdam, The Netherlands: Elsevier.

Jamieson, M. (1999). The Place of Counterfeits in Regimes of Value: An Anthropological Approach. *Journal of the Royal Anthropological Institute, 5*(1), 1–11. https://doi.org/10.2307/2660959

Jenß, H. (2004). Dressed in History: Retro Styles and the Construction of Authenticity in Youth Culture. *Fashion Theory, 8*(4), 387–403. https://doi.org/10.2752/136270404778051591

Jones, M. (Ed.). (1990). *Fake? The Art of Deception.* Berkeley: University of California Press.

Jones, M. (1992). *Why Fakes Matter: Essays on Problems of Authenticity.* London, United Kingdom: British Museum Press.

Kertész-Wilkinson, I. (1992). Genuine and Adopted Songs in the Vlach Gypsy Repertoire: A Controversy Re-Examined. *British Journal of Ethnomusicology, 1*(1), 111–36. https://doi.org/10.1080/09681229208567203

Kertész Wilkinson, I. (1997). *The Fair Is Ahead of Me: Individual Creativity and Social Contexts in the Performances of a Southern Hungarian Vlach Gypsy Slow*

Song. Budapest: Institute for Musicology of the Hungarian Academy for Sciences.

Kideckel, D. A. (1993). *The Solitude of Collectivism: Romanian Villagers to the Revolution and Beyond*. Ithaca, NY: Cornell University Press.

Kiesling, S.F., & Ghosh Johnson, E. (2010). Four Forms of Interactional Indirection. *Journal of Pragmatics, 42*(2), 292–306. https://doi.org/10.1016/j.pragma.2009.06.004

Kingston, S. (1999). The Essential Attitude: Authenticity in Primitive Art, Ethnographic Performances and Museums. *Journal of Material Culture, 4*(3), 338–51. https://doi.org/10.1177/135918359900400306

Kitzmann, A. (2005). The Material Turn: Making Digital Media Real (Again). *Canadian Journal of Communication, 30*(4), 681–6.

Kligman, G. (1998). *The Politics of Duplicity: Controlling Reproduction in Ceausescu's Romania*. Berkeley: University of California Press.

Klumbytė, N. (2010). The Soviet Sausage Renaissance. *American Anthropologist, 112*(1), 22–37. https://doi.org/10.1111/j.1548-1433.2009.01194.x

Knappett, C., & Malafouris, L. (Eds.). (2008). *Material Agency: Towards a Non-Anthropocentric Approach*. New York, NY: Springer.

Kopytoff, I. (1986). The Cultural Biography of Things: Commoditization as Process. In A. Appadurai (Ed.), *The Social Life of Things: Commodities in Cultural Perspective* (pp. 64–92). Cambridge, United Kingdom: Cambridge University Press. https://doi.org/10.1017/CBO9780511819582.004

Kornai, J. (1992). *The Socialist System: The Political Economy of Communism*. Oxford, United Kingdom: Clarendon Press. https://doi.org/10.1093/0198287763.001.0001

Korom, F. J. (1996). Recycling in India: Status and Economic Realities. In C. Cerny & S. Seriff (Eds.), *Recycled, Re-Seen: Folk Art from the Global Scrap Heap* (pp. 118–29, 190–2). New York, NY: Harry Abrams.

Kovács, B., Morris, J., Polese, A., & Imami, D. (2017). Looking at the "Sharing" Economies Concept Through the Prism of Informality. *Cambridge Journal of Regions, Economy and Society, 10*(2), 365–78. https://doi.org/10.1093/cjres/rsw046

Ladik, D., Carrillat, F., & Tadajewski, M. (2015). Belk's (1988) "Possessions and the Extended Self" Revisited. *Journal of Historical Research in Marketing, 7*(2), 184–207. https://doi.org/10.1108/JHRM-06-2014-0018

Lastovicka, J.L., & Fernandez, K.V. (2005). Three Paths to Disposition: The Movement of Meaningful Possessions to Strangers. *Journal of Consumer Research, 31*(4), 813–23. https://doi.org/10.1086/426616

Latham, K. (2002). Rethinking Chinese Consumption: Social Palliatives and the Rhetorics of Transition in Postsocialist China. In C.M. Hann (Ed.),

Postsocialism: Ideals, Ideologies and Practices in Eurasia (pp. 217–37). London, United Kingdom: Routledge.

Lave, J., & Wenger, E. (1991). *Situated Learning: Legitimate Peripheral Participation.* Cambridge, United Kingdom: Cambridge University Press. https://doi.org/10.1017/CBO9780511815355

Ledeneva, A. (1998). *Russia's Economy of Favours: Blat, Networking, and Informal Exchange.* Cambridge, United Kingdom: Cambridge University Press.

Ledeneva, A. (2006). *How Russia Really Works: The Informal Practices That Shaped Post-Soviet Politics and Business.* Ithaca, NY: Cornell University Press.

Lemon, A. (1998). "Your Eyes Are Green like Dollars": Counterfeit Cash, National Substance, and Currency Apartheid in 1990s Russia. *Cultural Anthropology, 13*(1), 22–55. https://doi.org/10.1525/can.1998.13.1.22

Lemon, A. (2000). *Between Two Fires: Gypsy Performance and Romani Memory from Pushkin to Post-Socialism.* Durham, NC: Duke University Press. https://doi.org/10.1215/9780822381327

Lempert, M. (2012). Indirectness. In C.B. Paulston, S.F. Kiesling, & E.S. Rangel (Eds.), *The Handbook of Intercultural Discourse and Communication* (pp. 180–204). Chichester, United Kingdom: Wiley Blackwell. https://doi.org/10.1002/9781118247273.ch10

Levi, J.M. (1992). Commoditizing the Vessels of Identity: Transnational Trade and the Reconstruction of Rarámuri Ethnicity. *Museum Anthropology, 16*(3), 7–24. https://doi.org/10.1525/mua.1992.16.3.7

Light, D., & Young, C. (2015). Local and Counter-Memories of Socialism in Post-Socialist Romania. In M. Beyen & B. Deseure (Eds.), *Local Memories in a Nationalizing and Globalizing World* (pp. 221–43). Basingstoke, United Kingdom: Palgrave.

Lury, C. (1996). *Consumer Culture.* Cambridge: Polity Press.

MacDougall, J.P. (2003). Transnational Commodities as Local Cultural Icons: Barbie Dolls in Mexico. *Journal of Popular Culture, 37*(2), 257–75. https://doi.org/10.1111/1540-5931.00067

Magee, C. (2005). Forever in Kente: Ghanian Barbie and the Fashioning of Identity. *Social Identities, 11*(6), 589–606. https://doi.org/10.1080/13504630500449218

Maida, C.A., & Beck, S. (2018). Introduction: Global Sustainability and Communities of Practice. In C.A. Maida & S. Beck (Eds.), *Global Sustainability and Communities of Practice* (pp. 1–19). Oxford, United Kingdom: Berghahn Books.

Mandel, B.R. (2009). Art as an Investment and Conspicuous Consumption Good. *American Economic Review, 99*(4), 1653–63. https://doi.org/10.1257/aer.99.4.1653

Marcus, G.E. (1995). Ethnography in/of the World System: The Emergence of Multi-Sited Ethnography. *Annual Review of Anthropology*, 24(1), 95–117. https://doi.org/10.1146/annurev.an.24.100195.000523

Marcus, G.E., & Myers, F.R. (Eds.). (1995). *The Traffic in Culture: Refiguring Art and Anthropology*. Berkeley: University of California Press.

Marx, K. (1909). *Capital: A Critique of Political Economy* (Vol. 1). Chicago, IL: Charles H. Kerr & Company.

Massino, J. (2012). From Black Caviar to Blackouts: Gender, Consumption, and Lifestyle in Ceaușescu's Romania. In P. Bren & M. Neuburger (Eds.), *Communism Unwrapped: Consumption in Cold War Eastern Europe* (pp. 226–45). New York, NY: Oxford University Press. https://doi.org/10.1093/acprof:oso/9780199827657.003.0009

Matras, Y. (2002). *Romani: A Linguistic Introduction*. Cambridge, United Kingdom: Cambridge University Press. https://doi.org/10.1017/CBO9780511486791

Matras, Y., & Leggio, D.V. (Eds.). (2017). *Open Borders, Unlocked Cultures: Romanian Roma Migrants in Western Europe*. New York, NY: Routledge.

Maynard, M. (2004). *Dress and Globalization*. Manchester, United Kingdom: Manchester University Press.

McCracken, G. (1986). Culture and Consumption: A Theoretical Account of the Structure and Movement of the Cultural Meaning of Consumer Goods. *Journal of Consumer Research*, 13(1), 71–84. https://doi.org/10.1086/209048

McCracken, G. (1988). *Culture and Consumption: New Approaches to the Symbolic Character of Consumer Goods and Activities*. Bloomington: Indiana University Press.

McLaughlin, E. (2007). The Equality Chameleon: Reflections on Social Identity, Passing, and Groupism. *Social Policy and Society*, 6(1), 69–79. https://doi.org/10.1017/S1474746406003344

Merkel, I. (2006). From Stigma to Cult: Changing Meanings in East German Consumer Culture. In F. Trentmann (Ed.), *The Making of the Consumer: Knowledge, Power and Identity in the Modern World* (pp. 249–70). Oxford, United Kingdom: Berg.

Miklóssy, K., & Ilic, M. (Eds.). (2015). *Competition in Socialist Society*. New York, NY: Routledge.

Miller, C. (1975). American Rom and the Ideology of Defilement. In F. Rehfisch (Ed.), *Gypsies, Tinkers and Other Travellers* (pp. 41–54). London, United Kingdom: Academic Press.

Miller, D. (1987). *Material Culture and Mass Consumption*. Oxford, United Kingdom: Basil Blackwell.

Miller, D. (1995). Consumption Studies as the Transformation of Anthropology. In D. Miller (Ed.), *Acknowledging Consumption: A Review of New Studies* (pp. 263–92). London, United Kingdom: Routledge.

Miller, D. (1997). Coca-Cola: A Black Sweet Drink from Trinidad. In D. Miller (Ed.), *Material Cultures: Why Some Things Matter* (pp. 169–87). London, United Kingdom: UCL Press.

Miller, D. (2001). Alienable Gifts and Inalienable Commodities. In F.R. Myers (Ed.), *The Empire of Things: Regimes of Value and Material Culture* (pp. 91–118). Santa Fe, NM: SAR Press.

Miller, D., & Parrott, F. (2009). Loss and Material Culture in South London. *Journal of the Royal Anthropological Institute, 15*(3), 502–19. https://doi.org/10.1111/j.1467-9655.2009.01570.x

Mills, B.J. (2004). The Establishment and Defeat of Hierarchy: Inalienable Possessions and the History of Collective Prestige Structures in the Pueblo Southwest. *American Anthropologist, 106*(2), 238–51. https://doi.org/10.1525/aa.2004.106.2.238

Moffitt, J.F. (1995). *Art Forgery: The Case of the Lady of Elche.* Gainesville: University of Florida Press.

Morgan, M. (2010). The Presentation of Indirectness and Power in Everyday Life. *Journal of Pragmatics, 42*(2), 283–91. https://doi.org/10.1016/j.pragma.2009.06.011

Morris, J. (2005). The Empire Strikes Back: Projections of National Identity in Contemporary Russian Advertising. *Russian Review, 64*(4), 642–60. https://doi.org/10.1111/j.1467-9434.2005.00379.x

Morris, J. (2007). Drinking to the Nation: Russian Television Advertising and Cultural Differentiation. *Europe-Asia Studies, 59*(8), 1387–403. https://doi.org/10.1080/09668130701655218

Morris, J. (2012). Beyond Coping? Alternatives to Consumption within a Social Network of Russian Workers. *Ethnography, 14*(1), 85–103. https://doi.org/10.1177/1466138112448021

Morris, J. (2014). The Warm Home of Cacti and Other Soviet Memories: Russian Workers Reflect on the Socialist Period. *Central Europe, 12*(1), 16–31. https://doi.org/10.1179/1479096314Z.00000000020

Morris, J. (2016). *Everyday Post-Socialism: Working-Class Communities in the Russian Margins.* Basingstoke, United Kingdom: Palgrave Macmillan. https://doi.org/10.1057/978-1-349-95089-8

Morris, J., & Polese, A. (Eds.). (2013). *The Informal Post-Socialist Economy: Embedded Practices and Livelihoods.* London, United Kingdom: Routledge.

Morris, J., & Polese, A. (Eds.). (2015). *Informal Economies in Post-Socialist Spaces: Practices, Institutions and Networks*. Basingstoke, United Kingdom: Palgrave Macmillan. https://doi.org/10.1057/9781137483072

Munn, N.D. (1986). *The Fame of Gawa: A Symbolic Study of Value Transformation in a Massim (Papua New Guinea) Society*. Cambridge, United Kingdom: Cambridge University Press.

Myers, F.R. (1991). Representing Culture: The Production of Discourse(s) for Aboriginal Acrylic Paintings. *Cultural Anthropology, 6*(1), 26–62. https://doi.org/10.1525/can.1991.6.1.02a00020

Myers, F.R. (1998). Uncertain Regard: An Exhibition of Aboriginal Art in France. *Ethnos, 63*(1), 7–47. https://doi.org/10.1080/00141844.1998.9981563

Myers, F.R. (2001). Introduction. In F.R. Myers (Ed.), *The Empire of Things: Regimes of Value and Material Culture* (pp. 3–61). Santa Fe, NM: SAR Press.

Myers, F.R. (2002). *Painting Culture: The Making of an Aboriginal High Art*. Durham, NC: Duke University Press. https://doi.org/10.1215/9780822384168

Myers, F.R. (2004a). Unsettled Business: Acrylic Painting, Tradition, and Indigenous Being. *Visual Anthropology, 17*(3–4), 247–71. https://doi.org/10.1080/08949460490468036

Myers, F.R. (2004b). Ontologies of the Image and Economies of Exchange. *American Ethnologist, 31*(1), 5–20. https://doi.org/10.1525/ae.2004.31.1.5

Myers, F.R. (2006a). "Primitivism" Anthropology and the Category of "Primitive Art." In C. Tilley, S. Kuechler, M. Rowlands, W. Keane, & P. Spyer (Eds.), *Handbook of Material Culture*. London, United Kingdom: Sage. 267–84. https://doi.org/10.4135/9781848607972.n18

Myers, F.R. (2006b). Collecting Aboriginal Art in the Australian Nation: Two Case Studies. *Visual Anthropology Review, 21*(1–2), 116–37.

Myers, F.R. (2006c). The Complicity of Cultural Production: The Contingencies of Performance in Globalizing Museum Practices. In I. Karp & C. Kratz (Eds.), *Museum Frictions* (pp. 504–36). Durham, NC: Duke University Press. https://doi.org/10.1215/9780822388296-025

Myers, F.R. (2013). Disturbances in the Field: Exhibiting Aboriginal Art in the US. *Journal of Sociology (Melbourne, Vic.), 49*(2–3), 151–72. https://doi.org/10.1177/1440783313481520

Nelissen, R.M.A., & Meijers, M.H.C. (2011). Social Benefits of Luxury Brands as Costly Signals of Wealth and Status. *Evolution and Human Behavior, 32*(5), 343–55. https://doi.org/10.1016/j.evolhumbehav.2010.12.002

Nemeth, D.J. (1991). A Case Study of Rom Gypsy Residential Mobility in the United States. *Yearbook – Association of Pacific Coast Geographers, 53*(1), 131–54. https://doi.org/10.1353/pcg.1991.0001

Nemeth, D.J. (2002). *The Gypsy-American: An Ethnogeographic Study*. Lewiston, NY: E. Mellen.

Nemeth, D.J. (2010). Introduction. In C. Gianferro (Ed.), *Gypsy Interiors: Contemporary Roma Portraits* (pp. 7–10). Rome: Postcart Publishing.

Nemeth, D.J., & Gianferro, C. (2009). Prestige Mansions of the Affluent European Roma: Magnets for Hatred? In *Proceedings of the 2009 East Lakes Division Association of American Geographers Conference*, October 24. Dayton, OH.

Nemeth, D.J., & Gianferro, C. (2010, Fall). The Magical Realism of Postmodern Gypsy Palaces. *Aether: The Journal of Media Geography 6*, 55–65.

Newman, G.E., Diesendruck, G., & Bloom, P. (2011). Celebrity Contagion and the Value of Objects. *Journal of Consumer Research, 38*(2), 215–28. https://doi.org/10.1086/658999

Ngai, P. (2003). Subsumption or Consumption? The Phantom of Consumer Revolution in "Globalizing" China. *Cultural Anthropology, 18*(4), 469–92. https://doi.org/10.1525/can.2003.18.4.469

Obeng, S.G. (1997). Language and Politics: Indirectness in Political Discourse. *Discourse & Society, 8*(1), 49–83. https://doi.org/10.1177/0957926597008001004

O'Guinn, T.C. (1991). Touching Greatness: The Central Midwest Barry Manilow Fan Club. In R.W. Belk (Ed.), *Highways and Buyways: Naturalistic Research from the Consumer Behavior Odyssey* (pp. 102–11). Provo, UT: Association for Consumer Research.

Okely, J. (1983). *The Traveller-Gypsies*. Cambridge, United Kingdom: Cambridge University Press. https://doi.org/10.1017/CBO9780511621789

Okely, J. (2013). Constructing Culture through Shared Location, Bricolage and Exchange: The Case of Gypsies and Roma. In T. Fillitz & A.J. Saris (Eds.), *Debating Authenticity: Concepts of Modernity in Anthropological Perspective* (pp. 196–210). Oxford, United Kingdom: Berghahn Books.

Olivera, M. (2012). The Gypsies as Indigenous Groups: The Gabori Roma Case in Romania. *Romani Studies, 22*(1), 19–33. https://doi.org/10.3828/rs.2012.2

Olsen, B. (2004). Steps Towards a Defense of Things. *Nordisk Museologi, 2*, 25–36.

Oprea, A. (2005). The Arranged Marriage of Ana Maria Cioaba, Intra-Community Oppression and Romani Feminist Ideals. *European Journal of Women's Studies, 12*(2), 133–48. https://doi.org/10.1177/1350506805051234

Osei-Kofi, N. (2012). Identity, Fluidity, and Groupism: The Construction of Multiraciality in Education Discourse. *Review of Education, Pedagogy & Cultural Studies, 34*(5), 245–57. https://doi.org/10.1080/10714413.2012.732782

O'Sullivan, D. (2009). *Wikipedia: A New Community of Practice?* Farnham, United Kingdom: Ashgate.

Pantea, M.-C. (2009). Performing the Border of Child Labour: Roma Working Children. *Romani Studies*, 19(1), 19–48. https://doi.org/10.3828/rs.2009.2

Parsons, E., & Maclaran, P. (2009). "Unpacking Disposal": Introduction to the Special Issue. *Journal of Consumer Behaviour*, 8(6), 301–4. https://doi.org/10.1002/cb.294

Patico, J. (2002). Chocolate and Cognac: Gifts and the Recognition of Social Worlds in Post-Soviet Russia. *Ethnos*, 67(3), 345–68. https://doi.org/10.1080/0014184022000031202

Patico, J. (2008). *Consumption and Social Change in a Post-Soviet Middle Class*. Stanford, CA: Stanford University Press.

Pels, P. (1998). The Spirit of Matter: On Fetish, Rarity, Fact, and Fancy. In P. Spyer (Ed.), *Border Fetishisms: Material Objects in Unstable Spaces* (pp. 91–121). London, United Kingdom: Routledge.

Pesarini, A. (2010, August). Romanian Gypsy Women in Rome – An Ethnographic Account. *Tsiganologische Mitteilungen* 51–63.

Philips, S.U. (2010). Semantic and Interactional Indirectness in Tongan Lexical Honorification. *Journal of Pragmatics*, 42(2), 317–36. https://doi.org/10.1016/j.pragma.2009.06.005

Phillips, R.B., & Steiner, C.B. (Eds.). (1999). *Unpacking Culture: Art and Commodity in Postcolonial Worlds*. Berkeley: University of California Press.

Piasere, L. (1985). *Mare Roma. Catégories humaines et structure sociale. Une contribution à l'ethnologie tsigane* [Mare Roma: Human Categories and Social Structure: A Contribution to Gypsy Ethnology]. Paris, France: Études et Documents Balkaniques et Méditerraneens.

Pine, F. (2002). Dealing with Money: Zlotys, Dollars and Other Currencies in the Polish Highlands. In R. Mandel & C. Humphrey (Eds.), *Markets and Moralities: Ethnographies of Postsocialism* (pp. 75–98). London, United Kingdom: Bloomsbury Academic.

Plainer, Z. (2012). "They Took Personal Data and Some Pictures, yet They Found Nothing for Us" – Misunderstanding and Suspicion in a Marginal Roma Neighborhood from Romania. *Journal of Comparative Research in Anthropology & Sociology*, 3(2), 111–28.

Price, S. (2007). Into the Mainstream: Shifting Authenticities in Art. *American Ethnologist*, 34(4), 603–20. https://doi.org/10.1525/ae.2007.34.4.603

Radnóti, S. (1999). *The Fake: Forgery and Its Place in Art*. Lanham, MD: Rowman & Littlefield.

Ráduly, J. (1978). Balladaéneklés a kibédi virrasztóban [Ballad Singing at Vigils in Kibéd]. In K. Kós & J. Faragó (Eds.), *Népismereti dolgozatok 1978* (pp. 245–51). Bucharest, Romania: Kriterion Könyvkiadó.

Rees, A. (1971). Information Networks in Labor Markets. In D.M. Lamberton (Ed.), *Economics of Information and Knowledge* (pp. 109–18). Hammondsworth, United Kingdom: Penguin.

Reisinger, Y., & Steiner, C.J. (2006). Reconceptualizing Object Authenticity. *Annals of Tourism Research, 33*(1), 65–86. https://doi.org/10.1016/j.annals.2005.04.003

Rhodes, J. (2012). The "Trouble" with the "White Working Class": Whiteness, Class and "Groupism." *Identities (Yverdon), 19*(4), 485–92. https://doi.org/10.1080/1070289X.2012.710548

Ries, J. (2007). "I Must Love Them with All My Heart": Pentecostal Mission and the Romani Other. *Anthropology of East Europe Review, 25*(2), 132–42.

Rogers, D. (2005). Moonshine, Money, and the Politics of Liquidity in Rural Russia. *American Ethnologist, 32*(1), 63–81. https://doi.org/10.1525/ae.2005.32.1.63

Salo, M.T., & Salo, S.M.G. (1977). *The Kalderaš in Eastern Canada.* Ottawa, ON: National Museum of Canada. https://doi.org/10.2307/j.ctv16rm1

Sassatelli, R. (2004). The Political Morality of Food: Discourses, Contestation and Alternative Consumption. In M. Harvey, A. McMeekin, & A. Warde (Eds.), *Qualities of Food* (176–91). Manchester, United Kingdom: Manchester University Press.

Sassatelli, R. (2006). Virtue, Responsibility and Consumer Choice: Framing Critical Consumerism. In J. Brewer & F. Trentmann (Eds.), *Consuming Cultures, Global Perspectives: Historical Trajectories, Transnational Exchanges* (pp. 219–50). Oxford, United Kingdom: Berg.

Sassatelli, R. (2007). *Consumer Culture: History, Theory and Politics.* London, United Kingdom: Sage.

Saunders, N.J. (1999). Biographies of Brilliance: Pearls, Transformations of Matter and Being, c. AD 1492. *World Archaeology, 31*(2), 243–57. https://doi.org/10.1080/00438243.1999.9980444

Schamberger, K., Sear, M., Wehner, K., & Wilson, J. (2008). Living in a Material World: Object Biography and Transnational Lives. In D. Deacon, P. Russell, A. Woollacott (Eds.), *Transnational Ties: Australian Lives in the World* (pp. 275–98). Canberra: The Australian National University Press.

Scheffel, D.Z. (2005). *Svinia in Black & White: Slovak Roma and Their Neighbours.* Peterborough, ON: Broadview Press.

Scheper-Hughes, N. (2000). The Global Traffic in Human Organs. *Current Anthropology, 41*(2), 191–224. https://doi.org/10.1086/300123

Scott, L., & Urry, J. (1994). *Economies of Signs and Space.* London, United Kingdom: Sage.

Setiffi, F. (2011). Reflections on the Cultures of the New and the Second Hand in Italy. *Italian Sociological Review, 1*(3), 12–20.

Shafir, M. (1985). *Romania: Politics, Economics and Society: Political Stagnation and Stimulated Change*. London, United Kingdom: Frances Pinter.

Siegelbaum, L.H. (Ed.). (2011). *The Socialist Car: Automobility in the Eastern Bloc*. Ithaca, NY: Cornell University Press. https://doi.org/10.7591/cornell/9780801449918.001.0001

Sigona, N. (Ed.). (2008). *The "Latest" Public Enemy: Romanian Roma in Italy. The Case Studies of Milan, Bologna, Rome and Naples*. Florence: osservAzione.

Silverman, C. (2007). Trafficking in the Exotic with "Gypsy" Music: Balkan Roma, Cosmopolitanism, and "World Music" Festivals. In D. Buchanan (Ed.), *Balkan Popular Culture and the Ottoman Ecumene: Music, Image, and Regional Political Discourse* (pp. 335–61). New York, NY: Scarecrow Press.

Silverman, C. (2011). Gypsy Music, Hybridity and Appropriation: Balkan Dilemmas of Postmodernity. *Ethnologia Balkanica, 15*, 15–32.

Silverman, C. (2012). *Romani Routes: Cultural Politics and Balkan Music in Diaspora*. Oxford, United Kingdom: Oxford University Press.

Silverman, C. (2014). Global Balkan Gypsy Music: Issues of Migration, Appropriation, and Representation. In S. Krüger & R. Trandafoiu (Eds.), *The Globalization of Musics in Transit: Musical Migration and Tourism* (pp. 185–208). New York, NY: Routledge.

Silverman, C. (2015a). Gypsy/Klezmer Dialectics: Jewish and Romani Traces and Erasures in Contemporary European World Music. *Ethnomusicology Forum, 24*(2), 159–80. https://doi.org/10.1080/17411912.2015.1015040

Silverman, C. (2015b). DJs and the Production of "Gypsy" Music: "Balkan Beats" as Contested Commodity. *Western Folklore, 74*(1), 1–27.

Slater, D. (1997a). *Consumer Culture and Modernity*. Cambridge, United Kingdom: Polity.

Slater, D. (1997b). Consumer Culture and the Politics of Need. In M. Nava, A. Blake, I. MacRury, & B. Richards (Eds.), *Buy This Book: Studies in Advertising and Consumption* (pp. 51–63). London, United Kingdom: Routledge.

Slater, D. (2000). Political Discourse and the Politics of Need: Discourses on the Good Life in Cyberspace. In W.L. Bennett & R.M. Entman (Eds.), *Mediated Politics* (pp. 117–40). New York, NY: Cambridge University Press. https://doi.org/10.1017/CBO9780511613852.007

Solimene, M. (2011). "These Romanians Have Ruined Italy": Xoraxané Roma, Romanian Roma and Rome. *Journal of Modern Italian Studies, 16*(5), 637–51. https://doi.org/10.1080/1354571X.2011.622471

Spooner, B. (1986). Weavers and Dealers: The Authenticity of an Oriental Carpet. In A. Appadurai (Ed.), *The Social Life of Things: Commodities in*

Cultural Perspective (pp. 195–235). Cambridge, United Kingdom: Cambridge University Press. https://doi.org/10.1017/CBO9780511819582.009

Steiner, C.B. (1994). *African Art in Transit*. Cambridge, United Kingdom: Cambridge University Press.

Steiner, C.B. (1995). The Art of the Trade: On the Creation of Value and Authenticity in the African Art Market. In G.E. Marcus & F.R. Myers (Eds.), *The Traffic in Culture: Refiguring Art and Anthropology* (pp. 151–65). Berkeley: University of California Press.

Steiner, C.B. (1996). Can the Canon Burst? *Art Bulletin, 78*(2), 213–17.

Steiner, C.B. (2001). Rights of Passage: On the Liminal Identity of Art in the Border Zone. In F. R. Myers (Ed.), *The Empire of Things: Regimes of Value and Material Culture* (pp. 207–31). Santa Fe, NM: SAR Press.

Steiner, C.B. (2002). The Taste of Angels in the Art of Darkness: Fashioning the Canon of African Art. In E. Mansfield (Ed.), *Art History and Its Institutions* (pp. 132–45). New York, NY: Routledge.

Stewart, M. (1994). *Daltestvérek. Az oláhcigány identitás és közösség továbbélése a szocialista Magyarországon* [Brothers in Song. The persistence of (Vlach) Gypsy community and identity in Socialist Hungary]. Budapest, Hungary: T-Twins – MTA Szociológiai Intézet – Max Weber Alapítvány.

Stewart, M. (1996). Vlach Gypsies of Hungary. Encyclopedia of World Cultures. *Encyclopedia.com.* https://www.encyclopedia.com/doc/1G2-3458000722.html

Stewart, M. (1997). *The Time of the Gypsies*. Boulder, CO: Westview.

Stewart, M. (1998). Brothers and Orphans: Two Egalitarian Models of Community among Hungarian Rom. In M. Stewart, S. Day, & E. Papataxiarchis (Eds.), *The Lilies of the Field: Marginal People Who Live for the Moment* (pp. 27–44). Boulder, CO: Westview.

Stewart, M. (2004). Remembering without Commemoration: The Mnemonics and Politics of Holocaust Memories among European Roma. *Journal of the Royal Anthropological Institute, 10*(3), 561–82. https://doi.org/10.1111/j.1467-9655.2004.00202.x

Strahilevitz, M.A., & Loewenstein, G. (1998). The Effect of Ownership History on the Valuation of Objects. *Journal of Consumer Research, 25*(3), 276–89. https://doi.org/10.1086/209539

Straight, B. (2002). From Samburu Heirloom to New Age Artifact: The Cross-Cultural Consumption of Mporo Marriage Beads. *American Anthropologist, 104*(1), 7–21. https://doi.org/10.1525/aa.2002.104.1.7

Sutherland, A. (1975). *Gypsies: The Hidden Americans*. New York, NY: The Free Press.

Szalai, A. (2010). *Átok, feltételes átok és társadalmi nem erdélyi roma közösségek nyelvi ideológiájában és gyakorlataiban* [Curse, Conditional Curse, and

Gender in Linguistic Ideologies and Practices of Transylvanian Romani Communities]. (PhD thesis, University of Pécs).

Szalai, A. (2013). A kínálás pragmatikája gábor roma közösségekben [The Pragmatics of Offer in Gabor Roma Communities]. In A. Benő, E. Fazakas, & E. Kádár (Eds.), "Hogy legyen a víznek lefolyása ..." Köszöntő kötet Szilágyi N. Sándor tiszteletére (pp. 461–73). Kolozsvár, Romania: Erdélyi Múzeum Egyesület.

Tannen, D. (1981). Indirectness in Discourse: Ethnicity as Conversational Style. Discourse Processes, 4(3), 221–38. https://doi.org/10.1080/01638538109544517

Téglás, I. (1899). Vándor czigányok kincse [The Treasures of the Wandering Gypsies]. Erdély népei. Az "Erdély" néprajzi melléklete 2(2):21–3.

Téglás, I. (1912a). Czigány-kincsek. Első közlemény [Gypsy Treasures I]. Néprajzi Értesítő, 13(1), 50–5.

Téglás, I. (1912b). Czigány-kincsek. Másdik közlemény [Gypsy Treasures II]. Néprajzi Értesítő, 13(2), 124–30.

Téglás, I. (1912c). Czigány-kincsek. Harmadik közlemény [Gypsy Treasures III]. Néprajzi Értesítő, 13(3–4), 268–73.

Téglás, I. (1913). Czigány-kincsek. Negyedik és utolsó közlemény [Gypsy Treasures IV]. Néprajzi Értesítő, 14(1–2), 135–42.

Tesăr, C. (2012). Becoming Rom (Male), Becoming Romni (Female) among Romanian Cortorari Roma: On Body and Gender. Romani Studies, 22(2), 113–40. https://doi.org/10.3828/rs.2012.7

Tesăr, C. (2016). Houses under Construction: Conspicuous Consumption and the Values of Youth among Romanian Cortorari Gypsies. In M. Brazzabeni, M.I. Cunha, & M. Fotta (Eds.), Gypsy Economy: Romani Livelihoods and Notions of Worth in the 21st Century (pp. 181–200). Oxford, United Kingdom: Berghahn.

Thomas, N. (1991). Entangled Objects: Exchange, Material Culture, and Colonialism in the Pacific. Cambridge, MA: Harvard University Press.

Thomas, N. (2001). Appropriation/Appreciation: Settler Modernism in Australia and New Zealand. F.R. Myers (Ed.), The Empire of Things: Regimes of Value and Material Culture (pp. 139–63). Santa Fe, NM: SAR Press.

Tibori Szabó, Z. (2001, November 16). Rudi bácsi Strasbourgba megy [Rudi Goes to Strasbourg]. Szabadság, 3.

Tilley, C. (2006). Objectification. In C. Tilley, W. Keane, S. Küchler, M. Rowlands, & P. Spyer (Eds.), Handbook of Material Culture (pp. 60–73). London: Sage. https://doi.org/10.4135/9781848607972.n5

Tremlett, A. (2009). Bringing Hybridity to Heterogeneity in Romani Studies. Romani Studies, 19(2), 147–68. https://doi.org/10.3828/rs.2009.8

Trigg, A.B. (2001). Veblen, Bourdieu, and Conspicuous Consumption. *Journal of Economic Issues, 35*(1), 99–115. https://doi.org/10.1080/00213624.2001.11506342

Troc, G. (2002). A State of Despair: Roma (Gypsy) Population during Transition: Transylvanian Case Studies. *Studia Europaea, 47*(1–2), 49–90.

Turgeon, L. (1997). The Tale of the Kettle: Odyssey of an Intercultural Object. *Ethnohistory (Columbus, Ohio), 44*(1), 1–29. https://doi.org/10.2307/482899

Vasile, M. (2015). The Trader's Wedding: Ritual Inflation and Money Gifts in Transylvania. In S. Gudeman & C. Hann (Eds.), *Economy and Ritual: Studies of Postsocialist Transformations* (pp. 137–65). Oxford, United Kingdom: Berghahn.

Veblen, T. (1899). *The Theory of the Leisure Class*. New York, NY: Macmillan.

Velthuis, O. (2005). *Talking Prices: Symbolic Meanings of Prices on the Market for Contemporary Art*. Princeton, NJ: Princeton University Press.

Verdery, K. (1983). *Transylvanian Villagers: Three Centuries of Political, Economic, and Ethnic Change*. Berkeley: University of California Press.

Verdery, K. (1991). *National Ideology Under Socialism: Identity and Cultural Politics in Ceauşescu's Romania*. Berkeley: University of California Press. https://doi.org/10.1525/california/9780520072169.001.0001

Verdery, K. (1995). "Caritas" and the Reconceptualization of Money in Romania. *Anthropology Today, 11*(1), 3–7. https://doi.org/10.2307/2783317

Verdery, K. (1996). *What Was Socialism and What Comes Next?* Princeton, NJ: Princeton University Press. https://doi.org/10.1515/9781400821990

Wang, N. (1999). Rethinking Authenticity in Tourism Experience. *Annals of Tourism Research, 26*(2), 349–70. https://doi.org/10.1016/S0160-7383(98)00103-0

Wang, Y., & Griskevicius, V. (2014). Conspicuous Consumption, Relationships, and Rivals: Women's Luxury Products as Signals to Other Women. *Journal of Consumer Research, 40*(5), 834–54. https://doi.org/10.1086/673256

Warde, A. (2005). Consumption and Theories of Practice. *Journal of Consumer Culture, 5*(2), 131–53. https://doi.org/10.1177/1469540505053090

Weiner, A.B. (1983). "The World of Made Is Not a World of Born": Doing Kula in Kiriwina. In J.W. Leach & E.R. Leach (Eds.) *The Kula: New Perspectives on Massim Exchange* (pp. 147–70). Cambridge, United Kingdom: Cambridge University Press.

Weiner, A.B. (1985). Inalienable Wealth. *American Ethnologist, 12*(2), 210–27. https://doi.org/10.1525/ae.1985.12.2.02a00020

Weiner, A.B. (1992). *Inalienable Possessions: The Paradox of Keeping-While-Giving*. Berkeley: University of California Press. https://doi.org/10.1525/california/9780520076037.001.0001

Weiner, A.B. (1994). Cultural Difference and the Density of Objects. *American Ethnologist, 21*(2), 391–403. https://doi.org/10.1525/ae.1994.21.2.02a00090

Weiss, B. (1996). Coffee Breaks and Coffee Connections: The Lived Experience of a Commodity in Tanzanian and European Worlds. In D. Howes (Ed.), *Cross-Cultural Consumption* (pp. 93–105). New York, NY: Routledge.

Weiss, B. (1997). Forgetting Your Dead: Alienable and Inalienable Objects in Northwest Tanzania. *Anthropological Quarterly, 70*(4), 164–72. https://doi.org/10.2307/3317223

Wenger, E. (1998). *Communities of Practice: Learning, Meaning, and Identity.* Cambridge, United Kingdom: Cambridge University Press. https://doi.org/10.1017/CBO9780511803932

Wilk, R. (1995). Learning to Be Local in Belize: Global Systems of Common Difference. In D. Miller (Ed.), *Worlds Apart: Modernity Through the Prism of the Local* (pp. 110–33). London, United Kingdom: Routledge.

Wilk, R. (2001). Consuming Morality. *Journal of Consumer Culture, 1*(2), 245–60. https://doi.org/10.1177/146954050100100211

Wong, N.Y., & Ahuvia, A.C. (1998). Personal Taste and Family Face: Luxury Consumption in Confucian and Western Societies. *Psychology and Marketing, 15*(5), 423–41. https://doi.org/10.1002/(SICI)1520-6793(199808)15:5<423::AID-MAR2>3.0.CO;2-9

Wood, D. C. (2005). The Polder Museum of Ogata-mura: Community, Authenticity, and Sincerity in a Japanese Village. *Asian Anthropology, 4*(1), 29–58. https://doi.org/10.1080/1683478X.2005.10552550

Woodward, I. (2007). *Understanding Material Culture.* London, United Kingdom: Sage. https://doi.org/10.4135/9781446278987

Yeoman, I. (2011). The Changing Behaviours of Luxury Consumption. *Journal of Revenue and Pricing Management, 10*(1), 47–50. https://doi.org/10.1057/rpm.2010.43

Yoon, J., & Seok, H. (1996). Conspicuous Consumption and Social Status in Korea: An Assessment of Reciprocal Effects. *Korea Journal of Population and Development 25*(2), 333–54.

Zhan, L., & He, Y. (2012). Understanding Luxury Consumption in China: Consumer Perceptions of Best-Known Brands. *Journal of Business Research, 65*(10), 1452–60. https://doi.org/10.1016/j.jbusres.2011.10.011

Zhang, B., & Kim, J.-H. (2013). Luxury Fashion Consumption in China: Factors Affecting Attitude and Purchase Intent. *Journal of Retailing and Consumer Services, 20*(1), 68–79. https://doi.org/10.1016/j.jretconser.2012.10.007

Index

African art, 53, 220–2, 235
agency, 154; of curses, 181; material,
263; of objects, 3, 77, 96, 263, 308;
of ownership histories, 4, 16, 106;
of things-in-motion, 18, 261, 264; of
women, 29
aging: of objects 226–7, 228
Anderson, Benedict, 34
antiques collectors, 3, 9, 60, 72, 86,
88, 106, 133, 177–9, 220–2, 224, 234,
320n1; vs Gabor Roma prestige
economy, 70–1. See also African art
antiques dealers, 9, 24, 70, 86, 105,
117, 130, 147, 177–9, 190–1, 216,
224–5, 226, 231, 235, 293, 301, 302,
320n1, 232n2, 335n3
antiques markets, 4, 8; as consumer
subculture, 177–9; vs Gabor Roma
prestige economy, 3, 61, 63–71, 85,
87–8, 89–90, 91, 92, 101–5, 108, 109,
116, 130, 133, 182, 235, 265, 293, 302,
322n7, 324n11, 327n1; interest in
beakers, 17, 177; pricing of beakers,
63–6, 105, 216, 218; purchases
from Gabor Roma, 178–9, 234; role
of authenticity in, 219; as source
of Gabor Roma prestige objects,
15–16, 17, 53, 54, 82–6, 93, 101, 114,
125, 133, 216, 223–5, 227, 320n1,
323n2; as target of research, 8–9;
value regime of, 16, 65, 72, 82–3,
87–8, 89, 91, 103, 108, 109, 130,
177–8, 235, 320n1. See also antiques
dealers
antiquity: shared value between
Gabor and Cărhar Roma, 182; as
value in Gabor Roma prestige-
object aesthetics, 53–5, 109, 110–11,
226–7, 281
Appadurai, Arjun, 3, 23, 137, 261–3,
265, 331n1
art history, 117, 178, 265, 302, 319n10;
Gabor Roma interest in, 54, 87,
321n4, 324n11; Gabor Roma
relation to, 16, 83, 87, 88, 90, 91,
103, 108, 109, 116, 130, 178, 265,
318n2, 320n1
auctions: catalogues, 63, 66, 71, 97, 177,
216, 264, 319n13, 320n1; catalogues,
54, 87, 91, 187, 188, 224, 318n2,
321n4, 324n11; Gabor Roma interest
in, 54, 318n2, 321n4; vs Gabor Roma
prestige economy, 60, 65–70; role of
authenticity in, 219; as source

of Gabor Roma prestige objects,
86; as target of research, 9. *See also*
antiques markets

authenticity, 51, 151, 174, 187, 218, 223,
224, 225, 228, 237; approaches to,
219; of ethnic identity, 75–6, 79, 116,
251–2, 255, 322n10, 331n7; fraud, 17,
222–35; in market for African tribal
art, 221–2; nominal, 122, 133, 136,
138, 143, 212, 229, 234, 235, 266, 268,
273–5, 276, 291; politics of, 219–22;
of prestige objects, 15, 53–5, 235,
318n2; verification of, 133, 135, 143,
268

automobiles, 56, 67, 80, 137, 161, 181,
242, 291, 299, 303, 304, 306, 330n2;
as assets, 24, 32, 77, 325n4; Cărhar
Roma ownership of, 242–3; as
novelty-oriented prestige goods,
15, 19, 215, 241, 243, 247, 249, 250,
251, 297, 300; used to convert
between currencies, 128–9

autonomy, 29, 31–2, 46, 48–9, 52

average standard of living, 4, 18, 215,
239–40, 242, 243, 248, 249, 253, 254,
297–8, 299

baro řom. See big man

bazaars, 60, 137–8

bazaar-style trade, 16, 136–49

beakers (*taxtaj*): authenticity of,
53–5; biography of, 127–9, 266–80;
conditions for ownership, 57;
decorations on, 55, 91, 110–12,
115, 125, 187–9, 266, 282; external
sources of, 86–7; Gabor Roma
preference for over tankards, 60,
185; inheritance of, 76–7, 162,
192–5; as luxury goods, 63–72, 182;
naming of, 90–3; role in Gabor

Roma politics, 24, 32, 78–9, 106–8;
seen as male, 62–3; shape and size
of, 54, 108–9, 112, 113, 115–16, 125,
178, 184–6; symbolic emptying of,
82–3, 87–90; symbolic recreation
of, 83, 90–4; value among Cărhar
Roma, 17, 182–92; value among
Gabor Roma, 3, 63–73. *See also*
material patina; prestige economy;
prestige objects; symbolic patina;
tankards

begging, 180, 213, 229, 247, 252–3,
278, 331n6

behaviour (*phirajimo*), 25, 26, 27, 28,
46–51, 152, 153, 154, 160, 171, 288,
315; among Cărhar Roma, 183, 201,
204–5; consumer, 239, 240, 256;
role in determining *patjiv*, 46–7,
151–2, 167, 172. *See also* ethics of
sociability; *patjiv*

Belk, Russell W., 96, 99

betrothals, 7, 26, 28, 39, 150, 161–6,
195, 270, 314n5; songs at, 162–6.
See also social gatherings

bibaxtalo (unlucky), 93

big man (*baro řom*), 30, 31, 37, 103,
104, 154, 171, 183, 190, 269, 300,
315n9. *See also* honorific titles

Bigvillage, 59, 233, 279, 334n13

biographical method, 3, 8, 18, 261,
264–5; examples of, 266–80, 281–96

Blasco, Paloma Gay y, 33–4, 38

Bloom, Paul, 99–100

Boissevain, Jeremy, 147

boldimo (compensation), 194–5,
328n10

Bourdieu, Pierre, 74, 82, 239

Boym, Svetlana, 335n8

Braşov, 226

Brenneis, Donald, 156, 172

bricolage, 16, 150, 172, 237, 326n15
brokers (*cenzar*): academic literature on, 147–8; as agents of persuasion, 142–3; in antiques market transactions, 323n2; chosen by local government, 30; competition between, 120; conflicting roles of, 139; desired characteristics of, 146–9; family relatives as, 120; influential men as, 131–2; in interethnic trade, 120–1; mistrust of, 138–40; as risk managers, 138–9; role in estimating value, 130–3, 142; role in loan transactions, 119; role in prestige-object transactions, 16, 118–22, 267–8; role in price bargaining, 143–5; role performed by a group, 120; as touts, 140–2; use of in fraud, 228, 229; used to make communication indirect, 132–3; verifying authenticity of prestige objects, 143; as witnesses, 145–6. *See also* interethnic trade
Brubaker, Rogers, 10–11, 15, 236
Bucharest, 111, 180
Bucholtz, Mary, 11
Budapest, 59, 63; antiques markets, 9, 63, 70, 93, 105, 179, 224–5, 234
bulibaš. See village leader
business ethics: among Cărhar Roma, 217, 246, 290; consequences of violating, 245–6, 290; curses and, 289–90; among Gabor Roma, 46, 49–50, 69, 94, 123, 145, 214, 265, 277, 279, 281, 284–8, 292–3. *See also mita*

čaladvezetăvo (family leader), 30, 31, 106, 149. *See also* honorific titles
Campbell, Colin, 237–8

Cărhar Roma: attitude towards material patina, 184–9; attitude towards symbolic patina, 189–92; business ethics among, 217, 246, 290; as creditors to Gabor Roma, 180, 208, 210–11, 285, 287–9, 293; economic activities of, 179–80; ethno-aesthetics of, 115, 184–9; face-work among, 231; Gabor Roma stereotyping of, 244–9, 256–7, 312; ideal family, 193; inheritance practices, 192–5; languages among, 179; marriage practices, 183, 195–207; preferences in beaker shapes, 184–6; preferences in decorations, 187–9; preferences in silver, 187–8; prestige economy of, 9, 182–4; prestige-object trade with Gabor Roma (*see* interethnic trade); rarity of prestige-objects sales among, 216; as Roma ethnic population, 179–82; stereotyping of Gabor Roma, 249–55, 256–7, 310
Caritas (pyramid scheme), 282–3, 285, 332n2
cash gifts. *See mita*
catalogues, 54, 60, 87, 91, 133, 187, 188, 224, 318n2, 321n4, 324n11. *See also* antiques markets
cenzar. See brokers
children, 316n19; in Cărhar Roma ideology of marriage, 193, 195–6, 197, 199, 201, 202, 203–4, 206, 327n8, 328n9; in Gabor Roma ideology of marriage, 24, 29, 30, 39, 40, 41, 43, 269–70, 280, 296, 316n20, 317n22, 317n27; inability to have, 201; silver objects from antiques market compared to, 102; in situations of divorce, 44, 202

činste, 204, 328n13
classification struggle, 17, 18, 236, 239, 240, 243, 248, 249, 254. *See also* politics of consumption
Cluj Napoca, 58, 268
coins: as decorations on beakers and tankards, 55, 91, 110, 111, 113, 125, 189, 282, 289; as form of investment, 333n7, 335n4; used in prestige object transactions, 287. *See also* ethno-aesthetics of prestige objects
commodity fetishism, 87, 89–90, 262
communities of practice, 3, 7, 14, 15, 38, 87, 314n2; definition of, 11–12
conditional self-curses, 140, 181, 229, 294–6, 324n13, 330n3, 334n13. *See also* curses
consumer goods, 96, 220; Cărhar Roma relation to, 240, 242, 246–7, 250–2; classification of, 254; Gabor Roma relation to, 240, 241, 243, 248, 249, 251–2, 299, 300, 306; proliferation in post-socialist period, 215, 297; as trust-building strategy, 241; value in Gabor Roma politics, 32
consumer subcultures, 4, 8, 15, 17, 177, 309; antiques market as, 3, 177–9; Cărhar Roma prestige economy as, 179–207; Gabor Roma prestige economy as, 3, 15, 53–81, 105, 224; role of authenticity in, 220;
consumer value preferences, 4, 18, 239, 240, 246–7, 251, 252, 253, 256–7, 297, 308, 329n5, 330n3
consumption studies: recent trends, 97, 236, 313n5
co-parents-in-law: as brokers, 120, 139, 280; honorific titles and,

31; involvement in prestige object transactions, 120, 166, 209, 277–8; motivation in choosing, 32, 43–6; roles of, 40; search for, 271; as sources of praise, 154; suspicion of, 200. *See also* marital alliances
coppersmithing: among Cărhar Roma, 179–80, 184; among Gabor Roma, 7, 311
Crewe, Louise, 98–9, 100
Csontváry Kosztka, Tivadar, 70
currency, 283, 317n24, 318n7, 335n7; conversions between, 127–9; devaluation of, 127, 282, 303, 305–6; legalization of possession of, 305–6
curses: and business ethics, 231, 246, 289–90; Cărhar Roma sensitivity to, 181; cursed (*armandino*) objects, 93–4, 290, 322n9; fear of consequences of, 290. *See also* conditional self-curses; public swearing

Dant, Tim, 89
Daunton, M.J., 236
Dawdy, Shannon, 322n1
debt, 73, 93, 121, 143, 209, 210–11, 217, 231, 233, 234, 245–6, 250, 251, 256, 299, 311; as cause for suicide, 285; as reason for employing brokers, 119; as reason for interethnic trade, 250–1; stories involving, 66–9, 128, 162–6, 266–77, 284–96
decontextualization, 16, 83, 87–90
definitional struggle. *See* classification struggle
Diesendruck, Gil, 99–100
divorce, 31, 50, 201–2, 204, 205, 207, 280, 317n22, 328n14
dowry, 41, 196, 197, 315n11, 328n13, 333n7. *See also* marriage payments

Easter, 134, 135
Eckert, Penelope, 11–12
Edwards, Elizabeth, 331n1
előkérés (request to view), 135–6, 268
ethics of managing social relations and interactions. *See* ethics of sociability
ethics of similarity, 48, 49, 52
ethics of sociability, 24, 28, 183, 201, 202, 204, 314n6, 317n28, 320n16; definition of, 46–51; and face-work, 150–3; and Gabor Roma politics, 13, 15, 17, 25, 51–2; in Gabor Roma politics, 30, 46, 151, 159; in Gabor Roma song practices, 166, 174; importance of respect in, 153; and significance of *patjiv*, 25, 50–1, 151. *See also* behaviour; *patjiv*
ethnicity: and authenticity, 79, 251–2, 255; construction of ethnic identity, 10–11, 12, 13, 14, 24, 34, 35, 48, 61, 79, 80–1, 87, 183, 190, 227, 239, 254–5, 304, 309, 310, 331n7; ethnic boundaries, 30, 34; ethnic endogamy, 41, 180; ethnic history, 33, 34, 35, 61, 76, 77, 80–1, 87, 146–7, 177–8, 183, 190, 234–5, 300, 309; ethnic pantheon, 16; ethnicization of beaker shapes, 185; ethnicization of prestige objects, 3, 7, 14, 15–16, 24, 48, 54, 60–1, 75, 79, 81, 83, 84, 90–4, 147, 151–2, 174, 183, 223, 227, 254, 292–3, 302, 307–8, 310, 331n7; ethnicized ownership history, 54, 101–8; prestige-object aesthetics as "invisible ink" of, 116–17; role in determining value, 234–5; in Roma politics, 23, 151–2; stereotyping of, 244–55, 312; use in fraud attempt, 235. *See also* Cărhar Roma; Gabor Roma; interethnic trade

ethno-aesthetics of prestige objects: of Cărhar Roma, 115, 184–9; changes in Gabor Roma preferences, 114–16; differences between Gabor and Cărhar Roma, 185, 187–9, 192, 213–14; of Gabor Roma, 54–5, 61, 87–8, 91, 108–12, 112–16, 281, 302; gender and, 62–3, 112–13, 189; as "invisible ink" of ethnic identity, 116–17; objects not modified to fit, 82; similarities between Gabor and Cărhar Roma, 182–4; uneven knowledge of, 146; value of antiquity among Gabor Roma, 55, 111; value-decreasing properties, 112–13; value-increasing properties, 108–12
ethnonyms: used by Cărhar Roma, 179; used by Gabor Roma, 4

face-work, 16–17, 44, 72, 79, 94, 136, 150–72, 210, 214, 230–1, 265, 280, 325n1; discursive political, 150–2; indirectness as technique in, 155–6, 166, 171–2; and interethnic trade, 214, 243, 256; involved in ethics of sociability, 47–50, 151–2; in marital alliances, 45, 204; neglect of, 152; in requests to view prestige objects, 136; and sales of beakers and tankards, 73, 107, 113, 141, 145–6; at social gatherings, 35, 48, 152–3, 155–6; use of songs in, 162–72, 174. *See also* ethics of sociability; political discourse
faluvezetăvo. See village leader
Fanselow, Frank S., 137–8
Faragó, József, 172–3
feminine: decorative elements of prestige objects, 112, 113, 189
folklore, 172–3

forgery, 182, 221; examples of, 229–32, 233–4; of material patina, 226–7, 233; of symbolic patina, 227, 233. *See also* fraud

forgetting, 87, 88–9

Foster, Robert John, 262, 264–5

Fowles, Severin, 263, 265

France, 6, 180, 229–30, 252, 327n, 331n6

fraud: directed towards the author, 234; discursive techniques used in, 227–8; examples of, 229–32, 233–4; between Gabor and Cărhar Roma, 17, 18, 223–32; between Gabor Roma and non-Roma, 232–5; money-oriented, 222, 223–35; political, 222, 273–5; secrecy in, 224–5, 230; as teasing technique, 222. *See also* forgery

funerals, 7, 26, 27, 28, 150, 161, 214, 314n5, 315n7; interethnic attendance at, 180. *See also* social gatherings

Gabor Roma: business ethics among, 46, 49–50, 69, 94, 123, 145, 214, 265, 277, 279, 281, 284–8, 292–3; Cărhar Roma stereotyping of, 249–55, 256–7; concept of rank, 36–8; ethics of sociability, 46–51; ethno-aesthetics of, 54–5, 61, 87–8, 91, 108–16, 185, 187–9, 192, 213–14, 281, 302; expectations for behaviour, 46–50; ideology of swearing, 140; inheritance practices, 51, 62, 76–7, 192–5; languages among, 4, 179, 295; marriage practices among, 39–46; overview, 4–7; politics of difference among, 13, 23–52; prestige economy, 53–81; prestige-object trade with Cărhar Roma (*see* interethnic trade); rise in status, 7; sensitivity to consumer culture, 240–1, 247, 251; stereotyping of Cărhar Roma, 244–9, 256–7, 312; transformation since 1970s, 126–7

Geertz, Clifford, 137

gender: in Cărhar and Gabor Roma family practices, 327n8; in Cărhar Roma prestige-object aesthetics, 189; in Gabor Roma prestige-object aesthetics, 62–3, 112–13; Gabor vs Cărhar Roma views of, 193; in gender-specific interethnic cooperation, 180–1; and patrilines, 29, 315n9; preference for sons, 40–1; in prestige economy, 62–3; in Roma politics, 29. *See also* masculinity; women

gilding, 59, 92, 102, 157, 159, 203, 209, 211, 212, 213, 217, 266, 269, 282, 328n14, 329n3; aesthetic preferences, 55, 82, 111, 112, 113, 123, 125, 189, 211, 322n8; forgery of, 229

globalization, 4, 99, 219, 220, 221, 261, 262, 265

Goffman, Erving, 47, 56, 79, 308

Gregson, Nicky, 98–9, 100

groupism, 10, 12, 15

Hand, Martin, 238

Harrison, Simon, 218, 239, 251, 310

Herzfeld, Michael, 249, 311

hierarchy, 3, 12, 13, 28, 49, 76, 236, 244, 246, 299, 304; mobility within among Gabor Roma, 38; of patrilines, 14, 24, 26, 27, 32–8, 46, 151, 315n13; of prestige objects, 150–1; soft, 29, 320n16

Hilton, Matthew, 236
historicization, 16, 83, 90–4, 111
honorific titles, 15, 29–32, 106, 183,
  315n9, 320n16. *See also baro řom,*
  bulibaš, čaladvezetăvo, faluvezetăvo
honour. *See patjiv*
horses (*grast*), 78, 147, 179, 217, 242,
  285, 325n4; as decorations on
  beakers, 110, 112, 188, 211, 325n5,
  325n6; used as metaphor for
  prestige objects, 157–74
Hoskins, Janet, 264
Hungary, 6, 7, 9, 33, 52, 57, 63,
  66, 70, 71, 86–7, 103, 132, 177–8,
  179, 210, 216, 224, 229, 233, 234,
  241, 270, 274, 275, 279, 317n28,
  331n6, 333n7
hybridity, 16, 150, 172, 326n15

inalienability, 68, 86, 105–6, 322n4; as
  ideal state in Gabor Roma prestige
  economy, 3, 15, 73–8, 79, 81, 124,
  320n15
individualism: limits to, 153
inflation: following post-socialist
  transformation, 127, 282, 306
inheritance: 51, 75–6, 322n3;
  Cărhar Roma practices, 192–5;
  Gabor Roma practices, 24, 27,
  51, 62, 76–7, 192–5; as means of
  constituting family history, 100;
  practice of *boldimo* in, 194–5; of
  prestige objects, 17, 57, 74, 76–7,
  79, 94, 102, 122, 125, 128, 157,
  160–1, 162, 166, 197–8, 199, 200,
  202, 205, 206, 211, 229, 233–4, 267,
  271, 274, 281, 283, 284, 286, 290,
  328n14; of prestige objects, as
  ideal, 182–3, 193
insults, 94, 204–5, 329n4; exclusion
  from sales transaction as, 273;

interethnic trade as means of
  avoiding, 214; linguistic indirectness
  in, 160–1; marital alliances as means
  of avoiding, 44; public mention of
  purchase prices as, 73; risks for face-
  work, 152–3; role in Gabor Roma
  politics, 35, 51, 84, 94, 107, 113, 155,
  170, 171, 218, 228
interethnic trade, 17, 85, 86, 208–18;
  examples of, 208–18, 245, 248; and
  face-work, 214, 243; framing of,
  243–57; fraud in, 223–35; history
  of, between Gabor and Cărhar
  Roma, 208–9; imbalance in, 208;
  intermediaries in, 118, 120–1, 141,
  147, 149; reasons for, 213–16, 239;
  role of Gabor Roma politics in,
  214; stereotypes in, 244–55. *See also*
  prestige objects
intermediary trade: as livelihood
  strategy, 6, 28, 85, 179, 241, 283,
  331n6, 333n6
invidious comparison, 96, 106, 152,
  155, 157, 301, 307, 325n3
Italy, 6, 179, 180, 213, 252, 327n2,
  331n6

Jehovah's Witnesses, 4
juššo. See marriage payments

kana. See tankards
kinship: discourse on, 35; politics of,
  24–5, 32–8, 39–46; primacy of father
  in relations, 48–9; scholars' views
  on, 33–4. *See also* marital alliances;
  patrilines
Kopytoff, Igor, 95, 264
Kornai, János, 218
Kula exchange, 75, 91, 318n5, 318n6,
  323n8, 324n10

Landscape in Trau at Sunset (painting), 70

languages: among Cărhar Roma, 179; found on prestige objects, 111; among Gabor Roma, 4, 179, 295; of songs, 28, 161, 170, 173–4; used in interethnic communication, 225

linguistic indirectness: examples of, 157–9, 163–5, 168–70; used in discussing prestige objects, 17, 150, 156–72. *See also* political discourse

loans, 40, 45, 50, 65, 67, 69, 73, 180, 183, 233–4, 250, 267, 270, 274, 276–7, 279, 282–92, 295, 296, 298, 308, 319n12, 323n4; brokers' involvement in, 119; between Cărhar and Gabor Roma, 180, 208, 210–11, 223; in Gabor Roma social ethics, 47–8. *See also* debt

luxury goods, 55–6; beakers and tankards as, 15, 63–72, 148, 215; Cărhar Roma relation to, 242, 247, 250–1, 256–7; in competition with prestige economy, 305–7; as contested symbolic field, 18, 240; criticism of, 250–1, 256–7, 310–11; Gabor Roma relation to, 32, 80, 251, 256–7; novelty- vs patina-oriented, 80–1; rise in possession post-1989, 241–2; shift in definition, 242–3

MacDougall, Paige J., 263

Marcus, George E., 8, 265

marital alliances: asymmetrical, 41; among Cărhar Roma, 181, 183, 193, 195–203, 328n12; and Cărhar Roma prestige objects as securities, 199–203; competition for, 39; among Gabor Roma 39–46; importance of patrilines in, 35; as livelihood strategy, 44–5; as means of social mobility, 43–4, 198–9; role in Gabor Roma politics, 24, 25, 27, 29, 30, 31, 34, 36, 37, 40, 44, 48, 50, 118, 150, 162–4, 167, 171, 268, 270, 271, 278, 280, 300, 315n12; as source of income, 268; stories involving, 203–7, 268, 269–70, 271, 278, 280. *See also* co-parents-in-law

marriage payments (*juššo*), 32, 35, 41–3, 44, 48, 49, 62, 162–4, 166, 193, 268, 270, 271, 280, 315n11, 317n22; currencies used for, 127, 197; as livelihood strategy, 45; practice among Cărhar Roma, 194, 196–8, 199, 200, 202, 204, 206; role of rank in determining, 46. *See also* dowry

Marx, Karl, 89, 262

masculinity: and decorative elements of prestige objects, 189; moustache as symbol of, 103; prestige associated with, 41, 62, 113, 317n27

material patina: Cărhar Roma attitude towards, 184–9; definition of, 54; forgery of, 226–7; Gabor Roma attitude towards, 16, 17, 95, 101, 108–17, 123–4, 225, 232, 233; importance vs symbolic patina, 114; varied effect on value, 113; verification of, 135. *See also* symbolic patina

Maynard, Margaret, 263

McConnell-Ginet, Sally, 11–12

McCracken, Grant, 95, 98–9, 117, 311–12

memorial rituals, 26, 28, 161, 191, 315n7

memory, 95, 98; genealogical, 27–8, 33, 35–6, 316n14; personal, 34, 145

methodological fetishism, 3, 18, 261–2, 265

migration: of commodities, 263–4; economic, 6, 180, 241, 327n3, 331n6; of objects, 8, 9, 261–5; of researcher, 8; as Roma way of life, 242

Miller, Daniel, 243, 298

mita (cash gifts), 38, 170, 273, 277–80, 316n18; and Gabor Roma business ethics, 279; and marriage politics, 39, 43, 45–6, 268, 270; as proper behaviour, 48; as "representations of joy," 48, 64, 158, 168–71, 217, 230, 265, 270–1, 277–80, 319n12, 326n13; as source of income, 279; as a wage, 295, 319n13

moralizing, 18, 48, 69, 112, 152, 153, 155, 156, 160, 172, 222, 236, 239, 240, 243–4, 246, 248–50, 252–7, 297, 310–11. *See also* politics of consumption

Morris, Jeremy, 313n5, 335n5, 335n8

multi-sited ethnography, 3, 7, 8–9, 14, 18, 264–5

Munn, Nancy D., 318n6, 323–4n8, 324n10

museums, 3, 88, 219, 226, 293; as buyers, 106, 177, 111, 234, 319n8; catalogues, 54, 87, 187, 188, 318n2, 321n4, 324n11; as objects of study, 9, 264, 265; as source of prestige objects, 86, 190, 191, 320n1

need: politics of, 17, 238, 247, 299

nemzetezinpe (talking "nations" [patrilines]), 27, 35

Newman, George E., 99–100

novelty-oriented consumption, 15, 19, 80–1, 97, 101

oath-taking. *See* public swearing

object ethnographies, 263–4

objectification, 76

Olsen, Bjørnar, 331n1

Orthodox Churches, 134, 285; Cărhar Roma membership in, 179

ownership history, 3–4, 53, 58, 59, 70, 83, 84, 85, 87, 92, 93–4, 124, 147, 187, 212, 264, 321n3, 322n4; Cărhar Roma interest in, 189–92, 218, 231; consumer interpretations of, 95–101; as extension of self, 96; Gabor Roma interest in, 104–5, 266, 281; manipulation of, 17, 222, 224, 231; as marker of second-handedness, 95; paying for, 101; and post-socialist prestige goods, 80; of second-hand goods, 95–101; singularity of, 125; as source of value, 81, 101–5, 114, 266, 302, 322n2; as symbolic pantheon, 16, 96, 105–8; as symbolic patina, 54, 90, 100, 314n8. *See also* agency; prestige objects

patina. *See* material patina; symbolic patina

patina-oriented consumption, 3, 80–1, 100–1, 105–6

patjiv (honour, respectability), 25, 46–51, 151–2, 154, 317n29–31; cheek as metaphor for, 79; contribution to Gabor Roma politics, 51; as intergenerational, 51; loss of, 68; role in acquiring honorific titles, 31; role in determining rank, 38; role in face-work, 47; role of behaviour in determining, 46–7; social significance of, 50; and women, 29. *See also* behaviour; ethics of sociability

patrilineal identity, 35, 48, 62, 76–7, 79, 80–1, 87, 106–7, 149, 161, 183, 218, 227

patrilineal prestige, 25, 27, 35, 36, 37, 38, 44, 45, 51, 78, 152, 171, 183
patrilines, 42, 43, 45, 78, 106, 152, 315n8, 315n12, 317n29, 327n8; as determinant of rank, 36–7; fraudulent claims of, 227–8; Gabor Roma knowledge of, 36; and gender, 29, 315n12; hierarchy of, 14, 24, 26, 32–8, 46, 76, 151, 162, 167, 244, 246, 299, 315n13; importance in Gabor Roma politics, 25, 27, 29, 30, 35, 43–4, 316n14; prestige objects as symbols of, 106–7, 234, 309; prestige relations between, 15, 23, 24, 27, 30, 32, 57, 78, 104, 135, 150, 171, 182, 269, 304, 316n15; role in constructing ethnic identity, 34–5; and self-pantheonization, 171
pawning: brokers' involvement in, 118–19, 121–2, 132; of prestige objects, 9,17, 57, 59, 62, 63, 123, 124, 134, 163–6, 180, 183, 208–11, 212, 213, 225, 228, 232–4, 250, 267, 270, 274–5, 276, 282–5, 286–7, 288, 289, 296, 323n4, 329nn1–3, 334n12; as strategy to avoid sale, 73
Pels, Peter J., 262
Pentecostalism: among Gabor Roma, 4
phirajimo. See behaviour
police, 11, 61, 67–8, 205, 230, 245, 294, 295, 302, 314, 316n16
politeness, 153, 155, 156, 157, 167, 212, 325n2
political discourse, 16, 28, 35, 36, 38, 48; and the ethics of (self-) representation, 152–5; and face-work, 150–2, 155–6; Gabor Roma synonyms for, 26; indirectness in, 156–61; intraethnic, 301; as masculine practice, 62; prestige objects in, 150–5; and songs 161–72
politics of aesthetics, 116–17
politics of consumption, 18, 236–40; Cărhar Roma discourse of, 249–53; and consumer moral superiority, 253; Gabor Roma discourse of, 244–9
politics of fairness: as aspect of politics of consumption, 236, 238
politics of identity: as dimension of politics of authenticity, 220; as dimension of politics of consumption, 236–8, 253
politics of normalization: as aspect of politics of authenticity, 221; as aspect of politics of consumption, 236, 238, 253–5, 297, 330n3
pollution, 97–8, 239, 251, 257, 310
post-socialist consumer revolution, 18, 80, 215, 240–3, 297–8, 308
post-socialist transformation: changes in prestige-object aesthetics, 115, 116, 184; economic changes following, 80; effects on Cărhar Roma, 242–3, 247–51; effects on Gabor Roma, 4, 240–3, 247–8, 250; effects on Gabor Roma prestige economy, 61–2, 86, 297–301, 305–12; effects on interethnic trade, 215; hyperinflation following, 127
power, 11, 29, 31, 32, 44, 69, 77, 89, 110, 124, 131, 150, 181, 199, 237, 240; bargaining, 130, 216; buying, 81; economic, 16, 124; explanatory, 12, 15, 261, 264; purchasing, 97, 126, 127, 133, 139, 191, 307, 308; ratifying, 131

praising, 120, 135, 136, 153–6, 159,
160, 166, 167, 171, 172, 325n2, 325n3
prestige economy: of Cărhar Roma, 9,
182–207; changes in post-socialist
period, 18–19, 297–301, 305–12;
decline in popularity, 216, 298,
300–1, 306–8; effect of Romanian
socialism on, 303–5; ethnicized
nature of, 87–94, 101–5, 116–17,
185, 218, 302; of Gabor Roma,
15, 53–81, 106; Gabor Roma vs
antiques market, 61, 65–9, 70–1,
105, 178; genderedness of, 62–3;
general characteristics of, 53–81;
as identity practice, 4, 10, 12, 34,
38, 79, 256; informality of, 61–2,
301–3; involvement with other
political arenas, 265; knowledge
of as symbolic capital, 149; and
masculinity, 62, 112–13, 189; role in
Gabor Roma Politics, 24, 32, 78–9,
106–8; role of curses in, 289–90;
role of witnesses in, 145; Romanian
government's ignorance of,
302–3; translocal, 7–8, 57–9. See also
beakers; interethnic trade; prestige
objects; tankards
prestige objects: authenticity of,
53–5, 133, 143; and Cărhar Roma
marriage payments, 197–8;
cultural biographies of, 59, 77–8,
101–8, 266–80, 281–96; cursed,
93–4; difficulty of determining
value, 122–33; inalienability as
ideal state, 73–8; indirectness in
referring to, 156–61; inheritance
of, 76–7, 162, 192–5; as "invisible"
and mobile goods, 303–4, 308;
metaphors used for, 157–9, 162,
163–6, 168–70; novelty-oriented,

15, 19, 80–1; patina-oriented, 15, 19,
80–1; pawning of, 163, 166, 210–11;
as political trophies, 78, 110, 148;
post-socialist, 80–1; ranking of,
124, 131; restrictions on viewing,
81, 133–4, 301, 324n11; role in
Gabor Roma politics, 24, 32, 78–9,
106–8; as securities among Cărhar
Roma, 199–203; singularity of,
125–6; social definition of, 53–81,
124, 182–92; as symbol of patriline,
106–7; as symbol of prosperity, 79.
See also beakers; ownership history;
prestige economy; tankards
proprietary contest, 16, 56, 60, 77, 81,
93, 100, 106, 158, 183, 185, 191, 218,
221, 265, 281, 298, 304, 320n17
public swearing, 181, 265, 294–6,
334n13

Ráduly, János, 173
rank (rango), 25, 27, 36–8, 162, 167,
316n15, 316n16; in determining
marriage payments, 46; mobility
within, 38, 77–8, 108; ranking of
loyalties, 139; ranking of prestige
objects, 123, 124, 131, 184,
266, 281
recontextualization, 15, 16, 82, 83,
90–4, 242, 264, 321n2, 326n15
Reformed Church: fraudster posing
as member of, 225; as source of
Cărhar Roma prestige objects, 182;
as source of Gabor Roma prestige
objects, 82, 86, 320n1
Reisinger, Yvette, 219
reputational profit, 24, 74, 84, 163,
215; marital alliance as source
of, 45, 200; ownership history as
source of, 106; prestige objects and,

35, 85, 106, 143, 144, 172, 215, 282,
    294, 320n14
respectability. *See patjiv*
risk management, 16, 118, 136, 138–9
Roma, 313n2; academic research on,
    12–13; Djurdjovaje Roma, 286–8,
    333n6; Gitanos, 33–4; Masari Roma,
    33–4; stereotyping of, 14, 33, 172–4,
    244–57; theories of origin, 34,
    316n16; value of the past for, 33–6.
    See also Cărhar Roma; Gabor Roma
Roma politics: conditions for success,
    24–5; definition of, 23–9; and
    discourse, 16, 28, 35, 36, 38, 48,
    62, 150–5, 155–6, 156–61, 161–72;
    and ethics of sociability, 13, 30, 46,
    52, 151; ethnicized character of,
    51, 151–2; and face-work, 150–6;
    and gender, 29; and genealogical
    discourse, 27; honorific titles in,
    29–32; importance of patrilines
    in, 25, 27, 32–8; and indirectness,
    156–61; in informal conversation,
    28; insults in, 35; marital alliances
    and, 24–5, 39–46; vs national
    politics, 23; role in interethnic
    trade, 214; role in value estimation,
    130–1; role of prestige objects in,
    78–9, 281–2; significance of *patjiv*
    in, 51; and songs, 161–72; symbolic
    arenas of, 24–5
Ŕomani kris, 202, 205, 206, 314n5
Romanian socialist state, 61–2, 86,
    301–3, 305–6, 335n4; nostalgia
    for, 311
roofed tankards. *See* tankards
Rupuno, 181, 184, 185, 186, 190–1,
    194, 217, 327n3, 328n10

Sassatelli, Roberta, 238–9, 240
second-hand cultures, 3, 105

second-hand goods, 6, ownership
    histories of, 95–101, 101–5, 105–8,
    189–92; symbolic emptying of,
    87–90, 98–9, 321n6
second-hand markets, 6, 7, 28, 42,
    314n6; as place of interethnic
    interaction, 182
secrecy, 145, 230, 273, 285; economic,
    39, 43, 45, 86, 133–4, 136, 139,
    200, 223, 224–5, 229, 231, 233,
    234, 270, 271–3, 276, 278, 280,
    287, 288, 290
self-glorification, 106, 171, 253
separat marriage: among Cărhar
    Roma, 196–7, 199
Seventh-Day Adventism: among
    Gabor Roma, 4, 28, 134, 150, 161,
    283; hymns, 161–2
Shove, Elizabeth, 238
Sibiu, 180, 209, 213
silver: Cărhar Roma preferences in,
    186–7; Gabor Roma preferences in,
    54–5, 109
silversmithing, 9, 87–8, 91, 112, 211,
    226, 229, 327n6; in antiques market
    value regime, 177–8; involvement
    in fraud, 229; origins of Cărhar
    Roma prestige objects, 182, 185;
    origins of Gabor Roma prestige
    objects, 82
singularization, 53, 80, 81, 83, 92, 125,
    126, 183, 333n7
skimbo marriage: among Cărhar
    Roma, 196–7
Slater, Don, 238
social gatherings: in author's
    research, 314n6; face-work in,
    152–3, 155–6; political issues
    discussed at, 150; as site of Gabor
    Roma politics, 26–8, 31; songs at,
    161; viewing of prestige objects at,

135. *See also* betrothals; funerals; wakes; weddings

socialism, 61, 86, 116, 127, 129, 241, 242, 247, 249, 254, 256, 297, 300, 302, 304–5, 306, 307, 311

songs: at betrothals, 162–6; and ethics of sociability, 166, 174; examples of, 162–6, 167–72; Gabor Roma use of Hungarian, 174; as tool in Gabor Roma politics, 16, 17, 28, 150, 156–61; and transcultural recycling, 172–4; types of, 161–2; at wakes, 28, 167–72. *See also* political discourse

Spooner, Brian, 220

Steiner, Carol J., 219

Steiner, Christopher B., 221–2, 234–5

Stewart, Michael, 33–4, 35, 38, 52, 132–3, 147, 317n28

symbolic alchemy, 82

symbolic patina, 95–101, 114; Cărhar Roma attitude towards, 189–92; forgery of, 222, 223, 227; Gabor Roma ownership history as, 16, 35, 54, 81, 90, 101–5, 218, 314n8; importance vs material patina, 114. *See also* material patina

Szalai, Andrea, 38, 325n1

tankards (*kana*): authenticity of, 53–5; biography of, 281–96; Cărhar Roma interest in, 185; conditions for ownership, 57; external sources of, 86–7; Gabor preference for beakers over, 60, 185; inheritance of, 76–7, 162, 192–5; as luxury goods, 63–72, 182; naming of, 90–3; role in Gabor Roma politics, 24, 32, 78–9, 106–8; seen as female, 62–3; shape of, 54, 108–9; symbolic emptying of, 82–3, 87–90; symbolic recreation of, 83, 90–4; value among Cărhar Roma, 17, 182–92; value among Gabor Roma, 3, 63. *See also* beakers; material patina; prestige economy; prestige objects; symbolic patina

Târgu Mureş, 57, 67, 159, 211, 226, 294

taxtaj. *See* beakers

teasing, 222

things-in-motion, 3, 18, 261, 262, 263, 265. *See also* agency

tinsmithing, 6–7, 47, 113, 311

touts, 216, 224, 225; brokers as, 140–2

translocal, 3, 7, 8, 12, 14, 15, 53, 55, 57–8, 59, 60, 70, 113, 117, 121, 183, 314n2. *See also* prestige economy

transnational, 9, 331; biographies of objects, 18, 82, 83, 86, 87, 93, 265; commodities, 263, 264; movement of things, 3

Turkey, 6, 241, 331n6

"unexplainable animals", 55, 110–11, 113, 178, 188, 327n7. *See also* ethno-aesthetics of prestige objects

value regime, 3, 8; of the antiques market, 16, 65, 72, 82, 83, 87, 91, 103, 108–9, 130, 177–8, 235, 320n1; of the art history, 16, 83, 91, 103, 108–9, 177–8, 320n1; of the Cărhar Roma prestige economy, 17; of the Gabor Roma prestige economy, 17, 65, 72, 82, 87; objects moving between, 82–94, 261–5

Veblen, Thorstein, 133

Verdery, Katherine, 282

veste (renown): as a source of value for prestige objects, 101–5, 189–92, 266–7, 281–2

village leader (*bulibaš, faluvezetăvo*), 30, 31, 106, 149, 205, 271, 279. *See also* honorific titles

vurdon (cart), 36, 242, 325n4; used
   as metaphor for prestige objects,
   157–8, 159–60, 162, 169–70, 174,
   325n5

wakes, 26, 27, 31, 152, 155, 315n7;
   songs at, 28, 158, 161, 167–72. *See
   also* social gatherings
weddings: among Cărhar Roma,
   195–206, 328n15; among
   Gabor Roma, 31, 39, 40, 43,
   45, 62, 155, 162, 163, 270, 271, 294,
   315n11. *See also* marital alliances;
   marriage payments; social
   gatherings
Weiner, Annette B., 75–8

Weiss, Brad, 89
Wilk, Richard, 240, 255
women, 63, 189, 270, 317n27;
   clothing, 41–2, 48, 62, 102, 136,
   225, 242, 243; depictions of on
   prestige objects, 112, 189; economic
   activities, 180, 181, 247, 252–3; in
   inheritance practices, 62, 193, 202;
   and *patjiv*, 29; in Roma politics, 29,
   315n12; tankards viewed as, 62–3.
   See also agency; feminine; gender;
   marital alliances
Woodward, Ian, 331n1

xanamik. See co-parents-in-law
xanamikimo. See marital alliances

Anthropological Horizons

Editor: Michael Lambek, University of Toronto

The Varieties of Sensory Experience: A Sourcebook in the Anthropology of the Senses / Edited by David Howes (1991)

Arctic Homeland: Kinship, Community, and Development in Northwest Greenland / Mark Nuttall (1992)

Knowledge and Practice in Mayotte: Local Discourses of Islam, Sorcery, and Spirit Possession / Michael Lambek (1993)

Deathly Waters and Hungry Mountains: Agrarian Ritual and Class Formation in an Andean Town / Peter Gose (1994)

Paradise: Class, Commuters, and Ethnicity in Rural Ontario / Stanley R. Barrett (1994)

The Cultural World in Beowulf / John M. Hill (1995)

Making It Their Own: Severn Ojibwe Communicative Practices / Lisa Philips Valentine (1995)

Merchants and Shopkeepers: A Historical Anthropology of an Irish Market Town, 1200–1991 / P.H. Gulliver and Marilyn Silverman (1995)

Tournaments of Value: Sociability and Hierarchy in a Yemeni Town / Ann Meneley (1996)

Mal'uocchiu: Ambiguity, Evil Eye, and the Language of Distress / Sam Migliore (1997)

Between History and Histories: The Making of Silences and Commemorations / Edited by Gerald Sider and Gavin Smith (1997)

Eh, Paesan! Being Italian in Toronto / Nicholas DeMaria Harney (1998)

Theorizing the Americanist Tradition / Edited by Lisa Philips Valentine and Regna Darnell (1999)

Colonial "Reformation" in the Highlands of Central Sulawesi, Indonesia, 1892–1995 / Albert Schrauwers (2000)
The Rock Where We Stand: An Ethnography of Women's Activism in Newfoundland / Glynis George (2000)
"Being Alive Well": Health and the Politics of Cree Well-Being / Naomi Adelson (2000)
Irish Travellers: Racism and the Politics of Culture / Jane Helleiner (2001)
Of Property and Propriety: The Role of Gender and Class in Imperialism and Nationalism / Edited by Himani Bannerji, Shahrzad Mojab, and Judith Whitehead (2001)
An Irish Working Class: Explorations in Political Economy and Hegemony, 1800–1950 / Marilyn Silverman (2001)
The Double Twist: From Ethnography to Morphodynamics / Edited by Pierre Maranda (2001)
The House of Difference: Cultural Politics and National Identity in Canada / Eva Mackey (2002)
Writing and Colonialism in Northern Ghana: The Encounter between the LoDagaa and "the World on Paper," 1892–1991 / Sean Hawkins (2002)
Guardians of the Transcendent: An Ethnography of a Jain Ascetic Community / Anne Vallely (2002)
The Hot and the Cold: Ills of Humans and Maize in Native Mexico / Jacques M. Chevalier and Andrés Sánchez Bain (2003)
Figured Worlds: Ontological Obstacles in Intercultural Relations / Edited by John Clammer, Sylvie Poirier, and Eric Schwimmer (2004)
Revenge of the Windigo: The Construction of the Mind and Mental Health of North American Aboriginal Peoples / James B. Waldram (2004)
The Cultural Politics of Markets: Economic Liberalization and Social Change in Nepal / Katharine Neilson Rankin (2004)
A World of Relationships: Itineraries, Dreams, and Events in the Australian Western Desert / Sylvie Poirier (2005)
The Politics of the Past in an Argentine Working-Class Neighbourhood / Lindsay DuBois (2005)
Youth and Identity Politics in South Africa, 1990–1994 / Sibusisiwe Nombuso Dlamini (2005)
Maps of Experience: The Anchoring of Land to Story in Secwepemc Discourse / Andie Diane Palmer (2005)
We Are Now a Nation: Croats between "Home" and "Homeland" / Daphne N. Winland (2007)

Beyond Bodies: Rain-Making and Sense-Making in Tanzania / Todd Sanders (2008)

Kaleidoscopic Odessa: History and Place in Contemporary Ukraine / Tanya Richardson (2008)

Invaders as Ancestors: On the Intercultural Making and Unmaking of Spanish Colonialism in the Andes / Peter Gose (2008)

From Equality to Inequality: Social Change among Newly Sedentary Lanoh Hunter-Gatherer Traders of Peninsular Malaysia / Csilla Dallos (2011)

Rural Nostalgias and Transnational Dreams: Identity and Modernity among Jat Sikhs / Nicola Mooney (2011)

Dimensions of Development: History, Community, and Change in Allpachico, Peru / Susan Vincent (2012)

People of Substance: An Ethnography of Morality in the Colombian Amazon / Carlos David Londoño Sulkin (2012)

"We Are Still Didene": Stories of Hunting and History from Northern British Columbia / Thomas McIlwraith (2012)

Being Māori in the City: Indigenous Everyday Life in Auckland / Natacha Gagné (2013)

The Hakkas of Sarawak: Sacrificial Gifts in Cold War Era Malaysia / Kee Howe Yong (2013)

Remembering Nayeche and the Gray Bull Engiro: African Storytellers of the Karamoja Plateau and the Plains of Turkana / Mustafa Kemal Mirzeler (2014)

In Light of Africa: Globalizing Blackness in Northeast Brazil / Allan Charles Dawson (2014)

The Land of Weddings and Rain: Nation and Modernity in Post-socialist Lithuania / Gediminas Lankauskas (2015)

Milanese Encounters: Public Space and Vision in Contemporary Urban Italy / Cristina Moretti (2015)

Legacies of Violence: History, Society, and the State in Sardinia / Antonio Sorge (2015)

Looking Back, Moving Forward: Transformation and Ethical Practice in the Ghanaian Church of Pentecost / Girish Daswani (2015)

Why the Porcupine Is Not a Bird: Explorations in the Folk Zoology of an Eastern Indonesian People / Gregory Forth (2016)

The Heart of Helambu: Ethnography and Entanglement in Nepal / Tom O'Neill (2016)

Tournaments of Value: Sociability and Hierarchy in a Yemeni Town, 20th Anniversary Edition / Ann Meneley (2016)

Europe Un-imagined: Nation and Culture at a French-German Television Channel / Damien Stankiewicz (2017)

Transforming Indigeneity: Urbanization and Language Revitalization in the Brazilian Amazon / Sarah Shulist (2018)

Wrapping Authority: Women Islamic Leaders in a Sufi Movement in Dakar, Senegal / Joseph Hill (2018)

Island in the Stream: An Ethnographic History of Mayotte / Michael Lambek (2018)

Materializing Difference: Consumer Culture, Politics, and Ethnicity among Romanian Roma / Péter Berta (2019)